# THE HANDBOOK OF
# COMMODITY CYCLES

# THE HANDBOOK OF COMMODITY CYCLES

## A Window on Time

JACOB BERNSTEIN

A Ronald Press Publication
JOHN WILEY & SONS
New York   Chichester   Brisbane   Toronto   Singapore

***Library of Congress Cataloging in Publication Data:***

Bernstein, Jacob, 1946-
   The handbook of commodity cycles.

   "A Ronald Press Publication."
   Includes index.
   1. Commodity exchanges—Handbooks, manuals, etc.
I. Title.

HG6046.B39     332.64'4     81-14814
ISBN 0-471-08197-3     AACR2

Printed in the United States of America
10  9  8  7  6  5  4  3  2  1

There is no need to run outside
For better seeing,
Nor to peer from a window. Rather abide
At the center of your being;
For the more you leave it, the less you learn.
Search your heart and see
If he is wise who takes each turn:
The way to do is to be.

BYNNER, W.
*The Way of Life According to Lao Tzu.*

# Preface

We live in uncertain times. Hardly a day passes without leaving its mark on the pages of history. The pace of life appears to be on a never-ending upward spiral that goes hand-in-hand with technology. And yet, at the base of all sophistication lies simplicity. Cyclic analysis offers the opportunity to return to basics. It is my firm belief that repetition is the key to analysis in virtually all areas of science, philosophy and art. Were we to know all of the cyclic variables in a given area we would predict with near 100 percent accuracy. But the state of knowledge is itself governed by complex cycles and alternates from low to high and back to low again, hence making our task even more difficult. The history of humanity is the history of cycles. We have moved from humble one-celled beginnings to complex mega-celled human machines only to now sit on the verge of possible self-destruction and a return to the one-celled form. Technology itself tends to undo progress just as complexity eventually self-destructs leaving only gears, springs, wires, nuts, and bolts.

My efforts in writing this book have been to return commodity trading to basics before its growing illusion of computerized complexity self-destructs. There are no guaranteed answers, assured profits, totally safe methods, or ultimate systems in this or any other speculative or investment area. We are all subject to emotion, confidence, self-doubt, conceit, and overconfidence. In the proper measure these traits can be valuable, but in extremes they can undo even the most promising method of market analysis. Cyclic analysis and the methods I discuss in this book have definite limitations. There will be times when they are more effective than usual, and there will be times when their results are less than desired. But these results can be significantly altered for better or for worse by the human factor. And the human psyche itself is subject to cyclic variation. The world of cycles is at one and the same time complex and simple.

JACOB BERNSTEIN

Winnetka, Illinois
November 1981

# Acknowledgments

The planning, writing, and final editing of this book took many months of preparation and years of experience. Special words of appreciation go out to the people at Commodity Research Bureau, Commodity Price Charts, Commodity Perspective, and CYCLES, for permission to use charts from their various publications. In particular, I would like to express thanks to the following friends and associates for the reasons(s) stated: Steve Kippur for extensions of time; Marilyn Kinney for constructive comments, final editing, preparation, and screening of calls; Lucia Ringler for cover copy suggestions and art; Phil Tiger for his contrariness and expertise on cycles and spreads. Lee Baker for his never ending faith and persistence; Joe Krutsinger for his ability to get the job done quickly; Jan Greene for her typing and patience; and, of course, my daughter Rebecca for providing a never-ending source of delightful distraction.

J.B.

# Contents

# Credits

Several organizations, in response to the author's requests, supplied illustrations that were invaluable to the presentation and development of the subject matter. For their permission to reprint the Figures listed below, I wish to express my sincere thanks.

Commodity Research Bureau, Inc., 1 Liberty Plaza, New York, NY 10006

| | | |
|---|---|---|
| 3-10 | 5-29 | 7-1 |
| 5-7 | 6-2 | 8-21 |
| 5-10 | 6-3 | 8-22 |
| 5-11 | 6-4 | 9-7 |
| 5-13 | 6-5 | 9-8 |
| 5-14 | 6-7 | 12-8A-D |
| 5-15 | 6-9 | 13-5 |
| 5-16 | 6-10 | 13-6 |
| 5-21 | 6-11 | 16-17 |
| 5-22 | 6-12 | 17-4 |
| 5-23 | 6-13 | 17-6 |
| 5-24 | 6-14 | 18-7 |
| 5-25 | 6-20 | 18-9 |
| 5-26 | 6-29 | 18-11 |
| 5-27 | 6-31 | 18-13 |
| 5-28 | | |

The Foundation for the Study of Cycles, 124 S. Highland Ave., Pittsburgh, PA 15206

| | | |
|---|---|---|
| 2-6 | 5-3 | 5-18 |
| 5-1 | 5-4 | 5-34 |
| 5-2 | 5-9 | 9-9 |

xiii

Commodity Price Charts, 219 Parkade, Cedar Falls, IA 50613

| | | |
|---|---|---|
| 3-8 | 8-11 | 14-1 |
| 3-11 | 8-13 | 15-3 |
| 3-12 | 8-14A | 15-4 |
| 6-1 | 8-15 | 15-5 |
| 6-17 | 8-19 | 15-6 |
| 6-19 | 13-1 | 16-1 |
| 8-4 | 13-2 | 16-16 |
| 8-7 | 13-3 | 17-1 |
| 8-8 | 13-4 | 17-2 |
| 8-9 | | 17-3 |

Commodity Perspective, 327 South La Salle, Chicago, IL 60604

| | | |
|---|---|---|
| 3-1 | 6-30 | 9-13 |
| 3-2 | 6-32 | 10-1 |
| 6-6 | 8-5 | 10-2 |
| 6-8 | 8-6 | 10-3 |
| 6-15 | 8-10 | 12-6 |
| 6-16 | 8-12 | 13-7 |
| 6-18 | 8-13B,C | 14-2 |
| 6-21 | 8-14B | 16-4 |
| 6-22 | 8-16 | 16-7 |
| 6-23 | 8-17 | 16-11 |
| 6-24 | 8-18 | 16-12 |
| 6-25 | 8-20 | 16-13 |
| 6-26 | 9-4 | 16-14 |
| 6-27 | 9-5 | 17-5 |
| 6-28 | 9-11 | |

Lambert-Gann Publishing Co., Richman Gulch, Pomeroy, WA 99347

| |
|---|
| 8-1 |
| 8-2 |
| 8-3 |

**CHAPTER ONE**

# Introduction

I have written this book with two intentions in mind. First, and foremost, it is my goal to teach you an approach to commodity analysis that I believe has the potential to keep you on the right side of the market most of the time. Second, and almost as important, I would like to increase public awareness of cyclic price behavior in the commodity futures markets. What follows is written to maximize your understanding of the concepts presented. My only responsibility in writing this book is to present the information clearly, concisely, and accurately. Once that is done, I will have no control over the manner in which the techniques expressed are actually employed. It is unfortunate that so many investors and speculators tend to lack the necessary discipline to implement this or any analytical method. If you have even the most limited investment or trading experience, then you will know how important self-discipline is in the overall success of any trading system or method. I have addressed myself to this topic in an earlier book, *The Investor's Quotient—The Psychology of Successful Investing in Commodities and Stocks* (1980). If you have even the slightest suspicion that your self-discipline or personal attitude toward the market may be in need of help, then I urge you to read it.

Several other points must be mentioned at the outset.

## THE IMPORTANCE OF ORGANIZATION

I cannot overemphasize the importance of being organized in your approach to this material. Concepts are presented here that will be totally new to many readers. Several levels of market analysis must be learned. A number of timing indicators must be thoroughly understood in order for you to benefit fully from the overall concept and methods. To achieve this end, I suggest that you keep clear notes on the material. Even though I have attempted to be highly organized in my presentation, you will most likely benefit from your own notes as well.

## THE IMPORTANCE OF PRACTICE

It is impossible to learn most things effectively unless you use and/or practice them. Occasionally in the text I suggest that you practice various techniques. I emphasize the importance of doing so. The development of my cyclic methods has taken over 12 years, and I am still learning! You can significantly reduce the amount of time it takes *you* to learn the cyclic analysis methods if you become totally skilled through intensive practice. There are a number of ways in which this can be achieved. They will all be discussed at the relevant point in a later chapter. Appendix 4 contains many examples of cyclic analysis to help you understand the concepts.

## THE IMPORTANCE OF IMPLEMENTATION

Implementation is another prime consideration once you feel comfortable with the material. I am not suggesting that my techniques are best for you. From your study of my analytical methods, you may discover several additional ways in which your own technical or fundamental timing may be improved. If so, then it will be important to implement what you have learned in order to test it in "real time." There is a world of difference between a concept that works well on paper and one that works well in reality. This is why I am not in favor of so-called *paper trading*. If a method seems to work well on historical data, and if you have accounted for such things as poor entry and exit, commission costs, practical limitations on data availability, and lag time between order entry and execution, then you should immediately test the method in real time, with a predetermined amount of dollar risk or number of trades. If you believe that the indicators and signals presented here could prove valuable, then begin implementation on a test basis in real time. If you believe that your own timing could be improved as a function of what I discuss, then make certain that you examine all possible limitations and/or errors that may result from a change in your approach.

## SUPPLEMENTAL READINGS

Supplemental readings are suggested from time to time. I do not believe that any of the recommended books is a prerequisite to your understanding. I *do*, however, believe that your overall understanding of cyclic events can be greatly improved by studying the references. The value of such an education rests not only in the new ideas that it may inspire, but moreover in the philosophical insights that can be achieved. There is a much higher purpose in life than speculation in commodity futures and the profit it can bring. I have found that students of cycles appear to have a much better understanding of the world around them. Somehow the mental internalization of universal cyclic truths tends to solidify previously disconnected pieces of life experience into a visionary whole. By learning about the pervasive nature of cycles, a new *Weltanschauung* is achieved, one that can serve us well in all aspects of life.

## THE ORGANIZATION OF THIS BOOK

The organization of this book is designed to make learning enjoyable and complete while progressing through a series of logical steps that build on one another. There is only minor emphasis on theory, but considerable attention is paid to the pragmatics and real life problems encountered in the implementation of any trading system. In many ways this aspect of the book makes my coverage unique in the commodities field. Not only have I attempted to present you with a unified approach to the use of cycle concepts, but, having studied the markets extensively, I am well aware of the problems that can beset you.

I have attempted to prepare you for them, and the best way I can do this is to follow a logical approach that moves from the simple to the complex and the historical to the contemporary. Essentially, the following outline is maintained:

1 Historical background.
2 Introductory concepts.
3 Working tools and definitions.
4 Levels of analysis—long term, short term, intermediate term.
5 Seasonal cycles.
6 Integration of concepts—timing.
7 Implementation.
8 Limitations and pragmatic considerations.
9 Guidelines for further study.
10 Summary of methodology.

Throughout the discussion considerable space is devoted to examples. When a specific indicator is discussed, I provide many illustrations of its occurrence, as well as an operational (written) definition.

## OTHER METHODS

For those wishing to study the many other approaches to cyclic analysis I have provided references, condensed notes, and a number of examples at the appropriate points. Those wishing to obtain an overview of advanced mathematical models can do so by thoroughly studying the many references listed. It has been my personal experience, however, that for practical purposes there is a point of diminishing return in the application of what is generally considered advanced cyclic technology. All too often the mathematical work involved becomes immense, complicated, and frequently esoteric. Until recently, the implementation of advanced technology has been limited to those having access to computer facilities. The late 1970s have witnessed the arrival of such technology into the home. The once expensive computer is rapidly becoming a home fixture in the 1980s. Even so, there are decisions to be made in trading with cycles that cannot as yet, in my opinion, be committed to an effective software regimen. I am possibly being a bit old-fashioned in my approach. Having had considerable experience with computers and in using my own in-house computer system, however, I have come to respect the assets and liabilities of this massive technological tool.

## WHAT THIS BOOK CAN DO FOR YOU

It is impossible to write a book that will satisfy all levels of readership. Being a pragmatist, I have not attempted to please everyone. Because the experiential exposure of most traders varies considerably, it is necessary to cover a number of basics in order to bring these concepts into the reach of as many traders as possible. My primary purpose, as stated earlier, is to teach you something that I sincerely believe will help you trade the markets in a way that may be more effective than anything else you have been using. Certainly I am not so presumptuous as to assume that what I have to teach is better than anything else being used out there in the speculative world. I accept the fact that many successful traders are using methods either better, or just as good, as my approach. Therefore, I cannot assume that you will indeed do better. I do know, however, from many years of personal observation and experience, that well over 90 percent of all commodity traders are losers, have been losers for many years, and will continue to be losers. Possibly I can help change this by presenting a logical and organized approach to the markets, one that I believe has not been previously set forth in such precise fashion, or with as much care, in any other text. What, then, can this book do for you? I have made a list of what you can expect in order to keep you from developing any misconceptions or disappointments. This book will:

1  Explain the cyclic theory of commodity analysis.
2  Provide historical references and examples of cyclic behavior.
3  Provide suggestions for further increasing your knowledge of cyclic analysis.
4  Explain several methods of cyclic trading in the commodity futures market.
5  Provide examples of how such methods may be used in your own trading.
6  Outline and explain some of the limitations, assets, and liabilities of the cycle technique.
7  Suggest avenues of further research or combinations of cyclic methodology with more traditional fundamental and/or technically based systems.

## WHAT THIS BOOK CANNOT AND WILL NOT DO FOR YOU

It is not my intention to sell you on the cyclic method of trading. Nor is it my intention to convince you that cyclic trading is the best thing for you. I know from personal experience that cycles add a highly important feature to any trading approach, fundamental and/or technical, because they add the dimension of time expectation to data. But my job ends as soon as I have finished my presentation. I would like you to understand that this book cannot and does not attempt to do a number of things. There are no attempts to:

1  Guarantee you profits in any way, shape, or form.
2  Assist you in developing self-discipline.
3  Help you overcome any emotional limitations you have in the marketplace.
4  Give you all the answers to trading success.
5  Provide you with an education in commodities if you are not already schooled in the basic concepts.
6  Cater to any approach of market analysis other than those cyclically based.
7  Teach you fundamental analysis.
8  Help you directly with your own trading system.

**FOLLOWING AS OPPOSED TO PREDICTING THE MARKET**

There is a vast difference between predicting (or forecasting) the market and following the market. Unfortunately, awareness of this distinction does not come to most traders until late in life. I was blessed with this insight at a relatively early age, albeit somewhat late in my "trading life." It took me about nine years to realize that, although it may be a romantic and ego-gratifying goal, forecasting is not necessarily synonymous with profit. The act of determining *where* a market is going and *when* it will get there poses for me and for most traders a distinct *disadvantage* in profitable trading because it predisposes one to particular expectations. Expectations are what lead us to misperceive events, misread indicators, lose confidence in our signals, and avoid implementing decisions that we should know will "work."

It is the job of an economist to understand the many inputs that comprise the markets. After having made their judgments of fact, within a theoretical orientation (which is, by the way, an expectational error), economists make forecasts based on their collection of evidence. Very often the evidence used is provided by government sources. Time lags in the collection of such data can be as long as 4 months, if not, in fact, longer. Hence, any prediction based on old data is an old prediction. This is why so many economists are 180 degrees out of phase with reality. Unfortunately, their techniques have been extended, seemingly quite naturally, to the stock and commodity markets. After all, don't these markets respond to economic forces and conditions? In reality, the markets tend to *lead* economic events. It is a well-known fact, for example, that while the economy itself is zigging, the stock market may be zagging. This is why supposedly bad economic news may not make stock prices fall. It is the same with commodity markets.

What should a trader do? I believe that Joseph Granville, stock market technician supreme, has one answer. The thing to do is simply and exclusively to follow the market, because it is the market we are using as the trading vehicle. Granville (1980) says:

> *Following Wall Street analysts will seldom make you money but following a good stock market analyst will. We don't buy and sell the economy. We buy and sell stocks. Why do people forever try to link the economy with the stock market? Economics have nothing to do with stock market timing—and timing is everything. Yet the Press will forever clutter up their market commentary with discussions of the economy.* [Vol. XVIII, No. 37]

> *the first thing to do about the market is get in gear with it. . . . It is never too late to buy stocks as long as the market traffic light is green. That remains true even if you are buying stocks one day before a top. Who cares? You would simply follow the market sell signal, sell everything and then go 100% short across the board. That is called following the market.* [Vol. XVIII, No. 25]

In short, it is absolutely necessary to follow the market without attempting to impose upon it any preconceived notions. I believe that a market technician can only be a market technician, nothing more, nothing less. I believe in the purity of approach to the exclusion of all other methods. I have rarely found successful traders who can wear several hats at once. In my work I have attempted to wear as many hats as possible, as often as possible, and frequently all at the same time. I reasoned that the more information I had, the better off I would be on the so-called bottom line. The result of wearing too many hats at once? A very heavy head with not much profit to show for it.

This is why I strongly suggest you do your work in isolation. I have found it counterproductive to accept input from any source other than my own indicators. For the purist who seeks to achieve total discipline this means avoiding news reports, brokerage house opinion, newspaper coverage, comments from the floor, or input from any other "expert" who attends to such news. This is, of course, a radical approach. But it appears to work, and it seems to have many beneficial side-effects when profits are tallied. Some will argue that I am proposing we all trade like horses, wearing blinders. If that's what it sounds like, then so be it, at least initially. Until you have learned to keep your eyes on the road and your mind on the goal, you will need to ignore all peripheral inputs that may distract you from following the market. If the market is a carrot which we must follow to attain our goal, then let us be horses with blinders! As soon as we have mastered the art of working toward a goal, without distraction and with total discipline, we can discard the saddle, reins, and blinders, and ride into the face of the wind.

In my years of writing the *MBH Commodity Letter*, a widely read commodity publication, I have constantly been plagued with the *predicting* issue versus the *following* issue. On one hand, it is popularly acceptable and even praiseworthy to make predictions. After all, the public wants to know *where* gold is going and *when* it will get there. It is not sufficient to say, "Buy gold." Humans all too often resist trends. Possibly this is true primarily of Western man. It is difficult for most of us to become part of the flow, part of the process of life, accepting fortune and misfortune, not questioning, moving with the tide where it will take us, and blending in with the harmony of market trends, wherever they may go. To do so is, to most people, a very threatening experience. But I believe otherwise. To become part of the market, to become part of the cycle, to ride on the wave, is the path of least resistance and the path of greatest profit! It is the flow of market tides that my cyclic trading analyses are designed to uncover. Become one with the market and there will be no need for news, no need for brokers' opinions, input from friends and relatives, preachings of economists, or distractions from the government. The readings of Zen will help you achieve this state of harmony with the market if you cannot do so on your own. If there *is* a secret to the market, then I have just given it to you, and it has not cost you dearly. It is up to you, the individual, to develop this aspect of your internal being. My preaching is intended to set a philosophical background to the cyclic approach. It is often uncanny how cycles relate to reality and news. You will see this as you read on. In the words of the late American Zen philosopher Alan Watts:

> *The Yin-Yang view of the world is serenely cyclic. Fortune and misfortune, life and death, . . . come and go everlastingly without beginning or end. . . . The forces are so interdependent that no one can exist without all the others, just as there can be no yang without yin.* (pp. 31–33, 1975)

## WHAT YOU NEED TO KNOW IN ORDER TO BENEFIT FROM THIS BOOK

Certainly, a good education in market basics is necessary. What do I mean by market basics? Because space is valuable and all too many books begin by running through the very boring facts about each market (such as contract size, value of a tick, specifications, etc.), I will not bother doing so. I assume that you already know most of the following:

1   How to calculate the value of a one tick or unit move.
2   The concept of the futures market as a trading vehicle.
3   The meaning of such terms as margin, margin call, limit move, stop loss, open order, market open, high, low, last settlement, opening range, short sale, liquidation of position, buy stop, sell stop, market-if-touched order, and so on.
4   How to read a price versus a time chart (standard bar or closing basis chart).
5   And most other necessary terms used in conjunction with everyday trading.

If you do not have an adequate working knowledge of the foregoing, then I suggest you acquire it by referring to any of the basic texts on markets recommended at the end of this book.

## SOME TOOLS YOU NEED TO HELP LEARN THE CONCEPTS

In order to obtain the necessary practice and experience working with cycles, charts, and signals, it would be helpful for you to have the following:

1   Chart paper (blank), preferably K&E (Keuffel and Esser) No. 47–1810, Commodity Prices 53 weeks of 5 days × 10 divisions, and/or K&E No. 47–1650, Security Prices 53 weeks of 5 days × 8 divisions. You can also use National No. 12–188 paper (10 millimeters to the centimeter). Any good equivalent will do. Such paper is widely available in many office supply stores, direct from the manufacturer (see Appendix 1), or at an engineering supply house.
2   A high-quality transparent ruler or straight edge, at least 12 inches long.
3   A precision set of compass points, which will be used for measuring and marking. This instrument is available at a drafting or engineering supply house.
4   A binder or folder in which to store charts, preferably a ringed binder designed to fit the graph paper you are using.
5   Three drafting or mechanical pencils containing red, blue, and black writing lead, and a sharpener.
6   A number of historical price charts showing daily, weekly, and monthly price behavior. Weekly and monthly price charts can be purchased from Commodity Research Bureau (see Appendix 1 for instructions) in their *Commodity Year Book.* They also publish commodity charts showing daily price action. Many of their charts are used in this book. *Commodity Price Charts* in Cedar Falls, Iowa (see Appendix 1) also publish clear and

very usable commodity charts, as does *Commodity Perspective* in Chicago.

7  You also need a price record book such as an accountant's ledger, or one that allows you to list five columns of numbers and has room for commentary on the right-hand side. Figure 1-1 clearly illustrates this type of ledger.

8  This item is optional. I strongly suggest that you acquire a fairly large record book or diary with space for daily entries in which to record signals, prices, and so on.

## HOW TO USE THIS BOOK

To get the most out of this book there are several things you should remember. The style in which I present the complex topic of cycles reflects an academically oriented approach the goal of which is primarily pragmatic. Rather than spend a great deal of time in philosophical or theoretical discussions, I give my greatest attention to utilitarian details. I attempt to teach you something that can be of great value. Hence, the book should be approached as a cycles analysis course, designed to get you started in a given technical direction. Many examples, explanations, reviews, definitions, and techniques are covered in considerable detail. When an important point relates to another significant concept, I stray from the initial topic. Each chapter builds on the next. And each concept depends on a thorough understanding of what came before.

The structure of what follows makes it necessary for you not merely to read this book but, rather, to study it. In many cases I suggest practice. I also give guidelines as to organizational and practical details that are formulated to assist in your attainment of a full understanding. When practice is advised, you would do well to comply. Occasionally you may need to read a given section or chapter several times until you understand it. You should, by all means, take notes, keeping a list of all important concepts and definitions. It is a good idea to test yourself periodically on new information. When a reference to another text or source is given, you might wish to obtain that source for further reading and study.

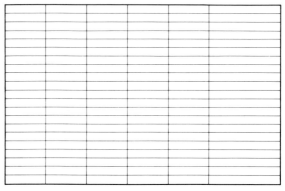

Figure 1.1  **Sample layout of price record paper.**

A glossary is also provided. This brief definitional review of terms should not be used as a substitute for reading but, rather, as an adjunct to the learning process. Many of the definitions are general and cannot be fully understood without the text examples. The glossary should be used as often as necessary. Not all items are contained in the glossary, however, because their definition might be redundant with what has already been explained in the text. Remember that some of the glossary terms differ in definition from standard English language usage.

Above all, remember that this book is not designed to serve as a substitute for practical experience. There is no way in which any book can supplant the role of trial-and-error learning, particularly in a field so intricate as commodity trading. The methods I discuss are not suitable for use by every individual. In fact, some traders may find other indicators and cyclic tools more reliable for their particular purpose. But if they can be inspired to discover even one new market tool, then I will have been successful. I cannot make guarantees about the cycle work because much of it is in its infancy. What may be a reliable tool today could easily fail to work effectively tomorrow. The nature of methods is itself cyclic. Therefore, the interested trader must always look for new patterns, new timing signals, and new trends in cyclic analysis.

No single individual or group of traders has a monopoly on market knowledge. Although there are those who claim to be market masters, they do not in fact possess the knowledge needed to earn this title. Those who have attained true perfection in this, or any other field do not seek public recognition or following. Those who have yet to approach the ultimate state of knowledge, however, will learn by teaching, because in teaching we test what has been studied and we learn from our students. I am as much a student as I am a teacher. And I do not have all the answers. If I had only 60 percent of all the available knowledge, I would be truly happy. My efforts in writing this book are to set the stage for even more meaningful cyclic research and to open the eyes of many disbelievers. To make the best of my efforts, you must let this book inspire, motivate, and educate you in a topic that has for too long been either ignored or ridiculed. Your inputs and experiences are just as valuable as mine. By keeping your eyes, ears, and mind open to new ideas, you will benefit. By not allowing yourself to follow false market prophets, you will maintain your independence as a student and speculator. By being separate from the crowd and by not identifying with any one approach to cycles, you will always be open to new experiences that will help you progress on the road to more profitable trading.

# CHAPTER TWO

# What is a Cycle?

The history of mankind is the history of cycles. Since the beginning of recorded time civilizations have grown, matured, and disappeared leaving only artifacts as remembrances of their existence. Time and time again the process of birth, growth, maturity, and death has woven its finality into the fiber of man's being. Indeed, cycles are all around us—the passing of night into day, the sunset and a return to night, only to be followed once more by day; the rise and fall of ocean tides; planetary movement; the arrival and departure of seasons.

Even religion speaks of a cycle-like process. When the physical body dies, it passes to another state and is, in effect, reborn. The teachings of Buddhism, Shinto, and Eckankar can be viewed from a cyclical standpoint. Although the form of life may change, the process is endless and repetitive. "The Thing that hath been, it is that which shall be, and that which is done is that which shall be done: and there is no new thing under the sun" (Ecclesiastes 1.9). The history of mankind is the history of cycles. To understand cycles is to understand life.

Our daily lives are ever influenced by the limitations of our environment. And our environment is, in turn, regulated by repetitive patterns such as light/dark, warm/cold, and wet/dry. Within these constraints our social, psychological, and economic systems operate, seemingly in a random dance of events. Once we gain awareness of the world around us, we realize, often in amazement, how the patterns of our lives repeat themselves, time and time again. And so it is in the world of commodities. Contemporary science is clearly aware of biological clocks within the animal kingdom but somehow hesitant to accept their existence in the social and economic worlds. Indeed, considerable study is necessary to isolate the role of cycles from random events. The academic pursuit of cycles has not yet attained a role of prominence in the scientific community; it is an idea that is ahead of its time. Simple as cycles may be to comprehend, man may not yet be prepared to accept their ramifications. The day will come, however, for man to fully comprehend and appreciate the role of cyclical science in all phases of life. I have spent many hours and considerable effort in an attempt to bring that day closer for the world of commodities.

There are many ways in which a cycle can be defined. One can use the standard dictionary definition, or one can refer to a series of highly complex mathematical expressions. The extent of our definition is very much a function of the manner in which it is to be employed. If we were about to enter into a purely scientific research program on cyclic tendencies, then our definition will necessarily be more complex and concise. For the purpose of our study,

**Figure 2.1  The symmetrical cycle.**

only a general definition is required. As a starting point, let's define a cycle in a fashion similar to the one used by Edward R. Dewey, whose definition was simply: "... the tendency of events to repeat themselves at more or less uniform intervals ... the pulsations of distant stars ... the prevalence of sunspots ... weather conditions ... the abundance of mammals, birds, insects and fish, and the prices of securities" (Dewey, 1970). Given this simple definition, we can see that cycles are everywhere around us. With so many events being cyclical in nature, it seems only logical that the course of commodity prices would also be relatively rhythmic in its movement. There are many different types of cycles. They can be defined as a function of their regularity, independence, and/or magnitude. Let's take a look at some rather elementary examples of what I mean.

1.  *The symmetrical cycle* is one that varies regularly over time. Each repetition of the pattern looks exactly like the one before it. In other words, if the price of corn hits a low point every 5 years, without fail, there would be a 5 year symmetrical cycle in corn prices. This, however, is not the case in commodities, or for that matter, in most other cycles. Graphically, we could depict a symmetrical cycle as shown (Figure 2-1). A symmetrical cycle is at its high point exactly halfway through the pattern.

2.  *The assymetrical cycle* is more representative of what happens in the markets. We may get repetitive patterns that are closely related in their length but not necessarily constant all the way through. The high point of the cycle can be hit at any time, as you can see (Figure 2-2). This category of cycle is very similar to what we see in the commodity markets.

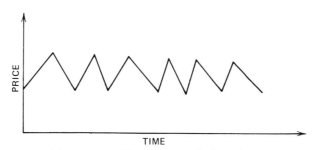

**Figure 2.2  The asymmetrical cycle.**

**Figure 2.3   Cycle and trend combined.**

3.   *The cycle and trend are often combined,* and we typically have combinations of cycles occurring within other cycles (Figure 2-3). Along with these we also have added-in random features (called "noise") that are not part of a cycle. There are many statistical techniques either for removing or for filtering out the effects of noise and/or trend (this is called *detrending*). In highly sophisticated analysis this is necessary, particularly if one wants to arrive at all the possible cycles within a given market. When working on short term patterns, this type of data treatment is also helpful because of the effect of such things as seasonal patterns. Much of this will become clear later on in our discussion.

### HOW DO WE MEASURE CYCLES?

Cycles are measured by their magnitude (up or down movement) and by their length. In this analysis I measure cycles primarily by their length in years, months, and/or weeks. I speak of such things as "the 7 year cycle in soybeans."

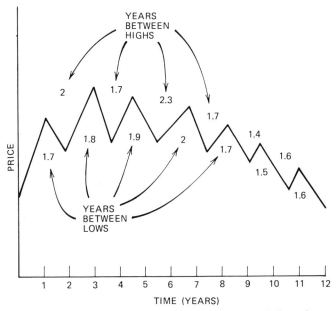

**Figure 2.4   A simple way of measuring cycle length.**

What this means is that about every 7 years the price of soybeans is at a low point from which it moves higher for about $3\frac{1}{2}$ years following which it moves lower for about $3\frac{1}{2}$ years, only to repeat the process or cycle once again. In reality, few if any commodity cycles are perfectly regular. There is considerable variation from one cycle to the next, but by taking an average of the time lengths and by following them over a long period of time we can become reasonably confident of their reliability. Details of several different cycle measurement techniques are given in later chapters. See Figure 2-4 for an example of cycle measurement.

## TAKING AN AVERAGE OF CYCLES

One way to arrive at a cycle's length is to take an average of the various lengths of each cyclical repetition. Here is a specific example of what I mean. The corn market has a 68.1 month repetitive pattern. In order to arrive at the average length of this cycle we need only add up all the cyclical lengths, divide by the total number of repetitions, and we have our answer. I refer to the average cycle length as "$\bar{X}_c$" read "x bar c" (mathematical notation for arithmetic average). There are other ways in which cycle lengths can be manipulated. They are all valid means of analysis, but within the constraints of this study they need not all be analyzed. Figure 2-5 shows how the basic method of averaging is used.

## WHAT DO WE COUNT AS A CYCLE HIGH OR LOW?

Cycles are not perfect. I have said this before, and I will say it many times again. How do we know what to count as a high or a low? Essentially, you

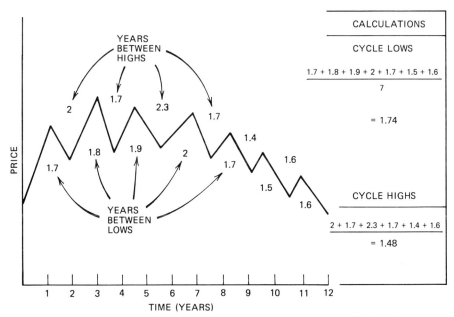

**Figure 2.5   A simple method of computing average cycle lengths.**

should know that more often than not many cycles can be easily identified by visual inspection. You need simply find what appears to be a cycle, measure it, go back in time and see how valid it is, project it into the future, and await the result. This is a "cheap and dirty" way of estimating cycles without the use of a computer. And I maintain that most of us can profit by a simple visual analysis or inspection. Chapters 9–14 cover the balance of this subject in considerable detail.

## CATEGORIES OF CYCLES ACCORDING TO LENGTH

I refer to several classes of cycles in this study. A brief explanation of each will help you keep a proper perspective on my comments.

1. *The Seasonal Cycle.* In a previous study (*Seasonal Chart Study 1953–1977*) I outlined in detail the seasonal cycle or pattern for each cash commodity. There are some markets that follow very well-defined and repetitive patterns each year, such as the egg market. And there are some that do not follow seasonals very well. For shorter term moves it is imperative to have a command of seasonals and their monthly or weekly probabilities.

2. *The Long Term Cycle.* The long term cycle is generally any cycle that averages more than one year in length. I do not find cycles of more than 15 years in length to be useful in my forecasting of long term trends. Data going back more than 100 years is difficult to obtain on many markets. A cycle of 54 years, for example, would require at least 432 years of data before a reliability factor could be isolated.

3. *The Intermediate Term Cycle.* The intermediate term cycle is measured in weeks and generally runs no less than 6 months but no more than 1 year in length. Combined with short term cycles, they help isolate timing of trades.

4. *The Short Term Cycle.* Short term cycles are measured in days and generally do not run more than 3 months or 90 days from low to low.

## HOW TO INTERPRET THE CHARTS

Many of the markets discussed in this book are also shown graphically. Some charts go back to as early as 1900. These charts contain several different kinds of information, as do most of the charts regardless of length, as follows:

1  The price for each market is plotted against time. When possible, charts have been updated to include the most recent figures.
2  Along the left axis is the price as indicated.
3  Along the bottom axis are the years, months, days, and so on.
4  The cyclical patterns for each market are drawn in. These cyclical patterns *do not* indicate prices. They merely indicate trends. The potential prices for each projected trend are discussed in the text when applicable.
5  The precise tops and bottoms of each cycle are indicated with a dot as they occurred in the past and as they are expected to occur in the future.
6  Contained within each cyclical repetition is the number of days, weeks, months, or years between the cycle lows or buy points for the actual cycle.

7   Each chart is discussed in detail, and further information on the specifics can be found in the corresponding text.

## CHARACTERISTICS OF CYCLES

A number of traits are common to most, if not all, cycles. Whether we are studying a repetitive pattern in interest rates, or in the population of Canadian lynx, the underlying characteristics of each cycle are similar. In the same way that a chemist studies the relationship between various substances as well as their individual properties, the cycle analyst studies individual cycles and their interrelationships. To do so successfully, it is necessary to define in operational terms the various common cyclic elements. Those persons interested in a more comprehensive analysis of the items should consult Dewey (1970, Chapter 2).

### PERIOD

Period, time span, or length are the terms used to measure the distance in time from one cycle turn to the next. Traditionally, you measure from low to low. Assume, for example, that a market makes a low in price, rises, and then makes a second low about 23 weeks later. Prices then rise again, make a peak, and come down to another low about 27 weeks later. A third wave up now begins, and prices climb, begin to fall, and make a low about 21 weeks after the second cyclic low. The time span, low to low, in each case is defined as the length of this cycle. Each repetition need not be exactly the same length as those before it, but the repetitions will cluster at or about the same general length. A cycle might also be measured from high to high, or from low to high (a half cycle). Generally, you will find that low-to-low measurements are the most stable.

### RELIABILITY

The reliability of cycles is another common element. The more often a cycle has repeated itself, the greater is its reliability. Some patterns have been present for hundreds, if not thousands, of years. Generally, you should require at least four repetitions of a given cycle before you conclude that a cyclic tendency exists.

### SYNCHRONICITY

Synchronicity is another common characteristic. It is not uncommon to find many markets, seemingly unrelated, whose cycles cluster around the same general lengths. This type of relationship is termed synchronicity (see Figure 2-6). It is difficult to explain why this happens, but it is not within the scope of this book to speculate on causes. We are interested only in presenting facts without conjecture as to their rationale.

### HARMONICS

Harmonics are another common element of cycles. We frequently find that a cycle may be broken into equal units of shorter cycles whose combined length is equivalent to a longer cycle in the same data series. As an example, we might divide the 54 year cycle in wheat into six patterns of 9 years each. The 9 year cycles might in turn be divided into three patterns of 3 years each. This process

THEORETICAL CYCLE LENGTHS

(Double and Triple Progression Up and Down Using 17.75 as a Base)

AND ALLEGED CYCLES WHICH ARE IDENTICAL OR CLOSELY CORRESPOND

| Theoretical Cycle | Found In | Observed Length |
|---|---|---|
| 479.3 yrs. | Not yet found | |
| 319.5 | Not yet found | |
| 213.0 | Not yet found | |
| 159.8 | Pig Iron Prices | 159 yrs |
| 106.5 | Women's Fashions | 105 |
| 142.0 | Number of International Battles | 142 |
| 71.0 | Not yet found | |
| 53.3 | Arizona Tree Rings | 54 |
| | Prices, U.S.A. | 54 |
| | Prices, Germany | 54 |
| | Prices, Great Britain | 54 |
| | Coal Consumption, France | 54 |
| | Coal Production, England | 54 |
| | Lead Production, England | 54 |
| | Number of Textile Workers, England | 54 |
| | Wages of Agricultural Workers, England | 54 |
| | Value of French Rente | 54 |
| | Value of English Consols | 54 |
| | Pig Iron Production, England | 54 |
| | Copper Prices, U.S.A. | 54 |
| | Cotton Acreage, U.S.A. | 54 |
| | Deposits in Savings Banks | 54 |
| | Foreign Trade (Imports & Exports) | 54 |
| | Interest Rates, U.S.A. | 54 |
| | Oat Acreage, U.S.A. | 54 |
| | Ship Building, U.S.A. | 54 |
| | Devaluation in England | 54 |
| | British Wheat Prices | 54.0 |
| | Railroad Stock Prices, U.S.A. | 54.6 |
| 35.5 | Abundance of Lynx in Canada | 35.2 |
| | Frequency of Aurora | 35.9 |
| | Frequency of Earthquakes in China | 35.2 |
| | European Weather | 35.5 |
| | Barometric Pressure of Batavia | 36 |
| | Manufacturing Production, U.S.A. | 36 |
| | Wheat Prices in Western Europe | 36 |
| | Immigration into U.S.A. | 35 |
| | Plant and Tree Growth in England | 35 |
| | Thickness and Thinness of Tree Rings in England | 35 |
| | Harvests in Europe | 35 |
| | Value of English Consols | 36 |
| 17.75 | Industrial Stocks | 17.78 |
| | A large mail-order house | 17.75 |
| | Failures | 17.75 |
| | Sunspots, alternate cycles reversed | 17.66 |
| | Pig Iron Prices | 17.69 |
| | Cotton Prices | 17.75 |
| | War | 17.73 |
| | Earthquakes | 17.66 |
| | Tree Rings, Arizona | 17.75 |
| | Variable Star, Scorpius V 381 | 17.724 |

| Theoretical Cycle | Found In | Observed Length |
|---|---|---|
| 8.875 | Pig Iron Prices | 8.9 |
| | Widths of pre-glacial tree rings | 8.85 |
| | Sunspots - Lane | 8.76 |
| | Sunspots - Stumpff | 8.8 |
| | Sunspots - Clayton | 8.94 |
| 5.916 yrs. | Cotton Prices | 5.91 yrs. |
| | Pig Iron Prices | 5.91 |
| | Copper Prices | 5.91 |
| | Sunspots with alternate cycles reversed | 5.91 |
| | Tree Ring Widths | 5.91 |
| | Railroad Stock Prices | 5.9 |
| | Industrial Stock Prices | 5.93 |
| | Dozens of other series of figures | 6. |
| | Wheat Prices in Western Europe | 5.96 |
| | Liabilities of Failures | 5.90 |
| | One half of the time it takes the planet Jupiter to go around the sun | 5.931 |
| | One fifth of the time it takes the planet Saturn to go around the sun | 5.892 |
| | One forty-second of the time it takes the planet Pluto to go around the sun | 5.915 |
| 4.438 | Sales of Company G | 4.37 |
| | Industrial Common Stock Prices | 4.4 |
| | Railroad Stock Prices | 4.4 |
| | Pig Iron Prices | 4.44 |
| | Advertising Effectiveness of Pinkham Medicine Company | 4.41 |
| | European Wheat Prices | 4.41 |
| | Temperature | 4.41 |
| Months | | Months |
| 35.5 mo. | Factory Sales of Passenger Autos | 36.0 mo. |
| | Common Stock Prices | 35.6 |
| | Common Stock Prices | 36.2 |
| 26.63 | Not yet found | |
| 23.6 | Factory Sales of Automobiles | 23.6 |
| | Industrial Stock Prices | 23.7 |
| 17.75 | Industrial Stock Prices | 17.8 |
| 13.31 | Industrial Stock Prices | 13.3 |
| 11.83 | Industrial Stock Prices | 11.9 |
| 8.88 | Sales of Company G | 8.8 |
| | Bank Debits | 9. |
| 7.89 | Sales of Company G | 7.92 |
| 5.92 | Electric Potential of Trees | 6. |
| | Industrial Stock Prices | 5.9 |
| 3.94 | Electric Potential of Trees | 4. |
| | Sales of Company G | 4.05 |
| | Industrial Stock Prices | 3.937 |
| 2.63 | Not yet found | |

**Figure 2.6    Synchronicity in Cycles (Dewey, 1970).**

can be carried on until the shortest reliable cycle has been found. Not all cycles can be reliably reduced to their harmonics, but most of them have definite harmonic elements.

## INTERRELATIONSHIPS

Interrelationships are also a common characteristic of cycles. It makes sense that the metals should all share generally similar cycles. Fat and feeder cattle futures, live hogs and pork bellies, soybean meal, oil and soybeans also have numerous cyclic interrelationships. It is not easy to explain other cyclic relationships, such as the overall 9 to 11 month cycle present in almost every commodity market. But then, again, our job is merely to state the facts, not to interpret them.

## MAGNITUDE

Magnitude of cycles may vary within the same data series. Whereas cycle length is a measure of time, magnitude is a measure of degree, or relative height. Whereas one cycle may bring prices much higher or lower than the next, the cycle length may still be approximately similar in each case. Although some cycle analysts study magnitude as well as periodicity, our concern in this book is with time alone.

## INDEPENDENCE FROM FUNDAMENTALS

Independence from fundamentals is another common element of cycles. Although there may be occasions that witness cyclic peaks and troughs correlating well with the current economic situation, cycles tend to lead economic events. Cycles seem to make their lows when most of the current news is negative and to make their peaks when the news couldn't be more bullish. It is the nature of cycles to turn well ahead of actual events. It is not uncommon for cycles to be 180 degrees out of phase with public and professional thinking and expectation.

## PERSISTENCE

The persistence of cycles is another important feature. Although certain influences, the most frequent among them being major wars, will distort a cycle, the cycle will then slowly but surely correct itself in order to compensate, as it were, for the previous deviation from the norm. If a cycle runs longer than the norm, then the next repetition will usually be shorter as a compensatory mechanism.

These are a few of the common cyclic features. Many more will become clear to you as you continue with your readings. Remember that the state of cycle science has not as yet attained the firm footing that is common to the physical sciences. Much of what is said herein will need to be adjusted and restated as our studies and knowledge increase.

# CHAPTER THREE

# A Window on Time

To effectively apply cycle analysis it may be necessary to change your orientation to market interpretation. Rather than attempt to make predictions about the future of market trends, you must become an observer of market action, reading its symptoms during critical times and acting accordingly in response to specific signals. Prices move within trends, which are themselves part of longer trends, which are in turn trends within secular patterns. Only a very small percentage of the time will be spent in changing trend. Most commodity traders, therefore, fail in their attempts to "pick" a top or a bottom that are based on such rationalizations as "prices are too high," "the market is overbought," or "prices have climbed too rapidly."

If, for every 100 days, the market only spends 8 to 10 days in changing trend, the probability of your successfully selecting the precise day of a trend change will be very low, particularly if you are not following a systematic selection method. There are several approaches you as a commodity trader can take. You can concentrate on selecting trend changes early in their inception, you can seek to capture only a portion of any given trend once it has clearly established itself, or you can take positions in advance of a trend change, earning, it is hoped, a maximum profit by particularly early entry. Of the three, it is especially risky to base your attempt to make entry prior to expected market turns. In other words, if you believe that a market will begin a strong upmove and if you buy well before the current downmove has terminated, you run the risk of riding prices down until either you have been forced out of the market because of accumulating losses, or you have run out of time. The story is told of the speculator who prayed to the Lord for guidance in the commodity markets. After many months of prayer, a vision of higher wheat prices came to him in a dream. This, he knew, was the signal for which he had waited. He started to buy wheat futures. To his dismay, the market did not turn higher. Before too long, he was riding a fairly large loss. And yet he knew in his very soul that his expectation was correct. And knowing this, there was only one thing to do, buy more and average down the cost. And so he did. Stubbornly, the market refused to turn. Our friend borrowed money and bought more wheat, knowing that one day soon it would turn. But day after day the market refused to comply. Finally came the day of reckoning, and our visionary was forced to abandon his positions, penniless but still believing that he was correct in his expectations. As the story goes, several days after he liquidated his position the market began to move higher. The uptrend continued virtually uninterrupted until prices had more than doubled. The speculator's feelings were correct, but he had nothing but losses and frustration to show for all his prophetic accuracy. And though the story changes just a bit, and the names of the players are different, the same scenes are acted out almost daily. The problem, as you can see, with establishing positions in the futures market before a turn is expected, is that unless your time and funds are virtually unlimited, you will reach a point beyond which you can no longer hold your position. More often than not, this point will be at or close to the start of the expected move. This is when the market typically experiences its greatest volatility. And this is when the temptation to give up is greatest.

A second and much more productive way of doing things is to identify a change in trend very early in its life, thereby establishing a position *not* at the precise top or bottom but certainly soon enough to permit substantial profit. This is what most market systems are designed to do. A moving average system, for example, signals, by certain specific indicators, a buy or sell *after* the trend has established itself. The most popular type of moving-average system, there-fore, typically gets you into a move after the move has been established. Figures 3-1 and 3-2 show exactly how the three moving averages, with their combination of signals, tend to work. There are many different combinations of moving-average, or trend-following, systems. See *Commodity Trading Systems and Methods* by Perry Kaufman for an excellent discussion of the many trend-following systems, their assets, and their liabilities.

Regardless of the type of trend-following system you use, the advantages of following a trend outweigh the disadvantages. And yet, for all the usefulness ability of such systems to get you into the right side of a trend, there are few traders who can use them successfully. In sideways or rapidly changing mar-kets, the moving-average system can give many false signals. By the time a signal appears in a relatively trendless market, the market move may be over. This is due to the time lag of moving average indicators.

It is not my intention to find fault with other technical approaches to com-modity trading. In the long run, each of you will settle on a method that you find both profitable and pragmatic within the constraints of time and effort. Ultimately, you will reach a point of harmony at which your effort and the return per unit of effort are balanced to your satisfaction. My goal, as earlier stated, is to present you with a method that I use, one that I believe is both logical and effective, as well as specific, operational, and objective.

At the beginning of this chapter I mentioned the importance of timing as a prerequisite to successful trading. When margins are small, timing is even more important. Hence, timing must always be as precise as possible. There are many false timing signals—indicators that may be wrong almost as often as they are right, and that requires subjectivity at times when signals should be very clear. The cyclic method attempts to maximize effective timing through the use of a bilevel market entry system. The first level, or *time window,* as I call it, allows you to make several conclusions about a market and its behavior. First, the time window can assist a long-term trader (investor) and/or hedger in making judgments about time periods that may bring important highs or lows. The seasonal pattern is only one example of how such individuals might use the time window in their transactions. A specific example explains what I mean.

It is a well-researched and well-documented fact that most commodity mar-kets exhibit seasonal price tendencies (Bernstein, 1978; Gruschcow & Smith, 1980). At certain times of the year, prices fluctuate because of various funda-mental factors such as planting, harvesting, weather, and so on. Livestock

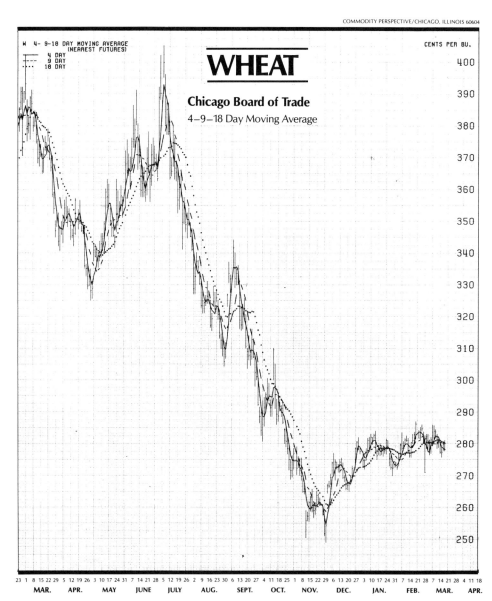

**Figure 3.1   Three short-term moving averages plotted against daily price. Moving average systems tend to use several such averages plotted against price. In this case a 4-, 9-, and 18-day combination is being used. The details on computing moving averages are available in any standard text (e.g., *Commodity Trading Systems and Methods*, P. Kaufman (1979)).**

markets tend to follow similar patterns, with prices rising early in the year, increasing in upward momentum through May, June, and July, reaching peaks in August or September, and falling rather sharply through year end, only to repeat the same process next year. The seasonal charts of Figure 3-3 depict what generally happens.

The meats, as a group, based on average expectations over the past 25 or

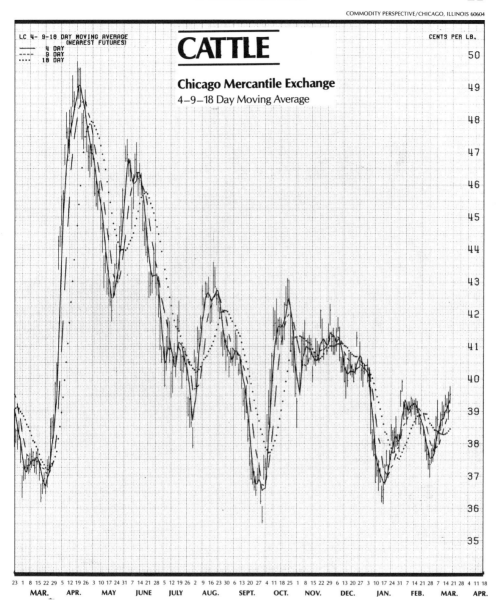

**Figure 3.2  Moving averages and live cattle futures.**

more years, have shown a highly reliable tendency to act in certain ways at certain times, thereby earning the reputation of being seasonal markets. A seasonal indicator, however, is no more perfect than any other market indicator. Although it can be demonstrated that certain moves occur more than 80 percent of the time, it is when expected seasonal indicators don't occur that large losses *can* occur. There are various ways by which to determine when such *contra-seasonal* patterns will develop, and they are discussed later.

Getting back to the hedger for a moment, let's see how he uses the time window. Assume that a farmer who raises cattle knows that his animals will

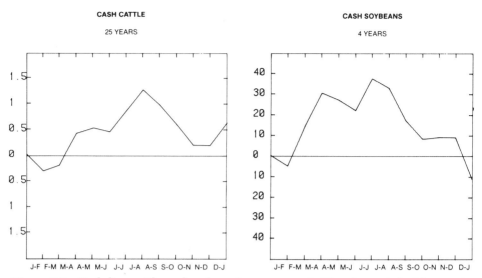

**Figure 3.3   Cash live cattle and cash soybean seasonals (Grushcow & Smith, 1980).**

be ready for market in December. Assume also that he has studied the seasonal tendency of beef cattle prices. If things go as anticipated, prices will most likely be at their peak in August (see Figure 3-3). However, his animals will not be ready until December and hence cannot be marketed until then. What to do? By knowing that the time window of highs in cattle is August/September, he can begin selling his cattle *in the futures market*. As you most likely know, this practice is called *hedging*. The farmer may not want to hedge all his production in August. He may want to begin in August, selling small amounts through September as prices move higher. Each market has its ideal seasonal top and bottom time window. Figure 3-4 shows what usually happens in the wheat market, for example.

The seasonal top or bottom period, by its very nature, involves a time span of from about four to as much as 10 weeks. During this period, a person who was trading futures could have been ruined many times over had he bought and held, or sold and held. The hedger who theoretically owns the goods has sold against his position. He has, in effect, locked in (or guaranteed) a price for his production because he can deliver against his short position when the futures contract comes due. Should the position go against him, he will still make the profit he has locked in, but he could buy back his short position should he wish to do so. The time window for a seasonal, top or bottom, then, is a rather broad one. It may vary from the ideal by several weeks, or even months.

Another time window, and one that involves a generally shorter length, is the weekly seasonal pattern. By studying the tendency of a given market during certain weeks of the year, it is possible to isolate several time frames during which reliable seasonals tend to occur. Does the wheat market, for example, usually move down during the last week of May? Do soybean prices tend to bottom early in October, or during the last week of October? What happens to

CHI WHEAT NEAREST FUTURES

10 YEARS

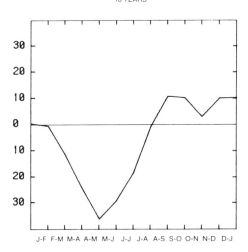

CHI WHEAT NEAREST FUTURES

4 YEARS

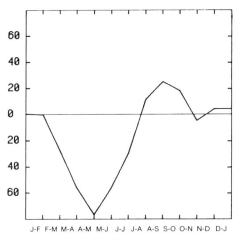

**Figure 3.4   10 year and 4 year cash Chicago wheat seasonals (Grushcow & Smith, 1980, p. 190).**

copper prices in the last week of December? By asking these questions, the speculator seeks to isolate a more specific or circumscribed period during which to buy or sell. In a previous study (Bernstein, 1979), I examined these tendencies in the commodity futures markets and found that there are indeed many weeks during the life of each futures contract that exhibited highly reliable up or down moves. In other words, I studied the historical behavior of commodity futures contracts in order to determine which way prices typically moved during certain weeks of the year. I discovered that there are specific periods in each contract month, some of which have had well over 90 percent reliability in the last 14 years or so. The cash markets could have been studied on a weekly basis as well.

An explanation of the method by which I chose to isolate weekly seasonal trends will help you gain a clearer understanding of the time window concept. In my introduction I made the suggestion that we examine the markets with "blinders." The function of the blinders is to block out our peripheral vision, helping us concentrate only on one sector of time. It is as if we were looking through a window of time. We can select a certain time frame for inspection, excluding all extraneous events, in order to isolate only those times that are truly important turning points.

Let's assume that you want to study monthly seasonal price patterns. You can approach your task in several ways. You can keep a notebook of what has happened each month, adding to it each time you have more data. W. D. Gann (1942) did something similar in his study of seasonality:

---

**Soy Beans—Months When Most High and Low Prices Have Been Reached**

This covers the period from 1913 to 1941, or 28 years.
During this period:

> January High 4 times—Low 7 times.
> February High 3 times—Low 7 times.
> March High 2 times—No Lows.
> April High 1 time—No Lows.
> May High 3 times—No Lows.
> June High 3 times—No Lows.
> July High 3 times—Low 2 times.
> August High 1 time—Low 2 times.
> September High 1 time—Low 1 time.
> October High 3 times—Low 11 times.
> November High 1 time—Low 5 times.
> December High 2 times—Low 5 times.

From the above you can see that most Highs have been reached in January, the month when seasonal Lows are usually reached in Corn and Wheat. Soy Beans have made High 3 times during May, June and July and 3 times during October and 3 times in February. The months when the least number of Highs have been made are April, August and September; also November. In each of these months only one High has been reached during the 28-year period. From this record you would expect seasonal Highs in January and February at certain times when the market was running opposite the seasonal trend. If Lows were reached in January and February, according to the seasonal trend, then you would watch the Highs in May, June and July and, if the crop was very short and the market running against seasonal trend, you would expect Highs in October. [p. 127]

---

Or you can approach the subject mathematically through the application of various seasonal techniques (see Kaufman, 1978). My method involves basically similar mechanics. Figure 3-5 shows how a simple monthly cash seasonal can be computed using nothing more than elementary mathematics. What we are

| Year | Jan. | Feb. | Mar. | Apr. | May | June | July | Aug. | Sept. | Oct. | Nov. | Dec. |
|------|------|------|------|------|------|------|------|------|-------|------|------|------|
| 1971 | 28.83 | 31.80 | 31.42 | 31.96 | 32.35 | 31.91 | 31.90 | 32.77 | 32.21 | 32.11 | 33.30 | 33.92 |
| 1972 | 35.35 | 35.74 | 34.73 | 34.20 | 35.29 | 37.48 | 37.65 | 35.18 | 34.69 | 34.68 | 33.38 | 36.58 |
| 1973 | 40.65 | 43.54 | 45.65 | 45.03 | 45.74 | 46.76 | 47.66 | 52.94 | 45.12 | 41.92 | 40.14 | 39.36 |
| 1974 | 47.14 | 46.38 | 42.85 | 41.53 | 40.52 | 37.98 | 43.72 | 46.62 | 41.38 | 39.64 | 37.72 | 37.20 |
| 1975 | 36.34 | 34.74 | 36.08 | 42.80 | 49.48 | 51.82 | 50.21 | 46.80 | 48.91 | 47.90 | 45.23 | 45.01 |
| 1976 | 41.18 | 38.80 | 36.14 | 43.12 | 40.62 | 40.52 | 37.92 | 37.02 | 36.97 | 37.88 | 39.15 | 39.96 |
| 1977 | 38.38 | 37.98 | 37.28 | 40.08 | 41.98 | 40.24 | 40.94 | 40.11 | 40.35 | 42.29 | 41.83 | 43.13 |
| 1978 | 43.62 | 45.02 | 48.66 | 52.52 | 57.28 | 55.38 | 54.59 | 52.40 | 54.26 | 54.93 | 53.82 | 55.54 |
| Total | 311.49 | 314.00 | 312.81 | 331.24 | 343.26 | 342.09 | 344.59 | 343.84 | 333.89 | 331.35 | 324.57 | 330.70 |
| Avg. | 38.94 | 39.25 | 39.10 | 41.40 | 42.91 | 42.76 | 43.07 | 42.98 | 41.74 | 41.42 | 40.57 | 41.34 |

Figure 3–5. Computation of a Monthly Cash Seasonal—Basic Method (The data below (Avg.) is plotted in Figure 3–6).

25

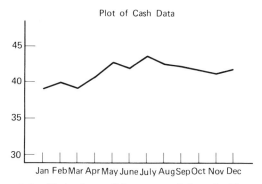

Figure 3.6    **Plot of monthly seasonal data in Figure 3.5.**

really doing in this case is segmenting each year into months, taking the price change direction from one month to the next, mathematically determining what percentage of the time prices move *up* or *down* from one month to the next, and making a judgment as to the apparent strength or weakness of the given time window. It is possible, for example, to look out your window and see a jumble of movement, motion in every which way, birds, dogs, trees, flowers, and more; or it is possible to look out your window and see a single rose bush in the glory of its bloom. The difference between what I call a reliable seasonal and a random price pattern is like the difference between these two scenes.

On the basis of my seasonal computations, I can now state with specific accuracy measures what the most probable time frame of *up* and *down* moves is for this market. Within the limits of my monthly computations, it is highly probable that history will repeat itself, and if I am truly brave and can withstand riding a position for one full month or more not knowing exactly when to enter on a daily basis, I can take a position based on my findings. Or I can become a little more sophisticated in my analysis by looking at the weekly cash or futures patterns. The procedure is similar; the only difference is that we are dealing with weekly data and not monthly data. When we complete the analysis, we'll end up with a series of weekly figures. See Figure 3-7 for an example of the weekly seasonal plot.

There is yet a third way in which time windows can be isolated, and that is by examining the various cycles that characterize each market. Certainly this is easier said than done. And certainly there are many different ways in which this can be accomplished. Perhaps the most thorough, time-consuming, and intensive method is through the construction of a systematic reconnaisance period record (SPR) as described in the studies published by the Foundation for the Study of Cycles (see Appendix 1).

Another and infinitely simpler way is to employ a number of commodity price charts that will help to isolate the cycles in each market. Once you have done this, you can determine a time window through which to look for cyclic highs and/or lows. Before moving on to some of the methods and procedures for determining the time window, I return to the question, "Why is it important to isolate the cyclic time window?" From the earlier discussions, you can see that it is not only important to know about the future direction of a market but

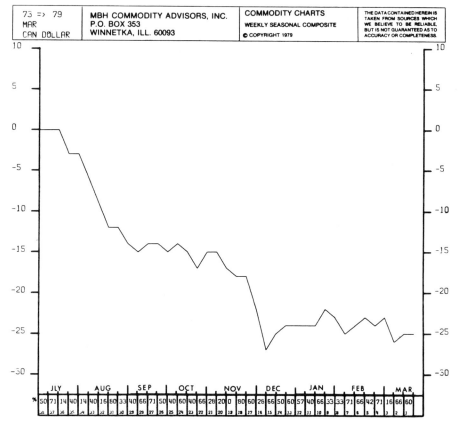

| 73 => 79 | MBH COMMODITY ADVISORS, INC. | COMMODITY CHARTS | THE DATA CONTAINED HEREIN IS TAKEN FROM SOURCES WHICH WE BELIEVE TO BE RELIABLE, BUT IS NOT GUARANTEED AS TO ACCURACY OR COMPLETENESS. |
|---|---|---|---|
| MAR | P.O. BOX 353 | WEEKLY SEASONAL COMPOSITE | |
| CAN DOLLAR | WINNETKA, ILL. 60093 | © COPYRIGHT 1979 | |

**Figure 3.7  Weekly seasonal tendency of March Canadian dollar futures.**

that it is possibly more important to know when the market will actually begin its move. It is for this reason that we must use a dual method of determining when to buy and/or sell. The remaining chapters of this book specifically discuss the following steps in sequence:

1  How to find the cycles.
2  How to isolate the time window.
3  How to find timing signals.
4  How to limit losses in conjunction with Steps 1 through 3.
5  Variations and adaptations of the cyclic method.

How can a commodity trader use the time window concept to trade the market? I now cite an example that should help to make very clear the idea at the very heart of my commodity cycles technique. Without digging too deeply into the mechanics of how a cycle is found, consider the 40 to 50 week pattern in pork bellies (Figure 3-8). Notice that the general cycle trend is depicted by a solid line, (zigzag) pattern running from low to high, and back down to low, and so on. The number that appears in each cycle (zigzag) is the approximate length of time in weeks between the lows. The dashed line that continues at

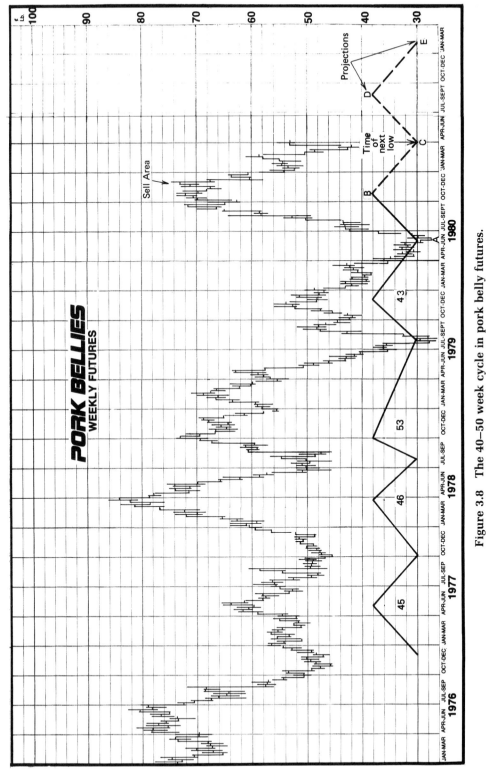

Figure 3.8  The 40–50 week cycle in pork belly futures.

the right of the chart is the projected, or ideal, continuation of the indicated cycle. It is this ideal pattern that constitutes part of the time window. Notice also that the number appearing in the dashed or dotted line continuation is the projected time span of the next cycle. In other words, this is how long you can expect it to be until the next low or high comes, counting the most recent actual low as the first week. The projected time span is a number we calculate using previous cycle lengths in a fashion that is explained later.

There are several significant things about the pork belly chart in Figure 3-8. First and foremost, notice that the general cycle (shown as zigzag) ignores the many up and down moves that occur during the overall trend. These smaller moves are part of another cycle or cycles that you will find later on. Second, and just as important, you can see that the length of each cycle is *not necessarily* exactly the same as the one before it, or the one after. Because commodity cycles are of only approximate lengths, very few are exactly the same. Some are exact, but most will vary. Generally, the variance will be about plus or minus 15 percent of the average cyclic length. A third thing to notice is that the measurement of cycles is primarily independent of price. Price itself is not an important consideration. Relative price is, however, very important. All we're concerned about is whether a certain price is higher or lower than it was at a certain time in the past. Another important thing about this chart is that there is more variability in time between cycle highs than there is between cycle lows. I'm not certain why this happens, although I have some plausible explanations. Let's remember that as commodity traders our goal is not to reason why, but rather to sell and buy. This is why I do not spend too much time discussing reasons, and a great deal of time discussing methods. Sometimes it's not too good to sit and think about why prices do what they do. We must accept the fact that what's happening is real, and we must act accordingly.

The next chapter describes in detail how we can "find" a cycle. Assume, for the time being, that the cycles I show in my pork belly chart have already been found and that they are reliable. Assume also that they have a history that goes back far enough to permit using them with confidence. By adding the cycle lengths, we get a total figure which is then divided by the number of cycles we have added together. This gives us the *average cyclic length*. The average cyclic length is then counted off from the last actual low *(A)*; then the next high *(B)* and next low *(C)* are projected. We then take a step back and calculate the *percentage of error factor*, which we do by simply taking 15 percent of the average cycle length, adding the percentage of error to the average cycle length, and then subtracting the 15 percent figure from the average cycle length. This provides us with an upper and lower time frame within which the cycle can top or bottom. The time frame during which a cycle can top or bottom is called the *time window*. Figure 3-9 is a step-by-step summary of what's involved in determining the time window.

The time window, in other words, gives you an idea of how early a low or high can come, or how late it can be seen within the parameters of the cycle(s) with which we are working. This is, or should be, the first step that any trader takes in determining what position he should take in the market. Because each market makes important turns only several times each year, if that often, it is important to know *when the most probable time* of the turn will be. Making

| Step Number | Goal | Method |
|:---:|:---|:---|
| 1 | Take cycle average | Add length of all cycles and divide by total number of cycles under observation |
| 2 | Project next cycle low | Place "P" (for projected low) at the *cycle average* number of time units into future from last low (use average from computation in Step No. 1) |
| 3 | Find percentage error factor | Multiply cycle average (from Step No. 1) by 0.15. Add this figure to cycle average, and subtract this figure from cycle average |
| 4 | Record Time Window | Take the two new figures, one larger than cycle average and the other smaller than cycle average, and place "W" on chart for each, showing time span of possible low or high (see accompanying chart figure) |
| 5 | Determine next high window | Same as Steps 1–4. |

**Figure 3–9.   Steps for finding time window.**

the time window projection is only about 25 percent of the process, however. Most cycle analysts have gone only this far, failing to realize the importance of three additional aspects in the use of cycles for commodity trading. And here is the key to how my analysis differs from any other method of cyclic trading. Once the time window has been found, there must be (1) a confirmation of the trend change, (2) a determination of other cyclic influences, and (3) a timing signal that allows for entry at a precise time or times.

Let's go back to our pork belly chart and see how this method can be used for trading. You will observe that a cyclic projection of the time window has been made on our original chart (Figure 3-8). The time window is, as earlier stated, a time range within which significant price change trends are most likely to occur. Hence, in determining our time window (Figure 3-8), we have in essence made a forecast, or have we? I told you earlier that our job is *not to forecast.* If you believe that we have made a forecast by determining a time window, then you may not be comprehending the concept fully. If you continue to study the examples presented, I believe you will begin to grasp the very subtle, but highly meaningful, difference between *forecasting* and *following.* At any rate, let's return to the pork belly chart (Figure 3-8). We have determined the time window. We believe that *if* a turn to the upside is indeed coming in pork bellies, *then* it will probably come within the time span of our time window. Anything that occurs earlier than our time window (*unless it is accompanied by a few specific exceptions* that are discussed in later chapters) is to be totally ignored. And this is where the self-discipline comes in! I repeat:

*Anything that does not occur within the time window, other than a few specific exceptions to be discussed later, is not to be considered.* You could, in fact, do your work on a market, set it aside until the time window date comes into focus, and then begin watching specific indicators.

What we have done, in effect, is to put a time reference on price behavior. This is not the way most people treat the market. Most people, as you have probably observed, are interested in where prices are going on a day to day basis. They are concerned with such things as how high prices will go next week, what will happen on tomorrow's opening, or whether prices will be higher today. These are dysfunctional and loss-producing attitudes. They are, however, a necessary part of the education in economics and trading as provided by schools and preached by most market experts.

Because we have an opening on time, we can begin to look for specific *timing indicators* that may help to confirm the cyclic low, tell us to wait for a more meaningful turn, or tell us that we had best not enter the market at this time. What we are doing, in effect, is screening the market. We are using a sort of filter designed to block out anything but the most meaningful moves. How does this work in real time? This will be discussed in detail later on, but for now let's continue with the pork belly example. You do not, as yet, know the combined timing indicators that should be used in connection with the time window, and you do not as yet know the various ways in which different cyclic lengths can be combined to give long term, short term, and intermediate term time windows. This is discussed later in the book, but for now pretend for a moment that you know the indicators. On the basis of the combined effect of the time window and the timing indicators, the belly chart we originally used allowed for the timing of a market entry to the short side at point B marked "sell" on Figure 3-8. Figure 3-10 shows what transpired thereafter. Remember that when we selected the time window we did, of course, not know what the future held in store. We did not know when, exactly, bellies would turn lower; we did not know how high they would go before turning lower; we did not know how low they would go after turning lower; and we did not know when to start selling. You can see, however, that with the proper combination of the time window and timing signals, it was possible to *follow* the market—not knowing any of the fundamentals, not knowing any of the underlying causes, and furthermore, not caring one hoot about these things. We selected the approximate cycle mid-point *(B)* as the probable top. This, of course, assumes a symmetrical pattern which is not always a correct assumption. I will provide you with more details later on, but for now this brief general example should give you an idea of the basic analytical approach.

One swallow does not a summer make. Were I able to give you only this one successful example, there would still be many unanswered questions regarding the cyclic method of price analysis. I will run through one more example of how the time window and timing signals function together at critical market turns (see Figures 3-11 and 3-12).

Figure 3-11 shows an approximate 28 trading day cycle in live cattle futures. The term *trading days* refers to days during which the market is open. This is, of course, distinctly different from calendar days. You will note that my references are to trading days when discussing short term cycles. From just

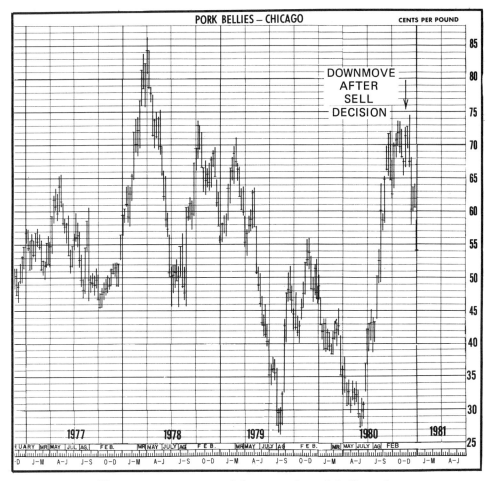

**Figure 3.10   Outcome of the 45 week pork belly cycle.**

prior to March 3 (see Figure 3-11) through July 14 there were four repetitions of the 28 day cycle. The previous history of this market strongly suggested that this was indeed a valid cyclic tendency. Therefore, on July 14 one might have assumed that another low was due to occur on or about August 18, approximately 28 trading days later. One could have made the further assumption that approximately 14 trading days after the July 14 low the market would have most likely made a high. An examination of the appropriate dates shows that prices did, in fact, make a low close to the August 18 date (see Figure 3-12). You will also note that there was a peak in prices about 10 days after the July 14 low. This was not exactly what we had expected, but it was fairly close to the projection. Don't forget that we made the projection based on the assumption that the cycle was symmetrical. In other words, we took exactly one-half the 28 day length (14 days), and counted forward in time. I pointed out earlier that this was not the best technique since it made the essentially incorrect assumption that cycles in commodity prices are symmetrical. This assumption

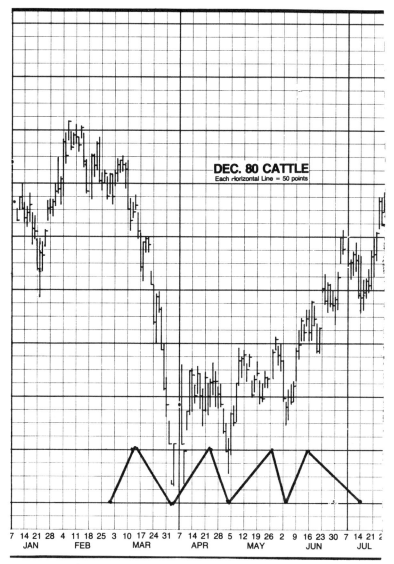

**Figure 3.11 Time window, cycles, and cattle.**

is reasonable now inasmuch as I am introducing the subject to you, but it will be rectified later on. Bear with me, however, as I continue with the example.

Following the August 25 low which came about 4 trading days later than our rough projection, we could have made another projection. Specifically, the next date for a probable low would be October 3. You will note from Figure 3-12 that the actual low in this case came about 4 trading days earlier than projected. It's interesting to note, by the way, that this low was about 4 days early whereas the previous low was about 4 days late. It is a common feature of cycles to correct themselves as time passes. A cycle that is too long, for

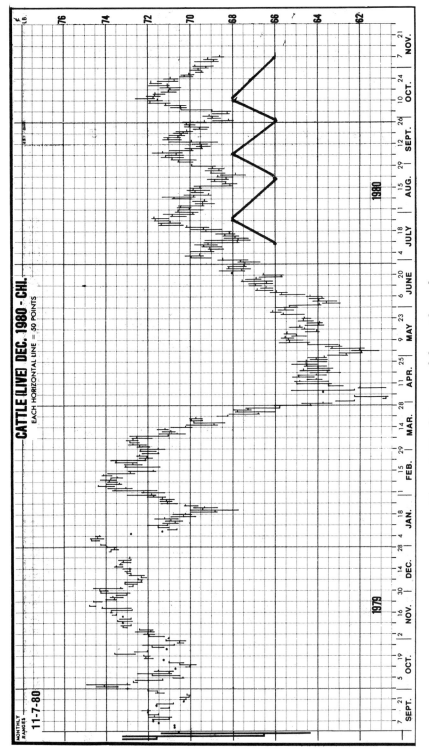

**Figure 3.12** Outcome of the cattle cycle.

34

example, might then experience an adjustment by running a bit shorter on its next repetition.

Continuing with our example, we can project the next peak to occur about 14 trading days after the current low. This yields a time target of approximately October 17. A look at Figure 3-12 shows that the actual top came a few days earlier than projected. We could now move forward in time and project the next low. We would do this by referencing back to the previous low, September 29, and counting forward. This gives the next probable low date as approximately November 6. Our chart does not permit a final determination of the actual low, but we are looking only at a general analysis at this time and will not concern ourselves with following this cycle to the present.

You will observe that several analytical techniques were employed in this short term analysis. They are outlined below.

1   Time span between lows was counted. In this case we used trading days as our cycle measure.

2   We assumed a symmetrical cycle. This means that one half of the length, low to low, was taken to be the approximate time of the next high.

3   In projecting the next cycle low we referenced back to the last actual low for our count.

4   The actual lows and highs were not exactly as we had projected, but they were within reasonable distance in time from our expectation.

5   We dealt exclusively with *time* in our projections. Price was used only as a measure of trend for plotting the cycle. Our main concern was the determination of probable time frame for lows and highs.

Let's review what has been discussed so far. First, and foremost, I explained the importance of following the market exclusively. The value of cyclic analysis was given primary consideration in this effort. Furthermore, I explained the concept of the time window, how it helps you to block out all extraneous market factors and how it helps you to isolate the very start of major changes in price trends. Finally, several examples were given of the manner in which the combined time window and timing signals (which have not yet been discussed) are employed in actually making a trade. What remains to be discussed is the exact fashion in which time windows of various interacting cycles are determined, the timing indicators that validate the time windows, and other indicators, methods, and procedures that are used in conjunction with the two main features of cyclic analysis.

Let me emphasize, before going any deeper into the subject, that this technique is not perfect. Although everything possible has been done to make it mechanical, objective, and specific, sometimes a major move starts and no signal is perceived. This is not a shortcoming of the system but, rather, of the inputs. Were we aware of all the cyclic factors that operate on the markets, we could easily be right over 90 percent of the time. Cycle analysis works only if the time window is accurate. For it to be accurate, we need to know and to take into account all relevant cycles. What this means in the long run is that we won't capture every move and that we won't be in every trend for the full duration of the trend. As I have said before, however, the goal is only to capture a piece of each trend. Many traders have gone to the poorhouse by getting in too soon or overstaying their position. Finally, all systems take losses. If you are not taking losses, then you are not trading. This technique will take losses as well, and I cannot and will not guarantee anything above and beyond the mere presentation of this material. Some readers will grasp the concepts and indicators especially well, and others will not get past step one. It's only human nature for people to have varying degrees of ability and success. That's what makes the market.

# CHAPTER FOUR

# Long Term, Short Term, or in Between?

I have met few traders in my time who are truly oriented to the long term. For one reason or another—primarily fear and/or greed—most commodity traders who start out with the best of intentions to trade over the long term usually fall by the wayside. Trading for the long term is like trying to give up a smoking or drinking habit. It is like maintaining a body-building program, or attempting to lose a considerable amount of weight. In short, it requires a tremendous amount of discipline. There has been much discussion through the years about the merits and shortcomings of various orientations within the ultra long term and "scalping" extremes. My working definitions, provided later, will, I hope, allow you to decide for yourself. No doubt you have already had your attitude shaped by experience, but it may not be too late to change, if you so desire.

## THE LONG TERM APPROACH

Generally, any position held for a period of more than six months is one that I would consider long term. There are, of course, those ultra-long term traders who can sit on a position for a year or longer, but they are few and far between. The advantages of such an approach are many. Notwithstanding the tax considerations, there are a number of other benefits in such an orientation. First and foremost, it takes much less time to trade for the long term. Decisions can be made using only long term and weekly cycle charts. Therefore, less time is required to determine which trades should be made. Another major consideration is the amount of profit that long term trades usually generate. Typically, a long term position yields very large profits compared to the average short term trade, and there is also less trading and therefore less commission. These facts should be obvious to most commodity traders. Remember, however, that I am talking about only a 6 month time span, which is really not a long time to hold a position. The facts seem to bear out my contention, however, that most traders are simply not capable of staying with a position for even three months. By the time a short term trader has agonized over signals, spent time studying charts, making charts, recording data, and paying taxes and commissions, the attraction of long term trading may begin to seem substantial and attractive. Let's face it, trend changes tend to last for a long time, and there is really no reason to trade any one market more than several times a year.

## THE SHORT TERM APPROACH

Generally, I would call *short term* any position held more than 2 weeks but less than 6 months. The nimble trader can take advantage of many short term cycles within secular trends, thereby maximizing profit from each move. In theory, this is the advantage of short term trading. In practice, however, this rarely is true. Why? There are a few prerequisites to short term trading that most speculators are either unable or unwilling to meet. These include, in order of importance, substantial time input, considerable self-discipline, close touch with the market, and highly effective methods of money management. Few traders depend entirely on the market for their income. Most people who trade commodities have other jobs and cannot devote the required degree of effort and time to maintaining up-to-date charts and signals. They are easily swayed by public opinion, fundamental analysis, news, brokers, friends, margin calls, and market hysteria. They are generally after the "quick kill," concentrating primarily on small prey rather than large game. To trade successfully for the short term requires total discipline and commitment. Even more than the long term trader, the short term trader is subject to extraneous influences and must be as totally isolated from them as possible (in my opinion). Yet the lure of short term trading is ever present. The thrill of knowing that 100 percent or more can be made on your money in just a few days provides an excitement and satisfaction difficult to surpass. For some traders, short term positions even fulfill a need to gamble that may be pathological. What is the outcome of this analysis? If you can make a total commitment, exercise near-perfect self-discipline, and have the time to fulfill these prerequisites, then you can consider short term trades. If not, then your success will be limited.

## THE IN-BETWEEN APPROACH

Is it possible to combine the positive aspects of each approach in a hybrid method that will serve you well? I believe it is. I recommend several guidelines for those who believe that long term trades are best but who feel the need or desire to trade for the short term as well. Here they are:

1 Keep two different accounts (at least). Trade long term signals in one and short term signals in the other. Remember that if you trade a short term position opposite from a long term position, do so in a different contract month.

2 Follow only a few markets for your short term trading, particularly if you have a full-time job other than the market. Get to know these markets well in terms of the cycles and timing signals. Generally, I recommend you trade only one each of the meats, metals, and grains, and possibly three of the remaining markets.

3 Maintain and follow specific rules for managing money in each of the accounts.

4 You must practice considerable self-discipline in not allowing your short term decisions to affect your long term positions.

| Approach | Taxes | Commissions | Time Input | Charts | Percentage of Profit | Commentary |
|---|---|---|---|---|---|---|
| Short-term | Usually higher[a] | Higher | Greater | More needed | Smaller percentage return[b] | More errors likely due to psychological factors |
| Long-term | Typically lower | Lower[c] | Lesser | Less needed | Larger percentage return | Decision making less crucial and psychological factors may be much less important |

[a]Tax considerations can be altered somewhat by the use of spreads or straddles in converting short-term to long-term gains.
[b]This holds true for a majority of traders. The experienced short-term trader will do just as well if not much better than the long-term trader.
[c]Commission-to-position ratio will be better because there is less trading overall.

**Figure 4.1   Assets and liabilities of various market orientations.**

Only you can decide what is best for you. If you are a long term trader and find the cyclic approach profitable, then do not change what you are doing. However, if you feel dissatisfied with your approach, whether it is long term or short term, make some effort to investigate what the other camp may hold. Figure 4-1 reviews some of the advantages and/or disadvantages of each method along various parameters.

The reason I have taken this brief side trip rests primarily in the importance of your having the proper attitude toward the markets. It is not my job to gain converts, but it is part of my commitment to let you know the pros and cons of each approach as I have personally experienced them while using the cyclic approach. You alone will make up your mind.

# CHAPTER FIVE

# Examining Some
# Long Term Cycles

Just as each person has a specific set of traits that characterize his or her personality, each market and group of markets has its own cyclic tendencies. Many of the markets move together as part of secular patterns and more pervasive economic forces. The approximate 54 year Kondratieff cycle, as it is called, although still controversial, tends to exert a major inflating and/or deflating effect on virtually all prices, stocks, and commodities. The long term interest rate cycles, which run about 54 years as well, also tend to have an impact on stock and commodity prices. The Foundation for the Study of Cycles has spent considerable time and effort examining many of these secular patterns. Some of their findings are cited in this work.

In order to be a well-rounded student of cycles, it is necessary to have a general knowledge of what the major patterns in each market have been, how they have acted in the past, and how they will most likely act in the future. The purpose of this chapter, and the three that follow, is to acquaint you with many of these patterns, to illustrate some of the important characteristics that accompany changes in trends, and to provide you with a set of tools you can use to analyze long range price behavior.

What is meant by the term *long term cycle*? There is no definitive rule as to what constitutes a long term trend. Some commodity traders consider a position held more than one week to be long term. An individual who trades only on seasonal patterns several times a year may regard a long term cycle as one that lasts more than several years. Unfortunately, the science of cyclic analysis is not sufficiently advanced to permit an operational definition. For the purpose of this discussion I consider a long term cycle to be one that runs 2 years or more from low to low or from high to high. I do not pay too much attention to patterns longer than 15 years in this analysis. I also avoid all manner of fundamental explanation pertaining to the cycles that I cover. I do not further fuel the controversy as to which came first, the cycles or the fundamentals. I simply present the facts as I see them, allowing you to judge.

In his excellent and classic work, *Cycles—Selected Writings* (1970), Edward R. Dewey compiled one of the most impressive lists of cyclically related events ever gathered together under one heading. Among the items studied were many commodities that have never been traded on the futures exchanges. In addition, Dewey investigated alleged cycles in everything from shoe production to variations in the depth of Lake Saki. If we are to believe the Dewey analysis, it

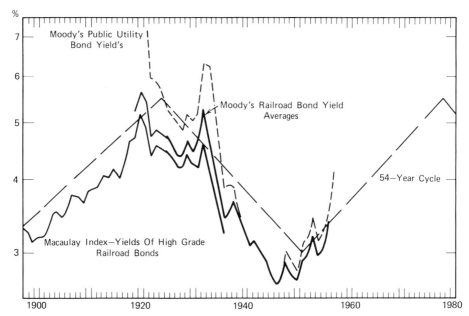

**Figure 5.1** **The 54 year cycle in interest rates, 1900–1957, and the projection of trend (dashed line) through 1980 (Dewey, 1970, p. 328).**

seems that virtually every aspect of life can be seen in terms of cycles. This does not, of course, negate the role of other forces. And it may not, in fact, be the ultimate explanation of change. It is merely one way of looking at reality.

 Take, for example, the 54 year cycle in interest rates (Figure 5-1). This chart was originally published in the December 1957 issue of *Cycles*. On the basis of several interest rate cycles it was possible to make a very general forecast about interest rates through the late 1970s, possibly on into the early 1980s. Here is a brief portion of what was said in the same *Cycles* issue that carried the chart of interests rates:

> *The 54-year cycle in interest rates is* upward [emphasis theirs] *at the present time. It suggests that, if this cycle continues to dominate, interest rates should work themselves gradually and irregularly upward until 1978.* [p. 327]

I cite this example because it has turned out to be an excellent projection, and it also points out the kind of long term work possible with cyclic analysis. The long term history of pattern is more completely shown later in this chapter. Another aspect of the 54 year cycle in interest rates is the approximately 33 month pattern in industrial bond yields. The chart of this pattern appears in Figure 5-2. As you can see, there are cycles within cycles within cycles, which could be extended to the point of absurdity. The important thing for our present study is the delineation of cycles that have a proven record of reliability. We *could* examine every possible pattern, but this would take considerable time, and it might in the long run prove to be a waste of effort. I have combined the work of other cycle analysts with mine to provide you with what

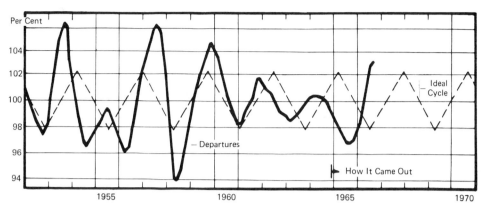

**Figure 5.2   The 32.94 month cycle in industrial bond yields (*Cycles,* May 1968, p. 106).**

I believe to be the most important cycles to commodity traders, farmers, economists, and hedgers.

## LIVE HOGS

Figures 5-3 and 5-4 are also taken from the May 1968 issue of *Cycles.* They show the cycle charts for three separate patterns in the "hogs on farms" data and the combined cycle of all three patterns (Figure 5-4). There are many such cycles in commodity data. Highly repetitive patterns occur in wheat acreage planted, wheat acreage harvested, livestock numbers, cotton acreage, housing starts, and the like.

These cycles are important, but in the long run they are expressed in the form of price fluctuation. Say, for example, that we are watching a cycle in hog production that suggests fewer hogs on farms, and we are also watching another cycle in pork consumption that suggests a lower meat demand during the same period. The net effect on price may be nil because the two factors are in a somewhat balanced state. A look at the demand or consumption side alone might lead you to expect lower pork prices, but a study of the supply cycle might lead you to alter your expectation. Why study all the underlying patterns if there exists a reliable price cycle?

We've been talking about the live hog market, so let's examine the long term cycle. In 1875 Samuel Benner, in his book *Benner's Prophecies of Future Ups and Downs in Prices,* made forecasts of rises and falls in corn and hog prices based on his studies of various cycles. His work was quite accurate despite the fact that he ignored the important fundamentals and attended almost entirely to the cyclic tendencies. Figure 5-5 shows the approximate 3.61 year, or 43.36 month cycle in hog prices (cash basis) since 1942. The Foundation for the Study of Cycles has traced this pattern back into the late 1800s, finding it to be valid. You will observe several interesting things about the cycle chart. First, the price plotted is average monthly cash price. Second, the time count runs from low to low. To obtain an average cyclic length, the individual cycle lengths are added together and a mathematical mean computed. Third, the maximum

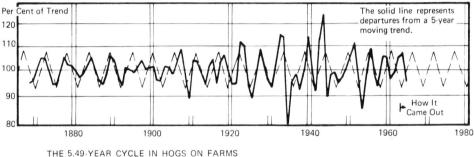

THE 5.49-YEAR CYCLE IN HOGS ON FARMS

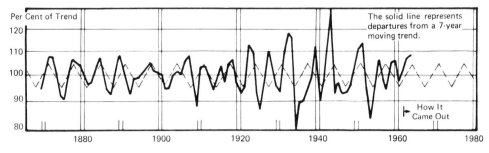

THE 6.06-YEAR CYCLE IN HOGS ON FARMS

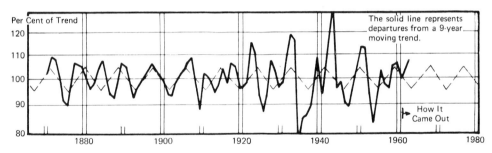

THE 8.78-YEAR CYCLE IN HOGS ON FARMS

**Figure 5.3   Several cycles in hogs on farms (*Cycles,* May 1968, p. 108).**

variation on this chart is 10 months from the average for the shortest cycle (marked *A*) and about 12 months from the average for the longest cycle (55 months). Notice in particular that the one cycle of 55 months is a bit distorted. This is common during periods of war. Subsequent to the 55 month pattern is a shorter cycle that tends to compensate for the longer one. The combined length is about 92 months, which averages out to 41 months, well within the 43.36 month mean cycle length. The shortest pattern, 33 months *(A),* cannot be totally explained at this time, but it is really one of the few anomalies in the hog cycle. Assuming that a trader was actually waiting for a turn that came early, he might have entered the market some 3 to 4 months after the actual low, still participating in a fairly large upmove.

  There are many different ways to depict cyclic patterns. I prefer the most simple. We could take the hog data, construct a moving average of it, subtract

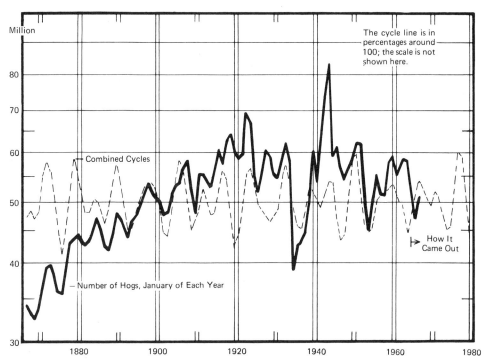

**Figure 5.4 Number of hogs on farms compared to combination of cycles (*Cycles*, May 1968, p. 107).**

from it a number of variant cycles, and arrive at a smoother chart, which looks better and supports our case more fully. We could also construct a chart of the percentage deviation from trend, which would smooth out the extreme highs and lows, again making the cycle both easier to find and more "pure." I have chosen not to do so because I believe that the closer we can stick to real data, the better off we are.

One final thing to note about the hog cycle is that it is not completely symmetrical. If we take a count of the time spans between the highs, we'll have a much more variable figure, but the cycles will still be evident. I have drawn a perfect 3.61 year zigzag (dashed line) to show how much deviation there might have been from an ideal cyclic pattern. Several things are clear about our chart, the most important being a fairly reliable cycle in hogs. A second factor is that the 3.61 year cycle tends to encompass most of the historically large up and down moves. As a result, it can be used in a predictive way for the purposes of trading, hedging, and/or forecasting. This is where *cycle expectation* and *timing signals* begin to work together. Having a cyclic expectation and trading on that expectation are two totally different things. I stress the importance of not using the cycle as a final determinant of what to do in any market. Any reliable or potentially reliable cycle must be combined with timing indicators that confirm the change in trend. In covering long term cycles, I am not making reference to the precise timing indicators that are a necessary part of trading. As I mentioned earlier, there is a great difference between

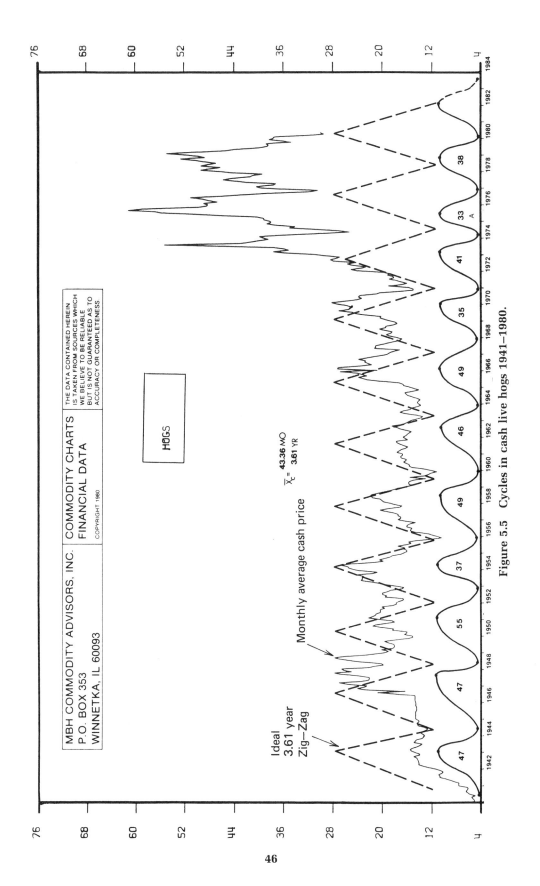

Figure 5.5  Cycles in cash live hogs 1941–1980.

forecasting and trading. The long term cyclic expectations cannot be used for trading purposes in and of themselves. For such things as hedging, planting intentions, expansion of herd size and/or facilities, and long range planning, the major cycles can be of value without precise timing, assuming that the individual using them is willing to take a position and is also capable of sitting with it until it has turned to the good.

## LIVE CATTLE

Another important cycle in the livestock sector is the long term cash cattle pattern. Figure 5-6 shows the approximately seven year pattern in cattle futures. As is the case in most long term cycles, this pattern is assymetrical. Notice also that the 3.61 year hog cycle, when doubled, gives us 7.2 years, the approximate length of the cattle cycle. Late tops characterize this long-range pattern. The cattle chart also shows another interesting characteristic that often appears in the study of cyclic data. Fairly reliable patterns can be found between highs as well as between lows.

A cycle, or repetitive pattern, need not be symmetrical. If we attempt to find cycle highs, we end up with a much less stable or predictable cyclic tendency. By averaging the lengths between lows, we arrive at the approximately 45 month tendency. Were we to use the cyclic patterns presented herein for simple forecasting purposes, we could extend the chart (see the dashed lines) to show the approximate timing of the next highs. Notice that our forecast does not permit the projection of prices. It is important to remember that time is critical, much more so than price itself. More on this point later.

How did we arrive at the next top and bottom forecasts? Here's a simple lesson in projecting top and bottom expectations. First, calculate the cycle low period by adding all the time spans between lows and taking their arithmetic average (mean). This is achieved as follows:

$$44 + 49 + 50 + 46 + 52 + 35 + 35 + 43 + 50 + 44 = 448$$
$$448 \div 10 = 44.8$$

The answer, 44.8, can also be noted as $\bar{X} = 44.8$. This is read "X bar equals 44.8," which in mathematical language stands for the mean, or average.

Next, we take the average that has just been calculated and count forward in time from the last recorded low. This marks our projected low for the next cycle (marked *PL* in Figure 5-6). The cycle high lengths are then treated the same way. We add the highs together, take their arithmetic mean, and project forward the next high (marked *PH* in Figure 5-6). The process can be followed for each and every cycle observed in the data. Some techniques that involve higher level mathematics combine the various cyclic lengths to arrive at one composite chart to reflect expected price trend action. This is a very reasonable way of dealing with cycles, and it also helps to account for cycles within cycles. Variations in length caused by influences of other cycles can also be factored in.

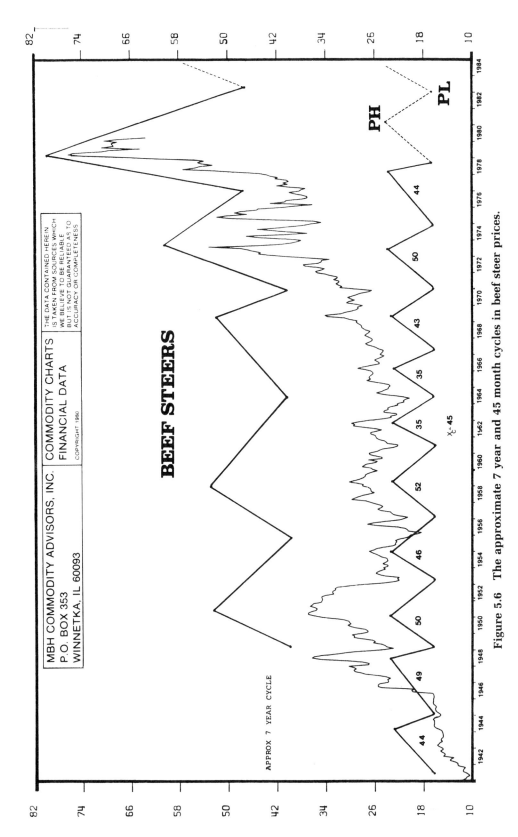

Figure 5.6   The approximate 7 year and 45 month cycles in beef steer prices.

BEEF STEERS

MBH COMMODITY ADVISORS, INC.
P.O. BOX 353
WINNETKA, IL 60093

COMMODITY CHARTS
FINANCIAL DATA

COPYRIGHT 1980

APPROX 7 YEAR CYCLE

PH

PL

$X_c = 45$

What conclusions can be drawn from the cycle chart of beef steers shown in Figure 5-6? Here are several that I feel are justified on the basis of our rather limited investigation:

1   There is a fairly reliable 7 year cyclic pattern, low to low, in prices for beef steers. It has repeated itself about 11 times since the early 1900's.

2   The 7 year pattern varies plus or minus 1.5 years on the average from its lows.

3   The top of this 7 year pattern most likely came in 1979. The next relative low should come in 1983.

4   The 7 year pattern has an approximately 45 month pattern within it. In fact, there are ordinarily two repetitions of the 45 month cycle within the 7 year pattern. The 45 month cycle is not very reliable across lows, but it is highly repetitive across highs. On the basis of the projection of highs according to this cycle, prices should peak in 1981.

And that is how we complete an elementary cycle analysis. The foregoing type of analysis could be done for every market you wanted to follow. By having long term information, many different ends could be achieved without the use of timing indicators. A livestock feeder, for example, could plan needs well in advance. If he knew that prices would most likely be higher in two years than they are today, he could plan the expansion of his animal population accordingly. Then, by moving to shorter cycles and seasonal trends, he could hedge his animals, locking in a profit, by selling them on the futures market before they are actually ready to be marketed. An end user of meat could also plan ahead. If he knew that meat prices would be relatively high in a year, he could buy futures contracts today, thereby locking in his costs and stabilizing his return on capital investment and profits. Certainly, the picture is not as simple as I have presented it. In the final analysis timing must be as accurate as possible, or substantial margin will be required if prices move too far against your position. Naturally, the overall prospects are improved the closer you can come to an actual top or bottom. This is where shorter cycles and timing come into play.

## PORK BELLIES

Let's go on to another cycle. If a cycle is found in one market, then it's highly likely that the same cycle will appear in related markets. Earlier we saw the 3.6 year cycle in live hogs and the corresponding 7 year pattern in cattle. We also note that the 3.6 year cycle is about 43.36 months long, which corresponds to the 45 month cycle in cattle also discussed earlier. It's understandable that markets such as these should move together. Later on I clearly show that many markets move together even though they are relatively unrelated. If we look closely at the pork belly market, then we should find a cycle similar in length to that which has been observed in hogs, and beef steers. Figure 5-7 shows the monthly high and low prices of pork bellies at a Chicago warehouse. I have marked the 3.6 year cycle in Figure 5-7, and you can see that it corresponds very closely to the hog and cattle cycles. Notice that the chart marks mid-1980

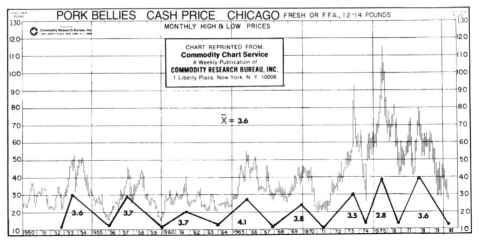

**Figure 5.7   The 3.6 year cycle in cash pork bellies.**

as the most recent low. An examination of prices since June 1980 clearly shows that the low has passed. Prices have more than doubled since then.

### THE LIVESTOCK INDEX

Carrying the relationship between cycles in different markets one more step, we can examine the livestock index cycle. By plotting the Standard and Poors monthly average livestock index data we arrive at a chart of the various ups and downs in the meats as a group. Figure 5-8 shows the chart and corresponding approximate 44 month cycle in this category. Notice that it is essentially similar in length to the 3.6 year pattern. After all, 44 months works out to be roughly 3.67 years. Because the index combines several meats (i.e., chicken, hogs, cattle), it is somewhat distorted for use in any one market, but it reveals the overall trend. You will notice that my cycle chart, drawn in on Figure 5-8, shows five fairly regular repetitions of the cycle. The last cycle, marked A, does not conform to the same regularity. Instead of the low coming at point B, which looks like a natural low, it does not actually come until point C. This gives the cycle a rather peculiar look. If the low had actually come at point B, this would have been too early for the low. The only thing that makes sense in terms of this pattern is to assume that the market made a low later on. Point C is the logical choice because it comes prior to the large upmove. The only way to know if the cycle has indeed shortened is by waiting for the next low. If it arrives on time, then no adjustment is necessary in our calculations.

Having completed our long-term analysis of the meats, we can draw several conclusions as follows:

1   Meats tend to move together as a group, generally exhibiting the same cyclic lengths.

2   The cattle, hog, and pork belly markets show approximately 3.6 year cycles.

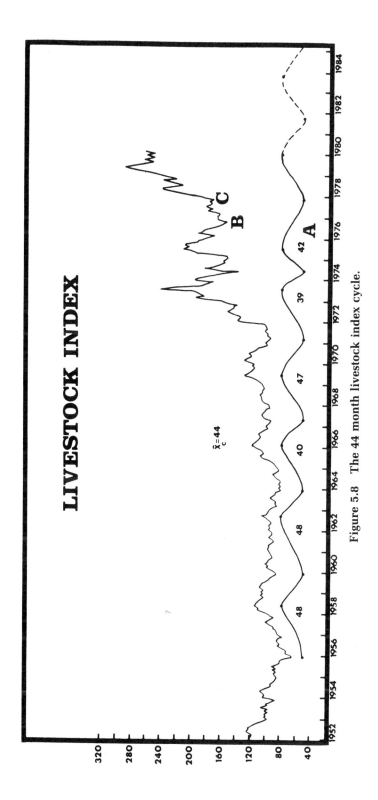

Figure 5.8 The 44 month livestock index cycle.

3  The cattle, hog, and pork belly markets show approximately 7 year patterns.

4  The livestock index generally reflects these patterns.

There has always been considerable speculation as to what causes cyclic variation in livestock prices. There is some validity in the biological explanations based on the period of gestation, but there are also other possible explanations. It has been noted, for example, that a 3.7 year pattern in temperature variation exists globally (Dewey, 1970). The similarity in length between the temperature cycle and the meat cycles is an important consideration because livestock is particularly susceptible to temperature variations.

## GRAINS AND FEEDS

The grain markets have price cycles as well, and in fact, the patterns in these markets have been studied extensively. Cyclic activity dating back several thousand years has been alleged to have existed. Dewey (1962) found several significant cycles in wheat prices running from 42 to 54 years in length. Figure 5-9 shows the percentage of deviations from trend plotted against an ideal 54 year zigzag for European wheat prices 1513–1856. There is reason to believe that the 54 year cycle (already mentioned earlier in this chapter in connection with interest rates) is a dominant economic force. Earlier I stated that I would give little attention to the very long-range cycles because of both their degree of potential error and their limited applicability. I discuss the 54 year pattern here in order to illustrate the harmonic principle of cyclic activity. Earlier we saw the 7 year cattle cycle and the approximately 45 month cycle within the 7 year pattern—about half the 7 year period. We could possibly find another important cattle cycle by taking a fraction of the 45 month pattern, which would result in an approximate length of 22 months, or 1.8 years. We could then go to our chart to see if a 1.8 year pattern did indeed exist. This procedure would require a weekly price chart, rather than a monthly chart. The process could be continued by looking for a cycle that was half the 22 month length, or 11 months.

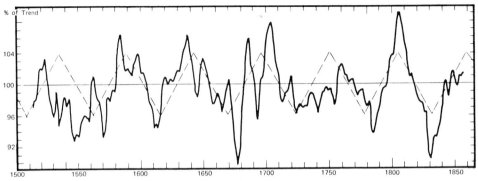

**Figure 5.9  The approximate 54 year cycle in European wheat prices 1500–1850 (Dewey 1962).**

If we take a half, a third, a sixth, and a ninth of the 54 year wheat pattern, we end with the following hints of possible cycle lengths: 27, 18, 9, and 6 (years). By examining these probable cycles visually (or mathematically), we should be able to isolate several reliable patterns. The best way to begin is by simple visual inspection. Figure 5-10 shows a monthly wheat cash price chart that goes back to the early 1900s. Now let's take some of the fractional cycles and see if they can yield any potentially positive results. First, examine the 27 year cycle across the bottoms and across the tops. I have placed letters on the chart showing my counts. Notice that the count began with either a prominent low or high. The 27 year pattern, beginning with the most prominent low on this chart, 1893.5, fails to yield any important repetitive lows. So we move to the next low, 1913.5 (marked *A* on chart). Add 27 years and you get 1940.5 *(B)*. Notice that an actual low came in 1939. Notice also that a very large upmove followed the 1940.5 theoretical low. Now add to 1940.5 the 27 year cycle to get 1967.5 *(C)*, which marked a low almost exactly. A move of over $5.25 followed. This was one of the largest moves in history. The next low of this cycle should come in approximately 1994.5. Now let's work backward from our starting point, 1913.5, subtracting from it 27 years, and we get 1886.5. There was indeed an important low in 1886 but not a major one. In actuality, the major low came in 1895.

So we have just a hint of a 27 year pattern across the lows of wheat prices. Now let's take a look at the 27 year pattern across the highs. Starting with a prominent high, 1920, *(D)* we work ahead in time to 1947 (1920 + 27). Notice that there was a high in 1947 *(E)*. Now add 27 years to 1947 and you get 1974

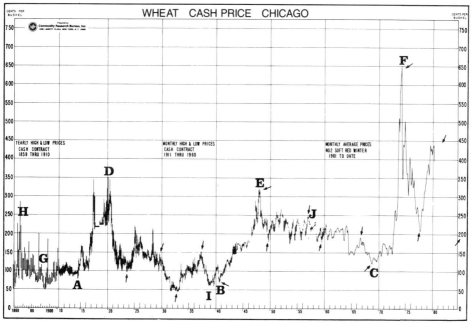

**Figure 5.10   Cash price and cycle turns in Chicago wheat.**

*(F)*, another prominent high in wheat prices. Working backward from 1920, subtract 27 years and get 1893 *(G)*, which is not a very significant result. Working back another 27 years, we get 1866 *(H)*, when there was another prominent high in wheat prices. To study this cycle more completely, we would need to go back as far as possible in order to make more detailed observations.

Let's look again at the 1920 high *(D)* as a starting point. Add to 1920 the 18 year cycle and you get 1938 *(I)*. Clearly this was not a high year. Add to 1938 another 18 and you get 1956 *(J)*. This was a minor high year because it was followed by a persistent decline through 1964. Now add to 1956 another 18 and you get 1974 *(F)*, the year of a very important high in wheat prices. If we work back in time from 1920 we get to 1302, which was not an important high in wheat prices. We can conclude from this analysis that the 18 year cycle does not work well across highs and is therefore not useful for such purposes.

Now let's take another look at Figure 5-10 (the same wheat chart we've been using). Examining the possible 9 year cycle, we find lows at the points indicated by arrows. Each is approximately 9 years from the first prominent low in 1913.5. The progression would read: 1922.5, 1931.5, 1940.5, 1949.5, 1958.5, 1967.5, 1976.5, 1985.5. Notice the indicated lows. Moving across the highs, beginning with 1920 as the most significant, we get 1929, 1936.5, 1947, 1956, 1965.5, 1974, and 1981. You will observe that many important tops came at the indicated or expected time. True, the 9 year pattern does not account for all the variability in wheat prices, but it does help to pick many of the tops and bottoms.

Now let's briefly examine the probable 6 year cycle. Beginning with our prominent low in 1913.5 and referring to Figure 5-11, we add 6 to 1913.5 and

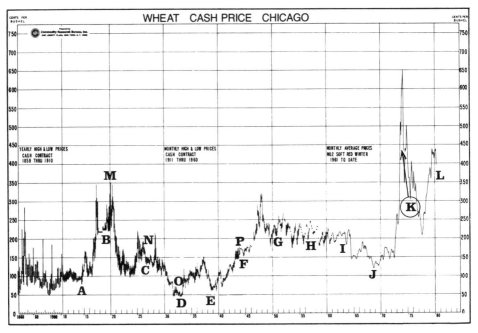

**Figure 5.11   Cycles in cash wheat; an approximate 6 year pattern.**

get 1919.5 *(B)*. Notice that in 1919.5 there was a significant low prior to an upmove of almost $1 per bushel. The next period of 6 years brings us to 1925.5 *(C)*, not a significant time in terms of a low. Adding again the 6 year period, we get to 1931.5 *(D)*, which is clearly a low period. Add another 6 years to the figure to reach 1937.5 *(E)*. This was also a low period and was, in fact, followed by a fairly persistent upmove of over $2.40 in the next few years. The next low in our series would ideally be 1943.5 *(F)*. Observe that this is also a relative low which, by the way, led to an upmove of over 1.50 and was also tested about one year later. Continuing to the next ideal 6 year cyclic low, we get to 1949.5 *(G)*. The actual low came a year earlier, and this bottom proved to be a secondary low. It did, nevertheless, lead to an upmove of more than $0.50 per bushel. The series continues to 1955.5 *(H)*, which, albeit a low, was not one that lasted long because prices moved in a sawtooth pattern for several years thereafter. The progression continues with 1961.5 as the next in our series *(I)*. This, in fact, turned out to be a high rather than a low. Notice that this is the first total deviation from the cycle seen so far. The next low, 1967.5 *(J)* is a number we've seen before. It's that very important low which several other variants of the 54 year cycle have picked. The upmove that followed was a classic and historical one. The next number in our cyclic pattern is 1973.5 *(K)*, which you will notice on close observation is not a significant low on the price chart. The actual low came in mid-1974 after a substantial drop from the 1974 highs. Prices bottomed in May and rebounded almost $2.00 per bushel in a matter of months. By using shorter cycles in conjunction with the 6 year pattern, the move might have been very profitable. The next number in our series is 1979.5 *(L)*, which means that mid-1980 should have seen a relative low in prices. From a low of about $3.80 in May of 1980 prices moved well above $5.00 over the next few months.

This completes the analysis of lows according to the 6 year cycle. Bear in mind that we have not said anything about symmetry. Nor have we given any attention to forecasting highs when looking only at the lows. Now we'll turn to the highs and see what we can accomplish with our very simple cyclic analysis. Going back to the prominent high in 1920 *(M)* (in Figure 5-11), we cound forward to 1926 *(N)*. Notice that there is a small top early in 1926 but nothing important thereafter. The next in this series in 1932 *(O)*, which actually is a low rather than a high. That's two misses now for the 6 year cycle across tops. The next high should have come in 1938, which also shows a low. Moving ahead we come to 1944 *(P)*, which again yields nothing in the way of positive results. Hence, we'll drop our analysis of the 6 year cycle across highs. It was clearly not a reliable pattern and, as a consequence, we have no use for it. The process I have explained in this analysis could be carried out for every market. In fact, it should be, if you want to obtain the most comprehensive analysis possible. Earlier I mentioned that this same basic method could be completed with much greater detail by a computer. The Foundation for the Study of Cycles has several computer programs that allow analysis on a much more sophisticated level, but I do not believe it is necessary to use a computer if you do not have access to one. I believe that most important cycles and their variants can be found by simple visual analysis.

What can we conclude from the foregoing analysis? First, we have observed the way in which a major cycle can be broken up into components, each of which has fairly good reliability across the highs and lows of a long term price move. By examining all the important patterns, we can account for a high percentage of the price variation in a given market. We have also seen that cycles in the commodity market are not necessarily symmetrical and, in fact, do not have to be regular. The same analysis can be applied on a shorter-term basis and is explained in a later chapter.

## CORN

A similar analysis can be completed for the corn market. Although I do not go into as much detail for corn prices, I do present the major cyclic patterns. Earlier in this chapter I mentioned the work of Samuel Benner. Benner (1875) had the ability to divorce himself from the fundamentals, studying only the cycles. In 1875 he discovered the 5.5 year corn cycle. In the March 1965 issue of *Cycles*, Edward R. Dewey discussed Benner's work and constructed a hypothetical record of corn purchases and sales from 1875 to 1955 according to the predictions of Benner's 5.5 year cycle. Dewey (1970) ended with a total gain of 542.3 percent! He went on to predict the next important highs and lows in corn through the year 2000, assuming a perfectly symmetrical cyclic pattern.

Figure 5-12 shows cash corn prices back to the early 1940s. The lows and highs of an approximate 5.5 year (68 month) cycle have been marked accordingly. In his original work Dewey picked the years 1955, 1960, 1966, 1971, 1976, and 1982 for lows. Examining the record, we see that lows actually came in late 1955, late 1960, late 1965, late 1971, and late 1977. Ideally, the next low should come in mid- to late 1982. You will also notice that the record of Dewey's forecast may be a bit off schedule in terms of the next low. Now let's look at the projected highs. The forecast called for highs in 1952, early 1958, 1963, late 1968 to early 1969, 1974, and late 1979 to early 1980. The actual highs were late 1951, mid-1956, 1963, 1970, and 1974. The record has not been as good regarding highs.

We can see, however, that a forecast made so far in advance has performed rather well considering the absence of what many economists would believe to be vital information regarding the fundamentals of corn. It is highly likely that the 5.5 year cycle will continue to work in years ahead. On the basis of my calculations, the cycle actually runs about 5.675 years, low-to-low average, which might get our projection a bit closer than if we had used a 5.5 year repetitive cycle. The corn market can also be studied in terms of an approximately 26 month pattern, which is also shown in Figure 5-12. This is a cycle that runs about 2 years; we examine it in greater detail later on.

## THE SOYBEAN COMPLEX

Few commodities have attracted as much interest and speculation over the years as has the soybean market. There are several long term patterns in beans that deserve study. Figure 5-13 shows the monthly average cash price of soybeans in Chicago back to the early 1900s. First let's examine the same 27 year approximate pattern across highs as was seen in the wheat market. We see tops marked *A*, *B*, and *C*, all within the approximate time frame. There are still

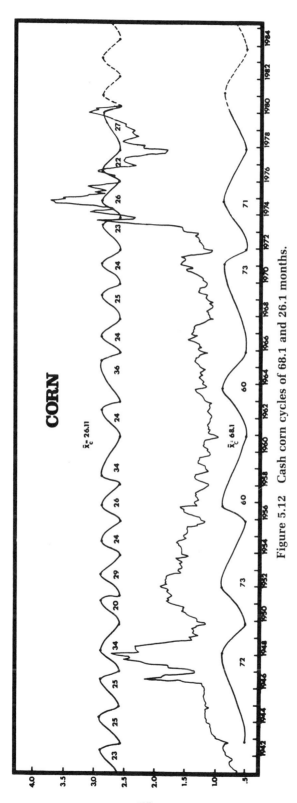

Figure 5.12   Cash corn cycles of 68.1 and 26.1 months.

57

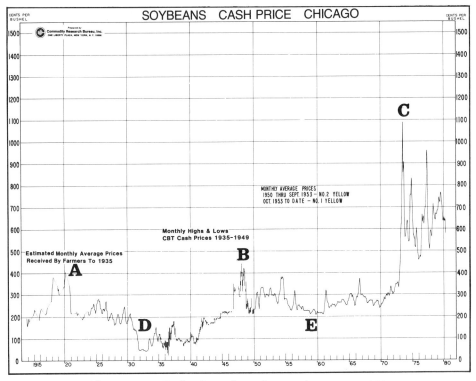

**Figure 5.13   Cycles in cash soybean prices 1913–1980.**

insufficient data to permit conclusions about the validity of this pattern. Now taking the low in 1932 *(D)* and adding 27 to it, we get point E, which marks another low. Projecting this forward we arrive at 1985–1986, the probable next low if this cycle is valid. There is insufficient evidence to confirm a 27 year cycle across lows because data are limited. We can only hypothesize that such a pattern exists. There are several other alleged cycles in the soybean market. The approximately 36 month and 24 month cycles account for most of the price change in soybeans. There is also the shorter 9 to 11 month cycle, which is discussed in Chapter 7. There is reason to believe that these three patterns have been valid as far back as 1935. They are extremely important to both the hedger and the speculator and are shown and discussed here in detail. The first hint of a possible 36 month pattern can be seen in the monthly high–low chart of soybeans (Figure 5-14), which covers 1935 to 1952. The very first pattern *(ABC)* ran 37 months, low to low (as indicated). Let's assume, for illustrative purposes, that the next low, which came 36 months later (cycle *CDE*), is indeed a valid one even though the high came very late. Remember that there is a tendency for cycles to become elongated during, or close to, periods of international war or major conflict. Futures trading was suspended from February 19, 1943 through July 7, 1947. Beginning with the low after trading was resumed, we continue our 36 month count (low marked *F*). The top of this cycle *(G)* and the next low *(H)* came within the time span to complete a somewhat shorter, but still valid, 31 month pattern.

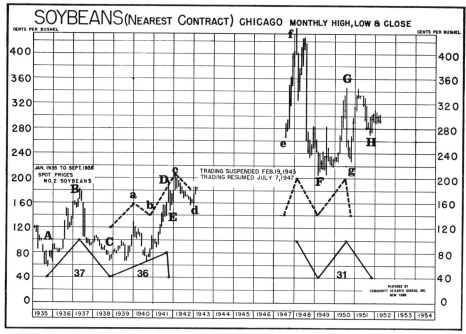

**Figure 5.14   The 36 and 24 month cash soybean cycle, 1935–1951.**

Let's step back now and take a look at the approximately 24 month cycle to see how it fits into the analysis. The first cycle is marked *Cab*. It ran about 22 months, low to low. The next cycle is marked *bcd* and ran about 26 months. (Please make certain you are reading the cycles correctly. Notice that I have used upper and lower case letters to illustrate them. A cycle may be denoted by a combination of upper and lower case letters). Again, we enter the period of trading suspension. Resuming our count with cycle *efF*, which ran about 20 months, we now have three repetitions of the approximately 24 month cycle. Cycle *FGg* ran 20 months as well. It's interesting that Figure 5-14 contains a combined total of 15 major tops and bottoms, 13 of which have been accounted for by our cycle analysis.

Were we doing initial research on the soybean market, we would have ample reason to believe that the two patterns under study are indeed reasonable for further investigation. Let's move to another chart now (Figure 5-15) to see how the cycles acted from 1956 through 1968. Instead of running through the individual analyses for all cycles, I present only several in order to help you familiarize yourself with the manner in which these charts are read. Let's work with only the 24 month cycle. Taking them in order we have *ABC* = 25 months, *CDF* = 24 months, *FGH* = 22 months, *HIJ* = 23 months, *JKL* = 18 months (a short cycle to be explained), and *LMN* = 24 months. The *JKL* cycle was very short. A certain amount of variation is reasonable in working with cycles because they are not, after all, perfect. You will notice that the 36 month cycle low of pattern *HKL* came at about the same time as the low of *JKL*. The *HKL* low had a profound effect on shortening the time span of *JKL*. This is a common

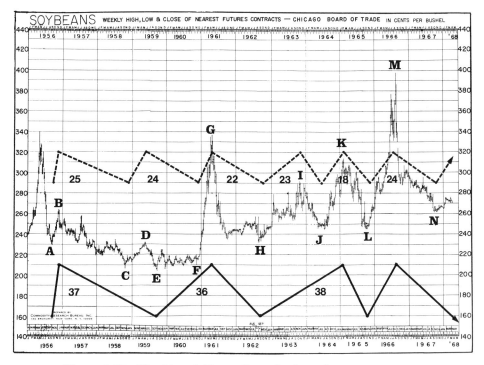

**Figure 5.15   The 24 and 36 month cycles in soybeans, 1956–1968.**

type of variation in working with multiple cyclic patterns. A speculator looking for the low of a 36 month cycle *(HKL)* would have been aware of this possibility in making his analysis. He would have picked the period in late 1965 to early 1966 as one during which a significant cyclic upmove was to start. This did indeed happen; prices moved from bottom *L* to top *M* in one of the largest moves since 1961.

The approximately 36 month cycles are also shown in Figure 5-15. Their lengths are marked accordingly. The manner in which cycles converge is also clearly demonstrated in this chart. Tops *B, G, K,* and *M* are all double cyclic highs. Notice the large and persistent downmoves—*BE, GH, KL,* and *MN*—which followed the convergence tops. Notice also that bottoms *A, H,* and *L* are double cycle lows. Although there was not a large move from bottom *A,* there were large moves from bottoms *H* and *L.* It is always advisable to look for convergence tops and bottoms because they most often give the longest and strongest moves in any market.

Let's continue the analysis with Figure 5-16, which shows price action from 1971 through early 1980. If our assumptions regarding the approximately 24 and 36 month cycles are valid, then we should see a continuation of the patterns in reasonably reliable fashion. Several years are skipped in the transition to this chart, but they showed valid cycle lows—one in late 1968 on the 36 month cycle and a low of the 24 month cycle in September 1969. The continuation in Figure 5-16, therefore, fits our pattern correctly. The approximate 36 month cycles are *ADE, EHI,* and *ILM.* According to the chart, bottom *M* should have

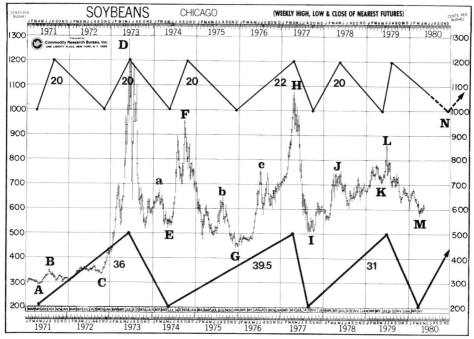

**Figure 5.16   The 24 and 36 month cycles in soybeans, 1971–1980.**

marked the beginning of a 36 month upwave ideally due to peak in June–July 1981, approximately. The analysis continued without any difficulty, except for the approximately 24 month pattern *IJK*, which does not seem to fit too well. Should this be a valid low, we'll see the next bottom in late 1980 to early 1981, marked *N* (top right of chart). On the basis of price behavior to date, it appears as if the analysis will indeed be correct. It should be noted that from late 1980, both the 36 and 24 month patterns should be in a general uptrend.

Regarding convergence, we can clearly see that tops *D, H,* and *L* are convergence tops, followed by concerted downmoves—in fact, they are among the largest downmoves of the decade. Bottoms *A, E,* and *I* are convergence bottoms, each of which was followed by either a sharp upmove in price or a long steady rise. Hence, the importance of convergence at major cycle turns is again validated.

As you can see, the approximately 24 and 36 month cycles in the soybean market are highly important in determining price trends. Several harmonic and seasonal patterns also have a direct bearing on the price behavior of soybeans. Between the 36, 24, and 9.5 month overall commodity cycle (discussed in a later chapter) and the seasonal price tendency, it should be possible to account for over 85 percent of all major tops and bottoms in soybeans. If we could combine these patterns with accurate timing indicators, we would have one of the most valuable tools for commodity analysis ever constructed. The serious student of cycles should continue with my analysis, investigating such things as a possible cycle between tops. Although there is not enough evidence as yet, you may want to look at the following tops in Figure 5-16 and their corresponding lengths—*D, a, F, b, c, H, J, L.* There seems to be a pattern here that's worth investigating, but I leave that up to you.

## SOYBEAN MEAL

The analysis for soybean meal is not as exhaustive as that for soybeans. Some of the long term cycles in meal are similar to those inthe bean market, but the meal has its own cycles in addition to those observed in soybeans. Figure 5-17 shows monthly average soybean meal cash prices. This analysis is based on cash prices and may not necessarily correlate well with what happens in futures. There are differences at times. I have shown a 31.3 month cycle that should be essentially similar to the 36 month cycle in beans, and a longer 49.4 month cycle (dots mark lows) that also helps to account for some of the bottoms and tops in meal. As a hedger or speculator, I would make most of my decisions on the basis of the soybean cycles, however, because they are much more reliable.

## SOYBEAN OIL

The soybean oil market has several patterns, all longer than those examined in the bean market. Although prices should move generally with trends in soybeans, there are times during which divergence is significant. The long term cycle in soybean oil runs about 83.3 months, and it has run as high as 103 months. These cycles translate to an approximate 7 year cyclic tendency, one that has received considerable attention in recent years. El Niño is the name given to the temperature changes in water current off the Peruvian coast. It is said that El Niño (the child) has a severe effect on the fishing yields of anchovies. Because anchovies are an important source of protein for feed, the fundamental effect on beans, meal, and oil is easy to grasp.

Within the approximately 7 year soybean oil cycle, there is a pattern that runs about 46 months, low to low. According to this cycle, early 1981 was projected as an ideal low with early 1982 projected as being an ideal high. The 7 year cycle is also due to peak in late 1980 to early 1981. This top could easily be elongated as prices trend with the 36 and 24 month soybean patterns.

If you examine a soybean oil cash chart dating back to the early 1900s, you'll find that the approximately 7 year pattern (actually 6.94) has repeated itself nine times. In analyzing trade over the long term, in either meal or soybean oil, it is always best to consider soybean price cycles as well. Because these markets are very closely related, there is certain to be a carryover of cyclic influence from one to the other.

## METALS

Metals also exhibit cyclic tendencies. Of these markets, copper is the one that has been studied most. It has the longest relatively uninterrupted history of trading. Dewey (1970) did considerable research on copper market cycles and isolated at least five distinct and reasonably reliable patterns running 32 months, 5 years, 8 years, 9 years, and 50 to 60 years. Figure 5-18 shows some

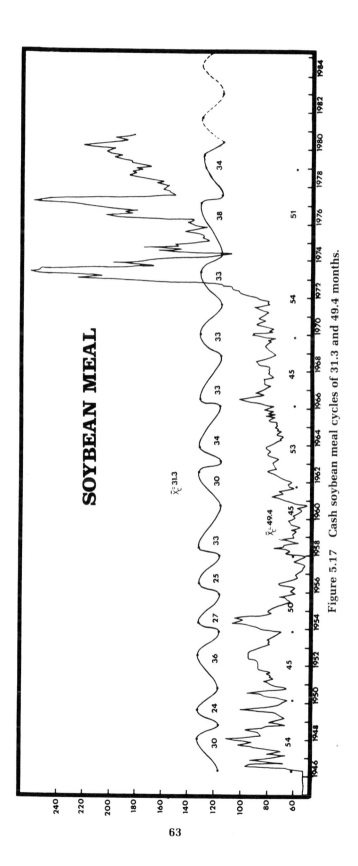

Figure 5.17 Cash soybean meal cycles of 31.3 and 49.4 months.

63

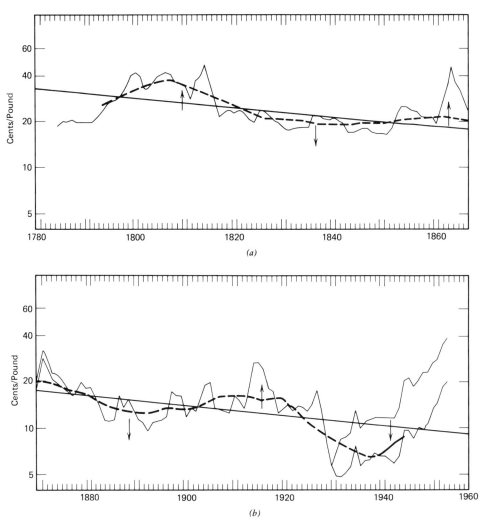

Figure 5.18 The 54 year copper cycle according to Dewey (1970, p. 578–9).

of the original Dewey work on the ideal 54 year pattern as it has behaved over the last several hundred years.

Perhaps the most important copper cycle, from a pragmatic standpoint, is the approximately 5.9 year pattern that I have been following. Figure 5-19 shows how this ideal pattern has acted in years past. You can see that there were several periods that showed little or no price movement because of government regulation of prices. The ideal lows on a 5.9 year pattern are marked accordingly. Notice the fairly high degree of regularity and predictability of the 5.9 year pattern. Making the reasonable assumption that 1977 was the last 5.9 year cyclic low, we should make another low in late 1982 to early 1983.

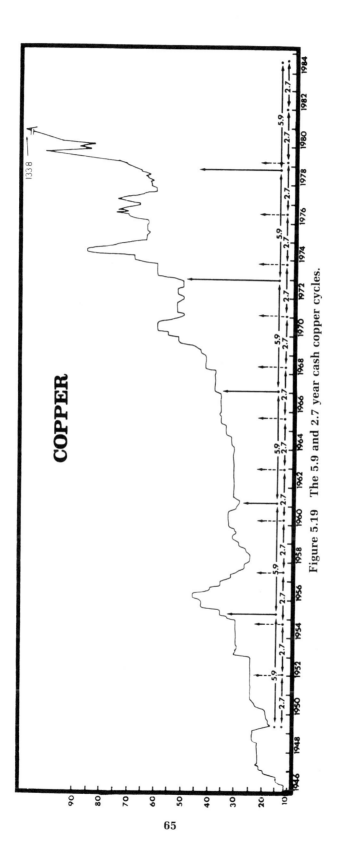

Figure 5.19   The 5.9 and 2.7 year cash copper cycles.

65

Within the 5.9 year cycle, we can also isolate a pattern that runs about 2.7 years, low to low. It is shown back to 1949 in Figure 5-19. By combining both the 5.9 and 2.7 year ideal patterns we can account for a large portion of the major bottoms in copper prices. How about the tops? The 5.9 year cycle works reasonably well across tops, but it is not nearly as reliable as it is across bottoms. We could examine several other cyclic patterns across the highs in copper, including a possible 10 to 12 year tendency, but with prices having gone through so many periods of government regulation, it is difficult to determine this cycle with sufficient accuracy. Because the 5.9 and 2.7 year cycles are highly reliable, we'll simply keep watching these until other tendencies become more evident.

## GOLD

Inasmuch as gold has been a favorite of metal buffs and inflationists over the years, there have been many attempts to find evidence of cyclical movement in this market. For many years, however, the price of gold was either regulated or fixed, making the cycle analyst's job more difficult since he had only sparse data or limited history of price change with which to perform an analysis. In such cases there are several alternatives. First, we can look at the price of gold in countries where such regulation did not exist, or we can construct a gold index that will reflect fluctuations in such things as gold share prices, which were not fixed by government policy in the United States. Figure 5-20 shows the gold index charts. Using the Standard and Poors index of gold stock prices, this chart conforms fairly well to the price of gold before its possession was again legalized in the United States.

There is still not much research on the gold cycle, and our work here can be considered only preliminary. Let's examine two segments of the gold index charts. The period from 1942 to 1948 shows a cycle of fairly good symmetry of about 6.9 years. The time frame from 1970 to 1976 shows a repetition of this cycle. Between these two lows, however, there are no distinct 6 to 7 year patterns. The two cycles we've already examined are so very close in length that we can make the assumption that there is most probably a 6 to 7 year cycle across lows in the gold market. Now we move back to the starting point and count ahead. Five years from the 1948 low brings us to the 1953 low (A). If, however, we count off approximately 7 years, we get to point B from which prices did move generally higher. We might have selected point C instead, which would give us a longer cycle period than what had been seen, hence making the next cycle shorter. There may be some disagreement with my particular selection of lows. It is, however, the only one that permits precise fitting of the two cycles we initially selected. We could go back and examine years previous to 1942 for additional repetitions of the 6 to 7 year gold cycle. We could also look at other price indexes for possible clues.

There are several cycles of shorter duration that yield considerably better results than the 6 to 7 year pattern, particularly in view of the brief period for which data can be obtained. These cycles are examined later on. In the interim we can look at several other precious metals in order to obtain a hint of cycles that could be related to those in gold.

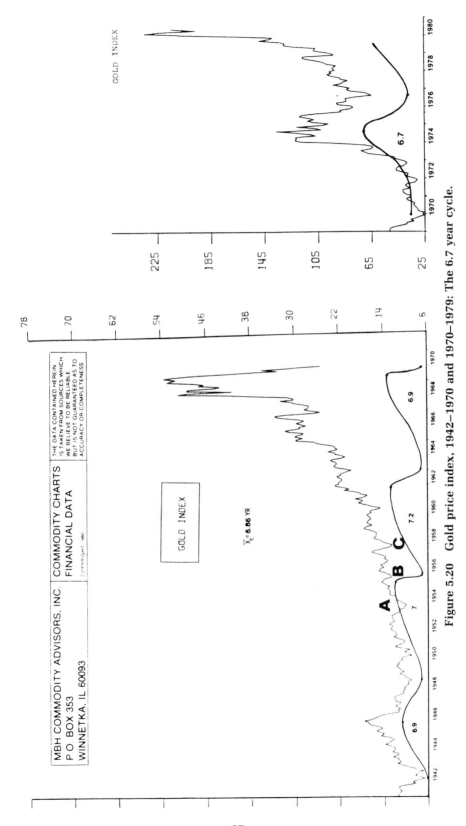

GOLD INDEX

GOLD INDEX

$\overline{X}_c = 6.86$ YR

**Figure 5.20  Gold price index, 1942–1970 and 1970–1979: The 6.7 year cycle.**

67

## SILVER

Silver prices have a lengthy history. In fact, some of the years during which there was no official trading in gold show data for silver. We can, therefore, gain some idea of the possible gold cycle by examining silver patterns during such times. There have been many attempts to isolate reliable cycles in the silver market. The Foundation for the Study of Cycles has published considerable work in this area. My work reveals at least one important long term pattern running approximately 5.5 years. Figure 5-21 shows how this pattern worked from the early 1900s through 1960. I detail some of the lows and highs here because they are especially valid, and clearly illustrate the reliability of silver cycles.

From 1902 through 1940 there were six repetitions of the cycle. The approximate length of each cycle is shown in Figure 5-21. Cycle 7 ran about 7.6 years, longer than had been the case until that time, undoubtedly because of war influences and several periods during which prices were not permitted to fluctuate freely. Thereafter, the market entered a period of stagnation lasting through the early 1960s. Notice in Figure 5-22 that a repetitive pattern was still present, although with not nearly as much symmetry or regularity. The last important bottom on this chart is the major 1971 low at about $1.35. Prices then rose sharply. Traders with knowledge of this cycle and its exceptionally reliable history should have known that prices were about to begin an upmove, with the next important low coming approximately 5.5 years later, in late 1976 to early 1977. This low (see Figure 5-22) was made in the range of $4.50 per ounce. The rest is commodity price history. Prices moved to over $50.00 per ounce as silver made its cycle high in early 1980. The next low, if our calculations are indeed correct, should come in late 1982 to early 1983.

The silver market is a classic example of the kind of cyclic activity that accounts for over 80 percent of all the price variation since 1903 and possibly earlier. There are a number of other alleged cycles that run longer than the 5.5 year pattern. What makes silver even more predictable from a cyclic standpoint is the fact that several other silver cycles (in particular, the approximately 42 week, 21 week, 10 week, 32 day, and seasonal) are also fairly reliable. These silver cycles are discussed in a later chapter. There can be no more dramatic evidence of cycles and their value than a hypothetical trading record of silver purchases and sales according to the long term pattern just discussed.

Carrying the silver cycle analysis one step further, we can see how patterns of various length fit into the 5.5 year cycle. Let's isolate one of these patterns, expand it to a larger chart, and examine the shorter cycles within. Figure 5-23 shows repetition of the 5.5 year cycle. Marked on the chart are several additional patterns (some to be discussed later). You can see how neatly the lesser lengths fit into the longer cycle. It is for this reason that so many students of cycles have chosen the silver market as their area of specialization. When we examine the shorter and intermediate cycles in the silver market, you may be even more impressed with our ability to forecast trends using only cycles. I must remind you, as I will do from time to time, that there has been no mention of such things as supply and demand, production and consumption statistics, industrial usage and application, or economic conditions. These fundamental facts are

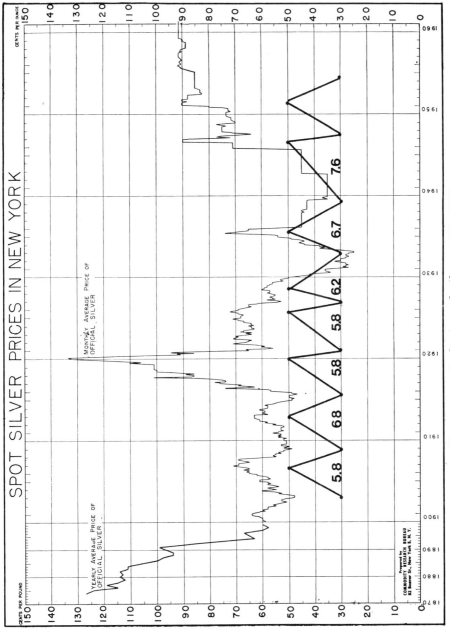

Figure 5.21 Cycles in cash silver, 1870–1960.

Figure 5.22   Cycles in cash silver, 1870–1977.

70

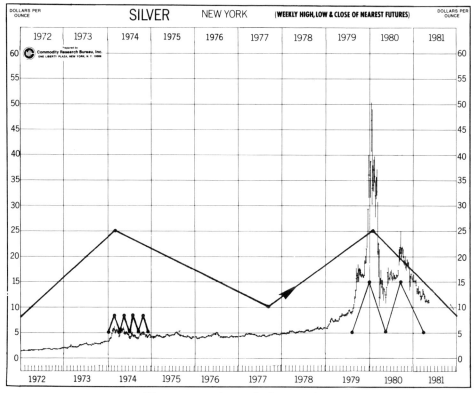

**Figure 5.23   Several silver cycles.**

not considered when making a cyclic analysis of prices. In fact, many cycle theorists consider knowledge of such facts as potentially detrimental to the pure study of cyclic tendencies.

## COTTON

One of the most volatile markets in recent years has been cotton. In fact, several periods historically have witnessed wide fluctuations in cotton prices. Many such periods have been associated with international and domestic warfare. Dewey (October 1954) did considerable work with cotton cycles, by isolating patterns in prices, consumption, and production. An entire text could be written on the cycles of cotton alone. I do not delve too deeply into many of the patterns here. I do, however, cover what I believe to be the most useful cycles from a trading and hedging standpoint.

The original work by Dewey revealed the presence of a cycle cluster. *Cycles,* October 1954 issue, summarized the findings as follows:

> *A 5.91 year cycle has characterized cotton prices for 224 years. . . . The cycle has been working better for the past 50 years . . . due to the concurrent presence of three other cycles of nearly the same length . . . 5.575 years . . . 6.11 years . . . and 6.45 years.*

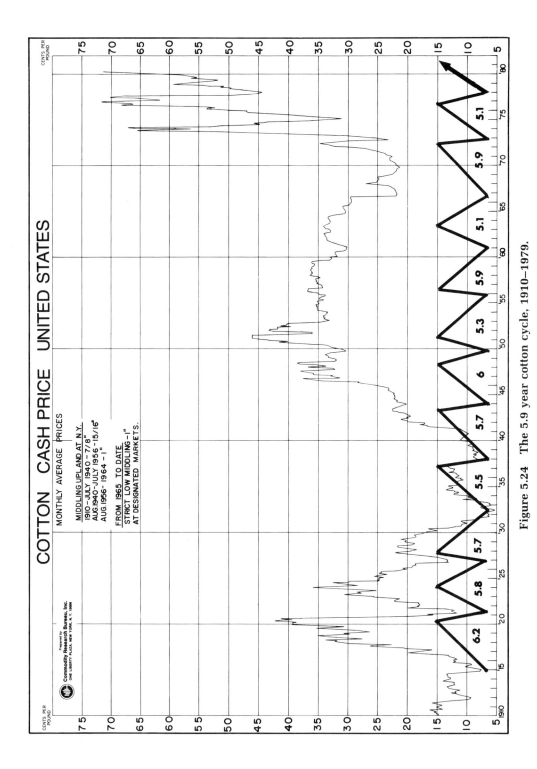

Figure 5.24   The 5.9 year cotton cycle, 1910–1979.

Figure 5.25 The 2.6 year cycle in cotton futures, 1970–1980.

On the basis of his findings, Dewey constructed a hypothetical buy/sell table for cotton back to 1731, using the ideal 5.91 year pattern as his parameter. His results showed a net gain of over 1400 percent. He concluded: "Behavior which persists over so long a period of time can not be the result of random forces."

Because this pattern is so very important, let's examine it back to the early 1900s, with details as to current functioning. Figure 5-24 shows the cotton cash market since 1910. I have marked off 11 repetitions of this cycle. The shortest ran approximately 5.1 years, and the longest about 6.1 years. Together, these patterns account for almost 100 percent of the major movement in cotton prices. Most of the repetitions were highly rhythmic. Even during a period of relatively stable prices, 1952–1970, there was close adherence to the cycle. It is important to note that cotton prices have fluctuated very widely in the last 80 years. The moves, once started, tend to carry on for long periods of time.

Within the 5.9 year cycle there is a fairly reliable pattern of about 2.6 years. This cycle runs for about half of the 5.9 year pattern and is also shown in Figure 5-25. If we expand the last few cycles and examine them for the 2.6 year cycle, we end up with another very workable and potentially profitable tendency. It is shown in Figure 5-25. Observe that in just the last four repetitions of this cycle we have seen the following approximate gains:

| February 1970 through May 1972 | +$0.17 | Uptrend |
| May 1972 through October 1972 | +$0.15 | Downtrend |
| October 1972 through October 1973 | +$0.68 | Uptrend |
| October 1973 through December 1974 | +$0.62 | Downtrend |
| December 1974 through July 1976 | +$0.57 | Uptrend |
| July 1976 through December 1977 | +$0.45 | Downtrend |
| December 1977 through February 1980 | +$0.42 | Uptrend |

This represents a total gain of $3.060 at $500 per cent, which works out to over $153,000 on a one-contract basis! Naturally, this ideal record assumes perfect timing and order fills. It is certainly not a realistic expectation. Even half this amount, however, on a one-contract basis would be considered an excellent record for only about six trades. There are also shorter patterns of a repetitive nature within the 2.6 year cycle. They are analyzed in Chapter 6.

## COFFEE

Among the more volatile markets is coffee. Several periods in its history have witnessed price freezes and/or the suspension of futures trading. In 1955 Dewey isolated the 16 to 16.6 year cycle (March 1955). It is interesting to note that this cycle correlates rather well with a number of other 17 year tendencies in unrelated natural events. We would suppose that the coffee market might also show a cycle about half of the 16 year pattern and possibly one that runs about 4 years, one-fourth of the 16 year cycle. On examining the coffee cash data, I cannot verify the Dewey findings exactly. Rather, I find three distinct cycles running from about 17 to 19 years, low to low, since 1902 (see large arrows in Figure 5-26). About 17 years previous to the 1902 low, there is the 1885 low (see Figure 5-26 for detailed cycle indications). There is also a distinct low in the 1868 period, about 17 years earlier. The cycle Dewey originally found seems to have been stretched out in the past 40 years, but my work tends to confirm a pattern running about 17 to 19 years.

We could subdivide each of the 17 to 19 year cycles into patterns of about three 6 year cycles. Looking once again at the long-term coffee chart (Figure 5-26), you will see the recent phasings of this pattern as well (small arrows). Remember that these are both long term cycles. If timing is incorrect by as little as 10 percent in either direction, we could be off by as much as 1.9 years or 0.6 years respectively, for each cycle. This may be an acceptable margin of error to those not trading futures, but it is an unreasonable degree of inaccuracy for those buying and selling on a margin of 3 percent or less. Hence, it is necessary in this and all other markets to refine cycle lengths to their most accurate terms. Timing indications are then applied to compensate for the degree of error in determining cycle length.

As you can see, a wide range of price variation within each cycle is acceptable. In fact, we are not concerned with what happens between major cycle lows and highs so long as the lows and highs themselves fall within shorter periods or cycles. A cycle could very well resemble Figure 5-26, showing wide price fluctuation within major highs and lows, but making important turns on time. What happens between these highs and lows can then be subjected to its own

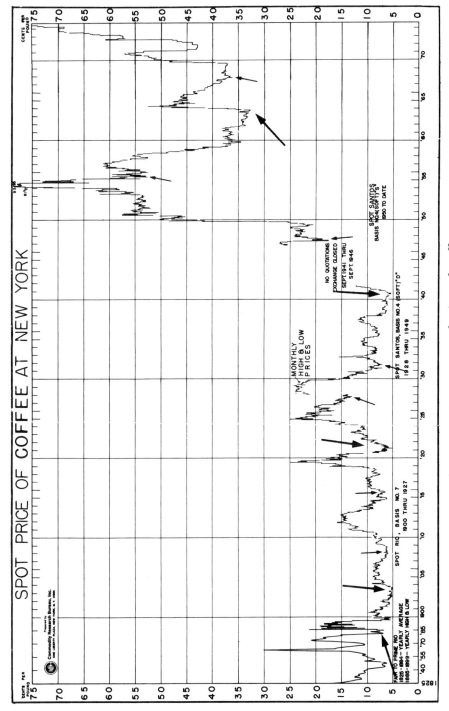

Figure 5.26   Long term cycles in cash coffee.

cyclic analysis in order to filter out the shorter term variations in price, as was done for the cotton market. You will recall that we first examined the 5.9 year pattern. We then looked at the 2.6 year cycle within it. Later on we'll examine the 20 to 24 week cycle within the 2.6 year pattern, the seasonal cycle within the 20 to 24 week cycle, and the 28 to 34 day tendency within the 20 to 24 week cycle. The silver analysis followed a similar course.

## SUGAR

There are at least two alleged long term cycles in sugar prices. Studies of the 6 year and 9 year approximate patterns date back to the 1800s and 1700s respectively (Dewey, 1970). A recent cycle is shown in Figure 5-27. It should be remembered that sugar prices did not vary much from 1946 to 1962. Nor did they vary much from 1964 to 1972. This makes precise determination of the lows and highs more difficult than if prices had fluctuated widely. There has been, nevertheless, a 6.2 year average pattern between lows in the sugar market. Between the bottoms marked A and C (Figure 5-27) there is a very clear

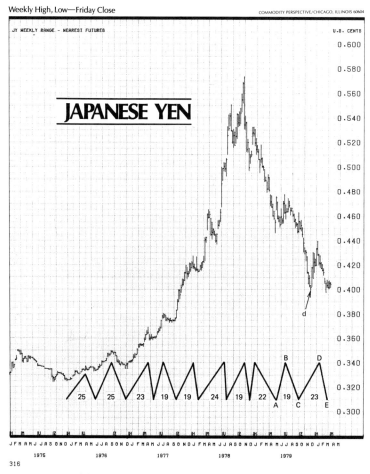

**Figure 5.27   The 6.2 year sugar cycle.**

cycle that is easily seen. Let's take a look at price action between 1957 and 1980 (Figure 5-28) to see how the cycle looks between these years. Notice that I have marked off an approximate 6.2 year pattern. Now we have examined at least two repetitions of this cycle. Figure 5-29 takes the pattern back before 1953. The basic 6 year cycle in sugar has maintained its reliability for many years now and continues to be the major force behind large price changes. The last low of this cycle came in 1977, and prices have been sharply higher since. If all goes according to schedule, we should see a peak in 1981 and another low in mid-1983. I will not give any space to the alleged 9 year cycle. Those interested can embark on their own course of research should they wish to learn more about this longer term pattern. Because the 6 year tendency accounts for so much of the long-range variation in sugar prices, there is no need, in my opinion, to search any further.

## RUBBER

Although not an active market in the United States, rubber is traded elsewhere in the world, and in years past has had wide price changes. There is also a fairly predictable cycle in the rubber cash market, which is depicted in Figure 5-30.

Using 1949 as our starting point we can begin measuring a cycle which runs 56.8 months on the average. Through 1977 the longest repetition of this pattern

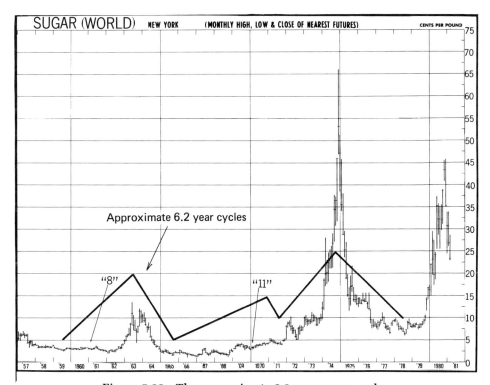

**Figure 5.28   The approximate 6.2 year sugar cycle.**

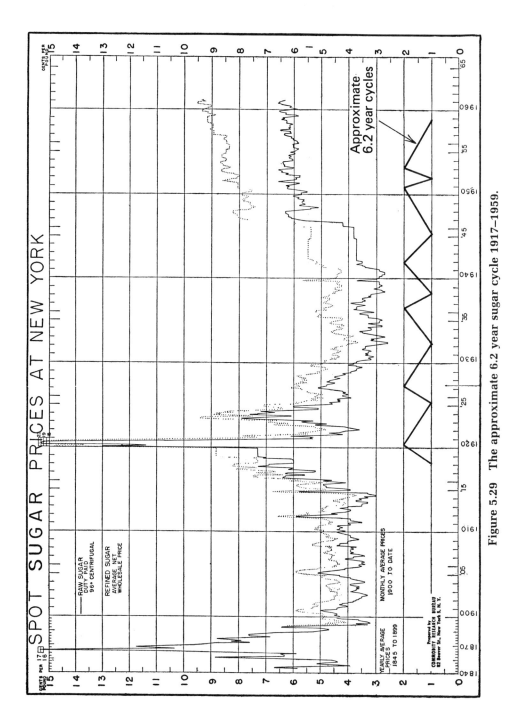

Figure 5.29   The approximate 6.2 year sugar cycle 1917–1959.

78

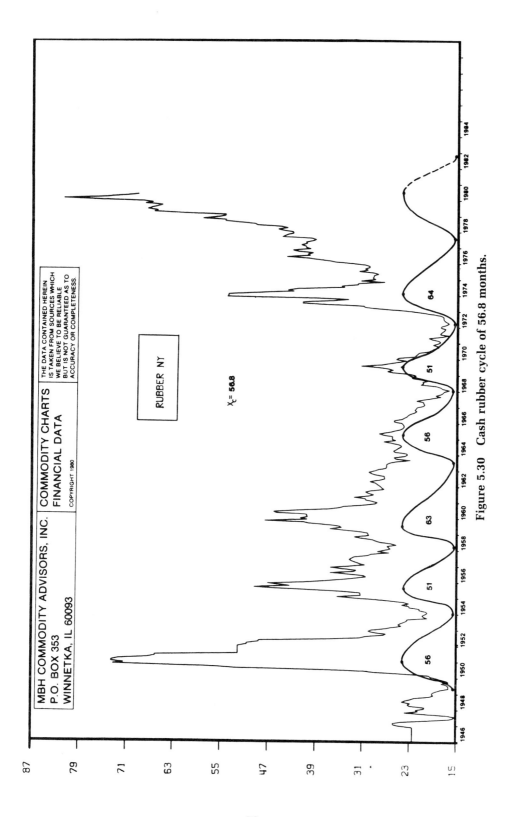

Figure 5.30 Cash rubber cycle of 56.8 months.

MBH COMMODITY ADVISORS, INC.
P.O. BOX 353
WINNETKA, IL 60093

COMMODITY CHARTS
FINANCIAL DATA
COPYRIGHT 1980

THE DATA CONTAINED HEREIN
IS TAKEN FROM SOURCES WHICH
WE BELIEVE TO BE RELIABLE
BUT IS NOT GUARANTEED AS TO
ACCURACY OR COMPLETENESS.

RUBBER NY

$X_t = 56.8$

has been 63 months, and the shortest 51 months. This is a variance of 6.2 months from the longest cycle to the mean (average) and 5.8 months from the shortest cycle to the mean. The variation from the shortest cycle to the longest cycle is 12 months. The cash rubber data illustrate an interesting long term cycle as well. You will note that from the mid-1947 low through the early 1972 low, prices moved through a long term cycle of approximately 25 years. There may, in fact, have been some important lows prior to 1946 which could stretch the cycle to about 27 years. In any event, the current cycle of 25 years (based on available data) represents a few years less than half the 54 year cycle we've seen in so many other markets.

An additional observation which could prove valuable is the tendency for a one-half cycle in the cash rubber data. Each approximate 56.8 month cycle could be divided into two cycles of about 28.4 months. As our analysis continues you will repeatedly observe clusters of cycles which aggregate during relatively similar time frames. That is to say that although many different markets and data series can be analyzed, it seems as if there is a central tendency for cycles to occur at relatively similar periods. Most long term cycles run from 50 to 54 years and there are many intermediate term cycles running from 9 to 11 months. This cyclic synchronicity will become an important consideration when we examine the commodity futures markets individually.

## CURRENCIES

It is reasonable to assume that currency markets also show cyclic activity. Although exchange rates were fixed for many years by government decree or policy, there was a profound change in the early 1970s when the U.S. dollar began to lose considerable ground. The effects of this, coupled with international instability, resulted in wide fluctuations of the exchange rate between both the U.S. dollar and other world currencies, and among world currencies themselves. It is somewhat too early to make a definitive statement about the precise cycles found in most foreign currencies, but there are initial bits of evidence to suggest some patterns. The Canadian dollar, for example, seems to have a 5.5 to 6.2 year cycle relative to the U.S. dollar. Figure 5-31 shows what has happened since 1950. With the exception of one elongated cycle (D) and one very early top (E), the tendency has been rather symmetrical. It suggests that late 1978 to early 1979 was the approximate 5.7 year low, and that rates should continue generally higher against the U.S. dollar through late 1981 if the cycle does not peak early.

Inasmuch as we have seen only five repetitions of this cycle, low to low, we cannot be entirely convinced that it is real. Should the next pattern work as anticipated, with a low in the 1984 period, we'll have more solid evidence of a true cycle. There also seems to be a fairly reasonable pattern across highs that runs about 2.3 years, high to high. The tops are marked accordingly on my chart. You'll notice that some of the peaks are a bit off schedule but that an overall tendency does exist. There have been about 11 repetitions of this top-to-top cycle. The cycles marked No. four and No. seven do not fit as well as we'd like. However, they are overcome in importance by the persistence of this pattern through the current time frame, which, if it persists as a workable and

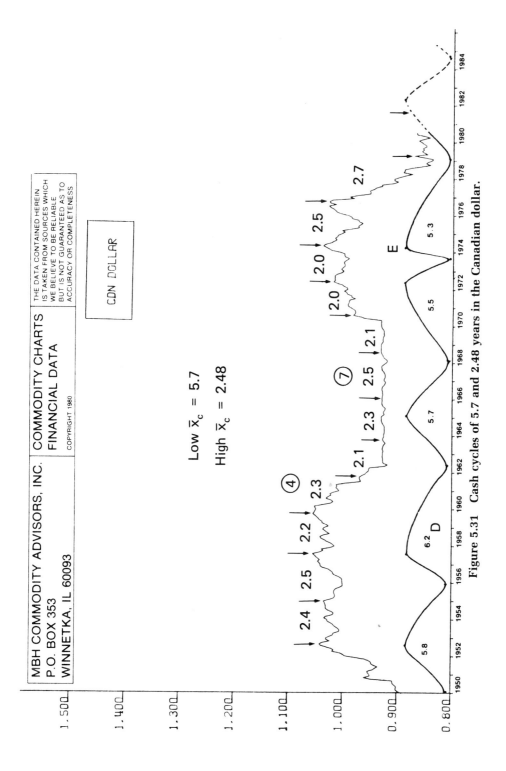

Figure 5.31  Cash cycles of 5.7 and 2.48 years in the Canadian dollar.

valid tendency, means we should see a peak in 1982, within several months of the 5.7 year cyclic top.

Other currencies have exhibited cyclic patterns as well. The Swiss franc and German mark show a cycle ranging from 3 to 4 years in length. At this time, there are insufficient data to permit a strong statement regarding the reliability of these possible patterns. In addition, the Japanese yen has an approximate cycle of 5.1 years, and the British pound has one of about 3.2 years, all low to low. Given the dearth of statistical evidence, I avoid making any definitive statements about these currency markets. The table below summarizes for the various markets not depicted in chart form several cyclic lows.

| Market | Cyclic Lows | Approximate Cycle |
|---|---|---|
| Yen | mid-1960, early 1964, late 1975, late 1981 (?) | 5.1 years |
| Mark | early 1969, late 1972, early 1976, early 1980 | 3.7 years |
| Swiss Franc | late 1970, early 1974, early 1976, early 1980 | 3.2 years |
| British Pound | late 1970, late 1973, late 1976, early 1980 | 3.1 years |

## WOOD

Lumber and plywood are highly seasonal, and there exists a number of fairly reliable long term cyclic forces. Among these is the approximately 51.7 month cycle, low to low, in monthly average lumber cash prices. The chart for this cycle is shown in Figure 5-32. Since 1946 there have been eight repetitions of the cycle. The shortest ran about 48 months, and the longest about 58 months. There appears to be a close relationship between this cycle and the 54 month average cycle in interest rates. There are several other shorter term price tendencies in the woods that are discussed in a later chapter.

## INTEREST RATES

At the beginning of this chapter I discussed some details of the approximately 54 year cycle in interest rates. As pointed out, a 54 year pattern is useful in determining secular trends, but it is not helpful in timing purchases and sales. To accomplish this end, we must examine possible cycles of shorter duration. One such pattern is the approximately 54 month cycle in 91 day T-bill yields, shown in Figure 5-33. There are several intermediate cyclic tendencies in long term bond yields. Interest rate cycles are important in analyzing many other related markets. Even a 54 month cycle is rather long when it comes to timing transactions in this highly volatile market. This is why the intermediate and short term cycles may be of greater value. Figure 5-34 shows the recent intermediate bond yield cycles.

Figure 5-33 also shows the tendency for prices to make two tops in forming the 54 month cyclic highs. Although this is not a cyclic event per se, it is still noteworthy. If you know that most tops of the pattern will be followed by a second top (which could be slightly above the first), then you may wish to wait for the secondary peak before making any trades or decisions on the basis of

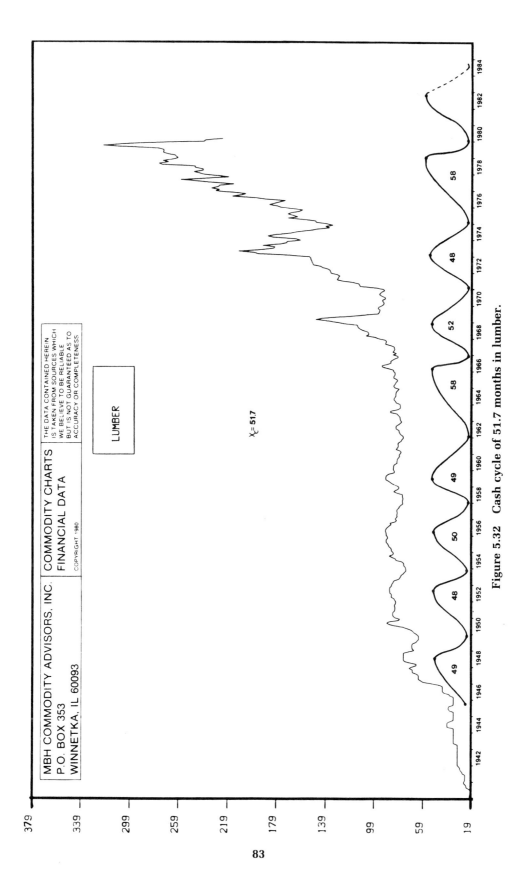

LUMBER

$X = 51.7$

Figure 5.32   Cash cycle of 51.7 months in lumber.

83

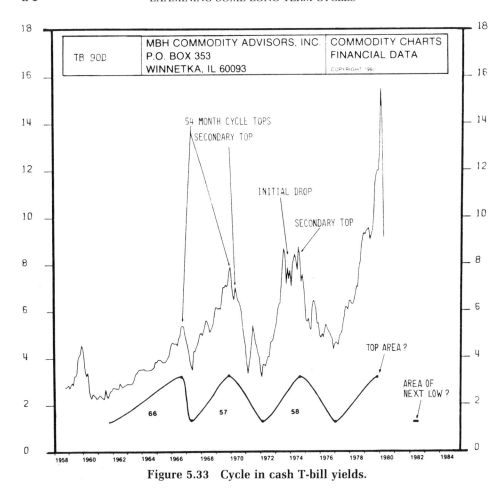

**Figure 5.33   Cycle in cash T-bill yields.**

the cycle. This is an important consideration in the interest rate market as well as in other markets that show the double peak tendency. More on this subject later on.

## DRAWING SOME CONCLUSIONS

The study of cycles is not yet an exact science. As you can see, there are many ways of looking at repetitive price tendencies, different interpretations of how to find such patterns, and varying opinions as to how they are best employed. Were it not for our still only limited knowledge about the many different cyclic inputs that eventually express themselves in the form of price change, we could possibly forecast to the very day, or even minute, of a low or high. Several conclusions are warranted on the basis of what has been expressed in the foregoing discussion. They are as follows:

1   Virtually every free market has a long term cycle that can be measured from low to low and/or from high to high.

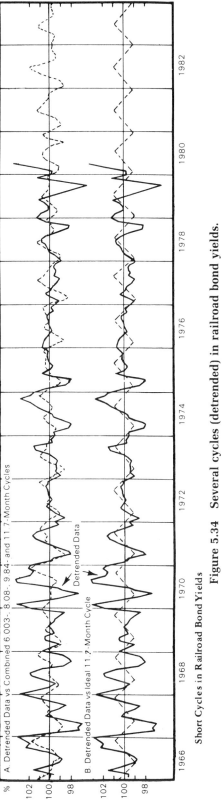

Short Cycles in Railroad Bond Yields

Figure 5.34   Several cycles (detrended) in railroad bond yields.

85

2   Markets have cycles within cycles. By analyzing each long term cycle and examining its component rhythms, we can eventually account for most of the price variation.

3   Although some markets do not at this point in time have a sufficient price history to permit valid conclusions regarding the presence of cycles, others have a long and well-documented history of repetitive price behavior.

4   Many long term cycles are statistically significant and cannot be explained as mere random variations.

5   Long term analysis of cyclic patterns represents only the first step in an overall program of explanation and extrapolation of price trends.

6   Pure cyclic analysis does not consider fundamental or economic events as causal explanations of price fluctuation. Such factors should not be given any role whatsoever in the determination of cycle lengths.

7   For more precise use of cycles, additional analysis is necessary until all important patterns for any one market have been determined and extrapolated.

8   Cyclic analysis is concerned only with determining the time period during which a price change, up or down, is likely. Price projection per se is not the goal of this text.

9   To accurately determine a cycle it is important to have as many observations as possible. The more repetitions of a given cycle, the more nearly valid our conclusions.

10  Timing of the precise turn in price direction is an additional tool that must be employed by persons wishing to use cycles for commodity trading or hedging purposes.

11  Cycles are not necessarily symmetrical in appearance. Frequently, they will peak or bottom well past their midpoints. It is characteristic for cycle tops and bottoms to vary because they are constantly being influenced by other cyclic forces.

12  Many cycles have similar lengths. Most meats, for example, have long-term tendencies that run for generally equivalent lengths.

13  Successful analysis of cycle patterns does not necessarily require the use of a sophisticated computer or advanced mathematics. Although these tools can help to isolate patterns that are difficult to find, most cycles can be visually determined by using elementary arithmetic skills.

# CHAPTER SIX

# Some Intermediate Term Patterns

Within each cyclic pattern we can isolate many other cycles of shorter duration, some of which are highly repetitive whereas others are merely general tendencies and not especially valuable from a predictive standpoint. Earlier I indicated the manner in which cycles are housed within cycles, which in turn were housed within other cycles. If we study the long-range patterns previously discussed, we will find that each contains many smaller patterns. The 5.5 year silver cycle, for example, contains within it about seven repetitions of the approximately 41 week cycle. The 5.5 year cycle is, in turn, part of a more pervasive tendency, such as the 54 year cycle. And the 54 year cycle is probably part of a much longer cyclic tendency. The 41 week cycle can be subdivided into about two 21 week cycles or four cycles of about 10 weeks each, and these, into segments of 32 days.

For the purpose of our current discussion we examine in this chapter cycles longer than 25 weeks but shorter than 2.5 years (or thereabouts). It is the intermediate term cycle that accounts for most of the potentially profitable futures trades, and it is the intermediate term cycle that is most useful to the hedger and the farmer. A subcategory of the intermediate term cycle is the seasonal price tendency, which is discussed in Chapter 18. As you can see, we are progressing from long term to shorter term, from macro to micro, from universal to specific, and from large time windows to smaller ones. This, by the way, is not the method followed by many market analysts and speculators who are, for the most part, concerned with events on a day-to-day or week-to-week basis. At times they are more concerned with what will happen to prices from one minute to the next than they are with where prices may be 2 or more years hence. I make no value judgment as to which method is better. In the long run, any method must be evaluated by results and results alone, but a method that seeks to determine price trends on a minute-by-minute basis must be limited in scope. It will have little value to the farmer or hedger, and less value yet to the longer term trader who wishes to capitalize on major moves, both for reasons of profit and potential tax savings. In addition, the individual who can follow the market minute by minute, or trade by trade is completely subservient to the market. Each method has its own merits and is best employed by those traders suited to its particular demands.

In making the progression from larger bits of time to smaller units, we also change from the long term cash chart that shows monthly average cash prices, to a weekly high, low, and close chart of the futures market. This change allows more resolution. It is as if we were switching from a telescope to a microscope of greater and greater power. The person who goes to an art museum and places his nose right against the canvas will see nothing but a blob of color. The color's unity with the rest of the masterpiece will go unrecognized, and the person will come away with virtually the same knowledge, appreciation, and understanding he had when he entered the museum. The person who first stands back, takes time to observe the total picture, and then moves closer to examine fine details of the work will leave with both a greater understanding and considerably more appreciation of the painting.

## LIVE CATTLE

The major cyclic force in cattle is the approximately 7 year cycle. It is comprised of about two 45 month patterns, the total length of 90 months being equal to about 7.5 years. The 45 month pattern is quite variable in length, running from a low of 35 months to a high of 52 months since 1942. It is basically similar to the 43.4 month or 3.61 year cycle in live hogs. Figure 6-1 shows how the approximately 30 week cycle, low to low, fits into the 45 month pattern previously analyzed (Figure 5-6). Examine first the approximate 45 month cycle from late 1970 through May/June 1974 (Figure 5-6). Notice that the high of this cycle came somewhat late. A low was then made and tested (1974). Prices thereafter moved up to another late top and lower to late 1978, completing a run of approximately 44 months, satisfying a low of the approximately 45 month cycle. Following the 45 month low, prices climbed sharply. A low can now be projected in the time frame marked *(PL)* (late 1982) should the cycle be running true to form.

Now let's take an individual 45 month average cycle and examine the approximately 30 week cycles. Remember the the 30 week patterns will not be exactly 30 weeks but, rather, will have a central tendency, or arithmetic mean, of about 30 weeks. In practice some will run longer and others shorter than the 30 week mean. The approximate length in weeks is indicated for each of the cyclic lows. The use of highs, lows, and closing prices is discussed thoroughly in Chapter 12. This (Figure 6-1) is the basic appearance of the approximately 30 week cycle in live cattle futures. There are certain timing considerations in entering the market at projected cycle lows. These are also detailed in Chapter 12.

Another important aspect of cyclic analysis is called *convergence*. Typically, when several cycles of different length either bottom or top within the same general time period, we have a convergence situation, which usually gives us a more definite and frequently more pronounced upmove or downmove. As an example, late 1976 marked the approximately 7 year cycle low in cattle. It was also the time frame of an approximately 45 month low and an approximately 30 week cyclic low. The upmove that followed was one of the largest in history (1976 through 1979). Prices more than doubled within a stretch of about 2 years. Convergence can happen at cyclic highs as well.

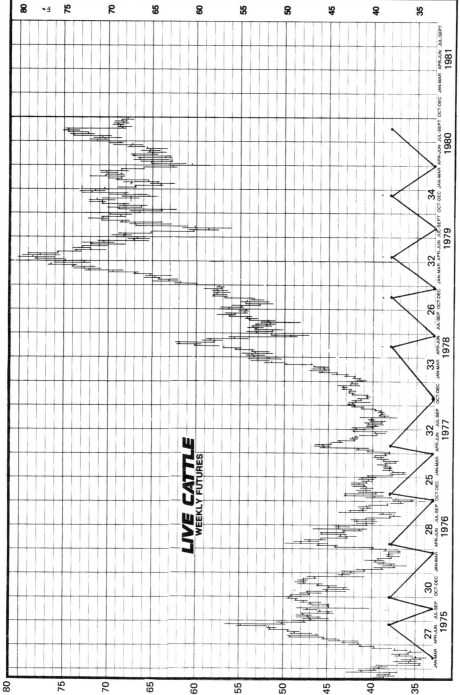

Figure 6.1   The 30 week cycle tendency in cattle futures.

89

## PORK BELLIES

The long-term cycles in bellies and hogs run about the same as those in cattle—3.6 years. Within the 3.61 year cycle there is evidence of a 40 to 50 week pattern in bellies. I gave the hog market considerable attention in the previous chapter, so I discuss the intermediate term pork belly pattern in this chapter. Figure 6-2 is a chart of belly prices on a weekly basis. The lows of the 3.6 year (A,B,C) and the 40 to 50 week cycles have been marked off accordingly. Notice the regularity in the approximately 45 week belly cycle as far back as 1971. There were several instances of variation from the ideal pattern, but the overall effect is quite impressive. Even had you blindly followed an ideal 45 week cycle, low to low, buying at the expected low and taking profits with a reversal in position at the expected top, the results would have been very good—assuming, of course, that no stops or money management tools were used. At times, a loss would have been carried for quite a few weeks before it turned profitable. In a true trading situation this is not, to be sure, recommended as a reasonable technique. Prior to 1975 the intermediate term cycle was shorter than 45 weeks; nevertheless, there were several repetitions (1971–1972) that ran about 45 weeks, low to low. At the time of this writing the 45 week cycle in bellies continues to be a viable and highly reliable pattern.

The 45 week cycle can also be divided into two cycles of approximately 22 weeks each, but they are not as precise in terms of tops and bottoms. Persons

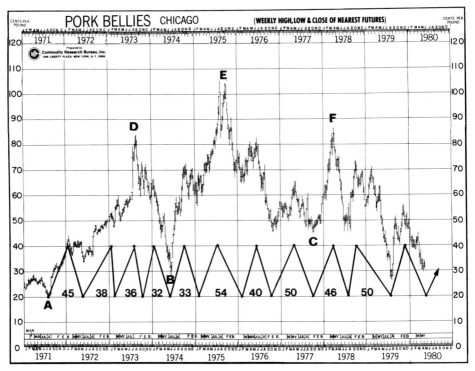

**Figure 6.2   Intermediate term cycle in pork bellies.**

who do not wish to trade the market by the 45 week cycle can consider this half cycle instead, but the accuracy of their results might not be as high.

Convergence of cycles is also easily seen in the belly market. Lows *A*, *B*, and *C* were all approximately 3.6 year cyclic bottoms. They were also 45 week cycle lows. In each case, the upmove that resulted was highly significant. Tops *D*, *E,* and *F* were approximately 3.6 year cyclic highs. They were also approximately 45 week cycle tops. In each case the drop subsequent to these tops was quite pronounced. It is for this reason that serious students of cycles will want to follow long term and intermediate term cycles. When there is a convergence of several patterns, the moves are generally more reliable and quite large. It is also possible for seasonal cycles to come at a time of convergence in other patterns. The more agreement we get between cycles of different lengths on or about the same time frame, the more likely and powerful we can expect the subsequent move to be.

## BROILERS

Although not nearly as active as many of the other meats, broilers have shown a remarkable cyclic pattern since 1969, with approximately 11 repetitions of the 11.5 month cycle. The effect is so powerful and predictable that I include it in my discussion despite low trading volume and open interest. The lows are marked accordingly, and the highs are marked as well (see Figure 6-3). The

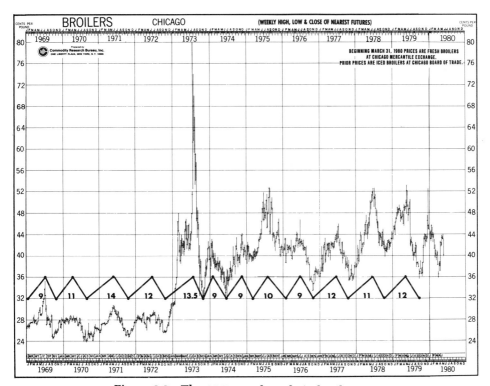

**Figure 6.3   The 11.5 month cycle in broilers.**

approximate cycle length is indicated within the pattern. The ideal zigzag cycle is also indicated. The pattern is so precise that it could also be measured in weeks, low to low and high to high. As is characteristic of top-to-top measurements, the time frames for this cycle are not as exact as those for low-to-low measurements.

There is also a highly repetitive seasonal pattern in broilers. The combined seasonal and cyclic effects in this market make for a highly predictable trend, one that could be highly profitable were it not for the thin trading volume in the broiler futures market. Recently, the Chicago Mercantile Exchange has added a broiler contract to its list of commodities, which could increase interest and volume. Should activity increase you might want to pay close attention to the market in view of the pattern I have just discussed. The switch may distort the cycle a bit, but it should get back on track within a year.

## EGGS

The egg market is also highly cyclic in its price pattern. Although I have not been able to isolate an especially worthwhile long term tendency, this market has two reliable intermediate-term cycles as well as a pronounced seasonal trend. Figure 6-4 shows the weekly high, low, and close chart of egg futures for 1970 through 1980. I have marked an approximate cycle that measures about

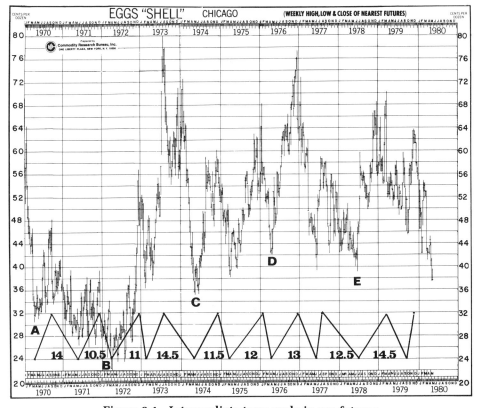

Figure 6.4   Intermediate term cycle in egg futures.

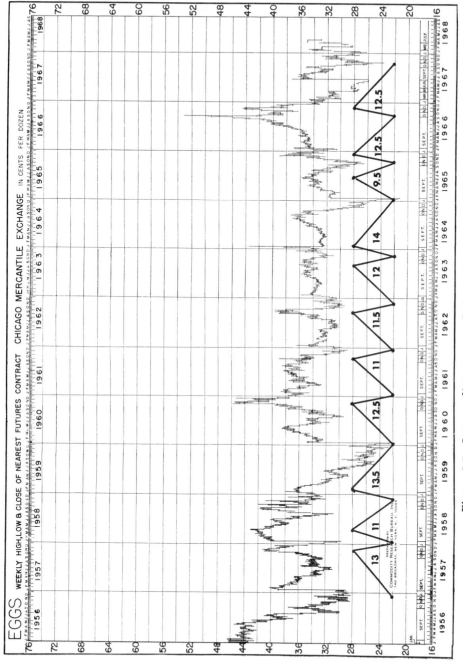

Figure 6.5   Intermediate term cycle in egg futures, 1956–1967.

93

11 months. To a certain extent this cycle is similar to what has already been discussed in the section on broilers. It is also part of the seasonal cycle. In the case of the egg market, the seasonal and 11 month intermediate-term cycle are about the same. The double cycle, or approximately 2 year pattern (marked A, B, C, D, etc. between lows) seems to be more reliable because it smooths out seasonal variation. Both patterns extend back to 1956 in Figure 6-5.

In many respects the low volume and open interest problems in the egg market are similar to the difficulty encountered in trading broiler futures. For those individuals who can trade low-volume markets, I suggest taking a close look at the egg cycles, both seasonal and otherwise. The low-volume problem in eggs has been cyclic as well. There have been periods of relative calm followed by periods of especially high volume and interest. It is likely that eggs will once again begin trading actively. I recommend following the cycles in eggs as preparation for such a volume and price explosion in the months ahead.

To appreciate fully the history of this cycle in eggs, examine Figure 6-5, which shows the pattern back to 1956. Although there were indeed a few cycles that ran on the short side, the overall tendency has remained valid for many years. Persons interested in trading the egg market should be completely familiar with this cycle because it accounts with a high degree of reliability for most of the intermediate term movement of prices.


## COTTON

In the previous chapter I discussed long term cycles in cotton. In particular, the approximately 2.5 year pattern was highlighted as being especially valid. The hypothetical results from trading this cycle were excellent. The cotton market has a short term cycle as well, however. In fact, there has been a tendency for cotton prices to make lows in an approximately 20 week cycle. Figure 6-6 shows the cycle since 1972. Many traders focus their attention on cotton because price swings are fairly large, the value of a $0.01 move is $500, and some of the cycles have been especially reliable. Before moving on to the approximately 20 week cyclic tendency (about five months), let's take a close look at how the approximately 2.5 year cycle fared from 1935 to 1951 (see Figure 6-7). My purpose is to demonstrate how especially valid the cotton pattern can be. I am not sure about the cause of such highly reliable cycles in cotton prices, nor do I really care about the reasons they exist so long as the patterns continue to be valid in the years ahead. There were seven repetitions of the 2.5 year cycle from 1935 to 1951. There were also seven important bottoms during this time, all of which were accounted for by the 2.5 year cycle. You'll recall from our previous discussion that a pattern of 5.7 years has also been isolated.

Within each 2.5 year move there are several approximately 5 month moves. Figure 6-6 shows how these cycles fit into the overall 2.5 year tendency. Cycles ABC and CDE have been included for reference purposes. Cycle ABC runs about 27 months, or 2.25 years (see Figure 6-7 for the larger picture regarding this cycle). Within the ABC cycle in Figure 6-6 I have measured off six patterns running from 17 to 23 weeks in length. Notice that as the overall upleg AB continues to dominate trends, tops of the approximately 20 week cycle come very late. Conversely, you will see that the downleg of this cycle BC causes

Weekly High, Low—Friday Close                                    COMMODITY PERSPECTIVE/CHICAGO, ILLINOIS 60604

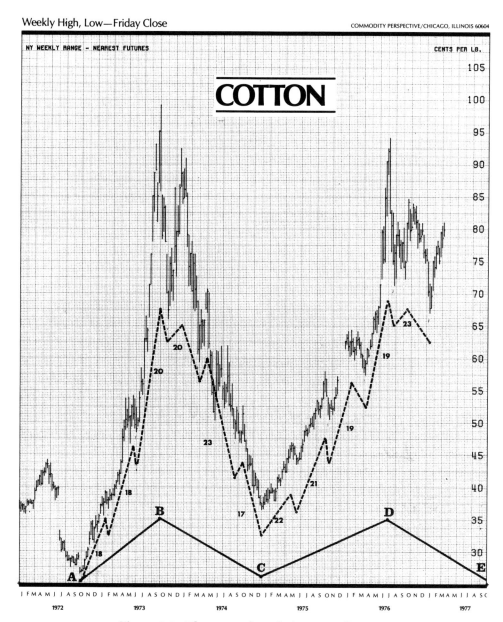

**Figure 6.6   The 20 week cycle in cotton futures.**

tops to come early in the 20 week pattern. The average length of this cycle is
19.3 weeks between lows.

Now let's look at the next longer wave, *CDE*, examining the approximately
20 week cycles in it. I have marked four cycles as part of upleg *CD*. Again there
is the tendency for tops to come late in the cycle. The average of these lengths
is 20.25 weeks. The average to this point (from low *A*) is 19.7. Observe also
that between cycles *ABC*, *CDE*, and the indicated 20 week patterns within them
we have accounted for almost every important top and bottom since 1972. The

**Figure 6.7   2.5 year cotton cycle, 1935–1951.**

analysis continues now with Figure 6-8, which completes the weekly cotton chart through early 1980. The arrow (upper center left) shows where we left off in our previous analysis. In Figure 6-8 we complete the previous cycle *CDE*, showing the downleg *DE* in its entirety. You'll see that it contains two repetitions of the 20 week pattern, measuring 22 and 21 weeks respectively. Tops come early inasmuch as the pervasive trend is down (*DE* downleg). The next 2.5 year cycle begins and runs as *EFG*. Low *G* is not shown but did, in fact, occur on schedule by mid-1980. Upleg *EF* poses a small problem in the cyclic analysis to this point. If we follow the cycles in order, we have (from the *E* bottom), 21 weeks and 23 weeks, low to low. The next count takes us to a low 21 weeks later (see Arrow 2). If we then continue with the count, we get past the next actual low because it does not fit our count. We move on to a low 20 weeks later that still does not seem to fit our pattern very well. Ideally, we should ignore the short cycle and begin with our count in the most logical point (Arrow 3). Time always resolves such problems in cycle analysis. There will be occasions when your count may go astray, and if this happens, consider one of several possibilities. First, you may not have counted properly. Go back and check your work on the previous cycles. If your count is indeed correct, then there may be another cycle causing the divergence. This is the most likely explanation of what happened. I am running through this step-by-step method with you to help you learn how an analysis is done by trial and error. How will we know where the cycles stand? If a cycle gets off course, will it get back on again in the near future? These considerations are discussed in later chapters as well, but here are a few points to consider:

1    When a cycle that has had a long history of reliability gets off schedule
     for one or two repetitions, it is not an indication that the cycle is no longer
     valid. It *is*, however, an indication that other cycles may be present that
     you may not as yet have found.

2    If a cycle gets off track, give it time. It will usually correct itself the very
     next time around. If more than three cycles in a row fail to fall on time,
     then there may very well be a major change in patterns.

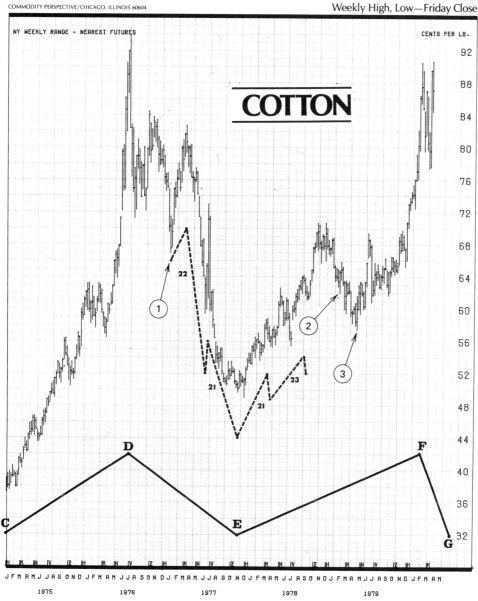

**Figure 6.8   The 20 week cycle in cotton figures.**

3   There is more than one cycle for each market. If the 20 week cycle in cotton goes astray for several repetitions, then the overall 2.5 year tendency should work. In our foregoing example this is exactly what happened.

## WHEAT

The approximately 9 year cycle in wheat was discussed in detail in Chapter 5. In addition to this pattern, there is also evidence of a 12.2 month tendency that dates back to the 1930s and earlier. There is also an approximately 45 month cycle that is not as reliable. Figure 6-9 shows the 12.2 month cycle since 1935. The period designated *ABC* is one repetition of the approximately 9 year cycle. It is shown to give you an idea of how the smaller cycles fit into the 9 year pattern. You'll note that most of the important intermediate term tops and bottoms have been accounted for by the 12.2 month cycle. If you take every fourth cycle beginning with the first shown (1935), you will end up with the approximately 45 month cycle mentioned earlier.

Now let's examine wheat price history through the 1956–1967 period (Figure 6-10). There were 11 repetitions of the cycle during this time frame. The average cycle length was 12.59, well within acceptable tolerance of the average cyclic length. The time span shown was one of relatively stable prices. During this period, the cycles were very stable as well. In fact, they can be seen quite plainly without any mathematical manipulation or guidelines. As a point of information, examine the yearly low. In most cases you will find that it came

**Figure 6.9   The 12.2 month cycle in wheat futures, 1935–1951.**

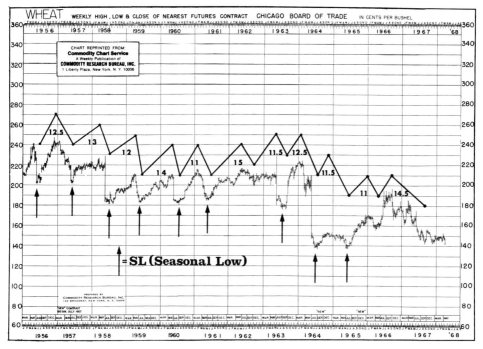

**Figure 6.10    The 12.2 month cycle in wheat futures, 1956–1968.**

in the April–June period. This constitutes the seasonal wheat cycle and is discussed later. I have marked some of the seasonal lows with arrows and the accompanying abbreviation *SL* for seasonal low.

The pattern continues from 1971 through early 1980, as is shown in Figure 6-11. The cycle during this period averaged 11.4 months, a bit shorter than in the past. The overall tendency, however, remains about 12 months. The arrows on this chart show the 1974, 9 year cyclic high and the 1977, 9 year cyclic lows respectively. You can see that in each case there was an accompanying elongation of the 12.2 month cycle. There have been attempts by other students of cycles to find shorter term patterns of value, and there are a few that can be watched closely on daily price charts. They range in length from 11 to 54 days and are discussed in Chapter 8. For illustrative purposes we later take a closer look at how wheat prices behave as they approach the time of a 12.2 month upturn. At this time, however, it should be noted that lows tend to occur more frequently in the April–June period, a time that normally marks the seasonal low.

## CORN

The long term corn cycle runs 5.7 years. Its behavior has been characterized in Chapter 5. Corn has a long history of reliable cyclic activity. The cycle of importance runs about 12.2 months, as it does in wheat, but the timing is not

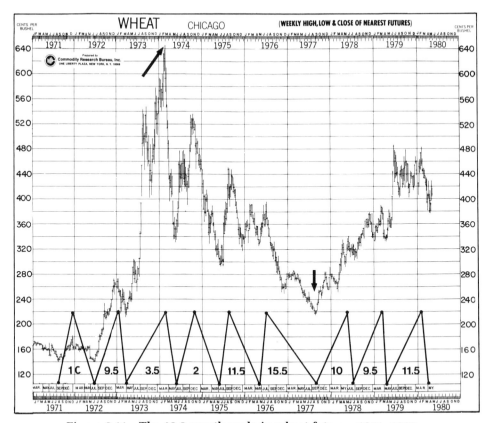

**Figure 6.11    The 12.2 month cycle in wheat futures, 1971–1980.**

necessarily similar. Figure 6-12 shows the cycle from 1956 to 1968. The cycle has been reliable and can be used successfully for trading purposes. It is the same pattern as the approximately 42 to 54 week cycle.

A cycle of equal importance, although shorter in length runs about half the length at 26 weeks, low to low. It is not especially reliable for trading purposes. The 12.2 month pattern is preferable. A number of short term cyclic tendencies are discussed in Chapter 8.

## POTATOES

In recent years there have been a number of problems in the potato market. Attempts at manipulation, highly erratic price moves, and various legal difficulties have made it difficult to trade futures with confidence. There has, nevertheless, been a fairly good cyclic pattern since 1956 that runs about 32 months, low to low, on the average. This approximately 3 year cycle accounts for a majority of the highs and lows since that time. It is included here as an intermediate term cycle although it is actually 3 years in length and could qualify as a long term cycle. Figure 6-13 shows the four cycles from 1956 through 1968, and Figure 6-14 shows the next four through 1980. Apparently the 1980 low came somewhat early.

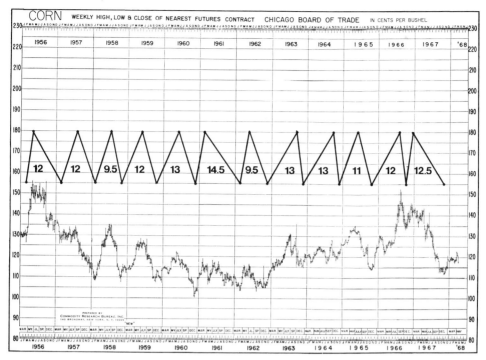

Figure 6.12   The 12.2 month cycle in corn futures.

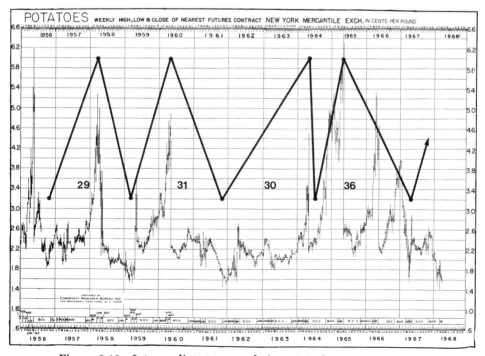

Figure 6.13   Intermediate term cycle in potato futures, 1956–1967.

101

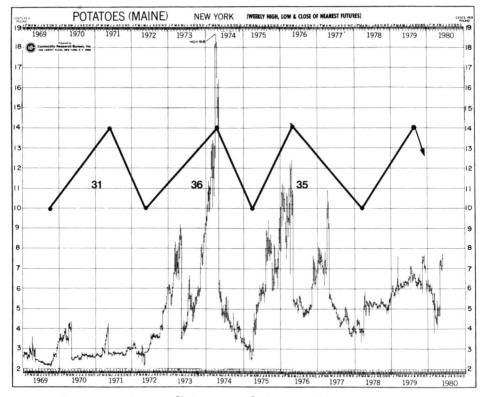

**Figure 6.14   Intermediate term cycle in potato futures, 1969–1980.**

## PLATINUM

Platinum should show cyclic lengths similar to what has already been observed in gold and silver. By examining the market closely, we can isolate a cycle that runs from about 25 to 39 weeks in length. It has persisted since 1972 and averages out at 30 weeks, low to low. There is a high degree of variability in the cycle length, but the mean period is still useful as a general guideline of major highs and lows. Virtually every important top and bottom in platinum since 1972 is accounted for by the approximately 30 week cycle. I have shown reversals down (R−) and reversals up (R+) as an additional feature of the platinum cycle (see Figure 6-15). These timing indicators are, as mentioned earlier, discussed in Chapter 12. You should also examine the half cycle that runs about 15 weeks, low to low, for possible reliability.

## PLYWOOD

For many years plywood and lumber have been known as highly seasonal commodities (seasonality is discussed in Chapter 18). A fairly reliable cycle in plywood dates back to the beginning of futures trading in this market. With only a few exceptions the cycle has averaged 47 weeks, low to low. The longest run has been 61 weeks and the shortest 42 weeks. The 61 week cycle deviated significantly from the tendency, but prices got back on track thereafter. The

# PLATINUM

**New York Mercantile Exchange**

Weekly High, Low—Friday Close

COMMODITY PERSPECTIVE/CHICAGO, ILLINOIS 60604

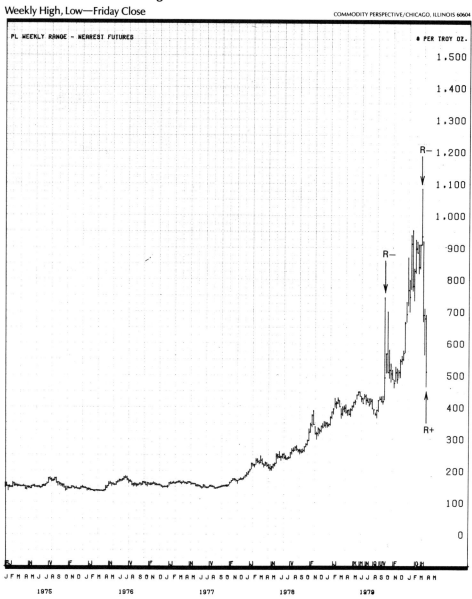

Figure 6.15   Intermediate term cycles in platinum.

Weekly High, Low—Friday Close                COMMODITY PERSPECTIVE/CHICAGO, ILLINOIS 60604

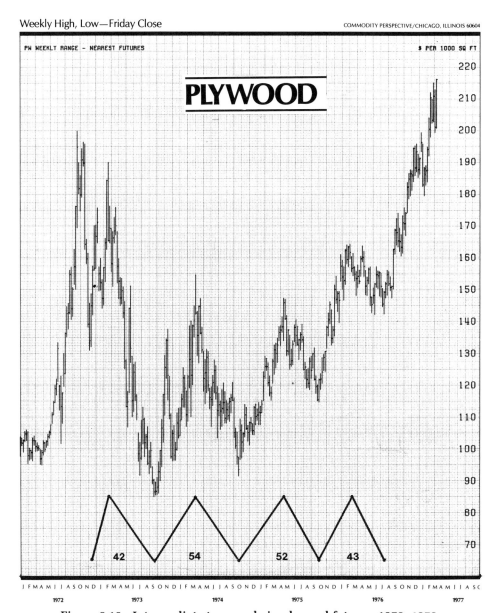

**Figure 6.16   Intermediate term cycle in plywood futures, 1972–1976.**

true test of this cycle came with the next bottom. Ideally, it was due in February 1981, although in actuality the low came in April 1981. In some cases, only time will tell if a cycle has changed its length. In this situation, however, it is unlikely, and I would venture a guess that the cycle will get back on course in 1981. Had you been trading the market based on an average 47 week tendency, you would no doubt have taken a loss when the cycle ran late. I have marked three bottoms at about the expected low time (arrows) (Figure 6-17). All were signals that failed. Situations such as these are discussed in Chapter 12.

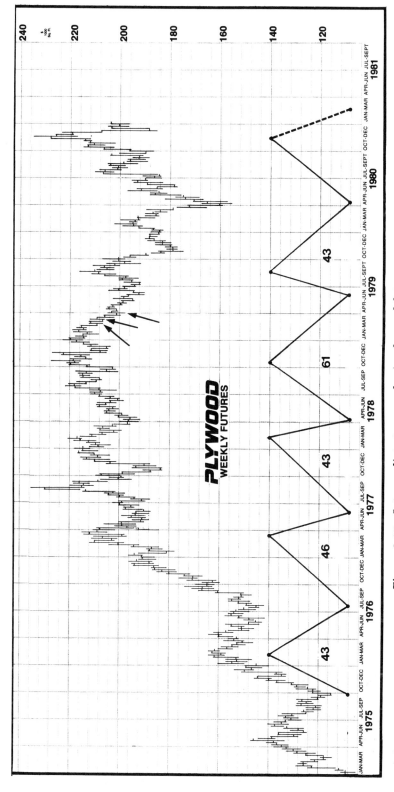

Figure 6.17  Intermediate term cycles in plywood futures, 1975–1980.

## ORANGE JUICE

The orange juice market has long been avoided by conservative traders. Its history has included many extended declines and severe rallies, functions of the market's sensitivity to weather conditions. Weather conditions also run in cycles. Hence, we would expect to find a fairly regular pattern in orange juice futures. This is, in fact, the case—at least on an intermediate term basis. From 1972 on we can isolate a cycle ranging in length from 43 weeks, low to low, to 61 weeks as the longest period (Figure 6-18). The average length is 51 weeks,

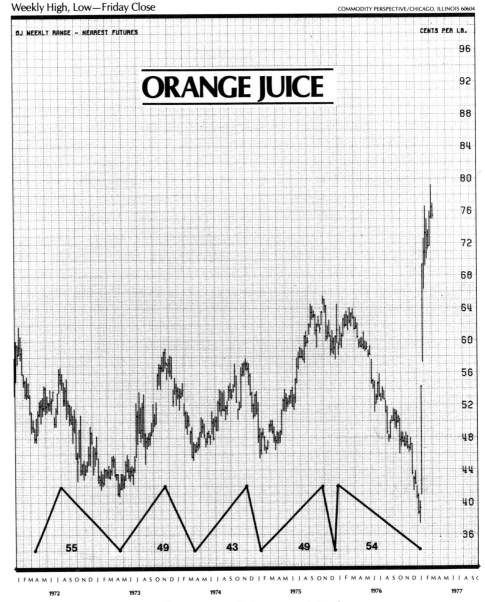

Figure 6.18   Intermediate term cycle in orange juice futures, 1972–1977.

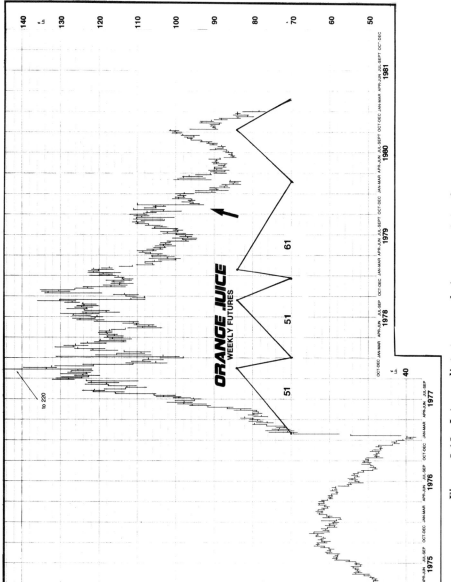

**Figure 6.19   Intermediate term cycle in orange juice futures 1975–1980.**

including the inordinately long 61 week pattern. Assuming you had bought the market (arrow, Figure 6-19) at the expected signal low, you would have taken a loss. The orange juice analysis is just another example of how a cycle can help keep you on the right side of the market. Even had you not been willing to buy orange juice futures, you would certainly have been cautious about holding a short position through this cyclic low period. Because the previous cycle ran longer than anticipated, you might have expected the most recent cycle to run a bit shorter than average.

## SUGAR

The approximately 6.2 year cycle in sugar has already been shown to be an important pattern in accounting for much of the price change in this market over the past 80 years. In addition, there is an approximately 12.5 month cycle dating back to the early 1950s and possibly earlier. Figure 6-20 shows the history since 1971 as well as the 6.2 year cycle, *ABC*. It also shows how the next 6.2 year pattern starts and how the shorter term cycles fit.

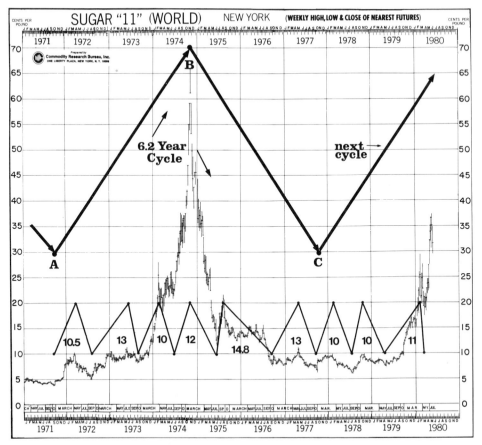

**Figure 6.20   The approximate 12.5 month sugar futures cycle 1971–1980.**

Of all the food commodities, sugar has had the most peculiar history—alternating between periods of extreme volatility and extreme dormancy. Many of the sugar cycles discussed in this text function well only when overall trading in sugar futures is relatively active. In addition, sugar futures have a history of extreme risk as well as profit potential.

## SOYBEANS

Among the grains showing an approximately 9 to 11 month cycle is the soybean market. In fact, allowing the usual variation at tops, the approximate 42 week cycle translates into a pattern of about 10.5 months. There is, to be sure, more than the desired amount of variation between tops of this cycle, but the lows are quite regular, and prices tend to put on an impressive show, particularly when all three important cycles bottom at the same time. Let's take a closer look at some of the patterns to see how they work. Figure 6-21 shows the price and cycle fluctuations from 1972 through early 1977. Figure 6-22 shows the continuation of this cycle through early 1980. The balance of this cycle can be updated by looking at a current chart. An important low in soybeans was made late March to early April 1980, which brought the cycle to a bottom. The next low should have been made in January to February 1981 but could have come as early as December 1980, at about the same time as lows in the 24 month cycle. In fact, there was a pronounced low in December 1980.

In Chapter 15 I discuss timing signals in conjunction with cyclic lows and highs. To give you an introduction to this topic, let's digress just a bit from the subject at hand. I am doing so because the soybean chart provides us with an excellent opportunity to give some advance instruction. In examining Figure 6-21 you will observe that I have marked a number of the lows and highs in beans with an arrow and the notation $R+$ or $R-$, abbreviations that are used later in this book. The abbreviations stand for *reversal up* $(R+)$ or *reversal down* $(R-)$. Each is a signal used to verify a low or high in the cycle. As you can see, most of the tops and bottoms since 1972 have given reversal signals. Reversal signals are not the only ones used to verify lows and highs of cycles. There are three other important indicators that I have not as yet discussed.

What is meant by a reversal signal? When a market trades lower than the lowest low it made in the previous week, but closes out the week higher than it did the previous week, it has made a weekly reversal up $(R+)$ signal. When a market trades higher than the highest high it made the previous week, but closes out the week lower than its closing price the previous week, it has made a weekly reversal down $(R-)$ signal. Timing signals are important because they let us know the exact week or day of a low or high. They are not always perfect, and the cycles are not perfect either, but they do help us zero in on the precise time period during which change in trend is most likely. The two reversal indicators are some of the signals to which I have referred in earlier portions of the text.

Certain markets are prone to give reversal signals, whereas others are likely to show less obvious confirming indicators. The soybean market has its own personality, if you will, part of which is characterized by the tendency toward frequent reversals. Cotton, on the other hand, is not usually a reversal signal

# SOYBEANS

**Chicago Board of Trade**

Weekly High, Low—Friday Close

COMMODITY PERSPECTIVE/CHICAGO, ILLINOIS 60604

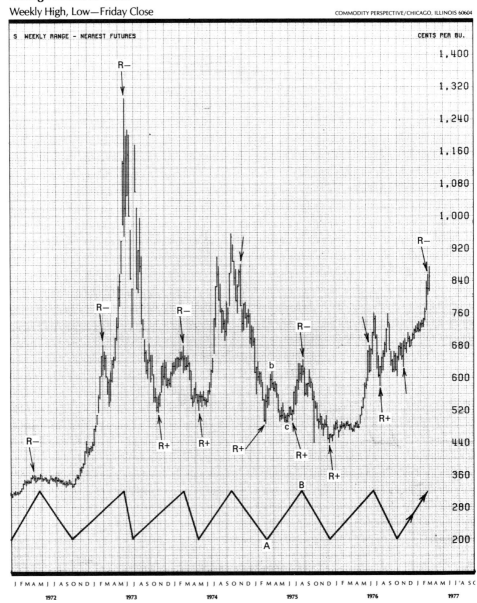

Figure 6.21   Intermediate term cycle in soybean futures, 1972–1976.

COMMODITY PERSPECTIVE/CHICAGO, ILLINOIS 60604                      Weekly High, Low—Friday Close

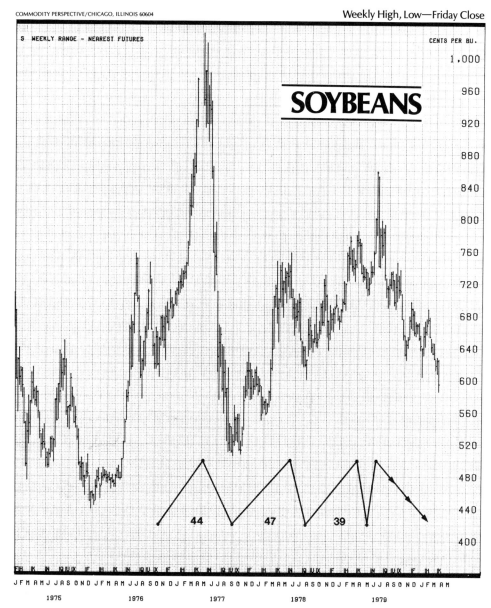

**Figure 6.22  Intermediate term cycle in soybean futures, 1975–1980.**

market but, rather, gives several other types of signals when turns come. It is important to keep this aspect of timing in mind. Changes through the years have occurred as the types of traders who participate in each market change, but there tends to be great consistency over long stretches of time. And you can take advantage of such stability in signals if you monitor them carefully.

As an exercise in correlating convergence tops and bottoms, I suggest you go back and examine the cycle charts of the 36 and 24 month tendencies, lining them up with the 42 week cyclic turns. You will probably be impressed with the magnitude of price movement when all three cycles are in line. Convergence of cycles has been discussed earlier. Its value is once again pointed out in order to impress upon you the importance of following as many reliable cycles as possible in all active markets. Later on I spend a little more time on this topic, particularly in relation to seasonality and cyclic convergence. For now, however, I advise you to examine with particular attention the cyclic tops made in 1973 and 1977 and the cyclic lows made in 1974, 1977, and early 1980.

Another exercise of value is to reduce the 42 week cycle into shorter patterns. For example, it could be fruitful to take one of the 42 week cycles, such as the one marked *Abc* in Figure 6-21. A quick inspection of the cycle shows that there seems to be a half cycle. Counting the time span between lows gives a period of about 14 weeks, low to low. To determine if this is a repetitive pattern, you would now move forward and backward, checking out lows and highs accordingly. If it proves to be a repeating tendency, or cycle, you can include it among those to be watched. You can also follow another procedure, which is to convert the new, shorter cycle into approximate days. Say, for example, that the cycle turns out to be 20 weeks, low to low. This translates into about 100 trading days. You could go to the daily price chart and look for cycles of approximately this length as your starting point in the short term analysis. In this fashion, the analysis of cycles follows the macro to micro chain as I have described earlier in this book.

There are several other important cyclic tendencies in the soybean market. Many of the cycles in soybeans are similar in length to those in silver cycles (discussed later in this chapter). Such interrelationships are common in cyclic analysis. I make no attempt to explain why this happens. It is best merely to accept the fact that there are rhythms in commodity prices that have persisted for many years. You can approach this fact from either an explanatory point of view or from the standpoint of a pragmatic motivation. Philosophical explanations will frequently be complex and can consume many chapters and thousands of hours in metaphysical exploration. This is a task that will be reserved for cold winter nights next to the fireplace.

**SILVER**

The long-range cycles in silver were discussed in Chapter 5. It was pointed out that silver is among the most repetitive markets when viewed from a cyclic standpoint. In fact, many students and analysts of silver find their work in this market especially gratifying because of the regularity and symmetry that have characterized silver for so many years. You'll recall the discussion of a 5.5 year tendency, which has been present since the 1900s (or earlier). Within this pattern there are also cycles that run approximately 30 to 40 weeks, 21 weeks, 10 weeks, and 32 days. Let's examine a few of these. Once again I have depicted the cycles on several charts that expand price action since 1972, making it easier to pick out the cycles. Figure 6-23 shows the weekly price of silver futures since the beginning of 1972. Figure 6-24 shows the continuation of this cycle through early 1980.

First, let's examine the 30 to 40 week cycle. Over the years it has been the most important trading cycle in the intermediate term. The 1979 explosion in

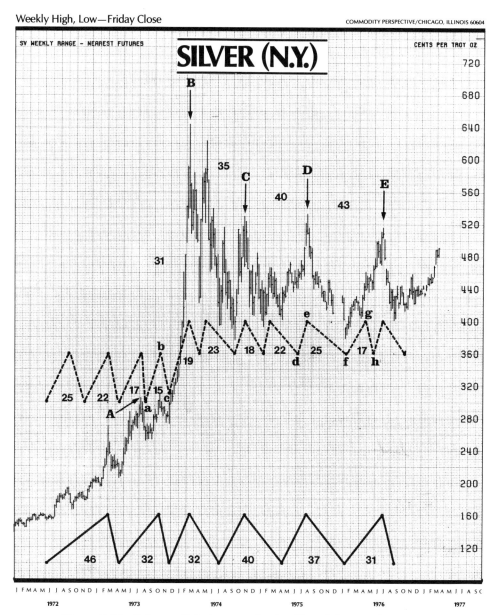

**Figure 6.23 Intermediate term cycles in silver futures, 1972–1976.**

prices has caused our chart to be a bit lopsided (in order to account for the move to $52), but the cycles are still visible. Figure 6-24 continues the 30 to 40 week silver cycle through early 1980. The shortest cycle length since 1972 has been about 31 weeks, and the longest cycle ran approximately 46 weeks. The average length works out to about 38 weeks, low to low.

Working with the next shortest cycle, 17 to 25 weeks, I have marked the lows and highs with time lengths indicated (Figure 6-23). For shorter term work you will need to go to the daily price chart, which is done in Chapter 8. For now,

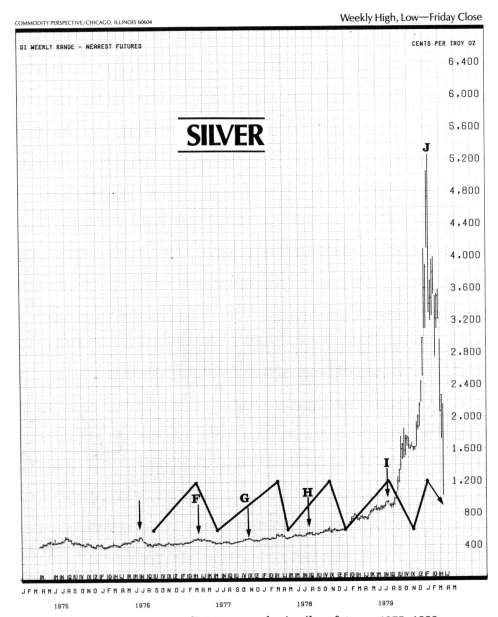

Figure 6.24   **Intermediate term cycles in silver futures, 1975–1980.**

however, suffice it to say that the 17 to 25 week cycle and the average 38 week cycle are the most important two patterns in silver. From 1972 through 1976 there were 12 repetitions of the shorter cycle, and with only a few exceptions it has been fairly reliable. Let's examine two of the irregular patterns. Cycle *abc* (Figure 6-23) ran only 15 weeks, low to low. Assuming that you were following the market with timing signals (to be discussed in detail later), you would not have been in on the move until about three weeks later when the high was penetrated. Notice that the subsequent move was very large. In addition, the approximately 38 week cycle made a low ahead of the expected low in the 17 to 25 week cycle, which would have been a much better buy indication. In Chapter 15, which discusses timing signals, you'll also see that the low of the 38 week pattern was made and confirmed by double timing signals. In previous sections I have stressed the value of following several cycles in each market to help minimize the effect of deviations from the expected pattern of any single cycle.

The next problem in the 17 to 25 week pattern comes with cyclic patterns *def* and *fgh* (Figure 6-23). Cycle *def* ran 25 weeks before giving buy signals. The chart is a bit deceptive because it appears as if *def* ran longer than 25 weeks. Several grids were left blank in the data to account for a contract switch. We are counting only the actual number of weeks, low to low, which totals 25. The next cycle, *fgh*, ran a bit short, as is frequently the case when a previous cycle has run longer than expected. Cycles tend to compensate. When there is a shorter or longer pattern that disrupts the overall tendency, the next cycle will usually change accordingly.

If you plan to use the approximately 20 week cycle for trading purposes, it would be best to use a daily price chart rather than a weekly chart. Although you will have room for only about three repetitions of the cycle on each contract, you may find it easier to pick out the highs and lows.

Also included in the weekly silver charts are cyclic highs A through J (Figures 6-23 and 6-24). These are all tops that fall reasonably close to one another. Some are 42 week tops and others are not. Notice the high degree of regularity between tops, which is another pattern that deserves further investigation. Earlier I pointed out the tendency for cycles to correct themselves when a given repetition has run either too long or too short. Notice, for example, that tops H and I (Figure 6-24) came about 49 weeks apart, much longer than any of the lengths since 1972. One would expect the next major top to come early as a compensation or correction of this late top. Notice that top J was, in fact, very early.

This completes the analysis for silver. When you work with the cycles in this or any other market, it is important to remember that combinations of cycles can also occur. Take, as an example, the average 38 week cycle. If you add two adjacent cycles, you'll arrive at an approximate 76 to 82 week cycle, which may have more appeal to the longer term trader. There are also a number of shorter term cycles in silver that are discussed in Chapter 8.

## GOLD

The long term gold cycle, discussed earlier in Chapter 5, has several component cycles that can be used for purposes of intermediate term trading. These patterns are marked accordingly in Figure 6-25. The longer of the two patterns ran about 47 weeks on the average, low to low, and accounted for most of the major highs and lows after 1975. The half cycle of this pattern ran about 23 weeks, low to low, and is also shown (as the dashed line). The shortest cycle ran 14 weeks and the longest, 24 weeks. The cycle that ran short bottomed during the time of a downtrend in the 47 week cycle. It is difficult to explain fully why this very brief cycle occurred, but things got back on schedule with the next two repetitions.

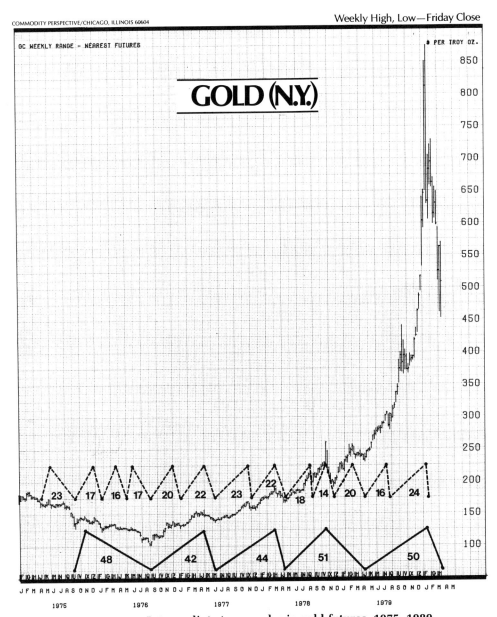

**Figure 6.25   Intermediate term cycles in gold futures, 1975–1980.**

## CANADIAN DOLLAR

The currencies have shown a high degree of cyclic reliability since futures trading in these markets began. As an example, the Canadian dollar, whose long term cycles I discussed in Chapter 5, has shown a highly reliable cycle of about 36 weeks, low to low, since 1975. It is fairly symmetrical, as you can see by examining Figure 6-26. There have been seven repetitions of the pattern with highs being only slightly less predictable than lows. Notice the tendency for early tops as prices moved in a longer term cyclic downtrend from 1976 to

Weekly High, Low—Friday Close                    COMMODITY PERSPECTIVE/CHICAGO, ILLINOIS 60604

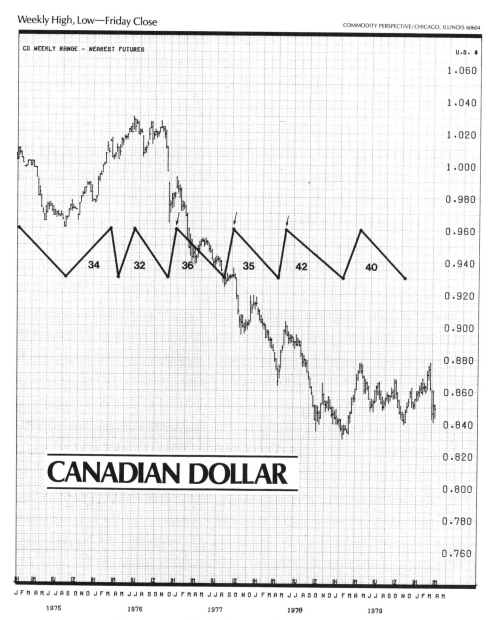

**Figure 6.26   Cycles in Canadian Dollar futures.**

1979. Each early peak in Figure 6-26 is marked with an arrow. This characteristic of cycles has been mentioned in previous chapters. As soon as the long term trend changed in early 1979, the tendency toward an early peak ended.

## JAPANESE YEN

Another market that has shown fairly high levels of cyclic reliability is the Japanese yen. Figure 6-27 shows the approximately 22 week cycle in yen fu-

Weekly High, Low—Friday Close                    COMMODITY PERSPECTIVE/CHICAGO, ILLINOIS 60604

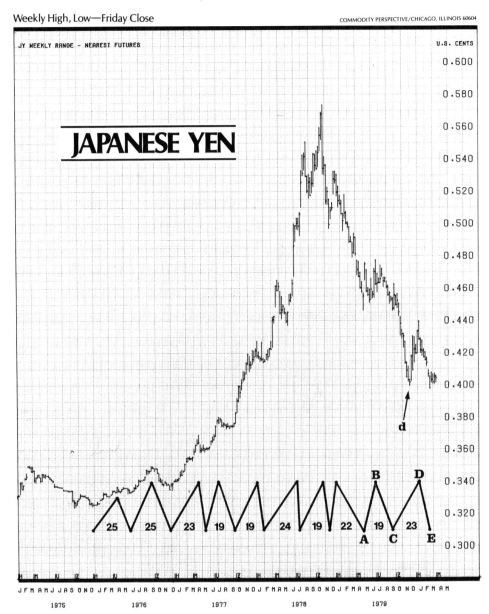

**Figure 6.27   Cycles in Japanese yen futures.**

tures. The double cycle would run about 42 weeks, which is about the same length as our overall 9.5 month tendency in most commodity markets. Since 1976 there have been 10 repetitions of the 22 week cycle, with a fairly high degree of variability between highs. On close inspection of Figure 6-27 you will see that with two exceptions each pattern fits the actual price behavior very well. The two possible deviations are cycles *ABC* and *CDE*—the last two on the chart. Let's run through a bit of explanatory material as an exercise in trouble-shooting cycles. This is how problems in selecting turns are resolved.

Notice that *ABC* made an early top after confirming a low 19 weeks from the previous bottom. The next major low is marked *d* with an arrow. This low came too close to the previous cycle bottom (*ABC*) and is not counted. We can only assume that it was part of another important low. Moving to bottom *E*, however, we *do* get a weekly count that fits the analysis well. The current results won't be known until recent price data are examined. When you analyze a cyclic pattern manually, it is sometimes necessary to backtrack if a cycle won't fit into its proper place within reasonable variation. The actual outcome cannot be definite until there are more price data. In this case, for example, the next lows were made in April 1980, August 1980, December 1980, and May 1981, all well within the limits of this cycle.

## GERMAN DEUTSCHE MARK

The Deutsche mark (D–Mark) has shown an approximately 32.5 week cycle, low to low, as seen in Figure 6-28. There have been seven repetitions of this cycle from 1975 through 1980. In an earlier section I mentioned the timing indicators for the weekly upside and downside reversal (R+ and R−). The indicators are discussed in considerable detail later on, but as a continued introduction to the topic observe the bottoms and tops marked with arrows (Figure 6-28). Each is a reversal top or bottom signal at or close to a major high or low in the cycle. The cycle ran well until 1979, at which time a small deviation occurred. In my discussion of the yen I gave some preliminary instructions on how to troubleshoot cycles when they are not as accurate as had been expected. The same technique can be applied in this case because the cycle went a bit astray in early 1980. Here is how you could deal with such a situation.

Assume that a low was made at *A* (see arrow Figure 6-28). The expected uptrend developed with a high about 17 weeks later (arrow *B*). The market might have then been sold short on the weekly downside reversal *(B)*. Arrow *C* marks the actual low. At the time, we did not know it was a low because it came too soon after bottom *A*. As a result we would not have covered the short position (were we actually trading the cycle). And there would have been no indication to get long. By the time bottom *D* arrives, however, we begin to suspect that something has gone astray, and by the time top *E* arrives, we are out of the short position—most likely with a loss. Having seen the cyclic count deviate, we have several choices. First, we could count *D* as the low of a cycle and project the next low about 32 weeks later. Second, we could assume that top *E* was the peak of another cycle, which would lead us to expect that the next cyclic low will be on time with *D* counted as a bottom. A third alternative would be to make no assumptions at all, stay out of the market, and analyze the next several months worth of data to see if the cycle will get back on schedule. The only way to be positive about the end result would be to await the actual outcome.

In this case we have considerable evidence as to what eventually developed. Figure 6-29 is an updated chart of March D–Mark futures (current through July

Weekly High, Low—Friday Close                    COMMODITY PERSPECTIVE/CHICAGO, ILLINOIS 60604

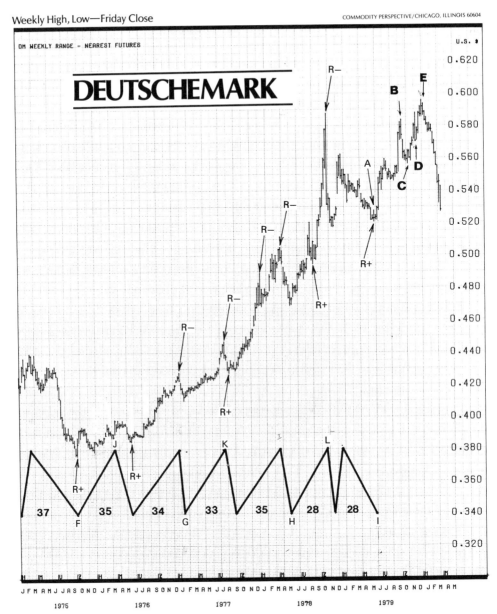

**Figure 6.28   Cycles in D-mark futures.**

11, 1980). Assuming a low at point *D* (Figure 6-28), we can project the next low 32 weeks later, which gives us a projected bottom in May 1980. The actual low (see Figure 6-29) came in April, still a bit too early for this cycle (about 20 weeks low to low). The only thing to assume in such a case is that the cycle has stopped working and will reappear later, or that an entirely new cycle has taken over. Regardless of what may eventually result, the market must not be traded on the basis of this cycle until this problem has been resolved.

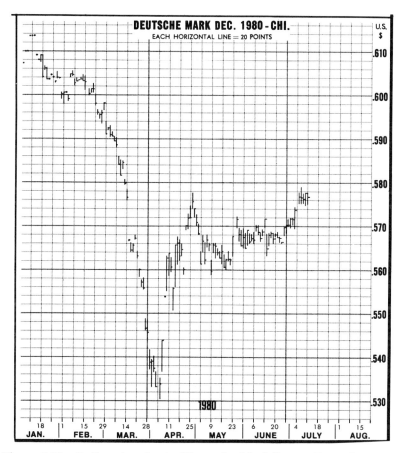

**Figure 6.29   Daily price chart of Deutsche Mark futures December, 1980.**

Failing to get any satisfaction from this cycle, we could examine the double cycle to see if any better results could be achieved. In this case we would use every other low of the approximately 32 week cycle as a low. I have marked the double cycle lows and highs with upper case letters accordingly (*F* through *L*). Assuming that *L* was the last low, we could project the next bottom about 65 weeks later. An important low in the D–Mark cycle actually came in December 1980, about 78 weeks after the last bottom shown in Figure 6-29. When a cycle fails to fit, there are a number of alternatives that can be explored. We can either look at the next longest cycle or the next shortest cycle.

## SWISS FRANC

The market in Swiss franc closely parallels price trends in D-Mark futures. Cycle lengths, however, appear to be more reliable, and tops seem to come at more regular intervals. Although the average cyclic length since 1975 has been slightly shorter than those of the D-Mark, overall price tendencies are similar in both markets. Figure 6-30 shows the approximately 29 week cycle through

Weekly High, Low—Friday Close                    COMMODITY PERSPECTIVE/CHICAGO, ILLINOIS 60604

**Figure 6.30   Cycles in Swiss franc futures.**

1979. The last few repetitions were a bit shorter than the average before that. The most recent two cycles (not shown) have run about 23 weeks, low to low. These are also a bit shorter than the average cycle length since 1975 but still within an acceptable degree of tolerance.

The double cycle can also be used, particularly by those seeking long term positions. Lows and highs (A to G of the double cycle) have been marked on Figure 6-30 accordingly. The last low on our chart is only half of the double cycle. It projected a low about 29 weeks later. The actual low came 22 weeks later, within the acceptable time frame. An approximately 3 year cyclic pattern in Swiss francs was discussed in Chapter 5. In studying intermediate cycles in Swiss francs you should take the earlier discussion into consideration.

## BRITISH POUND

British pound futures have also shown a cycle in the approximately 20 to 30 week range. Since 1977 the pattern has run as short as 23 weeks and as long as 27 weeks. The British pound cycle is perhaps the most stable of all intermediate market cycles in currencies, with tops having a high degree of regularity as well. Figure 6-31 shows the cycle since 1977. This chart is updated through late 1980, and it suggests that there should have been another relative low in the pound (the dashed line shows the projected trend). A double cycle could also be used here with equal success.

   I have earlier mentioned reversal timing signals. I also have pointed out the fact that not all markets make frequent reversal signals. Soybeans, for example, tend to make reversals at major lows and highs, but cotton does not. The British pound is another market in which reversals tend to occur rather infrequently. From 1977 through early 1981 there were only five signals although there was a total of 19 turns (tops and bottoms combined). This is why other timing indicators will be needed to confirm tops and bottoms in isolating cycles of the pound.

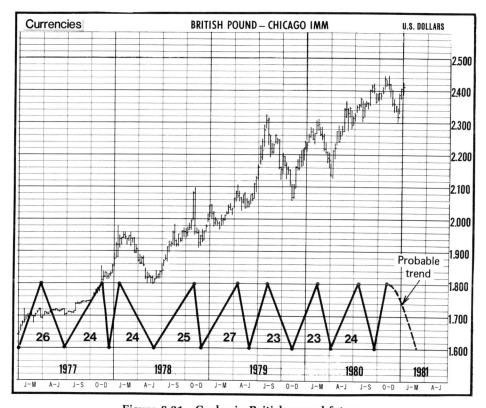

**Figure 6.31   Cycles in British pound futures.**

## TREASURY BILLS

The futures market in Treasury bills (T-bills) has rapidly become one of the most speculative of all commodities. With the large swings in cash interest rates and the economic uncertainties currently confronting virtually all free world powers, the trading volume of this market has rapidly expanded. Several reliable cycles in T-bills confirm the possibility that great profits may be made. Since 1976, when futures in T-bills first became active, there has been a per-

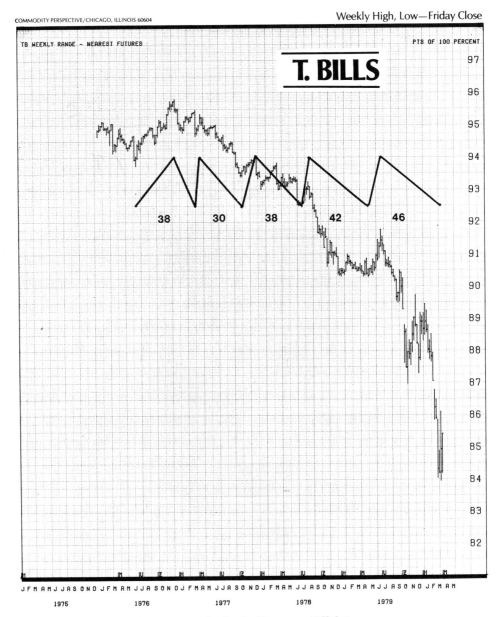

Figure 6.32  Cycles in Treasury Bill futures.

sistent uptrend in cash rates. T-bill futures move lower as cash markets move up. I have previously indicated the tendency for markets to make early cyclic peaks when the major trend is down. In approaching the cyclic analysis of T-bills, then, our first expectation is that just such a pattern will emerge.

Figure 6-32 shows the weekly high, low, and closing price since trading was initiated in T-bills. I have identified on the chart an approximate cycle of 38.8 weeks. This average includes the most recent cycle, which ran about 39 weeks, low to low. You can appreciate the high degree of volatility in T-bill futures by simply looking at this chart. There is also an approximate cycle of 26 weeks in T-bills, although it is not as reliable as the 38 week pattern. T-bills, as you will see later on, also have several short term cyclic tendencies. The interaction of the short term cycles makes this an especially good market to trade on the basis of the cyclic method. The behavior of other futures markets in interest rates should be basically similar.

# CHAPTER SEVEN

# The Nine to Eleven Month Cycle

The 54 year price pattern discussed in Chapter 5 constitutes an important long wave in virtually all commodity prices. The Kondratieff cycle named after its discoverer, N. D. Kondratieff, can be broken down into various shorter cycles, among which are included the Juglar and Kuznets, each named after its discoverer. Long term cycles are interesting, informative, and even applicable to planning years ahead, but their one major limitation is their degree of error. As pointed out earlier, a variance of $\pm 10$ percent in the 54 year cycle gives a 5.4 year time span on either side of an ideal high or low. This is an error factor of more than 10 years! Even in the case of such patterns as the 9 year wheat cycle, a variance of $\pm 10$ percent gives 0.9 years on either side of a low or high. The time frame during which the trend in wheat prices could change is therefore 1.8 years. This is a long period in which to watch for signs of change. There may be many false starts, many incorrect signals, and many losses during such a period.

Assume that an individual wishes to purchase land on the basis of a wheat price cycle. To him the 1.8 year time span may not be a limiting factor. If he begins to accumulate land slowly about six months before the ideal bottom and continues his program until about six months after the ideal bottom, he has stretched out his purchases over a 1.2 year period, anticipating an increase in land values as wheat prices rise over the next four years. This is a reasonable and probably profitable approach.

The individual who wishes to buy gold or silver bullion on the basis of the cycles in these markets can also fare well, provided he or she buys on a scale basis in regular time segments during the time frame most likely to be a low. The same holds true for the liquidation of holdings. Say, for example, that a low in gold prices is expected in 1983. We know from experience with cycles that the actual low might come in mid-1982. The investor would carefully watch prices. Come 1982, price trends are clearly lower. Not knowing exactly where and when the bottom will come, the investor begins to buy monthly or weekly in amounts that represent a fraction of his eventual position. This process continues until well after the expected low. Soon he recognizes that prices have indeed turned higher. At this point he stops the accumulation program.

The cycle begins its run, and an explosive upmove develops. Soon the cycle enters the time frame of an ideal high, and the investor slowly begins to divest his cash holdings on a scale-out basis. After the top comes, he will have left the market at an average price well within the bounds of respectability but certainly not at the exact top. The next bottom would then be projected and the same method followed. This approach can be applied to virtually all areas of investment, whether stocks, bonds, land, housing, or cash commodities. When long term accumulation is not possible, as in the case of commodity futures, timing must be much more exact because of the extremely low margins used in futures trading. To take advantage of the tremendous leverage in commodity futures it is, therefore, necessary to refine timing to its highest state of perfection.

One way in which refinement in timing can be achieved is by looking at short term price patterns within the long range patterns that characterize each market. I have already mentioned the 9 year pattern in wheat, the 3.6 year cycle in hogs and pork bellies, the 7 year and 45 month cycles in cattle, as well as others ranging in length from 11 months to many years. I have also shown that many markets move together. The 54 year Kondratieff wave, for example, seems to have an influence on virtually all commodity prices. In addition, the Juglar and Kuznets cycles also have an effect on price patterns. A shorter term cycle, which seems to affect virtually all commodity markets, is the 9 to 11 month pattern. We have already seen some evidence of this cycle in corn, broilers, eggs, sugar, lumber, and cotton. Let's take a closer look at this tendency with the eventual goal of using it in an overall trading strategy. Because of the importance of this pervasive pattern, this entire chapter is given to its discussion.

Assume that we wish to trade the commodity market from the standpoint of an intermediate term trend. Assume also that we use a 50 percent margin or more for each trade rather than the 3 percent or less required by exchange or government regulation. This means, for example, that a 5000 bushel contract of wheat at $5.00 per bushel, which represents $25,000 cash value, would require about $12,500 in margin as opposed to about $1500. What we are doing in this case is giving ourselves more leeway for each contract so that we can ride a loss longer if necessary. Hence, timing need not be as exact. We will not overextend our position by adding contracts against the margin already allotted to wheat. Theoretically, wheat prices would need to decline to $2.50 per bushel from $5.00 per bushel before our risk capital was gone and we were called for additional margin. This allows us the luxury of trading long wave cycles. It is rare that a wheat cycle is so far off base as to result in a contrary move of over $2.50 per bushel. In fact, it might even be possible to use 25 percent margin and still safely participate in the long term cycle.

Another technique is to watch the overall trend of commodity prices. In the same way that stock market students watch the Dow Jones or Standard and Poors averages, commodity traders can watch the Commodity Research Bureau or the Reuters commodity price indexes. In fact, since 1968 (and possibly earlier) there has been a fairly regular 9 to 11 month cycle in the overall index of commodity prices. This cycle could open many opportunities to the intermediate term trader using an approach similar to the one above, so let's examine it to see how well it has worked.

The Commodity Research Bureau Futures Price Index is comprised of the high, low, and close averages of 27 markets indexed on a scale that assigns a value of 100 to the year 1967. The markets included in this average are:

| | |
|---|---|
| Barley–WPG | Platinum–NY |
| Broilers–CHI | Plywood–CHI |
| Cattle–CHI | Pork bellies–CHI |
| Cocoa–NY | Potatoes–NY |
| Coffee–NY | Rapeseed–WPG |
| Copper–NY | Rye–WPG |
| Corn–CHI | Silver–NY |
| Cotton–NY | Soybean oil–CHI |
| Eggs–CHI | Soybean meal–CHI |
| Flaxseed–WPG | Soybeans–CHI |
| Greasewool–NY | Sugar 11–NY |
| Hogs live–CHI | Wheat–CHI |
| Oats–CHI | Wheat–MPLS |
| Orange juice–NY | |

The CRB Index Chart (Figure 7-1) shows what the index has done since 1968. A quick glance reveals that prices have, in general, exploded since 1972. Closer examination shows that a repetitive pattern has characterized the price trend since 1968. In fact, we can trace the index back to 1958 to find many more lows and highs within the acceptable time span. Looking at the waves, one by one, we see about 15 repetitions of this cycle. Figure 7-1 lists the approximate time span between lows of this cycle and the approximate month of low. It also projects ideal timing of the next cycle bottom and top. The cycle can also be expressed in terms of weeks. Again, notice that the time spans between the tops of this cycle vary more than the time spans between bottoms.

Let's take the analysis one more step. Assume that, from your studies of the CRB Index, you wish to take a position in some of the individual markets. How do you do this? Perhaps you are interested in the wheat market. Assume that your CRB Index chart is complete to the October bottom in 1973. You know that the pattern runs about 10.5 months, average low to low. You do not know what will happen next. You project the next low to come about 10 months after the October 1973 low, which means that you expect the next low in August 1974, or thereabouts (the actual low came in May/June). You know that cycles are never exact in the commodity market, so you begin buying March 1975 wheat about 10 percent ahead of the expected low. Because 10 percent of 10 months is about 1 month, you begin buying wheat in July 1974. *You did not know at the time that the low came early.* Now examine the March 1975 wheat chart, Figure 7-2. Notice that the contract low came in May. Your buying began in July (see Figure 7-2). You may have continued to buy on a fractional basis. A position might therefore have been accumulated in the area indicated.

The March 1975 wheat contract was selected because it would have allowed you to stay with your position for over five months, approximately one-half the length of the index cycle. Assume also that you projected a high in the cycle to occur about 5 months after the low. This would give you a projected high in November 1975, but the top on the wheat chart shows that it came late in October. Would you have sold at the top? No, you would not have sold all of your position at the cyclic top. You know that cycles are not exact, therefore

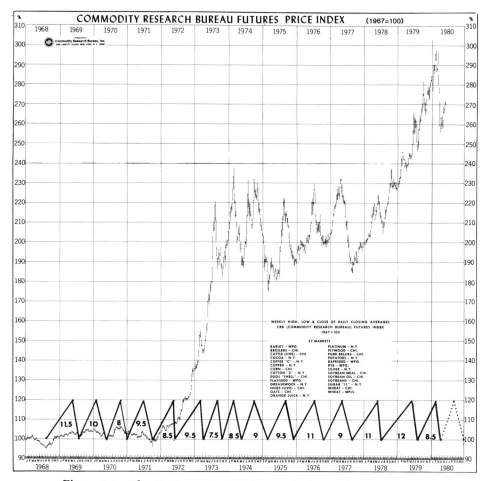

**Figure 7.1    The 9–11 month CRB futures index cycle, 1968–1980.**

you would have started selling in September and finished selling in November (see Figure 7-2). Your market entry in this case would have been near the $4.50 average cost, and your exits would have clustered in the $5.40 range. A total gain of about $0.90 would have been achieved. By using a 25 percent margin or even a 50 percent margin, your contracts would never have been in danger of being called for more margin in this case. The only thing you lost was leverage, but you gained considerable peace of mind and a large profit!

You might even have started to scale in a short position at the same time. Hence, you might have been selling short another contract month while leaving your long position. Let's take a look at another cycle to see how you might have fared using this technique. The CRB cycle low came in late 1975. The next top (Figure 7-1) came about seven months later, peaking a bit later than expected. Projecting the next low, we come to late October 1976. Assume you want to buy soybeans. You might wait until early November before starting, which would be 10 to 11 months after the last low. Figure 7-3 shows the September

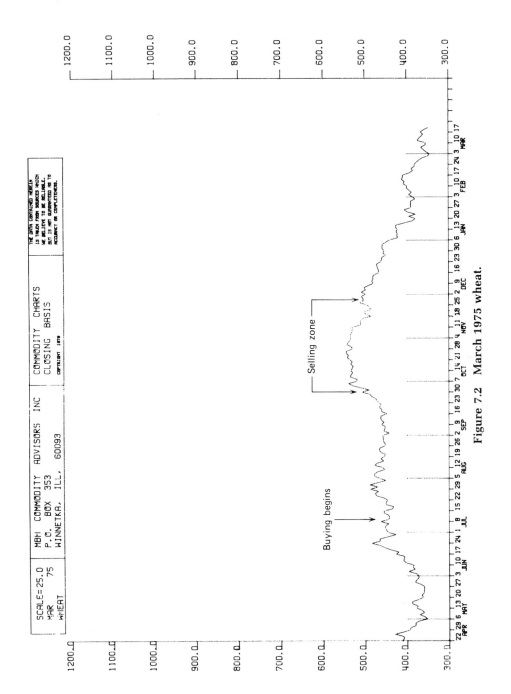

Figure 7.2  March 1975 wheat.

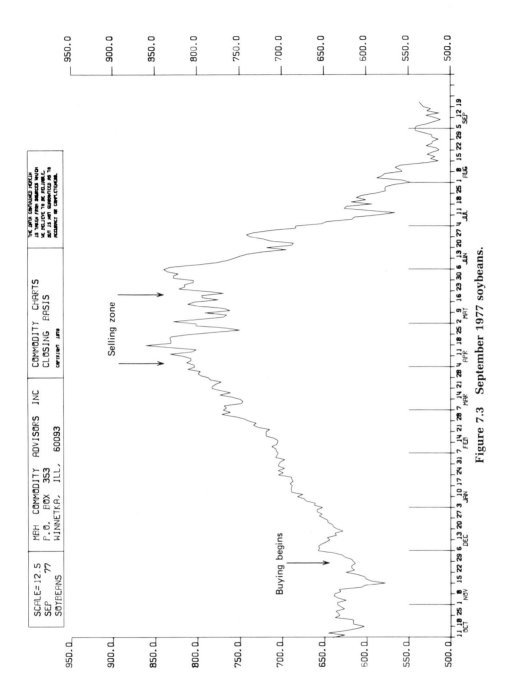

Figure 7.3 September 1977 soybeans.

131

1977 delivery of soybean futures. The start of a buying program in November 1976 would have been extremely successful. The projected high, about 5 months after the actual CRB low in December 1976, would have been May 1977. The actual selling might have started in April. In this case a very large profit could have been achieved with virtually no problem regarding margin if the 25–50 percent rule discussed earlier had been observed.

There are always exceptions to the rule, so let's see how you might have fared in a highly irregular cyclic period. Following the 1977 high the index made a low, reasonably on schedule in August/September 1977. Assume that you had started buying July 1978 soybeans during the low of August 1977. You continued your buying program into September and got in close to the contract lows (see Figure 7-4). You did most of the buying in the $5.40 area. You project a high about five months later, or February 1978, and you begin selling out in January 1978. You would leave your positions initially in the $6.10 area in January and in the $5.75 area in February. The actual high did not come until March 1978. Assume that you were also establishing short positions in the same time frame. Using the 25–50 percent margin rule, you would indeed have been riding a loss. The July 1978 delivery of soybeans (Figure 7-4) shows what might have happened in this case. Eventually you would have covered your short trade, possibly with a profit.

Clearly, there would have been some tense times in holding a short position through such a large move against you, no matter how much margin had been put up. This is one of the drawbacks of trading without more precise timing indicators. There might have been a way to forecast a late top in the cycle, which could have caused later entry of the long position and later entry on the short side. Your use of a combination of timing signals discussed in Chapter 17 would have avoided this problem. Notice also that you were treating the cycle as a perfect entity, which, of course, it is not. Also, had you been selling and buying on projected lows and highs, working from previous highs and lows rather than an ideal 9.5 month zigzag, you would have been better off.

Let's work a little more carefully with the cycle. Going back to 1968 in Figure 7-1, you can see that the time span across highs as well as lows can be calculated. The shortest time between lows since 1968 has been approximately 7.5 months, the longest, approximately 12 months. To determine the approximate cycle length between lows, we follow the same method explained in Chapter 2. The lows are added together giving a grand total of 143. The total is then divided by the number of observations—in this case 15. The result is 9.53, the average cycle length. Next, we compute the cycle variance by subtracting the shortest cycle length from the average and the longest cycle length from the average. This gives us $9.5 - 7.5 = 2$ months for the *variance from shortest cycle (VSC)*. Now we take $9.5 - 12 = 2.5$ *variance from longest cycle (VLC)*. This means that the cycle is likely to be as much as 2.5 months late in making a low. When it comes early, however, it is likely to be about 2 months early at worst. The total variance is 4.5 months. This is obtained by adding the *VSC* and *VLC* figures.

In predicting the next cycle low we would use the 9.5 average cycle length, counting forward from the last confirmed low. The same basic method is followed across the cyclic highs. First, we add all the cycle lengths across highs,

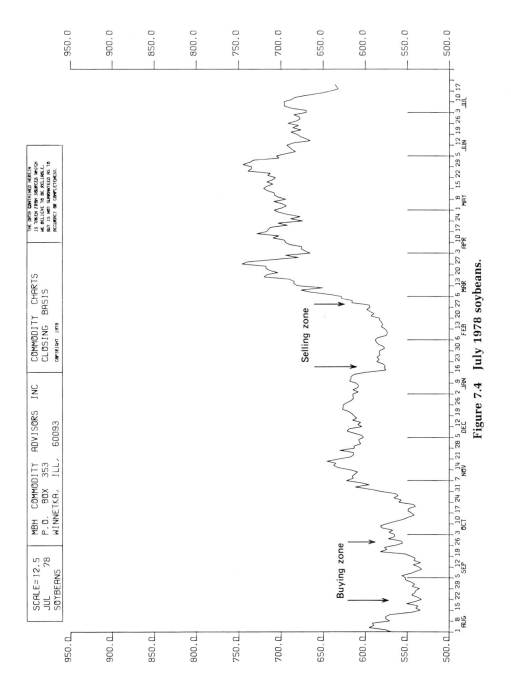

**Figure 7.4  July 1978 soybeans.**

133

for a grand total of 135. This is divided by the number of cycles observed, in this case 14. The cycle length across highs is 9.64. As you can see, it is slightly longer than the cycle period between lows. The variance, however, is larger. From the 9.6 average length we subtract the shortest cycle of 6 months and get 3.4 VSC. From the high of 13 we get 3.35, or 3.4 VLC rounded off. The cycle is more likely to be inaccurate at tops than at bottoms. What it amounts to is that more caution, better timing, and more risk are required when selling short. This stands to reason. A brief examination of this chart tells you that more time has been spent in the uptrends than in the downtrends over the past 12.5 years. This means that the chances of being right when long were higher than the chances of being right when short. In the final analysis, it means that we've been in a long term bull market, of which the 9.5 month cycle is merely a component of the shorter term. The force of a longer wave up has caused late peaks in the cycle.

Armed with this understanding, our job of taking profits and selling short is made that much easier. We know that the cycles are more likely to peak late, and we know that there is more variance at cyclic tops. Therefore, we can adjust our selling methods more suitably. The best method is to project a cycle high a bit later than the exact midpoint. If, for example, we made a low in the cycle, and a long position was taken, we project the next top ideally at one-half the 9.6 month top-to-top length. This gives us a top projection 4.8 months later, which we then adjust by 10 percent of the total top variance, or 0.34 (10 percent of 3.4 VLC). We then round off 0.34 and add 0.3 to our projected top, giving us about 5.1 months. True, this would prove to be a disadvantage if a top should come especially early, but the odds are in our favor if we project a late top. Of all the cyclic tops since 1968, only two were very early, running 6 and 7 months. The rest (six cases) were either 1.5 to 0.5 months ahead of the ideal top or on time. There were five late cycles that were from 1 to 2.5 months late. When the major cycle (of which the 9.5 month pattern is a small component) peaks, we'll most likely see early tops and late bottoms.

With this bit of added knowledge, let's examine another hypothetical case in which the CRB Commodity Futures Index cycle might have been used as a guide to trading one of its component markets. Let's trade some cotton this time, assuming that we have price history up to the 1978 bottom (July). The cycle ran about 11 months in actuality. Our buying might have started around 9.5 months from the last low. This means that we'd start buying in mid- to late June 1978. We would use the March 1979 contract because it was fairly active and still had plenty of time left until its expiration. Figure 7-5 shows the March 1979 cotton chart on which the initial buying point is indicated. An upmove of almost $0.10, or $5000 per contract, followed our hypothetical purchases. We know from past experience that the cycle is apt to run a bit late. A high is initially projected 5.1 months from our time of purchase. Remember that the high projection will change once it becomes clear that a bottom has been seen. We are buying now in anticipation of a bottom. Once the bottom has been confirmed, we will change the top projection. The bottom could come late, which should mean a later top. So, we have made our purchase, and we now initially project a top about 5.1 months later. This brings us to a late November as the ideal top. A bottom is confirmed within several weeks of our initial entry.

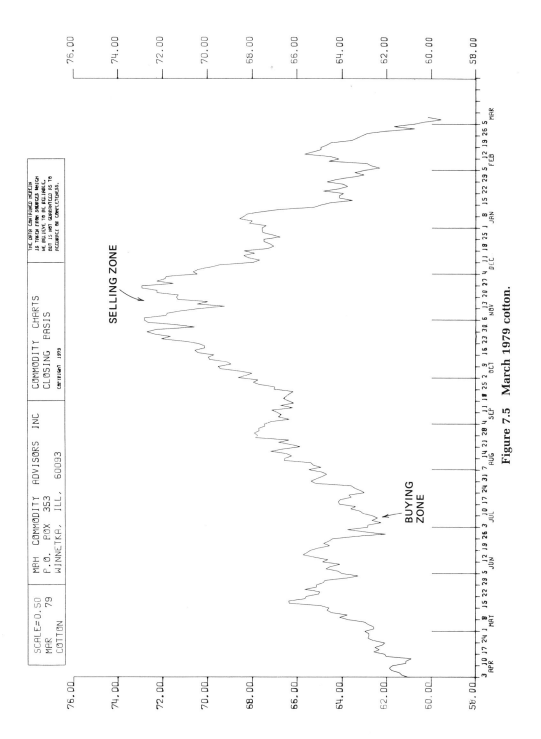

**Figure 7.5** March 1979 cotton.

We begin to sell out the position about 1 month before the ideal top and continue to sell until 1 month after the ideal top. This assumes that we have a multiple position, of course. What has been achieved? We started buying at about $0.63. We started selling in late October and early November at about $0.72, ideally, and we sold out the last position in late November and early December around $0.68. The total gain was excellent. The market never moved too far against us, and, best of all, we began selling short at the same time we started liquidating longs. We did not know that the 9.5 month cycle would actually peak very late. And neither did the cotton market! Prices dropped sharply even though the 9.5 month CRB cycle was still in an uptrend. The next low projection would have been about five months after the ideal top, or April 1979. From the November 1978 top to the expiration of the contract, a drop of more than $0.13 developed. There was indeed a low in the April 1979 period. In fact, it was a major low of one-half the 2.6 year cycle (previously discussed).

In the foregoing case we fared well on both sides of the move. Things do not always work this well. We have the good fortune of having 20/20 hindsight in all our examples. The purpose of running through some of the cycles and possible trades is merely illustrative. Each individual must decide how much risk and how large a position he or she wishes to assume. The general method discussed in connection with the 9.5 month Commodity Research Bureau Index cycle is one that could be refined considerably by the addition of several timing indexes. I caution against blindly trading the futures market on the basis of this or any of the information discussed in this book. The markets change, cycles become longer and shorter, risks become larger and smaller, and volatility increases and decreases. If you have the discipline to follow markets according to an organized and operational cyclic method, you will always be aware of the proper ratio of risk to reward. You will also know when cycles are reliable. There are too many people who begin trading futures with limited capital and limited net worth. Such individuals are doomed to failure before they start. My brief words of warning are just a few of many precautions you'll find throughout this book.

## REVIEW

A number of conclusions are warranted on the basis of what has been discussed in this chapter. They are as follows:

1   The commodity market has a general price cycle that runs about 9.5 months, low to low. It has done so since the 1950s and probably earlier.
2   The 9.5 month cycle is best studied using the Commodity Research Bureau (CRB) Index of commodity prices.
3   The cycle is not symmetrical. High-to-high measurements show that tops are less predictable than bottoms. There is more variance between tops than between bottoms.
4   One can trade individual component markets of the CRB Index using the 9.5 month cycle as a guide for buying and selling.

5   A general strategy for such trading, using 25–50 percent margin, was discussed with the caveat that it could be a suitable trading strategy for many traders but not necessarily for all traders.

6   A number of timing variations on this theme are certainly possible. Timing is the key to compensating for variation in length of cycles.

7   Note that when the major (secular) trend of commodity prices is up, it is likely that tops will continue to come late in the 9.5 month cycle. This trend should be reversed when the longer term cycle has changes direction.

8   The discussion of this cycle and the possible results of its use is preliminary and not intended to serve as a trading system or method. There are risks involved in every aspect of speculation, especially in the commodity markets.

# CHAPTER EIGHT

# Some Short-Term Cycles

The most attractive yet most difficult aspect of commodity futures is short term trading. The lure of low margin and large moves has tempted many a trader into positions of high risk. The two-edged sword of risk versus reward has also hurt many a trader. There is nothing wrong with short term trading from a technical standpoint. And there is nothing wrong with short term trading from the point of view of money management. There are, however, a number of prerequisites to short term trading, many of which are unknown to the average speculator. The ratio of losers to winners in the futures market should convince most of us that a majority of traders are not familiar with the tools required for successful speculation. Before taking a closer look at the short term cyclic patterns, I'll spend a little time laying some of the groundwork for money management that must accompany any successful program.

## WHAT IS A SHORT-TERM CYCLE?

A short term cycle can vary in length from several hours to several weeks. In many respects, the definition of short term is a matter of personal preference. For my purposes, I define *short term* as any cycle that runs less than 60 trading sessions. Some readers may argue this is too long a period, and others will consider it too short. Remember that it's just a matter of personal definition. We could call 60 days an intermediate term cycle if we wanted to, but the rules would be the same, regardless. Some speculators prefer to *scalp* or *day trade*, terms that refer to positions that last less than one trading day, and in some cases, less than one hour. I do not spend any time here discussing the ultra-short cycles, those that occur on an intraday basis. Although there *are* repetitive patterns within the day, I leave it up to the individual to research them.

## MARGIN, RISK, AND TIMING

In Chapter 7 I indicated the relationship between margin and risk. Low margin is an illusion that gives many traders a false sense of security. I suggested trading markets with considerably more margin than was required by the brokerage house and/or exchange. I proposed that this plan would allow the trader to hold on to an intermediate or long term trade with more leeway, thus minimizing the degree of error associated with all cycles. Timing, as you can see, is a key consideration in futures trading. The use of wider stops, larger margins, and positions of a longer term is one way of overcoming the limitations of cycle accuracy. When short term cycles are being traded, however, there is much less time. If a cycle averages 28 days, bottom to bottom, then a position based on this cycle might be held for about 14 days and certainly no more than 28 days. In practice, you would be trading approximately twice a month on the basis of such a cycle, which means that the expected move has less time to occur and is often relatively smaller. It also means that the time window or time frame during which a trade is to be established is shorter. All these considerations make timing important and necessitate a more effective method of limiting risk.

The best way to overcome the large risk accompanying low margin is to use more accurate timing indicators. The cycle length itself can take you only so far. Within a 15 percent time window, the cycle will either make a turn or it will not. What happens after the ideal time of a turn will either be unpredictable or it will involve more risk than you are willing to take. For example, a market may turn without giving an early indication of a change in trend. The price at which you enter may then be such that more risk is necessary. The relationship between timing and risk is, therefore, of greater concern to the short term trader than to the individual willing to risk more money with the intention of making more money. The better your timing, the less your risk. It's that simple, and it's that complicated. Outlined below are several guidelines for the short term trader. They should be considered by all individuals interested in the use of cycles.

## GUIDELINES FOR THE USE OF SHORT-TERM CYCLES

1 Timing must be as accurate as possible. Instead of market entry within a few weeks or months of a turn (as is acceptable in intermediate term and long term trading), you must enter within a few days or hours of the turn.

2 Daily price charts must be kept current at all times. If your charts are several days behind, you may miss an important cyclic turn.

3 Daily timing signals must be used. (Timing signals are discussed in Chapters 12–15.)

4 More trading will be required. Instead of trading several times a year or month, you may trade several times a week if you follow most of the active markets. Those who scalp or day trade may trade several times daily.

5 Each market entry exposes you to risk. Hence, the more often you trade, the more often you take risk.

6 Overall risk on any one trade must be much smaller than in short term or long term trading. If you trade six positions on the intermediate term during the year and risk $4000 on each, you have a total potential loss of $24,000. If you trade six times a month on the short term, however, your risk per trade must be less than $334 to equal the same total dollar risk.

7 You must enter and exit more quickly, as stands to reason because you are dealing with cycles that are much shorter. Your decisions must be

made more quickly, and as a consequence you will need to develop the psychological attitudes that facilitate quick decision making.

8  All the foregoing necessitate much more input of your time. Your overall effort may be five times greater than that invested by the intermediate term or long term trader. Unless your return on capital is considerably larger, your investment will not be paying commensurate dividends.

9  Another consideration is the cost of trading. Commissions vary from firm to firm (and so does service). If your total risk per trade is only $334, for example, then a difference of $30 in commission rates can be significant. Multiply this figure by the number of trades, and you end up with a fairly large amount of money each year.

10  Short term cycles are more likely to change in response to current news than are long-term and intermediate term patterns. An especially bearish government report, for example, could delay the start of a bull cycle by several days, which could be enough to cause a loss despite the otherwise accurate reading of your cycle work.

The foregoing are only some of the factors required for successful short term trading. Many others will become clear to you as you go through the text and examine the manner in which short term patterns work. Some patterns are, of course, more reliable than others, and they also have a longer history. Other patterns have a history of larger individual moves, but they also require larger risk. But more important than in any other form of trading is discipline, in every respect. When the decision-making process is called on more frequently, the potential for emotional response is greater. I have painted what I believe to be a realistic picture of the problems associated with short term trading. To represent fairly the possible benefits of short term trading, a brief list of them follows for your consideration.

POSSIBLE ADVANTAGES OF SHORT-TERM TRADING USING CYCLES

1  Frequent trading will keep your money working for you at all times.
2  By capturing all, or most, swings within a trend, your overall profit could be much greater than by simply establishing a position and holding on.
3  Short term trading may allow you to capitalize on the many sharp up and down reactions so common in intermediate term patterns.
4  You take less overall risk per trade.
5  By trading more often you are more likely to get in on reliable moves.
6  Short term trading will allow you to use low margins and obtain maximum leverage.
7  Those who trade more often can get substantial commission discounts thereby lowering the overall cost of doing business.

**LOOKING AT SOME CYCLES**

With the preliminaries out of the way, let's examine a number of short term cyclic patterns. As part of each discussion, I include a price chart showing recent behavior of the cycle. If the cycle has had a long history, I also show what the pattern has been in the past. In some cases there are several cyclic patterns. Those patterns having a reliable history are also mentioned. Remember that the cycles I discuss may have changed by the time you read this book, which is natural for short term cycles. The longer patterns—for example, the 9.5 month tendency previously discussed, should remain stable. Bear in mind that a pattern of 9.5 months can be divided into many different segments. There are about 38 weeks and 190 trading days in a 9.5 month span. The 190 day period can be split into three segments of about 64 days, or five segments of 38 days, and so on. Within the 9.5 month cycle there can be many different variations on a short term cyclic basis. At times a cycle that has shown one pattern may cease to function in its previous manner, assuming instead one of the many variant patterns possible on a short term basis. This is something for which you must be prepared.

## SOME GENERAL INFORMATION ON SHORT-TERM CYCLES

In working with short term commodity cycles, you must take several important considerations into account. Besides the greater degree of error in cycle periods, the increased importance of timing, and the greater frequency of trading, the range of acceptable variation is also somewhat different from that used in intermediate term trading. It is quite common for short-term cycles to peak or bottom much later than you expect. Assume that a cycle averages 29 days, low to low, for example. For 10 repetitions it may run on the average of 14 days, low to high. On the eleventh repetition, however, it may move up for 28 days and down for 1 day, with the next 29 day period starting after just a 1 day downside reaction. How is this possible? There are a number of explanations, all plausible but not all easily understood. The most parsimonious explanation, and to my way of thinking the most useful as well, is the fact that short term cycles are influenced by all the cycles above them. Hence, a short term cycle of 29 days may be influenced by a seasonal pattern of 11 months, an inter-mediate-term cycle of 17 months, long term cycles of 2.7 years, 5.9 years, 54 years, and the so-called super cycle of 165 years. The 165 year pattern may also be influenced by even longer cycles. The longer a cycle gets, the less sensitive it becomes. It is as if we were observing a tightrope walker. The wider and stronger his wire (i.e., longer cycles), the less he is influenced by other forces such as wind, air currents, rain, and his own muscular movements. The thinner his wire (i.e., shorter cycles), the more apt he is to fail in his efforts because of other influences. A gust of wind, a sneeze, a small muscle spasm, or an air current may set him off balance. This is how I view the short term cycle. To make short term commodity cycles work, you must be more agile, more responsive to changes in the market, more willing to accept variation in length, and hence, more flexible. Just as the tightrope walker on an ultrathin wire must be more skilled, more in touch with every aspect of his environment, and ready to shift weight on a second's notice, so must the trader in short term commodities be sensitive to his cycles. This is why there are few traders who can successfully use short term patterns, as appealing as their profit potential may be. Many brilliant analysts of cycles have met defeat in attempting to use only short term patterns.

There is yet another feature of short term cycles that bears mention. In working with intermediate-term patterns we noticed several interesting things regarding the similarity of cycle lengths in different markets. Why, for example, should cotton, corn, and copper all show a long term cycle in the 5 to 6 year range? Why do most commodities show a 50 to 60 year pattern? And why do most markets show a 9 to 12 month pattern? I am not so concerned about the reason as I am about the fact itself. If we accept the commonality or synchronicity of long term cycles as a fact, we would also expect to see this same characteristic in short term cycles. This is, in fact, the very situation we will find in our studies of the patterns of short term commodities. Many reasons are offered that vary from the astrological to the scientific to the religious. Some researchers claim that lunar effects are important. These attempts at explanation are by no means new.

In the 1930s, Burton Pugh published his findings in a series of six booklets entitled *Science and Secrets of Wheat Trading* (1933). In essence, Pugh maintained that most upmoves in wheat begin at or about the time of a full moon and most downmoves begin at or about the time of a new moon. In essence, Pugh was dealing with the average 28 day cycle that tends to affect most commodity markets. Here, from Pugh's original work, are a few of his thoughts about the lunar cycle:

> *Not one trader in a hundred thinks of the moon in making his deals or even notices what phase is in force. It is the general optimism that is in him, or the pessimism, engendered by outside forces and often his inspiration comes from the old, almost submerged, ancient moon complex that harks back to his ancestral days.*

> *Thus the moon effects are mild. They are gently, almost imperceptibly persuasive. The phases gain their power by widespread effect since they touch men in all lands and thus mildly affect world markets. They are so mild that they lose their effect during times of sudden or great stress. A declaration of war between two great nations or a killing hot wave or withering dust storm over wheat countries will completely upset the harmony of the market with the phases FOR A TIME. [1933, Book 5, p. 10]*

Pugh then goes on to warn, as I have, that this cycle is not a foolproof or perfect method by which wheat prices may be analyzed. In fact, he indicates that it is merely a tool to be used with other techniques and observations:

> *Astonishingly soon the options will fall in line with the phases again or will show enough obedience to them to the extent that they can be used to great advantage. The author again warns the student that, fascinating as this moon effect is, it has serious variations and must be used observingly. In the pages which follow every important variation is shown and the reason given why. Then the student is shown the styles of market action in which the two phases deliver their maximum effect and how they may be used to the greatest advantage.*

> *The author of this course uses the phases unceasingly. At times they afford no help. At other times they form the only means by which an*

*important move can be forecasted. The moon is not an independent method of forecasting movements but is of high value in locating the turning points.* [1933, Book 5, p. 10]

Figures 8-1, 8-2, and 8-3 show several of the charts from Pugh's original work. These show the response of wheat and corn prices to lunar phases, along with some of Pugh's observations. Pugh introduces his charts with the following explanation:

*The chart which follows gives the student his first graphic view of the normal action of the action of the two phases when the public is not worried or confused and when thed market is taking its natural course . . . small swings working in perfect harmony with the phases. Farther on will be seen a graph in which every dark and light phase of the moon for eight months followed the phases perfectly, fifteen successive swings.* [1933, Book 5, p. 10]

One of the most important warnings advanced by Pugh reads:

BECAUSE MOON EFFECTS ARE MILD IT OFTEN HAPPENS THAT EXCITING OR POWERFUL NEWS WILL INFLUENCE THE MARKET MORE THAN THE PHASES AND WILL TURN PRICES DIRECTLY AGAINST THE PHASE ACTION.

*On March 7 the market fell into perfect line with the new moon phase and broke to the 56–57 level by the time the full moon came in. The coming of the full moon halted the break and after a few days' work-out—as often happens—the normal advance started.*

*On March 22 the full moon started the advance properly and by April 5 the price was up six cents. The incoming new moon stopped the advance and in four days (from April 5 to April 9) forced a break of over three and one-half cents. The new moon was delivering its usual depressing effect when the very bullish Government report of April 9 came out proclaiming a loss of 340,000,000 bushels of winter wheat under last year's crop. The rise to $66\frac{3}{4}$ followed and was against the new moon phase. This is an instance when disturbing outside news was stronger than the milder phase effects.* [1933, Book 5, p. 19; capital letters, his]

Lunar phase or not, the fact remains that studies of short term cycles are not new. Most short term cycles fall into one of several periods. Among these are 14 to 21 days, 26 to 36 days, and 44 to 58 days. Longer and shorter cycles can be found. Some markets do not readily show cycles in these three major groupings, but the majority of markets, as you will see, tend to fall into these three categories of cycle. Some, in fact, show all three patterns with high regularity. Now let's take a look at some short term cycles in various markets.

Wheat was mentioned in the preceding quotation, so it might be fruitful to examine some of the recent short term patterns in wheat. Figure 8-4 shows the March 1981 wheat delivery (all our work is with the Chicago Board of Trade contract). The cycle here averages about 27 days, low to low. As you can see by close examination, not all the highs and lows came at the expected peak or

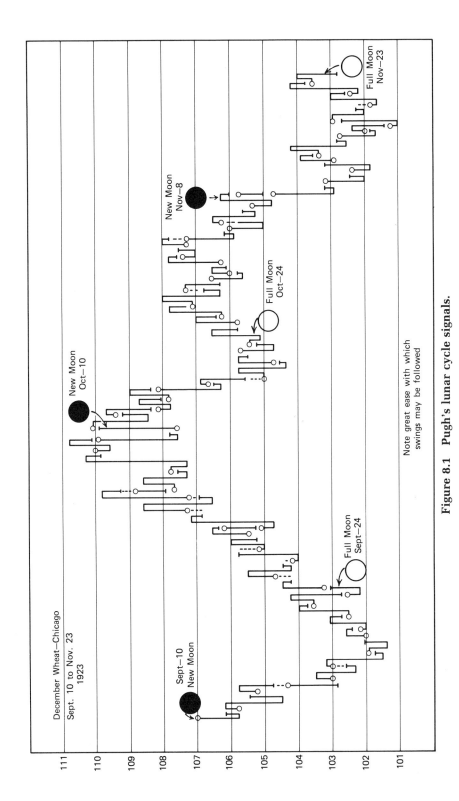

**Figure 8.1  Pugh's lunar cycle signals.**

144

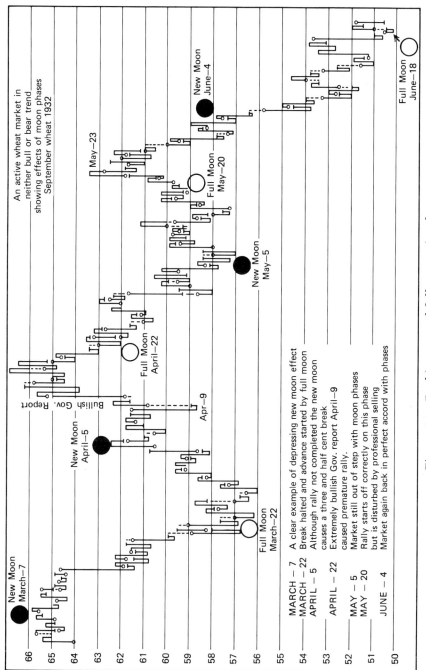

**Figure 8.2** Pugh's new and full moon signals.

145

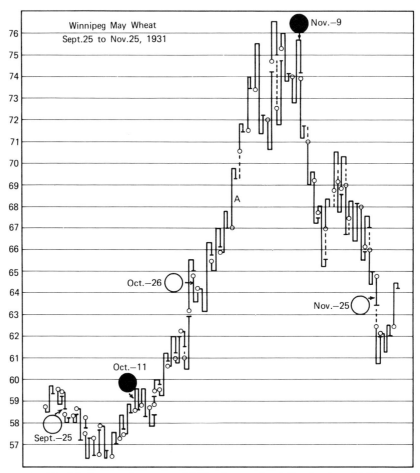

**Figure 8.3  Pugh's lunar phases and Winnipeg wheat September 25-November 25, 1931. (Pugh, 1933)**

trough, but the degree of regularity is truly impressive. Several things about this chart should be pointed out. Three bottoms (A, B, and C) are marked with arrows. Each denotes a confirmed low based on timing indicators (to be discussed in Chapter 12). Yet each one failed to produce a profit. The resulting downtrend was quite severe (two arrows), but you can see that it came during an expected cyclic downturn! Had we been trading wheat according to this short term pattern we would have either been short after failure to bottom (Arrow C) for the third time, or at least we would have been out of the market as a result of uncertain behavior of the cycle.

As a point of information, the new moon and the full moon dates since March 1980 are also marked on Figure 8-4. New moons are indicated by N and full moons by F. Although the lunar phases were not in perfect harmony with major tops and bottoms, there was indeed some degree of correlation with uptrends and downtrends. The severe December 1980 price break began during the new

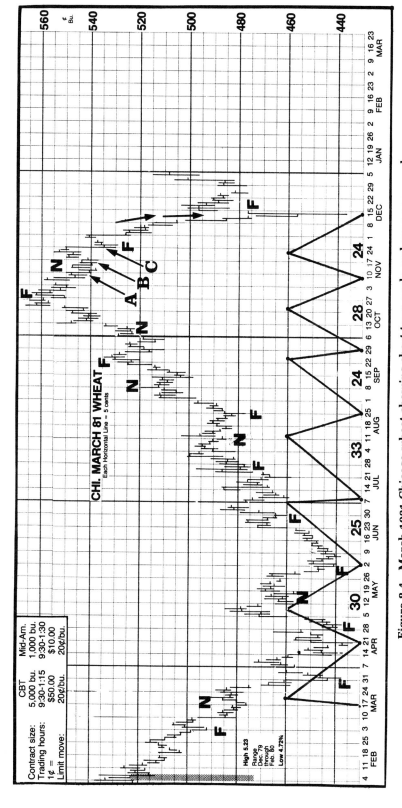

Figure 8.4  March 1981 Chicago wheat showing short term cycle and new moon and full moon dates.

147

moon phase and bottomed several days prior to a full moon phase. The full moon phase gave rise to a move from about 4.80 to 5.10. There are a number of instances in which the relationship went completely astray. It also appears that the buy indications of full moon were much stronger than the sell indications of the new moon. This is true because we were in intermediate term and seasonal uptrends during this time span. The fact that new moon and full moon dates were not as accurate as the 27 day cycle itself is another lesson in flexibility and its value in the analysis of cycles. When working with cycles,

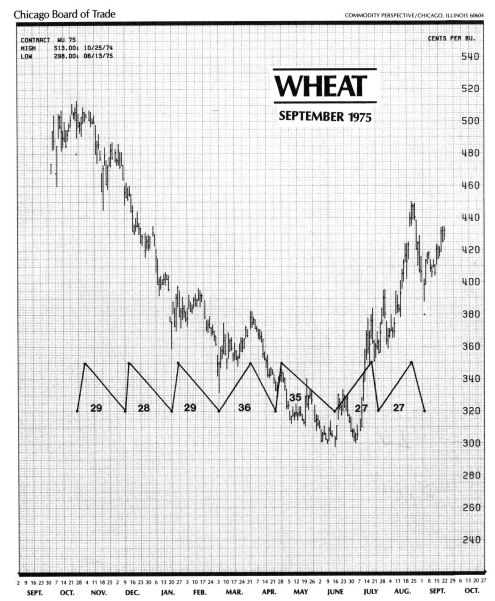

**Figure 8.5  September 1975 Chicago wheat cycles.**

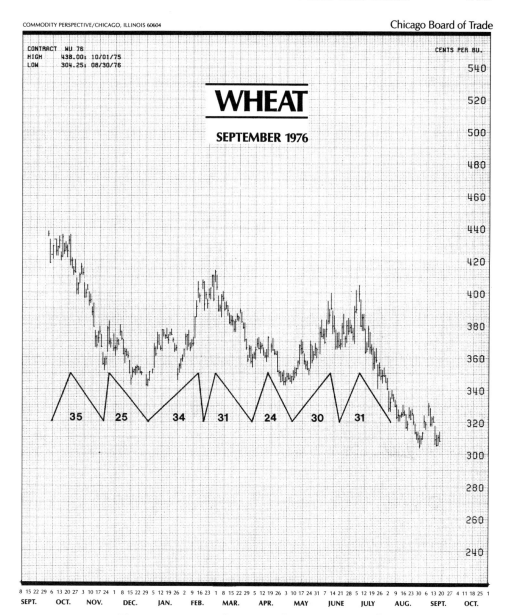

**Figure 8.6 September 1976 Chicago wheat cycles.**

you must be willing to follow the market and its cycles rather than adhere to a preconceived notion of what the market should do. Any trader who does the latter is doomed to failure.

Looking back several years, we can trace the approximately 27 day cycle to September 1975 and September 1976 wheat contracts (Figures 8-5 and 8-6 respectively). You'll see that the basic pattern was prevalent in both markets as it has been for many, many years. It is important to remember that short term cycles do not necessarily account for all the highs and lows in any market. The forces of other cycles come into play and will either stretch or contract short term cycles, which will make some tops come much later than expected and some bottoms much earlier than anticipated. In Chapter 2 I pointed out the difference between regularity and symmetry. *Symmetry* is reserved for geometry and mechanical drawing. It is not something for which we strive in cycle analysis. *Regularity*, on the other hand, involves patterns of a generally repetitive nature. Symmetry is reserved for geometric forms. Regularity, or repetitiveness within a given time frame, is what we look for in cycle analysis. The ultimate goal of all cycle analysis may be to isolate symmetrical patterns, but we are far from attaining this ideal.

## SOYBEANS

The soybean market tends to exhibit an approximately 27 day cycle, as well as one that runs about 54 days and one of a much shorter period of about 16 days, all low to low. Figure 8-7 shows the March 1981 delivery of Chicago soybeans and the approximate cycles of 20 to 32 days. In addition, the approximately 54 day pattern is marked. Arrows show the 11 to 19 day lows. Notice that arrow *A* was a late low in the 11 to 19 day cycle. Hence, we must assume that this was the important low of another cycle, probably the 9–11 month cycle discussed in Chapter 7. Cycles *bcd*, *def*, *fgh*, *hij*, and *jkl* are all repetitions of the 54 day pattern (approximately). Within this cycle fall the one-half, or 27 day patterns. The top *k* should be followed by a low in the projected time frame marked *l* if the cycle is indeed valid. This low will probably not fall below the 9 month cycle low marked *a*. Of course, time alone will validate or negate the cycle.

## OTHER GRAINS

Other grains display similar cycles. Corn and oats, for example, tend to move with soybeans and wheat, respectively. Corn cycles are frequently more regular and reliable, and they may be considered by those traders wishing to take less risk than soybean trading requires.

## GOLD

The gold market also provides many opportunities for short term cyclic trading. Figure 8-8 shows the approximately 28 day pattern in April 1981 gold (COMEX). Earlier I pointed out the fact that short term cycles may vary considerably in timing from low to low, high to high, low to high, and high back to low. In the case of cycle *CDE*, for example, there is an extended top *(D)* and a 1 day downleg to bottom *E*. Cycles *KLM* and *QRS* show similarly late tops. This is very common in short term cycles and should not be cause for concern. Remember that we are not looking for perfection; we are merely looking for a general guide as to time of probable up and/or down turns. Tops marked *1*, *2*, *3*, *4*, and *5* all seem to be part of an important cycle between peaks that runs about 12 weeks in length. This might also provide clues for the short term trader and should be investigated more thoroughly by those so concerned. Silver and platinum cycles are similar to those of gold.

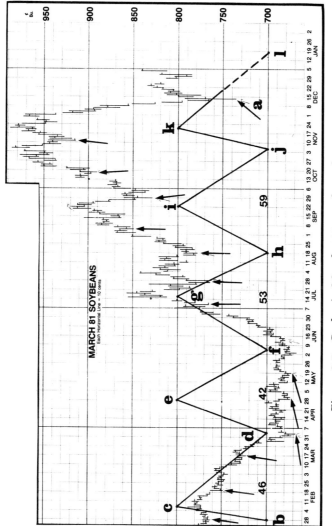

Figure 8.7   Cycles in March 1981 soybean futures.

151

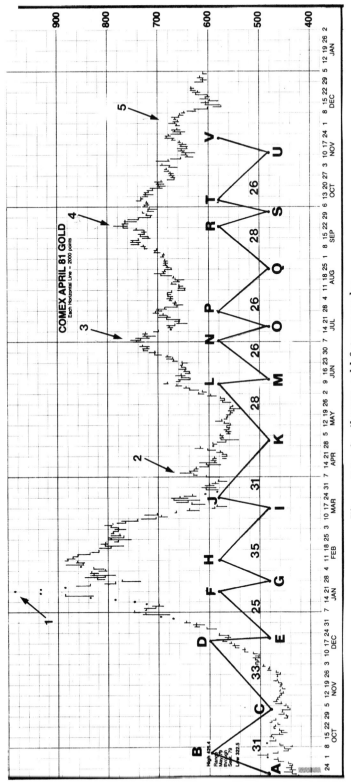

Figure 8.8   April 1981 gold futures cycles.

152

## COPPER

The copper market has several short term cycles worthy of mention. Figure 8-9 shows the March 1981 delivery of copper. This chart depicts two important cycles. The approximately 10 to 12 week, low-to-low cycle has dominated prices for many years. It is possible to examine a copper chart several years old and still find the same cycle. Figure 8-10, for example, shows the December 1978 delivery of copper and the approximately 10 to 12 week cycle. Notice that 10 to 12 weeks translates into about 50 to 60 trading days. Taking a fraction of the 50 to 60 day cycle, we get either two patterns of 28 days (approximately) or four patterns of about 15 days. This explains two other cycles found in copper. The preferred cycle for short term trading runs between 14 and 21 days, low to low, and is also shown in Figure 8-9.

These patterns could be projected into the future and other key dates for tops and bottoms of the 10 to 12 week cycle appropriately determined. The 10 to 12 week cycle accounts for most of the important tops and bottoms during any given contract year, and the 14 to 21 day cycles determine activity within the 10 to 12 week patterns.

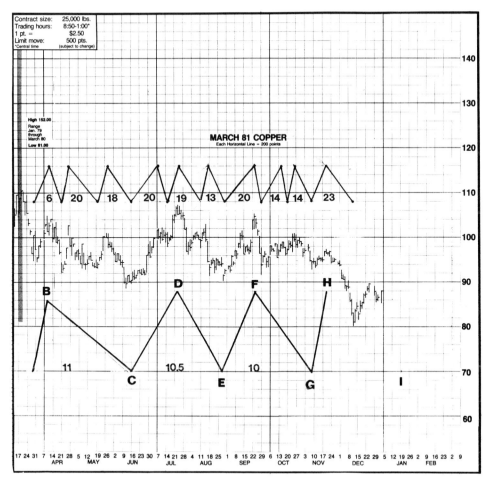

**Figure 8.9   Cycles in March 1981 copper futures.**

**DECEMBER 1978**

Commodity Exchange, Inc. N.Y.

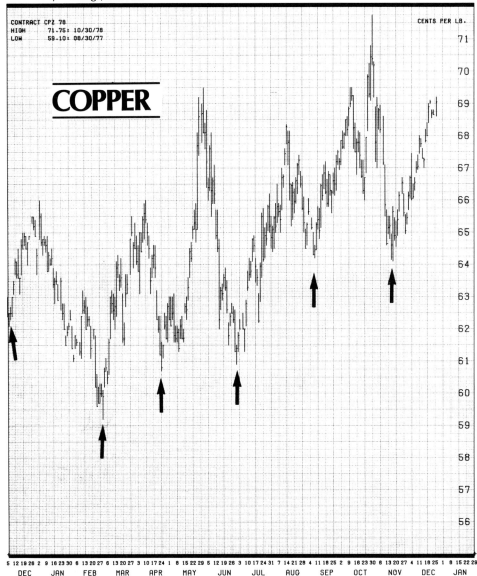

**Figure 8.10  Cycle lows (arrows) in December 1978 copper futures.**

## T-BILLS

Interest rate futures have shown remarkable adherence to periodicity since their introduction to the futures market. There have been several intermediate and short term patterns of high reliability. Some of these were discussed in the previous chapter. The short term cycles will now be analyzed. Figure 8-11 shows the approximately 32 day pattern in T bill futures within a cycle of longer duration. Cycles *BDC* and *DEF* show the longer cycle, which runs about

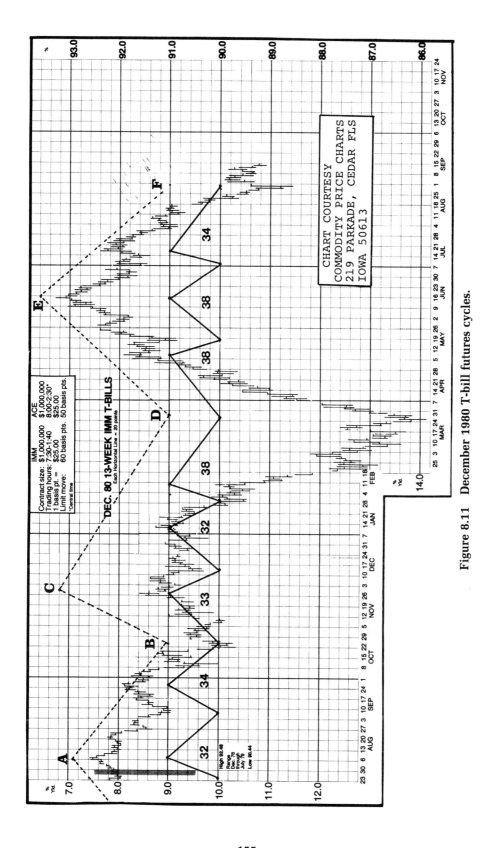

Figure 8.11   December 1980 T-bill futures cycles.

155

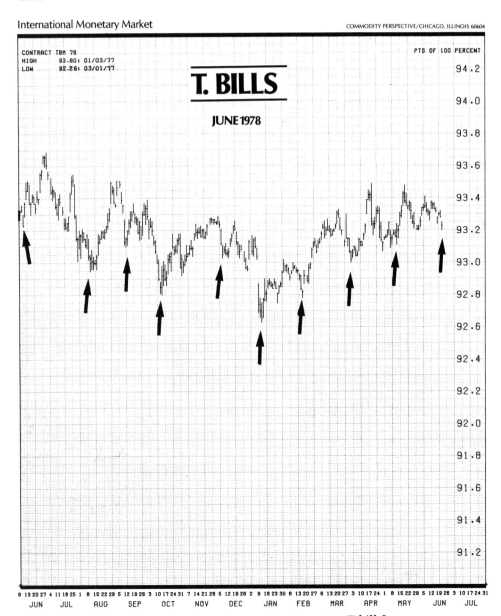

International Monetary Market                    COMMODITY PERSPECTIVE/CHICAGO, ILLINOIS 60604

**Figure 8.12   Cycle lows (arrows) in June 1978 T-bill futures.**

20 to 25 weeks, low-to-low. This longer cycle accounts for major peaks and bottoms within a given contract year, whereas the shorter cycle accounts for peaks and troughs within the 20 to 25 week period. You will see the high degree of reliability in short term T-bill patterns, as well as a large fluctuation in price within tops and bottoms. This is why the T-bill (T-bond and GNMA, as well) market is a favorite of traders in short term cycles. The cycle tops and bottoms are very pronounced and usually quite reliable. This contract (Figure 8-11) has shown no more than 6 trading days in variation between the longest

and shortest cycle. Things won't always work this well, so don't take this as a final statement about the short term T-bill cycle. A previous contract year (Figure 8-12, June 1978) is included to show you how the length has varied in past years.

## LIVE CATTLE

The live cattle market was discussed in considerable detail earlier. In addition, the short term cycle in feeder cattle was mentioned as being one of the most reliable patterns in recent years. Cycle lengths in cattle have varied through the years, but the persistence of an approximately 5 to 6 week (25 to 35 day) pattern is more than just a chance happening. Figure 8-13 shows the February 1981 delivery of live cattle futures. In addition, the lows and highs of the approximately 30 week cattle cycle (previously analyzed) are marked to show you how the picture fits together. Most of the short term peaks and troughs within the 30 week cycle are explained by the 25 to 35 day pattern. There is considerable stability between tops as well. Some cycle analysts also use the half cycle, which runs from 12 to 18 days. For most of us, the half cycle may be too variable and subject to error. I have, however, marked lows (arrows) of this extremely short term cycle accordingly for your information. Keep in mind the caveats I have given regarding the use of such extremely short term cycles.

Recently there has been a considerable amount of variation in short term live cattle cycles. Lengths of up to 45 days have not been uncommon. How would one go about dealing with such a situation? First, and foremost, it is important to recognize the fact that cycles will vary in length. Some periods will show much more stability than others. Over time, however, there should be a relatively consistent pattern of lengths from low to low and/or high to high. It is always a good idea to update cycle lengths periodically by working back through the last ten repetitions, or so, taking an arithmetic average, and determining whether there has been any significant change. If there has been a major lengthening or shortening of the cycle then you would do well to work with the new average. This is of particular importance when using short term cycles since they are most apt to show variations within any given year.

## COCOA

Cocoa prices have also shown an approximate cycle of 25 days, low to low. Figure 8-14 shows how this cycle acted in March 1981 cocoa futures. It ran from a low of 20 days in length to a high of 29 days in length. Also shown is an approximately 11 to 14 week cycle in cocoa futures, which has considerable potential. The market was still in an extended long term bear move, so tops of both the 25 day and 12 week cycle were made early. Most of the time was spent in downmoves.

Cocoa is a good example of what can happen to cycles when a long term cyclic low is approaching. This is particularly relevant to the events of 1981. During the March through July time-frame there were significant deviations from short term cyclic patterns. Peaks came very early and bottoms came rather late. This was due to the influence of a long term (approximately 8 year) cycle

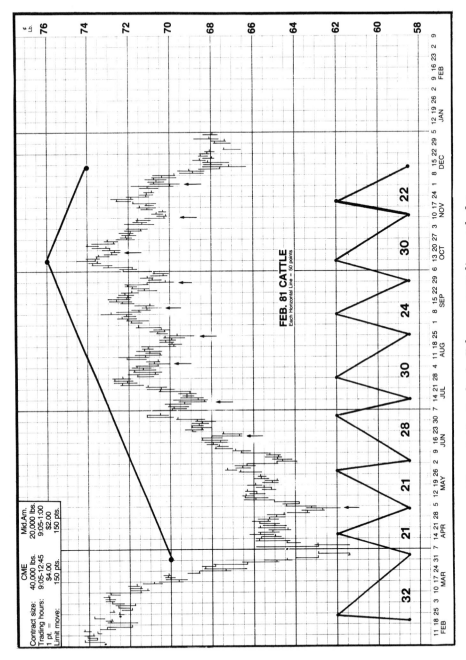

Figure 8.13   Cycles in February 1981 live cattle futures.

158

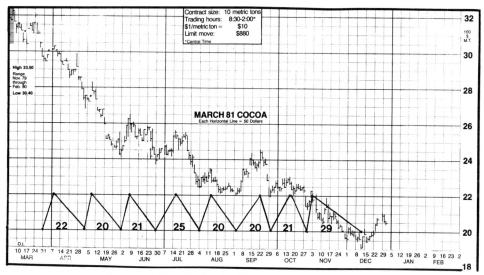

**Figure 8.14   Cycles in March 1981 cocoa futures.**

coming to a low in the same time-frame. The considerably bearish forces of this pattern were more than enough to distort and even mask entirely the short term cyclic tendencies. This type of distortion is not uncommon during important long term cycle change periods.

## PORK BELLIES

The belly market has shown many different short term cycles in recent years. Because it is an old-time speculative favorite of many traders, I have given considerable attention to its short term patterns. Those who have traded this market are quite familiar with the wide price swings, both daily and weekly. And those who have analyzed the cyclic patterns are also familiar with the relatively high reliability of timing signals. Let's start with a recent contract. Figure 8-15 shows two distinct cycles in bellies. Bear in mind that they function within the 40 to 50 week cycles, as well as the seasonal cycles. At the top of Figure 8-15 I have traced in a dashed line the 19 to 27 day cycle that constitutes about half of the 39 to 48 day cycle (at bottom of chart). Nine repetitions of the half cycle are shown. In bellies, reversal signals are especially valid. Several of these are marked with arrows for your examination. Large arrows show 39 to 48 day cyclic reversals and smaller arrows show 19 to 27 reversals. You'll note that there are many other reversals during the course of each cycle, but not all are reliable indicators of trend change. A reversal during an expected cyclic high or low period, on the other hand, is usually more reliable for confirming an actual trend change.

The heavy dashed line at far right bottom of Figure 8-15 shows the projected 39 to 48 day trend and the approximate time of the next low. Later we learn how to zero in on trend change signals during this time period, or time window, in order to maximize the reliability of timing. By combining timing and cycles,

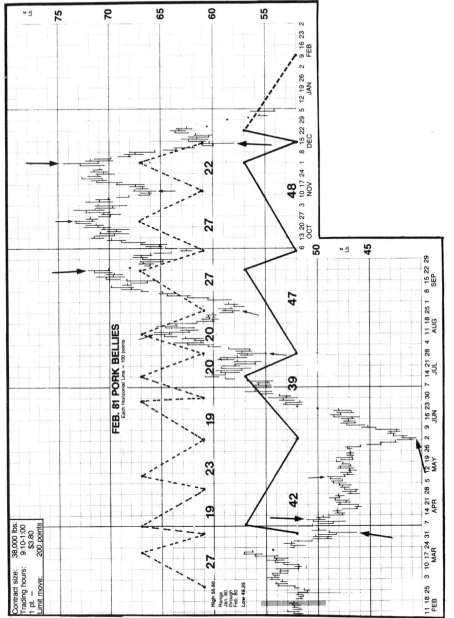

Figure 8.15   Cycles in February 1981 pork belly futures.

we ought to arrive at a much more useful combination of technical methods. This is discussed in complete detail later on. For now, however, I suggest that you spend some time observing the cycles and reversals. There are several other signals of trend change that can also confirm a cycle turn. Each of the signals helps to make the underlying cycle more valid for trading purposes.

Now let's examine several previous contract months in the belly market. Figure 8-16 shows the approximate 45 day cycle in May 1975 bellies, which varied in length from 38 to 52 days, low to low. Notice the large number of

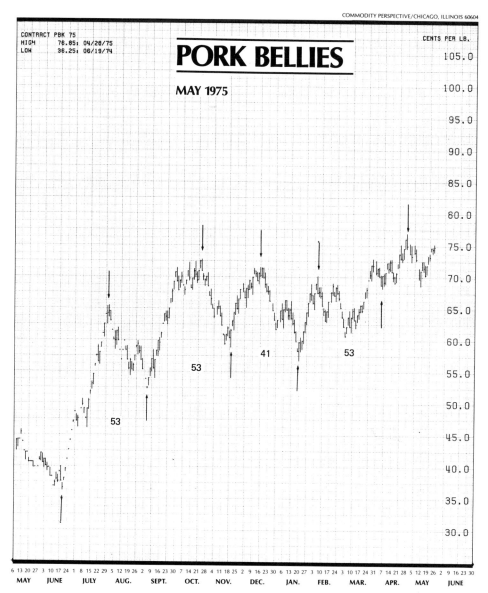

**Figure 8.16   Short term cycle in May 1975 pork belly futures.**

daily upside reversal signals at cyclic lows and daily downside reversals at cyclic highs. I have purposely left them unmarked so that you may gain some practice in spotting these timing indicators. You should also spend some time plotting out the half cycles to gain some valuable experience in finding repetitive price patterns. You can also study Figure 8-17, the August 1978 belly contract, and Figure 8-18, the July 1977 bellies. Although short-term cycles have varied somewhat in recent years, the fact remains that they are still valid in the overall process of projecting and timing market turns. Of all the markets,

**Figure 8.17    Short term cycle in August 1978 pork belly futures.**

Figure 8.18   Short term cycle in July 1977 pork belly futures.

that in pork bellies has shown the greatest stability of cyclic trends through the years. This is why I recommend you spend a good deal of time studying this market and its cycles.

## COTTON

Cotton has long been an attractive speculative market because of the large dollar value of a one-tick move. Trends in cotton are normally quite persistent. If one misses a market turn, it is difficult to jump in late in the game. We have already examined the long term and intermediate term cycles and their reliability. When these are combined with timing signals and short term cycles, the result is quite impressive. Although short term cycles have indeed shown some changes through the years, the most prominent short term tendency in cotton is an approximately 33 to 43 day pattern. On occasion this cycle has run as short as 28 days, but it is still highly reliable when combined with indicators of trend change. Figure 8-19 shows the March 1981 cotton delivery and four repetitions of the 33 to 43 day cycle. This pattern can, of course, be broken into a half (or 17 to 22) day cycle. Some of the lows of this half pattern are marked with arrows in Figure 8-19. With the exception of only one low (marked A), which came too early, the 17 to 22 day cycle was quite stable in March 1981 cotton. May 1975 cotton (Figure 8-20) is also included for your examination, and the 33 to 45 day cycle lows and highs are marked accordingly. Again, with few exceptions, these lows have been quite accurate.

How about market tops? You've probably noticed by now that most of my cycle work is centered on picking lows. This does not mean that I am always bullish. Nor does it mean that I must always be buying. Markets move up and markets move down in an inhale and exhale fashion common to all living entities. It is the nature of cyclic peaks, however, to be less predictable and regular than cyclic lows. It is for this reason that I spend most of my time and effort finding cycle lows. When cycle peaks exhibit a reliable pattern, they can also be used for trading purposes. More information on this aspect of cycles is presented in Chapter 12. In doing your own work, however, you ought to examine all the possible cycles, low to low and high to high.

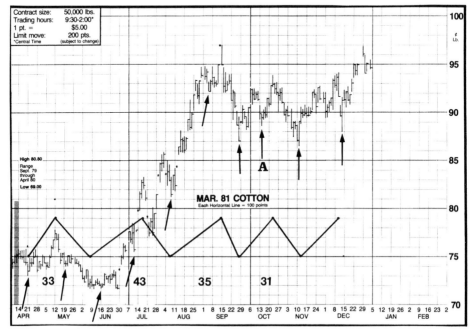

**Figure 8.19   Cycles in March 1981 cotton futures.**

New York Cotton Exchange                COMMODITY PERSPECTIVE/CHICAGO, ILLINOIS 60604

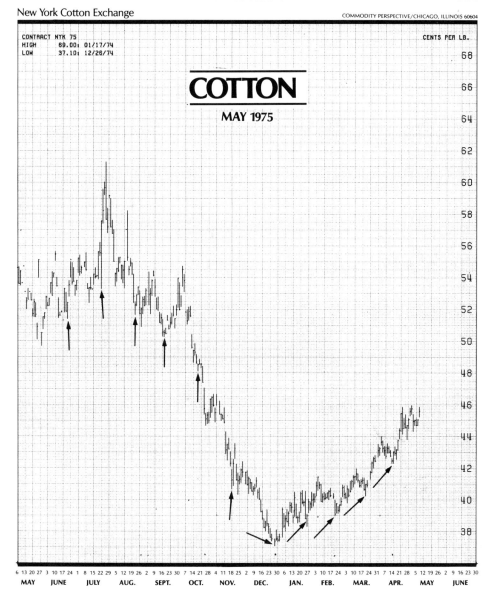

Figure 8.20   Short term May 1975 cotton cycles.

## SWISS FRANC

The currency markets also show short term cyclic behavior. In fact, some analysts believe that currencies are the most reliable markets when they are researched on a technical basis. Figure 8-21 shows a 20 to 27 day short term cycle in September 1980 Swiss franc. You'll note that there is a fairly high degree of reliability between cycle highs. Other currencies are also cyclic and show numerous short term patterns. Because these markets are closely interrelated on a fundamental basis, similar (i.e., synchronous) cycles can be found

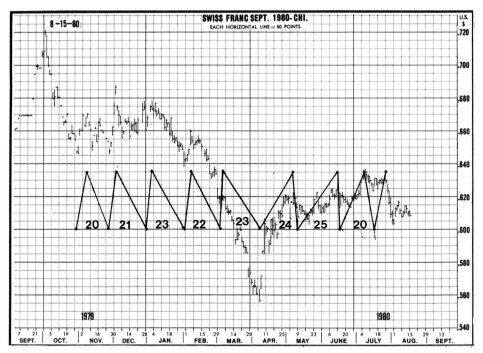

Figure 8.21   Cycles in September 1980 Swiss franc futures.

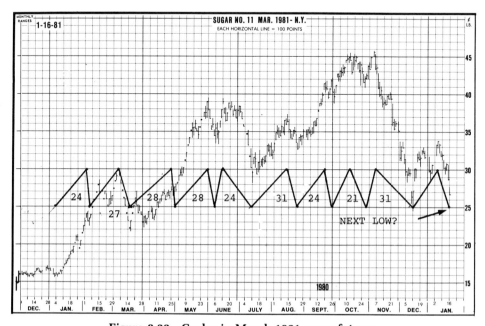

Figure 8.22   Cycles in March 1981 sugar futures.

166

in each. There is also a fundamental relationship between interest rates and currency rates. Hence, one would expect to find some synchronicity in these markets as well. Be forewarned, however, that there is considerable variability in the cycle due to the relative youth of futures trading in the Swiss franc.

## SUGAR

Sugar prices have gone through alternate periods of extreme tranquility and severe fluctuation. Virtually all the 6 year (approximate) turns have brought with them major intermediate and short term swings in price. This has placed sugar on the list of highly speculative markets. The current contract trades in $11.20 per tick increments, making daily price moves particularly substantial in terms of dollar value. Despite the large moves, sugar prices have shown a remarkably stable short term cycle in recent years. The pattern varies from about 23 days to 32 days in length, with most cycles falling in 24 to 28 days. Figure 8-22 shows this pattern in March 1981 sugar. Reversal signals are not as common in sugar as they are, for example, in the pork belly and soybean markets. However, other indicators of trend change are frequent in sugar. Among these are the LHC (low high close) and HLC (high low close) indicators, which are discussed later in Chapter 14. Figure 8-23 shows the short term cycle for May 1978 sugar. You will note that the shortest cycle ran 21 days, and the longest, 31 days. This is a total variance of 10 days from the shortest to the longest cycle. Although not all contracts will show such reliability, the overall pattern should prove rather useful in trading sugar futures on a short term basis.

# CHAPTER NINE

# Some Methods
# Of Finding Cycles

The earlier chapter on time windows was designed to help whet your appetite and motivate you for the task that you will encounter in this chapter. A prerequisite to determining the time window is the isolation of various cycles that permit such a formulation. Many different methods can be used in this effort, and some of the techniques are discussed in general here. Appendix 3 provides help for anyone interested in more complex mathematical approaches, although, as I have said earlier, I do not believe such high level methods are necessary. My experience has led me to the most parsimonious solutions in trading commodities. With each attempt to impose a more complex operation on my methodology, I find that profits tend to decline, or overall effort and profits reach the point of diminishing returns.

There are several approaches to the isolation of commodity cycles within a series of data. A trader who is not interested in doing this part of the work can refer to research done by others or to a service that pinpoints cycles in commodity data. This may not be the best way to go about the task because it removes you one step (and a very important step) from familiarity with the data. A second shortcoming in this "lazy man's method" is that there are very few services or publications that actually list the relevant cycles regularly. I publish one such weekly market letter, and I know of only two other publications that give cyclic time periods. Another problem with this approach is that some subtle but important differences in definitions of cyclic highs and lows are found among different experts. The theory of cycle analysis is not yet developed to the point of complete agreement on underlying principles. This is why I urge you to do your own work according to the guidelines I am providing, with any modifications you may find profitable. And one more thing before we plunge into finding cycles: the bottom line of any system, timing tool, method, or technique, is whether it generates profits. This is the one and only way of ultimately evaluating any approach. If you decide to make modifications on what I present here, then make certain they are profitable changes rather than losing alterations.

## COUNTING AND MEASURING

Examine the series of prices shown in Figure 9-1A. A simple scan of prices shows that there is considerable variability over time. Highs and lows are

```
LIVE CATTLE          7806LC
  DATE      OPEN        HIGH        LOW        CLOSE
 70177     42.52       42.52       42.17       42.17
 70577     42.50       42.60       41.65       41.70
 71177     41.65       41.85       41.20       41.25
 71877     41.20       41.97       40.82       41.75
 72577     41.85       41.95       40.20       40.40
 80177     40.35       40.35       39.10       39.40
 80877     39.30       39.47       38.70       38.72
 81577     37.75       38.55       37.40       38.42
 82277     38.67       39.17       37.85       39.10
 82977     39.00       39.10       38.55       38.90
 90677     38.87       39.30       38.72       38.95
 91277     38.90       39.15       38.67       38.95
 91977     38.95       39.57       38.95       39.37
 92677     39.47       39.65       39.02       39.55
100377     39.50       40.00       39.40       39.62
101077     39.50       39.80       39.05       39.17
101777     39.07       39.85       38.82       39.82
102477     40.00       40.20       39.62       39.65
103177     39.60       40.20       39.42       39.67
110777     39.55       40.55       39.40       40.47
111477     40.40       41.67       40.00       41.50
112177     41.70       41.85       41.15       41.72
112877     41.70       41.72       41.10       41.47
120577     41.60       42.15       41.52       42.07
121277     41.97       42.37       41.60       42.07
121977     42.15       43.27       42.00       43.22
122777     43.05       43.30       42.55       43.02
 10378     43.10       43.72       42.50       42.90
 10978     43.10       43.15       42.20       42.30
 11678     42.35       43.05       42.25       42.70
 12378     42.60       43.97       42.55       43.95
 13078     44.00       45.57       43.60       44.97
 20678     45.25       47.10       44.65       46.62
 21378     46.90       46.90       45.60       45.85
 22178     45.60       47.62       45.20       45.87
 22778     45.50       46.95       45.30       46.90
 30678     47.17       49.72       47.17       49.35
 31378     49.95       51.32       49.05       50.05
 32078     50.30       52.70       50.05       52.02
 32778     52.55       53.10       49.00       50.47
 40378     50.40       53.05       49.10       52.60
 41078     53.35       53.45       50.82       52.02
 41778     52.05       53.47       51.35       53.37
 42478     53.15       53.75       51.75       53.67
 50178     53.80       55.60       53.45       55.55
 50878     55.90       56.92       54.97       56.87
 51578     57.70       60.25       57.40       60.20
 52278     59.70       62.25       59.50       61.95
 53078     62.20       62.35       57.97       57.97
 60578     57.20       59.40       57.05       58.42
 61278     58.82       58.87       54.15       55.67
```

**Figure 9.1a    Counting cycles.**

169

```
LIVE CATTLE            7806LC
   DATE       OPEN       HIGH       LOW       CLOSE
  70177      42.52      42.52      42.17      42.17
  70577      42.50      42.60      41.65      41.70
  71177      41.65      41.85      41.20      41.25
  71877      41.20      41.97      40.82      41.75
  72577      41.85      41.95      40.20      40.40
  80177      40.35      40.35      39.10      39.40
  80877      39.30      39.47      38.70      38.72
  81577      37.75      38.55      37.40    L 38.42
  82277      38.67      39.17      37.85      39.10
  82977      39.00      39.10      38.55      38.90
  90677      38.87      39.30      38.72      38.95
  91277      38.90      39.15      38.67      38.95
  91977      38.95      39.57      38.95      39.37
  92677      39.47      39.65      39.02      39.55
 100377      39.50      40.00      39.40      39.62
 101077      39.50      39.80      39.05      39.17
 101777      39.07      39.85      38.82      39.82
 102477      40.00      40.20      39.62      39.65
 103177      39.60      40.20      39.42      39.67
 110777      39.55      40.55      39.40      40.47
 111477      40.40      41.67      40.00      41.50
 112177      41.70      41.85      41.15      41.72
 112877      41.70      41.72      41.10      41.47
 120577      41.60      42.15      41.52      42.07
 121277      41.97      42.37      41.60      42.07
 121977      42.15      43.27      42.00    H 43.22
 122777      43.05      43.30      42.55      43.02
  10378      43.10      43.72      42.50      42.90
  10978      43.10      43.15      42.20      42.30
  11678      42.35      43.05      42.25      42.70
  12378      42.60      43.97      42.55    H 43.95
  13078      44.00      45.57      43.60    H 44.97
  20678      45.25      47.10      44.65    H 46.62
  21378      46.90      46.90      45.60    H 45.85
  22178      45.60      47.62      45.20    H 45.87
  22778      45.50      46.95      45.30    H 46.90
  30678      47.17      49.72      47.17    H 49.35
  31378      49.95      51.32      49.05    H 50.05
  32078      50.30      52.70      50.05    H 52.02
  32778      52.55      53.10      49.00      50.47
  40378      50.40      53.05      49.10      52.60
  41078      53.35      53.45      50.82      52.02
  41778      52.05      53.47      51.35    H 53.37
  42478      53.15      53.75      51.75      53.67
  50178      53.80      55.60      53.45    H 55.55
  50878      55.90      56.92      54.97    H 56.87
  51578      57.70      60.25      57.40    H 60.20
  52278      59.70      62.25      59.50    H 61.95
  53078      62.20      62.35      57.97      57.97
  60578      57.20      59.40      57.05      58.42
  61278      58.82      58.87      54.15      55.67
```

Figure 9.1b  Marking highs and lows of probable cycles.

```
LIVE CATTLE              7806LC
  DATE       OPEN       HIGH       LOW       CLOSE
  70177      42.52      42.52      42.17      42.17
  70577      42.50      42.60      41.65      41.70
  71177      41.65      41.85      41.20      41.25
  71877      41.20      41.97      40.82      41.75
  72577      41.85      41.95      40.20      40.40
  80177      40.35      40.35      39.10      39.40
  80877      39.30      39.47      38.70      38.72
  81577      37.75      38.55      37.40    L 38.42
  82277      38.67      39.17      37.85      39.10
  82977      39.00      39.10      38.55      38.90
  90677      38.87      39.30      38.72      38.95
  91277      38.90      39.15      38.67      38.95
  91977      38.95      39.57      38.95      39.37
  92677      39.47      39.65      39.02      39.55
 100377      39.50      40.00      39.40      39.62
 101077      39.50      39.80      39.05      39.17
 101777      39.07      39.85      38.82      39.82
 102477      40.00      40.20      39.62      39.65
 103177      39.60      40.20      39.42      39.67
 110777      39.55      40.55      39.40      40.47
 111477      40.40      41.67      40.00      41.50
 112177      41.70      41.85      41.15      41.72
 112877      41.70      41.72      41.10      41.47
 120577      41.60      42.15      41.52      42.07
 121277      41.97      42.37      41.60      42.07
 121977      42.15      43.27      42.00    H 43.22
 122777      43.05      43.30      42.55      43.02
  10378      43.10      43.72      42.50      42.90
  10978      43.10      43.15      42.20    L 42.30
  11678      42.35      43.05      42.25      42.70
  12378      42.60      43.97      42.55      43.95
  13078      44.00      45.57      43.60      44.97
  20678      45.25      47.10      44.65    H 46.62
  21378      46.90      46.90      45.60      45.85
  22178      45.60      47.62      45.20    L 45.87
  22778      45.50      46.95      45.30      46.90
  30678      47.17      49.72      47.17      49.35
  31378      49.95      51.32      49.05      50.05
  32078      50.30      52.70      50.05      52.02
  32778      52.55      53.10      49.00      50.47
  40378      50.40      53.05      49.10      52.60
  41078      53.35      53.45      50.82      52.02
  41778      52.05·     53.47      51.35      53.37
  42478      53.15      53.75      51.75      53.67
  50178      53.80      55.60      53.45      55.55
  50878      55.90      56.92      54.97      56.87
  51578      57.70      60.25      57.40      60.20
  52278      59.70      62.25      59.50    H 61.95
  53078      62.20      62.35      57.97      57.97
  60578      57.20      59.40      57.05      58.42
  61278      58.82      58.87      54.15    L 55.67
```

Figure 9.1c   Additional work with the raw data.

apparent on closer study. Here's how to scan the raw data for evidence of a cycle. First, begin with the oldest date and read the prices moving toward the present time. Each time you see a new high or low (after looking at about 10 time units worth of prices), mark an *H* for new highs in the series and an *L* for new lows. The table would not look like Figure 9-1b. You can see that a natural rhythm has appeared in the data. Some of the highs and lows appear to be about the same distance apart in time units. These are the cycles we are looking for, and there are other cycles within the cycles. These too can be isolated. Figure 9-1c shows how this can be done. Let's take a look at one more price series to see if we can isolate another cycle by simply looking at it. Figure 9-2 shows the method I use as described. You will frequently encounter data that, at first examination, does not seem to have any apparent cycles, in which case the cycle is probably longer than the history you are using. Additional data must then be gathered or obtained. For practice I advise you to examine the raw data provided in Figure 9-1a, finding the cycles visually. Remember, you are looking for time spans of similar length within a plus or minus range of 15 percent. The initial visual inspection of data is not critical in terms of accuracy. All you want to observe is the general tendency of prices, which will alert you to some cycles. Notice that the prices I work with are closing prices. I use *only closing prices* for reasons discussed earlier. If you wish, you can use a daily, weekly, monthly, or yearly average price, low price, or high price. I have found the closing and/or average price best for my purposes. We will, however, use the high and low prices for other purposes later on.

Once you have isolated one or more cycles of reasonably similar duration, list them on a record sheet that you keep specifically for this purpose. Each market you follow should have its own record sheet. A ledger book or loose-leaf notebook is good for this purpose. List the cycles in the following order: long term, intermediate term, short term. For listing purposes I consider a long term cycle to be one greater than a year in length, an intermediate term cycle as one greater than 3 months in length but less than a year, and a short term cycle as one 3 months or shorter.

When you determine the length for each market, you may find several cycles of different duration in each of these three categories. Corn, for example, might have a 5.7 year cycle, a 3.3 year cycle, a 54 day cycle, and a 12 day cycle. Hence, allot sufficient room on your record sheet for recording several possible cycles. Figure 9-3 is a sample listing that, for organizing your data, is a good model to follow. Remember, in cycle analysis I always move from a long term to a short term orientation. The first step is to arrive at a "big picture" decision, and the next steps follow in time order. You must view every market from the "big picture" perspective to obtain the proper time orientation for your later work.

Another way to find a cycle is to plot the price data on a chart and measure the time lengths between lows or between highs. Experience has taught me that the time between lows tends to be more reliable as a measure of cycles than the time between highs. When I refer to the time span of a cycle, I am always talking about low to low (as I have pointed out earlier). Remember, also, that I count only those days for which there are price data—in other words, days on which the market in question was open. Some cycle analysts count calendar

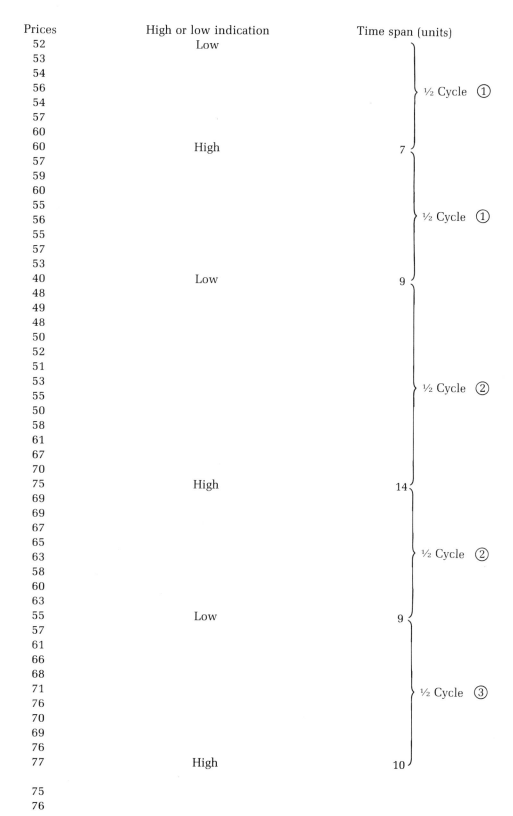

| Prices | High or low indication | Time span (units) |
|---|---|---|
| 52 | Low | |
| 53 | | |
| 54 | | |
| 56 | | ½ Cycle ① |
| 54 | | |
| 57 | | |
| 60 | | |
| 60 | High | 7 |
| 57 | | |
| 59 | | |
| 60 | | |
| 55 | | |
| 56 | | ½ Cycle ① |
| 55 | | |
| 57 | | |
| 53 | | |
| 40 | Low | 9 |
| 48 | | |
| 49 | | |
| 48 | | |
| 50 | | |
| 52 | | |
| 51 | | |
| 53 | | ½ Cycle ② |
| 55 | | |
| 50 | | |
| 58 | | |
| 61 | | |
| 67 | | |
| 70 | | |
| 75 | High | 14 |
| 69 | | |
| 69 | | |
| 67 | | |
| 65 | | |
| 63 | | ½ Cycle ② |
| 58 | | |
| 60 | | |
| 63 | | |
| 55 | Low | 9 |
| 57 | | |
| 61 | | |
| 66 | | |
| 68 | | |
| 71 | | ½ Cycle ③ |
| 76 | | |
| 70 | | |
| 69 | | |
| 76 | | |
| 77 | High | 10 |
| 75 | | |
| 76 | | |

**Figure 9.2   Sample Price Series and a cycle analysis.**

Market  ————————

### Long Term Cycle(s)

| Dates of Lows and Highs | Length | Comment | Next Low and High |
|---|---|---|---|

### Intermediate Term Cycle(s)

| Dates of Lows and Highs | Length | Comment | Next Low and High |
|---|---|---|---|

### Short Term Cycle(s)

| Dates of Lows and Highs | Length | Comment | Next Low and High |
|---|---|---|---|

**Figure 9-3    Outline for data record of cycles.**

days between market lows and/or highs. I do not. Either technique will probably work if you use it consistently. If you begin by using trading days as your measure, then do not switch to calendar days.

Figure 9-4 is a daily price chart of the weekly data shown in Figure 9-1a. Using essentially the same technique (namely, visual inspection), we now scan the chart for evidence of cycles. The task is much simpler this time because we are using a chart and can readily see the highs and lows. The current chart is one that allows for a relatively simple determination of cycles. I chose this chart as an example because it is obvious and not too much searching is needed to find the dominant cycle. I have marked the length of the cycle accordingly. As you can see, the length between lows is fairly regular. Not all cycles will be as easy to find as this one. Figure 9-5 is another price chart with cycles that are more difficult to determine. How can we isolate the patterns in a market such as this? There are two methods, both of which make use of a measuring device in the form of either a ruler or a set of compass points. When you approach a chart that you have never before analyzed, you need a starting point. After all, how can you know which cycles could be present if you have not had any experience with this chart? There could be, and most probably are, many different cycles. Here is the step-by-step method I recommend for finding a cycle by measurement alone. This is a trial-and-error technique that initially may take you quite some time to do. Once you have worked with many charts, it becomes a relatively simple task to find cycles using this procedure. Figure 9-6 details the steps involved.

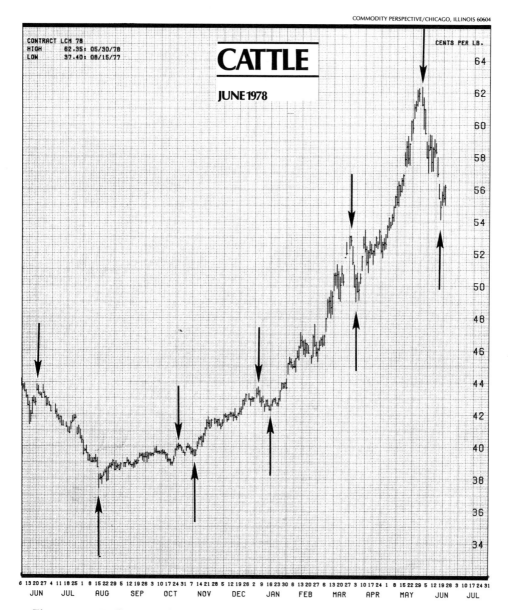

COMMODITY PERSPECTIVE/CHICAGO, ILLINOIS 60604

**Figure 9.4  Daily price chart of June 1978 cattle futures and 10 to 12 week cycle.**

Review the foregoing steps using the chart in Figure 9-5 as an exercise. To test yourself do not consult the chart in Figure 9-1a before completing the work yourself. A disagreement of one or two days between our work is no problem, but if you are not in close agreement with the cycles I have found, then study the steps once again.

Methods that employ higher mathematics for finding cycles use essentially the same technique. The only real difference is that we are doing the job manually, which takes more time. Typically, there is very little change in a

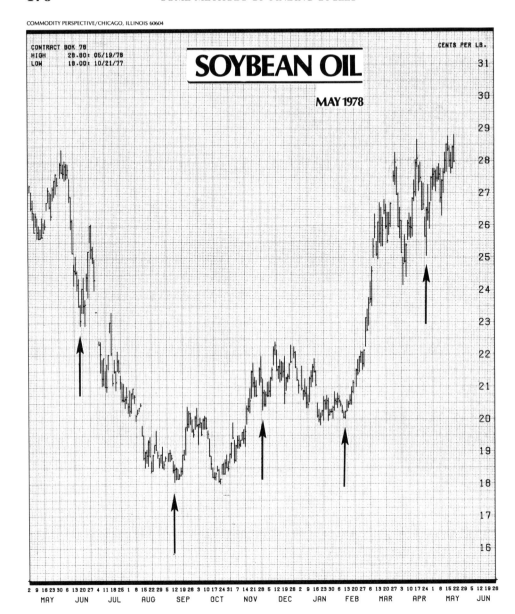

COMMODITY PERSPECTIVE/CHICAGO, ILLINOIS 60604

**Figure 9.5 Possible cycle lows in May 1978 soybean oil futures.**

cycle over extended periods. The longer a cycle runs, and the more times it has repeated itself, the more certain you can be that it is valid. It is usually best to wait for at least five repetitions of a given cyclic pattern before making a decision regarding its use in commodity trading. At the minimum, three complete repetitions should be used as the guideline.

Because the method of finding cycles is so important in our later work, I will run through several examples of how it is done according to the instructions I gave you earlier. Refer to figures 9-7 and 9-8. You will observe that in the

1   Visually inspect data or chart
2   Find a pattern of considerable length to amount of data being scanned
3   See if pattern repeats
4   If it does then check past data for repetition of cycle
5   If it does not then check cycle of shorter duration for repetitive pattern
6   Repeat Steps 1 through 5 for cycles of shorter and shorter length.

**Figure 9-6   List of steps to follow in finding a cycle**

illustrations I am demonstrating the weekly and daily analyses I progress from step one onward in sequence. There is absolutely no substitute for experience when it comes to finding cycles in this way. A tool that can help is the Cycle Finder, which is available commercially from the source listed in Appendix 1. See Chapter 10 for photos of the Cycle Finder. Essentially, this tool is nothing more than a set of multiple compass points that can be spaced to mark off equal intervals of time. Most cycles are not exactly equal in length, so this tool may

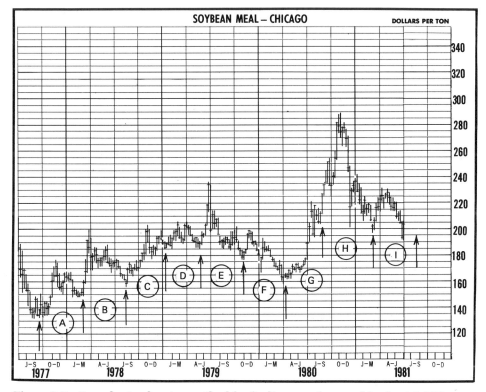

**Figure 9.7   Sample step-by-step method for finding a cycle—weekly chart. (a) Measure off first cycle by visual inspection. (b) Transfer same approximate count into future price period. (c) Count same approximate length forward and see if it marks a low. (d)–(f) Count forward and fit cycles to see if lows are valid. (g)–(h) Continue projection of low within ± 15 percent of time span. (i) Project next low and wait for it to be confirmed or negated.**

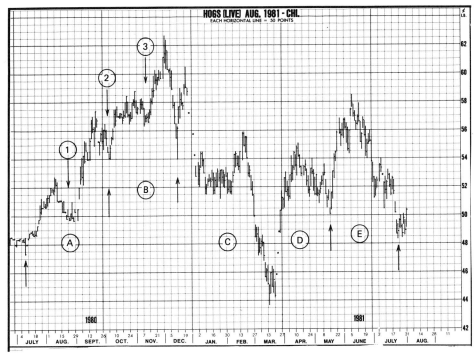

**Figure 9.8    Sample step-by-step method for finding a cycle—daily chart. (a) Find what appears to be a cycle. Lows 1, 2, and 3 constitute a shorter term cycle which could have been used instead. (b) Count forward and see if cycle length would have fallen on the next low or close to it. (c)–(e) Continue projection of cycle length.**

lead you somewhat astray because it will mark off only time spans that are exactly equal. It should be used only for making an approximate determination of possible cycles.

## DETRENDING CYCLES

A way to make the job of finding cycles more precise is the use of a mathematical tool called *detrending*. Any series of price data has elements of cycle and trend in it. *Trend* is actually part of a longer cycle that acts on the existing short term patterns. Figure 9-9 shows how cycle and trend are related. By subtracting elements of the longer trend from current short term cycles, you can remove the overall effect of trend. To do so, you must compute a moving average of the data and run through a series of additional steps. The technique is detailed in Chapter 11.

## A FEW MORE POINTS ABOUT FINDING CYCLES

Let's take several steps back now. I assume that you have had plenty of time to practice finding cycles. Now we'll talk about ways to keep your data organized. You need to keep several charts for each market. Specifically, I recommend the following:

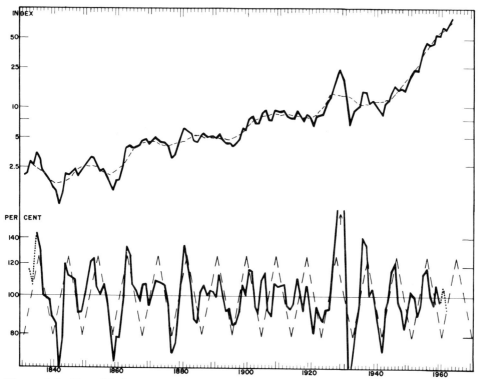

**Figure 9.9   Trend index (top) and detrended cycles (bottom) with ideal cycle zig-zag (dashed line).**

1    *A monthly average cash price chart* that extends as far back as data history allows. This item will help you to keep track of the long term cycles in each market. Of course, the chart should be updated monthly. Figure 9-10 is an example of how I keep my long term price chart for wheat, which shows the two important cycles.

2    *A weekly price chart* of the nearby contract month. Figure 9-11 shows a weekly price chart. Observe that cycles of several different intermediate lengths are recorded on this chart. In maintaining the weekly chart, you must remember a number of important rules as outlined earlier in this chapter.

3    *A daily closing price chart* must also be kept, particularly by persons interested in short term trading. Each closing price should be entered according to the sample in Figure 9-12. The price scale for this chart, as well as for all others, should be sufficiently large to allow detail work. The larger your chart paper can be, the more precise your analysis will be. I find the 11 × 17-inch paper manufactured by K & E (see Appendix 1) to be best suited for the job. It is best to follow at least two contract months for each market at any one time.

1.   Plot the closing price for each week on your chart. If the market is closed on a Friday, then use the Thursday price. You could plot high, low, and close if you wish.

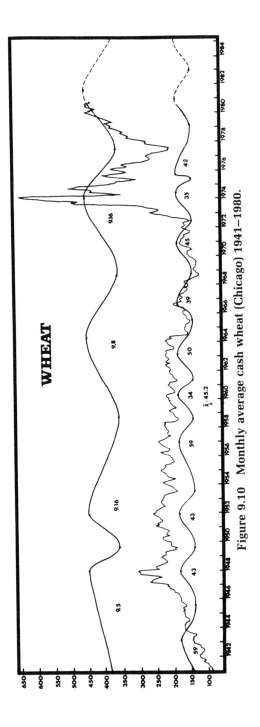

Figure 9.10  Monthly average cash wheat (Chicago) 1941–1980.

180

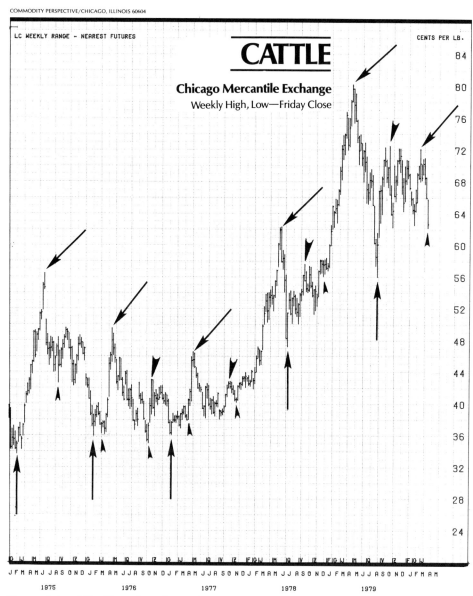

COMMODITY PERSPECTIVE/CHICAGO, ILLINOIS 60604

**Figure 9.11   Weekly price chart of cattle futures 1975–1980, showing several intermediate term cycles.**

2.   Chart only the closing price for the week. On occasion the exchange may list a "split close," or a range of prices within which the market closed. If the exchange lists a "settlement" price, then this is the price you should use. If a settlement price is not given, then use the exact mathematical average of the closing range prices. For example, if the June cattle closing is listed as 47.50–90, then you simply add the 0.50 and the 0.90 and take the average of this sum, which is 0.70. Hence, the price for your chart is 47.70.

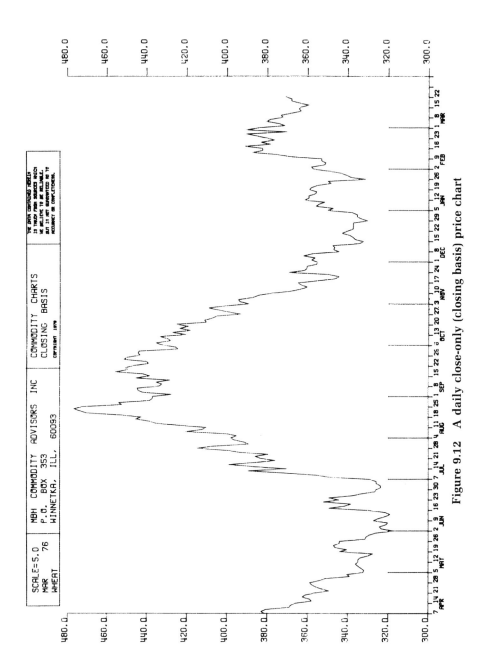

Figure 9.12  A daily close-only (closing basis) price chart

182

3. Do not plot the *open, high, or low* price for the week. These prices will be used for a different purpose later on, but they are not entered on the chart.

4. When each contract becomes the spot month, switch your plotting to the next option. For example, if the most current month (or lead month) in corn is September, and if you are currently in the month of August (actual time), then use the September contract price for your chart until the last Friday of August. Then switch to the next contract month, which is December. You may follow a different method, if you wish, as long as you remain consistent. You could follow a given contract month until the last day of trading, picking up on the very next listed month when the current contract expires. This may not necessarily give you different results, but it can cause more distortion in the chart. More on this later.

At first, compiling all the information on each market may be rather time consuming, but as your charts become current you will find that it is not much of a chore to keep them up to date, unless you become lazy or develop a bad attitude toward the market. It should take no more than an hour weekly to update the charts and about half an hour daily to work on the short term indicators (if you are looking for short term trades). It is a good idea to keep all charts, by market, in a binder or loose-leaf folder. Place the binders or folders in order, long term to short term, and examine them at least once weekly, if not more often. There are some sources of information that may substantially reduce the time it takes to get started with cycle charts. Commodity Research Bureau publishes *Commodity Yearbook*, which contains weekly high, low, close, and monthly average cash charts on most markets. The cash charts date back to the late 1800s, and the weekly high, low, and close charts go back about 10 years. You can make your own weekly closing chart by reading prices off the charts of the CRB. Although not as accurate as having actual prices, it can cut down considerably on the time it takes to get started. You can use a high, low, or close chart if you wish. It may make your task of cycle finding a bit more difficult, but it does save time.

## KEEPING THE CYCLE RECORD

Now that we have dispensed with the mechanics of keeping charts, we can go on to several practical aspects. Refer again to the foregoing paragraph on keeping a folder for each market you are following. Remember one should include all the cycles that have been determined as well as the time window calculation of the next high and low. This is very important for record-keeping purposes, but it is even more important for analytical reasons. At any time you should be able to quickly determine the time windows for each market, which is important because it provides you with a perspective on market activity. Notice also that there are a number of letters and comments entered on several of the charts I have used. This is part of the analysis I teach you later in Chapters 12–15. Sufficient room should be left for such purposes. Much of this information is also kept on your written record. As you change charts (for short term information) you will find that it is much easier if the record is right in front of you, all in one place. You can then say with certainty, for example, that "the 24 day cycle in pork bellies has repeated itself 32 times in the last 2 years."

## SOME PRACTICAL CONSIDERATIONS

It's one thing to find cycles. It is a far greater achievement to use them profitably in the market. When looking at a chart of cycles (or for that matter, any other technical indicator), it is common for people to say such things as, "We should have gone short last May," or "We should have bought and held when the cycle turned up." Such 20/20 hindsight is totally useless in our work. I caution you *not* to engage in "should have's, could have's, might have's, or would have's." In the market there is only "did or did not." When you sit before a chart and analyze it, you are not privy to anything but the present and the past. There are some important practical considerations in using cycles (or any other technical indicators) that must be learned and used in order for your work to be successful. Following are a few pragmatic considerations in cycle work:

1  *If you simply cannot find any cycles in a data series*, then stop trying. There are cases, however, that at first show no readily apparent cycles. Although this is the exception rather than the rule, there is no reason to labor over a market that you cannot analyze to your satisfaction. Simply stop working on it. Come back to the chart several days later and see if you can get anywhere. If you can't, then don't bother with the analysis for a few months, *but* keep the chart up to date. Try again at regular intervals. Sooner or later you will indeed find the pattern.

2  *The extension of highs and lows at the conjunction of turns in dominant cycles* is a very important consideration, and I urge you to keep it in mind at all times. When a short term cycle is due to turn within the same time window as an intermediate term cycle, there can be and often will be a distortion of the short term cycle. More often than not, the cycle will run longer than many of the previous cycles in this series. Figure 9-13 is an example of how this can happen.

When an intermediate term cycle is due to turn within the same time window as a long term cycle, the same thing may happen, as in the case of live hogs. Whereas the 3.5 year cycle was due to bottom in 1980, the 25 week pattern within the 3.5 year time window ran much later than usual. I mentioned earlier that you must keep a record of time windows for each and every cycle. One good reason for doing so is to see the extension of highs and lows. Once you have determined that a major turn is coming, it is best to examine the relationship between the cycle you have isolated for a turn and other patterns within the same market. Typically, a time frame within which cycles of different length all peak or bottom can yield a tremendous amount of profit. These are also time windows, however, during which cycles can be shortened and/or elongated. The timing indicators we discuss later in Chapters 12–15 alert you to situations such as these. Remember that I have covered about only 20 percent of the total trading technique.

3  *Few rules are ever perfect* in the market. The old adage, "When in doubt stay out," is useful in such cases. There is no reason to trade any market that gives you unclear, contradictory, or vague messages. I have tried to provide you with rules that are as automatic and mechanical as possible. There should never be any question in your mind as to what you need to do once the timing

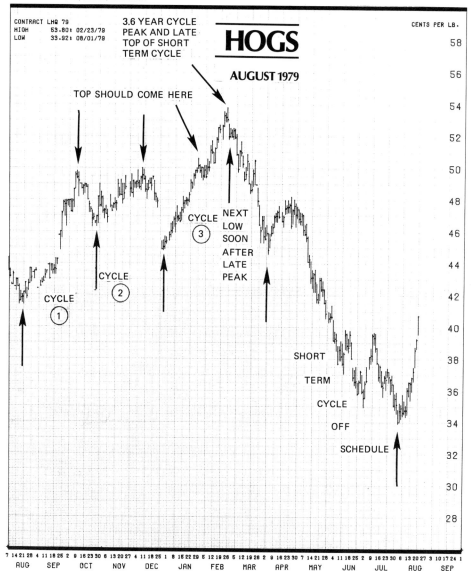

**Figure 9.13   3.6 year cycle top and late peak in short term hog cycle as a result.**

indicators have been understood. If there is a question, if there is any uncertainty, if there is any uneasy feeling, then stand aside. There are plenty of other markets and many other opportunities. I discuss this point later in Chapters 12–15 to clarify additional questions after I explain the timing indicators. Please remember that in the few cases that remain unclear, there may indeed be good reasons for staying out of those markets. The method I teach is designed to capture a large portion of most major moves, but it will not get you into every single move because of the limitations of technique.

4   *Avoid extraneous input* at all costs. I have stressed repeatedly (and will do so again) the importance of doing your market work in an information vacuum. In other words, I suggest you avoid other opinions and technical findings for reasons of self-discipline. You may not appreciate the value of this suggestion until you have been in the position of making an important decision and having it ridiculed or questioned by others.

5   *Experience is always the best teacher.* Do not attempt to overstep the limits of your knowledge. Trade slowly at first, making certain you understand the various combinations of rules, indicators, and signals.

# CHAPTER TEN

# A Tool for Finding Cycles

There are many paths by which one can attain a goal. In our age of advanced technology and computerization it has become more and more common for simple answers to be overlooked. I could easily have written this book in complex technical language. And I might easily have engaged in high level mathematical discussions on the subject of cyclic analysis. Some of this information is provided in Appendix 3 for those traders truly interested in chasing down the mathematics of cycles in its present (i.e., infantile) form. Some practitioners of cycle analysis attempt to glorify this tool, while practicing obfuscation in teaching their analytical techniques. I do not believe that any such nonsense is necessary. Because my only concern is making the method both pragmatic and profitable, I have structured my studies and experiences in the direction of parsimony. On the road to such simplicity I have examined solutions of considerable complexity, rejecting them as either inefficient or ineffective.

My searching, therefore, always leads to the inescapable conclusion that simple is always best. The point of this preamble is to reiterate that there are many methods by which cycles can be extracted from a data series. You can employ whichever method proves profitable, time effective, and cost effective. Several mechanical methods have already been mentioned. The use of a ruler or compass points is generally quite satisfactory. For those who have a flair for the more sophisticated, however, there is a simple tool that can provide invaluable assistance while saving considerable time and eyestrain.

Several years ago I had the good fortune to meet a commodity broker who shared with me an interest in cycles. His attempts to find a method for calculating cyclic periodicity led to the invention of a tool that might make the task less tedious for you. His efforts resulted in the Ehrlich Cycle Finder™, a device named after its creator. Traders who are mechanically and industrially inclined can construct their own model in their spare time.

Figure 10-1 depicts the Ehrlich Cycle Finder™ overlying a live cattle futures chart. This tool has several features. First and most important, the Cycle Finder points are always equidistant from one another. This means that if you stretch out two of the points and line them up between two lows or two highs, the other points of the Cycle Finder will also expand to the same distance. By then laying the Cycle Finder on the remainder of your chart, you can line up subsequent bottoms and/or tops accordingly. In other words, the Cycle Finder will average the cyclic pattern for you without the necessity of your counting. But remember that the Cycle Finder assumes perfect regularity of the cycle length. As you know, this can be misleading.

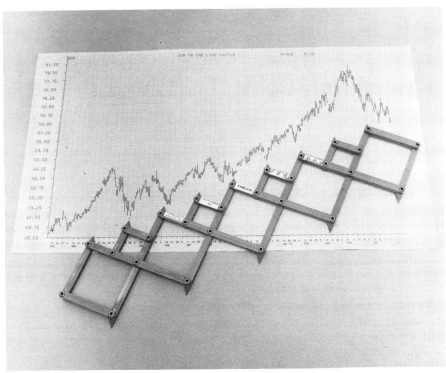

Figure 10.1    The Erlich Cycle Finder™ across lows in June 1979 cattle futures.

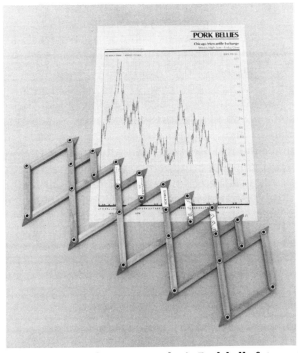

Figure 10.2    Finding the intermediate term cycles in Pork belly futures. (Chart courtesy Commodity Perspective)

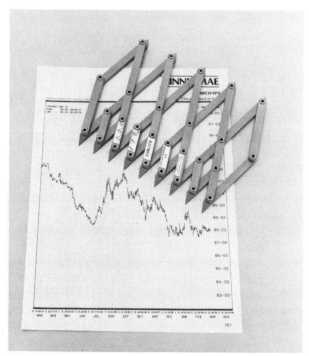

**Figure 10.3   Using the Ehrlich Cycle Finder™ to find highs. (Chart courtesy Commodity Perspective)**

By examining tops and/or bottoms during the time window close to each Cycle Finder point, you can overcome the tool's limitation. By expanding the Cycle Finder into the future, you can make a projection of the coming cyclic time windows quickly, accurately, and with a minimum of mental effort. Should you then wish to determine the actual cycle lengths, you can lightly mark each turn and proceed to count according to the methods described earlier. In Figure 10-2 the Cycle Finder is being used on an angle to capture the existing trend—another way the Ehrlich tool can be used. The value of this device is, therefore, twofold. First, it allows you to test, by trial and error, quickly and without any mathematics, many different cyclic periods until the most reliable one (or more) has been found. Second, and equally important, the Cycle Finder allows you to project the future high(s) and low(s) so that you may then take the all-important step of timing your market entry.

Figure 10-3 shows the use of the Cycle Finder in determining the highs of a given market, their cyclic period, and the most probable time of the next high. Information on the Ehrlich Cycle Finder™ may be obtained at the address listed in Appendix 1. Should you wish to construct your own model you must remember that this is a precision tool. Your work must, therefore, be exact if you wish the final product to accurately reflect the cyclic periods. There are various engineering and mechanical drawing tools which can be adapted to the same basic purpose. They are generally available from drafting supply stores.

# CHAPTER ELEVEN

# Detrending: Another Way To Find Cycles

There are many ways in which cyclic patterns can be isolated from a data series. Among these are such mathematical methods as the Box–Jenkins technique, spectral analysis, and Fourier analysis. These methods all have merit and should be carefully considered and studied by all serious students of cycles, but persons not well schooled in higher mathematics might find them somewhat difficult to handle without the use of a computer. The Foundation for the Study of Cycles has done considerable research with advanced mathematical models, including several not mentioned here. You can consult their work for guidelines, methods, and procedures if you wish to know more about their research. A simpler technique for isolating cycles is to use *detrending*. Detrending can be used to isolate seasonal patterns as well as cycles of all lengths in any data series. Here's basically how it works. As you have observed by now, every market or data series consists of many different cycles. Each cycle may contain within it many cycles of shorter length. Were we able to isolate each and every cyclic component we would probably be able to predict with close to 100 percent accuracy the future trend of prices. There will be some random elements in every data series, of course. We cannot consider every single variant, but we should ideally be able to account for most of the price variation by first isolating all possible cycles and then recombining them in order to simulate probable future trends.

To do this we must examine the data series without the influence of other cycles that may be affecting the particular pattern or patterns we wish to examine. Here's an example of what I mean. Assume that we want to determine the possible existence of intermediate term cycles without the overriding effect of a long term cycle. The only way in which we can be certain, or close to certain, that we are actually looking at the "pure" intermediate-term cycles is by filtering out the effect of the long term cycle. The filtering can be accomplished by subtracting our data series from a moving average trend as of the cycle we want filtered out. If we want to examine a 30 week cycle in cattle without the influence of a possible 45 month pattern, we construct a chart of deviations from a 45 month moving-average trend. This would, in theory, remove the possible effects of a 45 month cycle, giving us a look at the cycles we want to examine without concern about an underlying long term trend. What we are doing, in essence, is making other cycles more visible. The process is similar to finding a needle in a haystack, if I might use this old analogy. The pieces of straw are quite large in comparison to the needle. By constructing a mesh grating with holes too small for most of the straw, we allow only those pieces the size of the needle to pass through. Certainly, we'll pass some pieces of straw, but they can then be easily distinguished from the needle. Hence, our task has been made much easier. The same process can be repeated for cycles of any length. In other words, we look at a price chart of detrended data, first removing one cycle, then another, and then another. By using this method repeatedly you will probably find many cycles that you could not spot by simple visual inspection of the data without detrending.

The next step is to make a list of the cycles you have found by detrending the data. Then carefully check the list against the actual market to determine if it is indeed a valid pattern. This step compensates for any possible effects of random fluctuation that could produce artifacts, or unreal cycles, in the data. Remember that any manipulation of raw data tends to change what is there. The more you change what is there, the less reliable will be your output. Regardless of what you actually find when you detrend a data series, you will need to test the findings before you can make a definitive statement about the results. I have stressed repeatedly the importance of real time testing, and it is an issue that is given even more consideration in later chapters.

Let's take a close look at what can be achieved with a detrending approach. Figure 11-1 is a monthly cash average price chart of the Canadian dollar, plotted above an 11 month moving-average detrended chart. What it shows, in essence, is the way the Canadian dollar chart might look without the influence of an 11 month cycle. The detrended plot is more like a magnified version of the actual price plot. It permits us to observe, measure, and test the possibility of other cycles in the Canadian dollar data.

At the top of Figure 11-1 are several major bottoms marked a, b, c, and d; all represent a long term cycle in the Canadian dollar. The arrows on the bottom half of Figure 11-1 point to cyclic lows that might not have been easily observable from the unmanipulated cash plot. In particular, the time span from low b to low c was especially flat on the cash plot, but it is easily observed from a cyclic standpoint on the detrended plot.

You can see that some of the cycle lows on the detrended plot are, in fact, only minor lows. Low e, for example, is only a minor low in the untreated data although it shows up as a prominent low in the detrended plot. Another thing the detrended data allow you to do is to evaluate trends on a more effective basis. Notice that the trend in the Canadian dollar had two or more peaks in the first cycle. Tops h and i confirmed a cyclic high whereas the top on our detrended plot was made at j—much, much earlier. This high remained intact until bottom k and cycle low l arrived. In other words, the detrended data showed a downtrend even though the actual cash data (untreated) showed a sideways pattern. Notice also the behavior of our two plots at peaks m and n. Top m was higher than any of the previous tops since low c, but on the detrended plot there was a clear divergence from this pattern because top n was lower than the peak following bottom c. This was a clear warning signal that top m was a cyclic peak that might not be easily penetrated for some time to come.

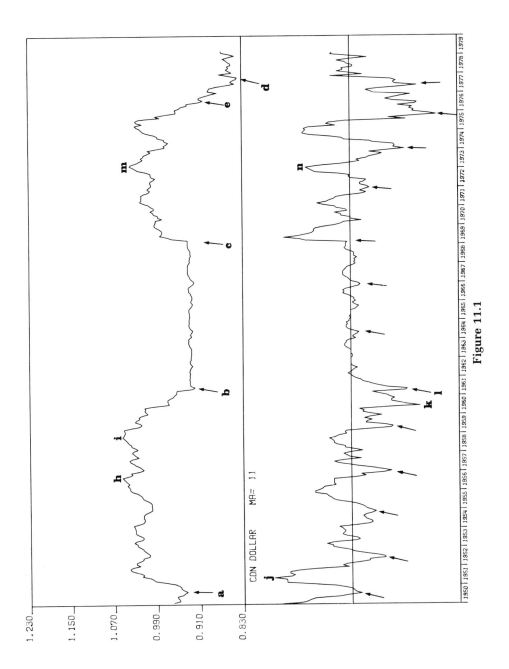

**Figure 11.1**

192

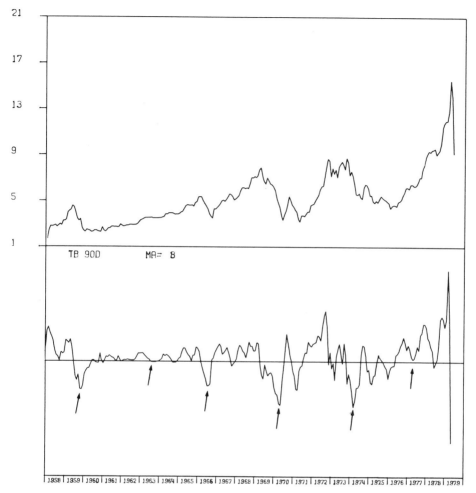

**Figure 11.2**

Now let's move to another detrended chart to see how prices would have acted on a normal and detrended basis. Figure 11-2 shows the monthly price cash of 90 day T-bills plotted above the detrended data. Figure 11-2 shows the deviations from an 8 month moving-average trend. I have marked lows on the detrended data that would otherwise not be easily visible on the actual price plot. The cycle runs about 4 years, low to low. Again, the actual determination of a cycle in this case would have been difficult, if not impossible, had the detrended data not been consulted.

Figure 11-3 shows the June 1978 cattle delivery plotted against a detrended 32 day moving average. Notice that the actual price plot (i.e., the daily close) shows no readily observable cyclic activity. The detrended data, however, show at least five important cyclic lows, of which four were highly valid. The fifth low came late in the contract and could not be verified for this delivery month. Again, it is important to observe how the detrended data allowed for deter-

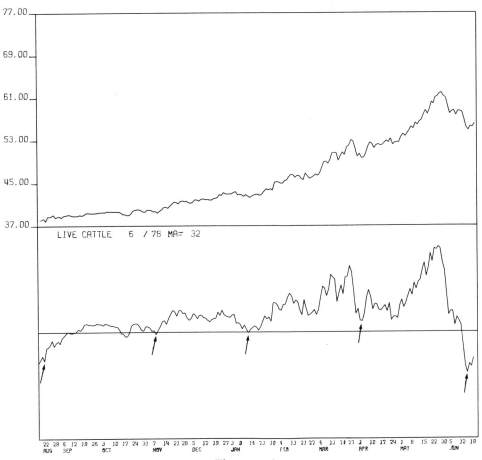

**Figure 11.3**

mination of a very clear cyclic tendency without any advanced mathematical tools. Simple visual inspection was the only thing necessary.

Now let's examine the same chart, June 1978 cattle, with a different detrended moving average. This time we'll remove the effects of a 14 day cycle (Figure 11-4). I have marked 16 cyclic lows that became evident only *after* the data had been detrended. You can see that not all of the turns came at precise lows in price, but they *did* come at important buying points. Again, the value of detrending is that it allows you to select cycles more easily. Furthermore, detrending can be performed on one market, using many different moving-average lengths. Traders interested in using a computer to aid in the moving-average technique of detrending can consult Appendix 2 for the specific programs I used to generate the results shown in Figures 11-3 and 11-4.

Let's take another look at the same cattle data as in Figure 11-3, but showing another detrended moving average. This time I have used the deviations from a 45 day moving-average trend. Figure 11-5 shows what resulted. There is not much difference between this detrended plot and the one shown in Figure

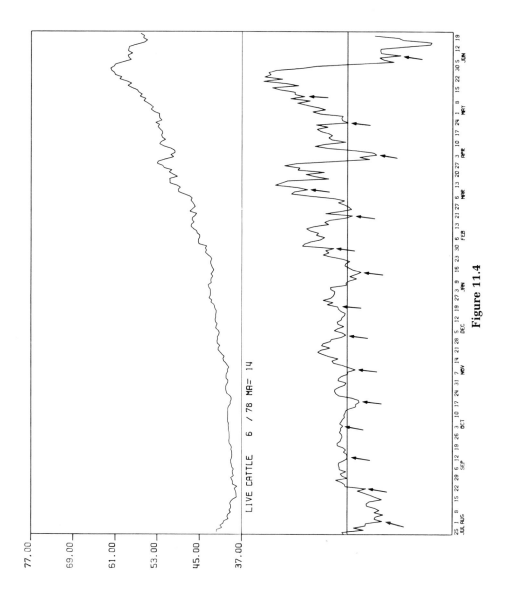

Figure 11.4

195

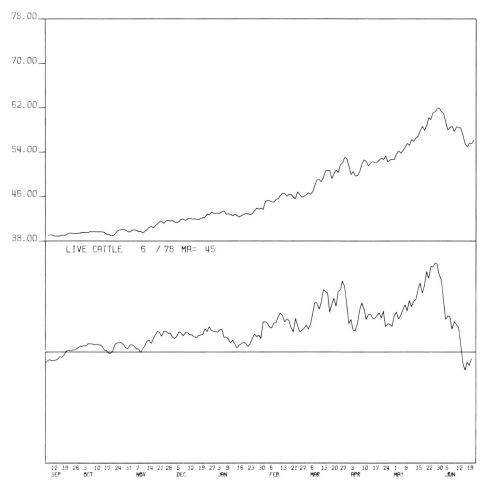

**Figure 11.5**

11-2, a result owing to the fact that the first plot used a 32 day moving average and the plot in this case was based on a 45 day detrended moving average. You might conclude that an even longer moving average might not have much of an effect on the ease with which cycles are isolated.

Now we move back in moving-average length and examine the pattern of a 6 day detrended plot, as shown in Figure 11-6. As you can see, there are many more short term patterns clearly visible in this short term detrending of the actual data. The short term detrending cycle would allow the more active trader many more opportunities than the trader who, for example, worked only with the longer cyclic patterns. In this market there would have been opportunity for a great deal of trading even though the trend was quite lasting. Also, the long term trader might have saved considerable money in commissions by trading the longer cycles (i.e., 32 or 45 days).

The values of detrending, then, are threefold. First, it allows you to examine a data series for cycles that you might not easily have seen had it not been for

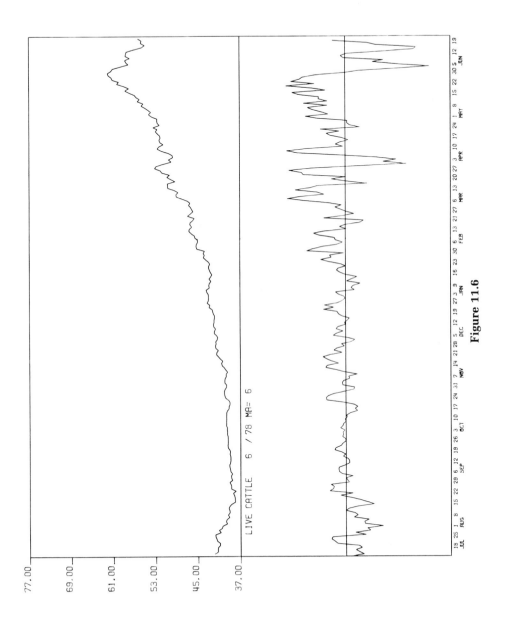

**Figure 11.6**

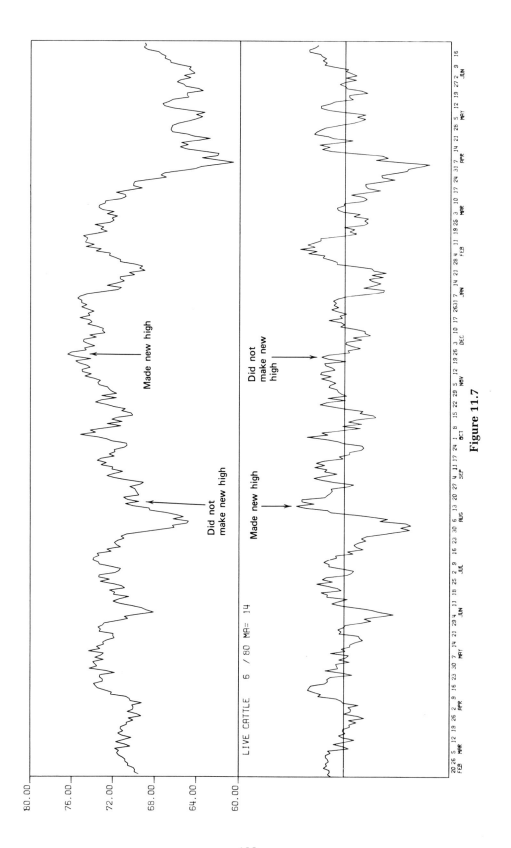

**Figure 11.7**

198

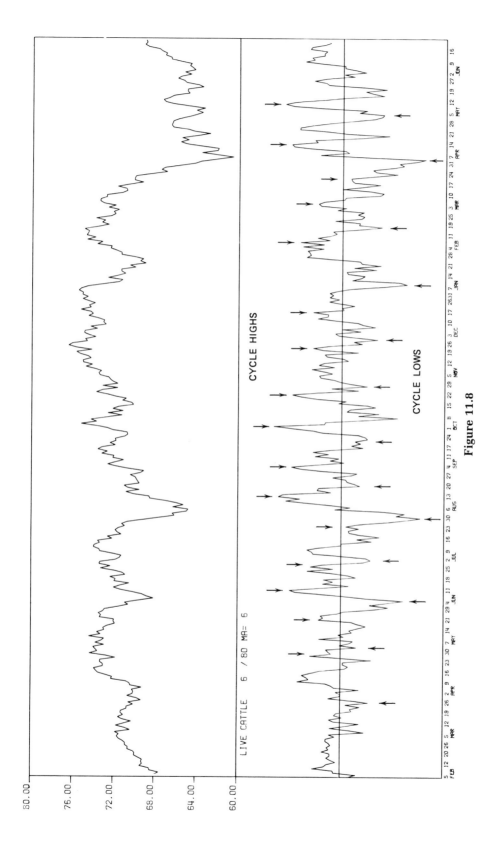

**Figure 11.8**

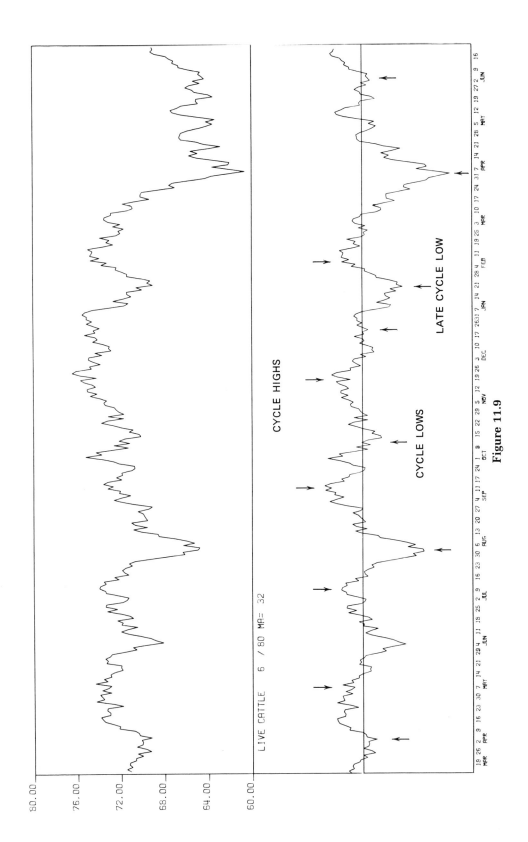

**Figure 11.9**

the detrending process. Second, it allows you to check for divergent patterns in lows and highs relative to the actual market plot. When the market makes a new high or low that is not confirmed by the moving-average detrend, there is reason to believe that the trend will reverse itself. Finally, the advantage of detrending data is that they permit examination of many possible cycles without the effect of other lengths. Hints about cycles of many different lengths can be obtained by the detrending process.

Now let's examine just a few more charts to see how detrending might have been used another delivery year of cattle futures. Cattle, as you know by now, has several highly reliable cycles. On a short term basis the cattle market can fluctuate considerably. As an exercise, examine Figures 11-7, 11-8, and 11-9 for hints of short term cycles. You will notice that there are many different cyclic possibilities. See if you can find them, and compare them to the actual price plot for verification of trading results. Can you see any other possible uses for the detrended data? I have made some notes on these charts to help guide you. Should you wish to apply more advanced detrending methods, you will find references in Appendix 3.

# CHAPTER TWELVE

# Timing Signals I

The next step in our study of cycles is the determination of timing signals that will either confirm or disprove changes in cyclic trends. Without a corresponding timing signal, no change in a cycle trend can be relied on with sufficient certainty to allow market entry. Without a cycle, the timing signal in and of itself is useless. It is for precisely this reason that many charting systems are not as profitable as they might be. Whereas the basic signals they use are sensible and valid, they are not as profitable as they might be because they contain no time reference. Without a time reference (cycle), there is a strong probability that the signal or combination of signals will not work. In other words, it is important to be in the right place *at the right time* when trading commodities. It is the timing signal in association with the time window that leads to profitable market entry. Without cycles, timing signals would be relatively useless and vice versa. This is where most trading systems go astray. They fail to combine the all-important element of time with their valuable signals. Except for cycle methods, most technical approaches to the market seek only to analyze chart formations, variations on price behavior alone or in combination with volume, and/or open interest. Point and figure charting systems concentrate exclusively on price and price change as do the various momentum and oscillatory approaches. It is highly likely that any technical tool that fails to take time into consideration could be markedly improved by adding cycles to its method.

## TIMING SIGNAL NO. 1: THE BREAKOUT

The first of four important timing signals is the *breakout*. There are a few important differences between my rules for determining breakouts and those used in standard charting techniques. First and foremost, we will use a closing basis chart for our work. This is no different from the procedure we've used until now. Most charting systems use a daily high, low close, or weekly high, low close chart. We could, in fact, use such a chart as well, but a closing basis chart makes signals easier to spot. Most charting systems look for breakouts at virtually any time. We will look for breakouts only at certain times. Before moving ahead, however, let's define what precisely is meant by a breakout, and the best way to do this is by graphic representation. See Figures 12-1 and 12-2 for examples of downside and upside breakouts. The lines drawn above prices in a downtrend are called *resistance lines,* and the lines drawn under prices in an uptrend are called *support lines.* Any support or resistance line must have at least three points to it. No lines consisting of two points are counted. See Figure 12-3 for a few more examples of support and resistance lines. Re-

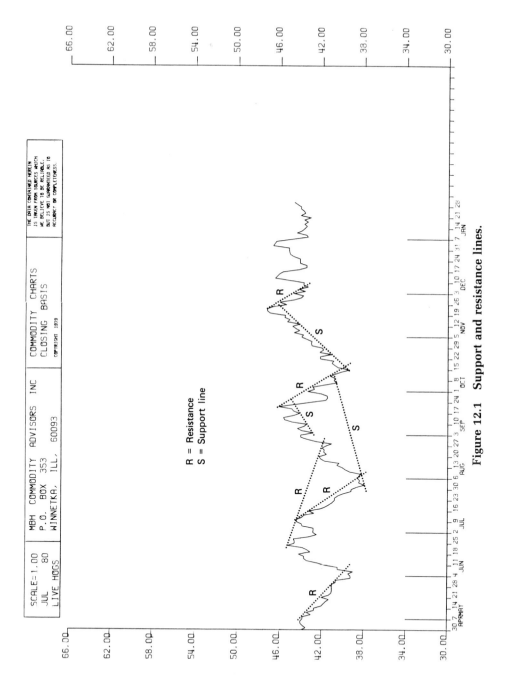

**Figure 12.1 Support and resistance lines.**

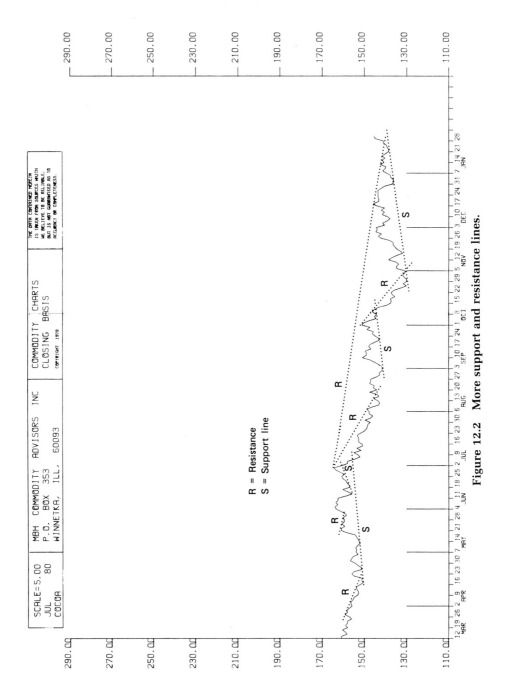

**Figure 12.2 More support and resistance lines.**

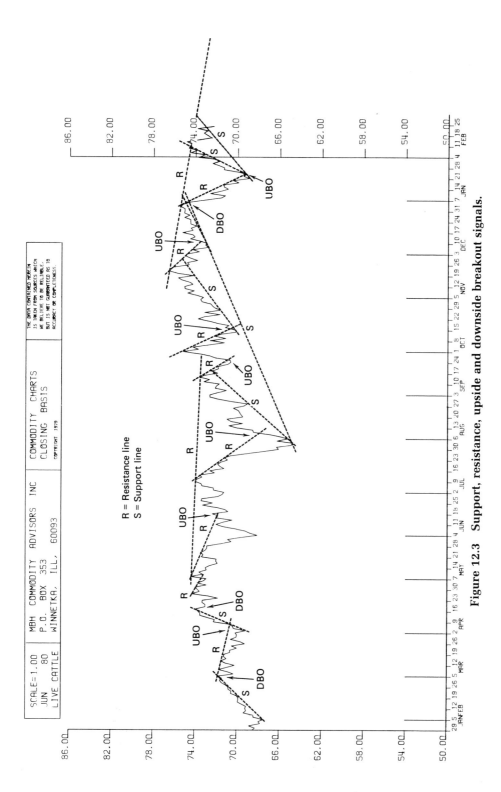

**Figure 12.3  Support, resistance, upside and downside breakout signals.**

R = Resistance line
S = Support line

SCALE=1.00
JUN  80
LIVE CATTLE

MBH COMMODITY ADVISORS INC
P.O. BOX 353
WINNETKA, ILL, 60093

COMMODITY CHARTS
CLOSING BASIS
COPYRIGHT 1979

205

sistance lines appear above the price plot and support lines appear below the price plot.

There will naturally be some disagreement about whether a point actually hits a line or not. Preferably, each point should be exactly on the line or not more than one price division away from the line. The support and resistance lines, so commonly used in most charting techniques, should be familiar to you. The breakout above or below a resistance line is equally common in charting methods.

## THE SIGNALS

An *upside breakout* (UBO) signal occurs when the closing price moves above the resistance line. A *downside breakout* (DBO) signal occurs when the closing price moves below the support line. Figure 12-3 shows several UBO and DBO signals. As you can see, prices usually continue in the direction of their breakout. Remember that we have not, as yet, combined cycles with UBO or DBO signals.

Let's review a few rules for determining support and resistance lines and upside or downside breakouts.

1  Three points or more are required to determine a line.
2  All points within one price square (smallest unit on graph) are counted as part of a line.
3  Any *one* price entry above the resistance or support line constitutes a breakout. If above the line, then it is an upside breakout; if below the line, then it is a downside breakout. Hereafter I refer to these terms by abbreviations UBO and DBO, respectively. Support line is abbreviated SL and resistance line, RL (or simply S and R).
4  Only UBO and signals in falling RLs and DBO signals in rising SLs are considered valid. In other words, a rising RL is not considered as part of our method. Similarly, a falling SL is not used.
5  Typically, the longer an RL or SL, the more valid a UBO or DBO signal is when it comes.
6  There may be several layers of SLs or RLs above and below the market, respectively. The more lines that are penetrated by a UBO or DBO signal at one time, the more lasting a move in the given direction is.
7  When marking your support and resistance lines, make as thin a mark (i.e., pencilled or inked lines) as possible. I prefer to use red for RLs and blue for SLs.
8  Always extend an SL or RL well into the future of your chart.
9  The same rules apply to monthly, weekly, and daily charts. All should be analyzed according to the same rules.

Figure 12-4 is a monthly average cash price chart of 90 day T-bills, which dates back to the 1950s. I have marked several RLs and SLs as well as UBO and DBO signals as they appear. Figure 12-5 is a monthly average beef steers cash chart. For illustrative purposes I have also marked a number of SL, RL,

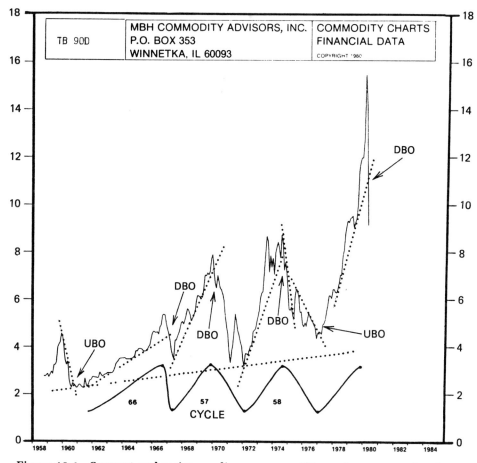

**Figure 12.4   Support and resistance lines on a monthly cash average price chart.**

UBO, and DBO signals for your edification. *Remember that the monthly, weekly, and daily charts are all treated the same way.* Figures 12-6 and 12-7 are weekly and daily charts respectively. It may seem from my selection of charts that UBO and DBO signals work a majority of the time. This is *not* true. I have chosen these charts for the specific purpose of illustrating my point. Be advised that there are many instances in which these signals alone will not necessarily be valid indicators of a price move. As explained earlier, the problem with UBO and DBO signals, as commonly used by most commodity (and stock) traders, is that they do not contain the necessary time element. The time element, or time window, must be included as part of the approach. Without it, there is not much we can achieve with the raw signals because signals alone tend *not* to work as often as they *do* work.

Let's take a big step now and combine a cycle chart with some RL, SL, UBO, and DBO indicators. First, let's take the pork belly chart in Figure 12-8a. Step 1 is to determine the cycle. Following the rules I gave you earlier, Step 1 has

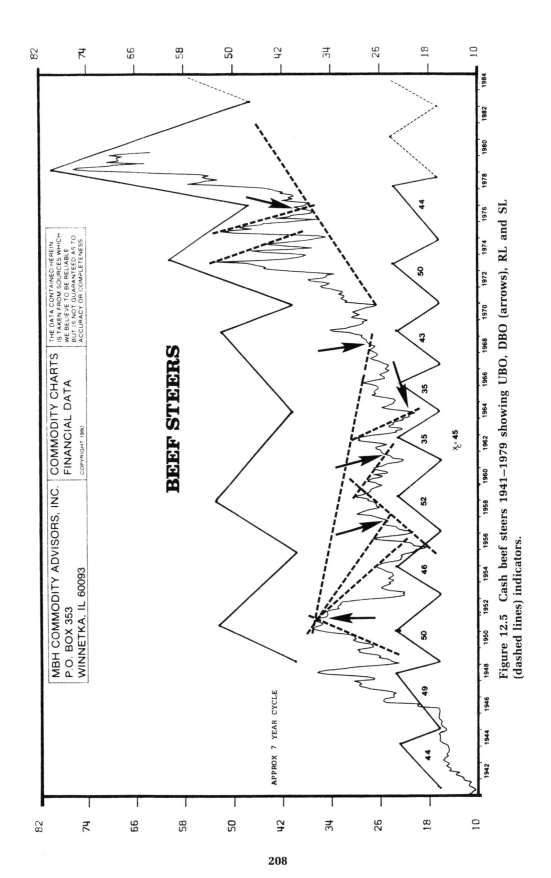

Figure 12.5  Cash beef steers 1941–1979 showing UBO, DBO (arrows), RL and SL (dashed lines) indicators.

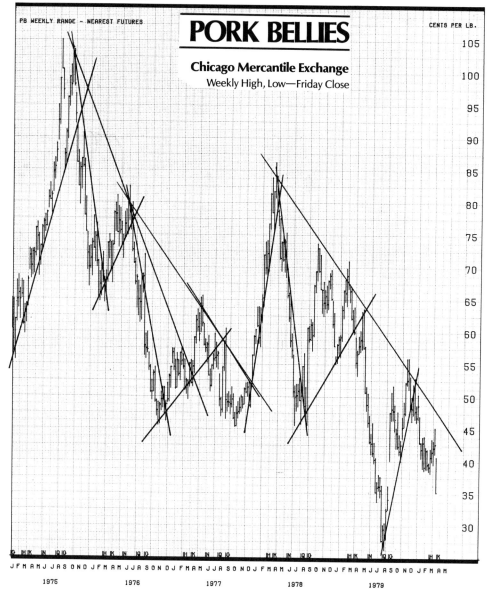

COMMODITY PERSPECTIVE/CHICAGO, ILLINOIS 60604

**Figure 12.6   UBO and DBO signals in weekly pork belly futures chart 1975–1980.**

been done in Figure 12-8A. Our next step is to project the appropriate time windows, which are also marked accordingly in Figure 12-8A. (Remember that we are doing this analysis in hindsight, which always makes decisions easier because we know the outcome.) The next step is to add SLs and RLs to our chart, as has been done in Figure 12-8B. Finally, we mark in the DBO and UBO signals, as in Figure 12-8C. What do we see now? Notice that there is a predominance of UBO and DBO signals at turning points of the cycle. In addition,

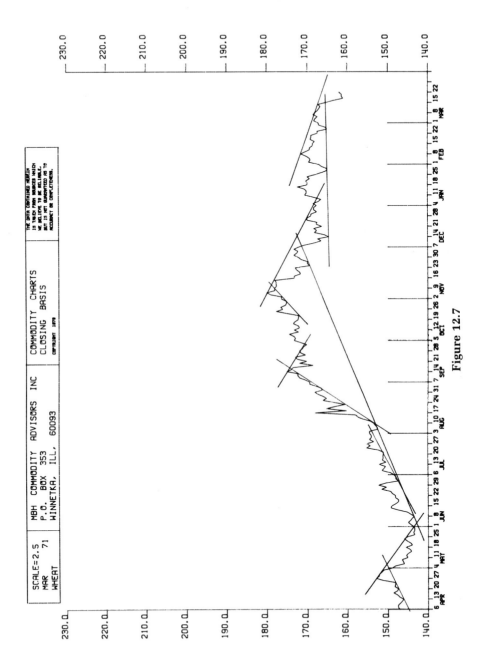

Figure 12.7

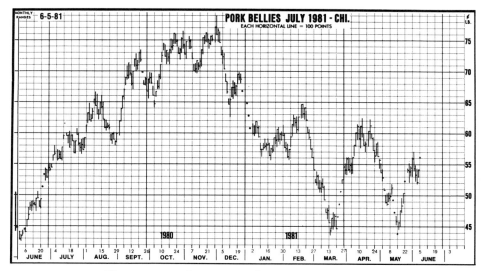

**Figure 12.8a   Step 1.   Mark UBO and DBO signals.**

**Figure 12.8b**

there are several UBO and DBO signals at cycle points that are *not* within the time window. Assuming that we had made all of the necessary decisions, with the correct technical analysis are the appropriate time, per the two tools I have taught, a total analysis for another market and contract would look like Figure 12-8D.

Note that the analysis moves ahead step by step. As you gain experience with the technique any one chart can be easily analyzed in a matter of minutes. In real time your chart will be updated daily, weekly, or monthly (depending on

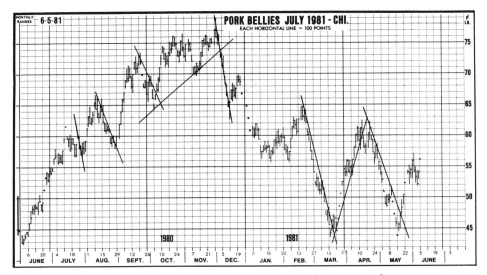

Figure 12.8c   Step 3.   Mark UBO and DBO signals.

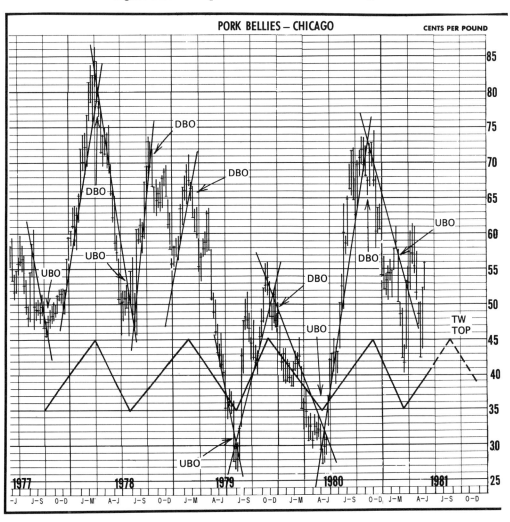

Figure 12.8d   UBO, DBO, AND cycles.

212

the length of cycle you were following). This will leave plenty of time for decision making and record keeping.

There you have it: a method that combines *time* with confirming signals of trend change! But before you run away with it, overuse it, abuse it, or trust in it implicitly, let me warn you that there is much, much more to learn. This small combination of tools is an effective one and should, for the most part, keep you well ahead of what a majority of traders are doing in the market. It is, by the way, uncanny how often this combination of signals comes at points in the market at which there is a high degree of public, political, economic, and/or media opinion to the contrary. All too often public opinion, media coverage, and even professional sentiment will only lead you astray, unless you teach yourself to believe the opposite at crucial time window periods.

Let's take a step back and see where we've come. First, I covered the basic concept of cycles in order to familiarize you with the time element in market analysis. I stressed the point that market work must be done in a vacuum without attention to economic considerations. The concept of the time window and the technical details of how to find cycles and determine time windows were discussed in detail. Examples were given, and you should have had considerable practice by now. The concept of upside and downside breakouts was discussed and differentiated from traditional approaches to this method. Some rules for UBO and DBO signals were given, and a number of examples were cited. The combined effect of the time window and UBO, DBO signals was discussed and illustrated. Now practice these principles on charts you either make on your own, or those provided for such purpose in Appendix 4.

A few details, however, are still missing from what has been taught so far. The use of *stop loss* orders, an important part of every trading system, has *not* been covered. There has been no mention of price objectives, adding to positions, reversal of positions, or overall money management. Most important, nothing has been said about the way in which longer cycles are combined with short cycles. Before doing so, however, I must alert you to a problem that every trader faces. Each individual must determine what his or her time orientation to the market will be. There are those who wish to trade only for the short term, and there are those who wish to look only at long term approaches to the market—for a variety of reasons from tax considerations to personal preference. Some individuals are not capable of sitting through major moves without trading actively. Each approach has its benefits. My bias is toward longer term trading. Through the years there has been much discussion of what precisely is meant by *long term* and *short term*. For our purposes, it is best to provide some operational definitions of these terms. Chapter 4 has already discussed these considerations.

# CHAPTER THIRTEEN

# Timing Signals II

Earlier I have discussed the importance of watching for timing signals at the appropriate time window. I have made the point repeatedly: A timing signal in the absence of verification by the time window is, in and of itself, relatively meaningless. This is why it is particularly important to understand the timing indicators that go hand in hand with time windows. The two are inseparable. Chapter 12 discussed how resistance and support lines give rise to upside and downside breakout timing signals. These are only a part of the overall picture of timing signals. There are a number of other signals that, if properly understood, can alert you to trend changes in timing windows. One is the *reversal signal*. Many traders have been using reversals for years, but they have been somewhat surprised at the relative inconsistency of such signals. Traders know that reversals are important. They know that certain types of reversals usually come at major market highs and lows, yet they do not know how to integrate reversals with the necessary time orientation.

What precisely do I mean by a reversal? The following operational definitions will help you understand precisely how such signals can be identified. (Notice that the definitions are for *daily* reversals. The same definition also applies to *weekly* and/or *monthly* reversals, with the time reference changed as necessary.)

*Upside Reversal (R +)*   If today's low price is lower than yesterday's low price *and* today's closing price is higher than yesterday's closing price, then a daily upside reversal has been made (see Figure 13-1 for graphic example).

*Downside Reversal (R −)*   If today's high price is greater than yesterday's high price and today's closing price is lower than yesterday's closing price, then a daily downside reversal has been made (see Figure 13-1 for graphic example).

In determining reversals the only things taken into consideration are the day's highs, lows, and closing prices. We do *not* pay any attention to the opening price in determining reversals. Nor do we look at open interest or volume in following my rules. It is important that you understand precisely what is meant by a *reversal*, up and/or down. A way of stating the definition mathematically would be as follows:

If     $H_1$ = high of day 1          And       $H_2$ = high of day 2
       $L_1$ = low of day 2                       $L_2$ = low of day 2
And $C_1$ = closing price of day 1              $C_2$ = closing price of Day 2
Then upside reversal is
$$L_2 < L_1 \quad \text{and} \quad C_2 > C_1 = R+$$
downside reversal is
$$H_2 > H_1 \quad \text{and} \quad C_2 < C_1 = R-$$

Let's take a look at some daily upside and downside reversals. For brevity, I will henceforth abbreviate them as R+ and R-. Figures 13-1, 13-2, and 13-3 depict actual R+ and R-, regardless of time window.

## KEY REVERSALS (KR+, KR-)

An important, but relatively infrequent, form of reversal is called the *key re-versal*. Many chartists and market technicians already know what these signals look like. For those who do not know, the following definitions are provided:

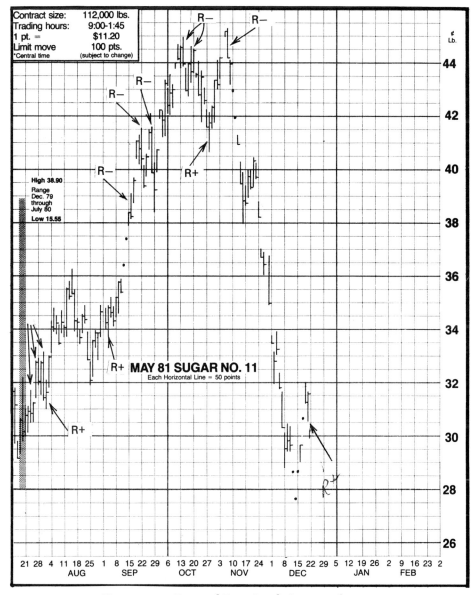

**Figure 13.1  R+ and R- signals in sugar futures.**

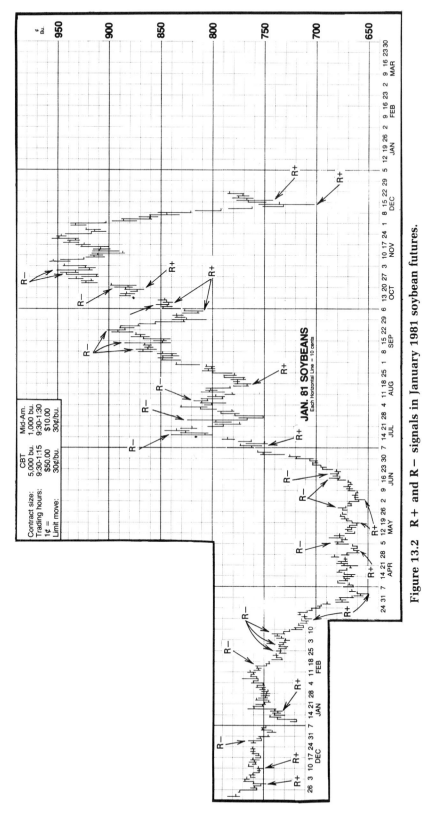

Figure 13.2  R + and R − signals in January 1981 soybean futures.

216

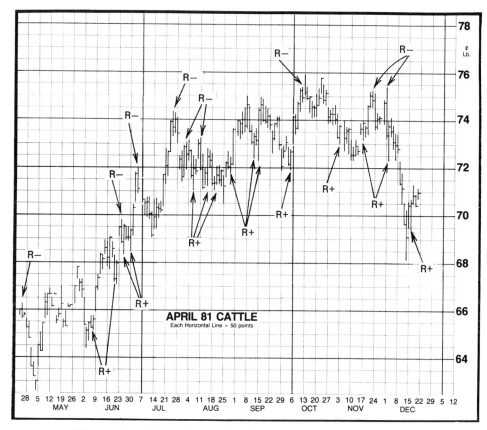

**Figure 13.3   R + and R − signals in April 1981 cattle futures.**

*Key Upside Reversal (KR + )*   Any day (week, month, etc.) during which prices trade above their previous day's high, below their previous day's low, *and* close *higher* than the day before.

*Key Downside Reversal (KR − )*   Any day (week, month, etc.) during which prices trade above their previous day's high, below their previous day's low, *and* close *lower* than the day before.

The key reversal is a special category of reversal signal and is considered much more important at major turning points of the market. Remember that I do *not* use volume and open interest in evaluating reversal signals, whether R +, R −, KR +, or KR −. Figure 13-4 shows a few KREV signals. Notice that many KRs seem to come at points of trend change. Some technicians believe that very high trading volume must accompany a KREV in order for it to be a valid signal. I do not make this stipulation. My only requirement is that a reversal of any kind occur during the appropriate time window, otherwise it is totally ignored.

## WHAT THE REVERSAL SIGNALS MEAN

During the time window, our attention focuses on the reversal signals as confirmation of a cycle turn. At a cycle low, the windows tend to give R + signals,

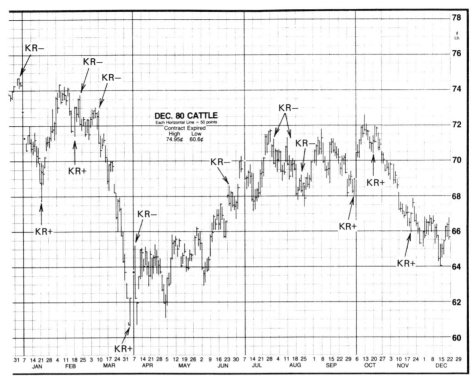

**Figure 13.4   KUREV KR + and KDREV KR − signals in December 1980 cattle futures.**

and at a cycle high, the windows tend to give R− signals. Let's put it another way. You've done your homework in constructing a cycle chart. It looks like Figure 13-5. You have projected a time window and know approximately when to begin looking for signals, which can take the form of either UBO, R+, and/or KR+. Anything that happens outside the time window will be ignored *unless*, of course, it is part of another time window. To determine this you must keep all charts up to date. Because not all tops and bottoms give breakout or reversal signals, we will miss moves. This is part of the game and must be accepted. If you cannot accept the fact that you will miss some moves, you are in for a big disappointment. To help in isolating as many trend changes as possible, I provide additional timing signals later on. Remember, we have taken only the third in a series of steps.

## PUTTING IT ALL TOGETHER

Now that we've examined reversal signals of various types, let's see if we can put the system together as it now stands. The best way to review is to list the step sequence that I have covered to this point. If you skip a step or if you do not understand one, then go back and review the appropriate chapter or section(s).

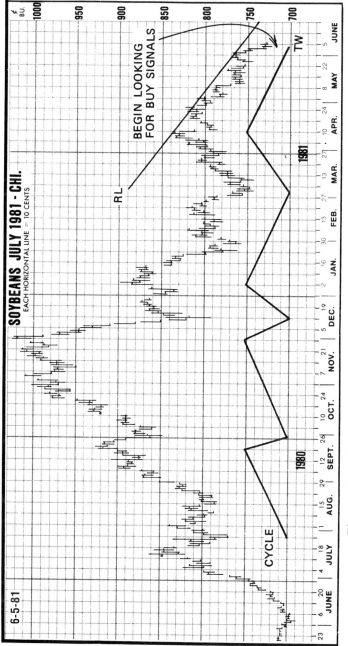

Figure 13.5 Time window, cycles, and reversal signals in soybean futures.

219

1  Maintain closing price chart (daily, weekly, etc.).

2  Determine cycle lengths and mark the various highs and lows accordingly.

3  Project the very next time window within the 15 percent tolerance as indicated.

4  Mark the various support and resistance lines.

5  Mark UBO and DBO signals within the time window.

6  Mark REV signals within the time window.

7  Determine buy and sell points accordingly (see next section).


## MARKET ENTRY

The single most important result of any trading system is to determine when the market should actually be entered and/or when to liquidate positions. The steps we have taken so far can give us some indications of when to buy, sell, or liquidate. Generally, we want to be buyers during a bottom time window when either an R+, KR+ and/or UBO timing signal appears. The more signals at any one point in time (or in close proximity), the more reliable the expected outcome. Figure 13-5 shows precisely what I mean, and pinpoints the exact time that buying might have been done on the basis of this combination of signals. Selling is determined by watching R−, KR−, and DBO signals at the proper time window. Figure 13-6 also shows how these signals are combined during the time window. The exact sell points are also indicated. It is important to remember that *only buy signals* are considered at bottom time windows and *only sell signals* are considered at top time windows. If a sell signal comes at the cycle low time window, then it is ignored. There *are* a few applications of contrary signals that I discuss later on, but for now we will ignore them. All we are looking for at bottom windows are *buy signals,* and all we are looking for at top windows are *sell signals.*

It's important to read a signal correctly, but it's a far more important thing to know exactly how and when to implement the signal. You must carefully and in a precisely detailed manner handle the many mechanical aspects of following signals. To understand these aspects, it is necessary for you to know the rules and vocabulary of placing orders. I assume that you are totally familiar with these methods and procedures. Buying can be done on the close if it is very clear that a UBO has come, which you can do by placing Market on Close (MOC) buy order. This course of action is only taken if there is almost no doubt that there will be a UBO signal. The order is placed as close to market closing as possible (within reason, out of respect to your broker). What if you buy on the close, almost certain that there will be a UBO, and it does not develop? Strange things can happen on the close, and you may have been too anticipatory. One way to avoid this problem is to wait until the next morning to buy. The problem with this is that a market will often "take off" the day after a UBO, and it may cost a bit more to get in. On the other hand, you will be 100 percent certain of the signal. If you have bought on the previous day's close, only to discover that the UBO did not occur, then you must *liquidate your position* immediately the next morning, whether the market opens higher or lower. Do

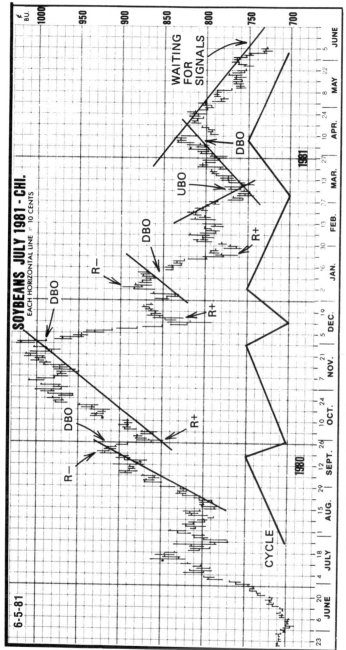

Figure 13.6   Cycles and buy/sell signals (UBO, DBO, R+, R−, KR+, KR−).

221

not be tempted by a higher opening. Get out at once and consider yourself lucky. Figure 13-6 shows some R+, UBO signal buy and sell points.

Selling on a DBO within the time window should be done according to the same rules as in buying on a UBO, only in reverse. Remember that if you buy too early, you will not know for certain whether a signal has actually occurred. As soon as you realize that an error has been made, liquidate the position promptly. This will usually be on the opening the next market day.

Contradictory UBO/DBO signals should not confuse you. Recall that we are following UBO signals only at window bottoms and DBO signals only at window tops. If a UBO comes and we buy, only to get a DBO several days later, this should not concern us *other than in a few special instances explained later.*

Buying on R+ and KR+ signals follows essentially the same method as buying on a UBO. What we're really interested in is the closing price, as long as the previous day's low price has been penetrated (in other words, today's low is lower than yesterday's). Should this be the case, you can buy on the close as long as there is little doubt that the market will indeed close higher, after the previous condition of the penetration of the low has been met. Should you buy on the close, expecting it to be higher, only to find that it is unchanged or lower after the settlement prices have been officially posted, then you must leave the position as soon as possible. All signals must be clear-cut and decisive. Every now and then an unclear signal will be effective, but we are looking for specific and well-defined conditions. If you miss the start of a move after an unclear signal, there will be plenty of opportunities to get in later on.

There are some cyclic traders who use R+ and KR+ signals very effectively during the day. Assume, for example, that we have an 11 to 16 day cycle in wheat. Assume also that we have projected a time window. Prices could bottom out at any time during the window. The astute trader will begin watching prices closely during the day, beginning with the first day of the time window and will trade the R+ and KR+ signals only. Before the market opens he will make note of yesterday's high, low, and closing price for the contract he is following. As soon as the low has been penetrated (i.e., today's low is lower than day before), he will place buy stop orders above yesterday's closing price. As soon as the market trades higher on the day and hits his price, he will be stopped into a position on what could be an R+ or KR+ signal during the proper cycle window. If, by the end of the day, the market fails to fulfill the condition for a REV signal (i.e., having a higher close), he will liquidate the position and follow the same method next day. The trader is, in effect, targeting the precise time of the cycle turn, down to the very minute, in some cases. Such a method takes total discipline, time, and close attention to the market. Many small losses may be taken in awaiting a turn, but when the turn comes, profits will typically be large and timing must be exact. This pivotal method has many other advantages and can be very profitable as a short term, or scalping, vehicle within the appropriate time window. More on this method later on.

If you do not buy into the market during the closing minutes of a UREV day, then you must follow the signal the next day on the opening. Frequently the market will "gap" higher the next day, and you may be tempted to wait for a pullback, or you may be afraid to buy. This is totally absurd reasoning. After all, what better indication of a bottom or trend change is there than strength? It is, or should always be, more comfortable to buy into strength than into weakness. If you fail to follow the signal as soon as you possibly can, then you must not act again until the next signal comes. To "chase" a market only results in losses and confusion. The same rules apply to buying on a KR+. More often than not, KR+s are rather obvious by the close of trading. It is not unusual to see a KR+ occur after several days of limit down trading with the close being up at limit the day of the KR+. In such an instance, buying near or at the close is very effective, particularly if the market gapped at limit up the next day and remained there.

Selling short on R− and KR− signals follows the same basic rules as buying on RT and KRT signals, only in reverse. There are many traders who are afraid to sell a market short. There is some justification for this fear because so-called "short squeeze" situations can be quite dramatic. The fact remains, however, that markets tend to decline much faster than they move up. You might think of this as akin to moving with, or pushing against, the forces of gravity. It takes considerable time and effort to climb a mountain. Falling from a height requires only the act of jumping, provided you do not apply energy to slow down. Markets often drop like the proverbial "lead balloon," and the opportunity for substantial profit over a short period of time always exists, particularly in markets that have moved up for a long time. In summary, entry on the short side when R− and KR− signals appear is often more critical. You must be there promptly, or miss much of the move because of the tendency of prices to gap down with successive limit-down moves. An example of how this happens is the behavior of silver prices during 1980. See in Figure 13-7 how quickly prices dropped, and without much opportunity to get short once the top signal came!

## COMBINED SIGNALS AND WHAT TO DO ABOUT THEM

Let's say you had both an R+, KR+, and two successive UBO signals within a short period of time, all within the time window. UBO and R+ signals often come on the same day. In fact, many REV and breakout signals (as well as a number of other signals to be discussed later) come on the same day. Your response in such a case should be very clear. If you've been following this discussion, if you understand the methods and techniques discussed so far, you'll know that this type of a situation should prove very effective. This is usually the time to become very aggressive in taking positions. This is often the time to buy more than usual, and this is also the best time to expect reliable moves that are larger than customary.

## COMBINED WINDOWS AND COMBINED SIGNALS

By now the wheels are really starting to turn as you begin to see the light at the end of the tunnel. In fact, you should have realized by now that if what I say is valid, the light has become very bright—in fact, overpowering. "What if many different cycles for a given market come together at the same time window, and you get a number of signals—weekly, daily, and so on?" This is the time to fasten your seat belt and prepare for the ride. This may also be the time to open several additional bank accounts to accommodate the potential

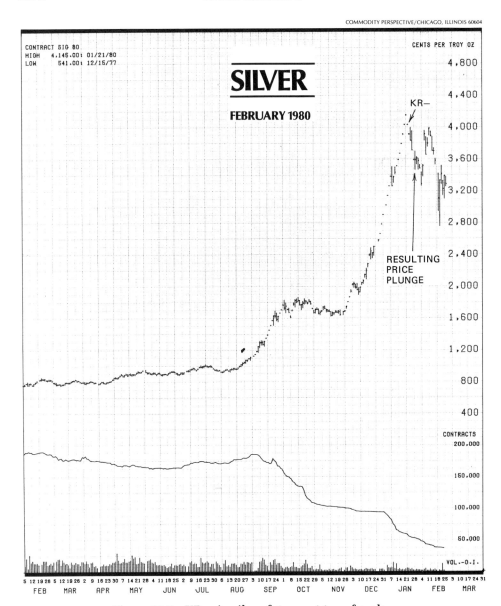

**Figure 13.7　KR − in silver futures at top of cycle.**

profit. Seriously, however, the more cycle and signal information you have within the same time frame, the more you can expect in terms of reliability and profit. The previous discussion of cycle synchronization is relevant in this respect and further attests to the validity of cyclic events.

## A FEW MECHANICAL DETAILS

Now it's time to take a step back, review what has been discussed, and dispense with a few technical matters. Where do we stand? First, we should know how to find, project, measure, and time the cyclic turns. We should be familiar with charting techniques, definitions of the various time window concepts, and the timing signals that are a symbiotic part of these windows. Everything should be perfectly clear as to method and concept, but let's not get too far from the actual mechanics. If you are keeping a chart based on closings, as I suggest, then you are not plotting the weekly or daily highs and lows. If this is the case, then how do you know when they've come, and how can you keep track of them? For this purpose I advise several methods. You can keep two sets of charts if you wish. On one chart you can plot closing prices and cycles, support and resistance lines, UBO and DBO. On the daily (or weekly) charts for high and low closes, you can plot the same cycles and windows, as well as REV signals. This requires too much work, in my opinion. I advise that you simply keep a written record for each market that shows highs, lows, closes, signals, and your own comments, in addition to the chart of closing prices that contains the signals.

We are following several signals, many cycles, and at least three levels of cyclic period, so organization is vital. At any time you should be totally familiar with what is expected in a given market. After a while, you will have most of the information in memory, but at first it must be available in black and white. In fact, it should always be available in written form. Provided your chartwork is clear and precise, you can keep all signals on a high, low, close chart.

## EXCEPTIONS TO THE RULE—SPECIAL CASES

I don't like exceptions to rules. I do not believe that the exception, as they say, makes the rule. It is always preferable to make a rule, follow it, and define it without exception. It is possible to do so with the rules I have given you. If you can allow for just a few minor exceptions or special cases, however, you may save some grief and money. To avoid confusing the issue I deal with exceptions as they arise. For now assume that there are no special cases, and do not bend the rules or accept as valid any signal that is questionable in any way.

## WHERE DO WE GO NOW?

Chapter 14 discusses another set of timing indicators designed to make your determination of market entry even more accurate and specific. Remember that I have said very little about the all-important subject of money management and virtually nothing about stop losses or techniques for limiting losses and defining risk. This is why the system presented so far is *incomplete* and should not be used in its present form. Keep an open mind until all the aspects of cycle trading have been presented. Without the added features that have not yet been discussed, there is no system. It is important to remember that many traders do not follow a system. Although they believe that they are disciplined in their approach, they are almost totally without organization or structure. If you operate this way, or if you are not organized in your approach to cyclic trading, then the techniques will not do you any good. Nor, for that matter, will any other system.

# CHAPTER FOURTEEN

# Timing Signals III

To fully appreciate and internalize the value of timing signals, it is a good idea to discuss the causes of market behavior. A signal, after all, is a roundabout way of determining public sentiment. Because people trade the market and because emotions rule people, signals are a way of evaluating the underlying emotions of the people who trade the market. Most of the time there is a reasonable balance between fact and fantasy, insanity and clearheadedness, fear and greed, winners and losers. In other words, the market is relatively stable. Bullishness and buying overpower selling pressures and negative sentiment, and the market starts an uptrend as a result. At times bearish sentiment prevails, rallies are short-lived, and trends are lower. At certain times, however, emotional response to economic realities, or perceived economic realities, is overbearing, affecting a majority of traders and resulting in actions that are fairly predictable. Such things as selling panics and buying climaxes are an expression of trader sentiment. If the majority of traders sell, the result is a sharp price drop. At such times the professional, organized, and rational traders will often be buyers. Their combined buying power can overpower the total selling of a panicked public, prices will have a sharp spike down and an almost immediate reversal up. Such action seems to come most frequently during cycle time windows and in response to news. Hence, the signals we are following are indicators of emotion and poor judgment. I do not wish to get too clinical about this explanation. More on the subject can be found in my earlier book, *The Investor's Quotient* (1980). The reversal up, for example, can easily be understood as an emotional reaction. The market has been moving lower, many traders are still long, having overstayed their position as usual, and the bad news the market has been anticipating finally becomes public knowledge. "Prices will most likely decline further, and we've held on too long" reasons the public. Massive selling begins. The previous day's or week's lows are penetrated as the avalanche of selling begins. Professional traders, floor traders, and commercial traders realize that there is a disproportionate move and begin buying. Prices are at levels that are too low in terms of economic reality. The market begins to turn, and because selling pressure has been exhausted, there is nothing for prices to do but rise. They end by closing higher on the day. An R+ or KR+ has occurred. A bottom has been seen!

Similarly, the close on high (COH) and close on low (COL) signals are measures of emotion and liquidation at critical points. Volume *can* be useful at such times, but it may also lead you astray too often. The COH and COL timing signals defined and discussed in this chapter may be used in conjunction with cycle windows, as are all signals discussed earlier. Let's take a look at the operational definition of these indicators.

For any given day (week, month, etc.):

*Close on High (COH)*    A closing price that is no more than 10 percent below the daily high price.

*Close on Low (COL)*    A closing price that is no less than 10 percent above the daily low price.

Figure 14-1 shows exactly what is meant by a COL or a COH. Let's take a look at the mathematics of figuring out the 10 percent variance. Let's say that the June live cattle contract had the following price range on a certain day:

|      |       |
|------|-------|
| High | 45.70 |
| Close | 45.65 |
| Low  | 44.25 |

You can see, simply by observation, that the close price is almost equal to the high price. If you take 10 percent of the daily price range, you get 14.5 points. Hence, if the close price is more than 14.5 points below the high price, the condition for a COH will *not* have been met. In other words, a close below 45.555 would *not* be acceptable, but a close at 45.56 (rounded off) would constitute a COH.

Close on low, or COL, is calculated in reverse. Simply compute the daily price range. Take 10 percent of the daily price range. Add it to the day's low, and arrive at your limit figure for COL. Figure 14-1 shows a few examples of COL signals.

What we are looking for in defining COH and COL signals is an emotional market response that results in liquidation and subsequent accumulation. The wider the price range, the more valid a COH or COL signal will be. In and of themselves, COH and COL signals do not have much meaning. There are a few ways in which they can be used individually for short term trading, stops, and the like, but COH and COL should be used together to form timing signals. The first condition of COH and COL is called *THE HIGH TO LOW CLOSE*, defined as follows:

*High to Low Close Signal (HLC)*    If a market gives a COH one day and a COL on the very next trading day, then an HLC signal has occurred.

*Low to High Close Signal (LHC)*    If a market gives a COL signal one day and a COH signal the next trading day, then an LHC signal has occurred.

Figure 14-2 shows some HLC and LHC signals. Bear in mind that sometimes we can get an HLC or LHC signal at the same time as an REV signal, which is a very significant combination. Notice that the LCH or HLC signal has absolutely nothing to do with penetrations of previous day high or low. See Figure 14-3 for visual representation of LHC and HLC signals.

## HOW DO WE USE THESE NEW SIGNALS?

Very simple. As you have probably guessed by now, the LHC is used at cycle low windows and the HLC at cycle high windows. The rationale here is also quite elementary (if you wish an explanation). Continuing with our earlier discussion of emotion and prices, we can take one more step. Assume that

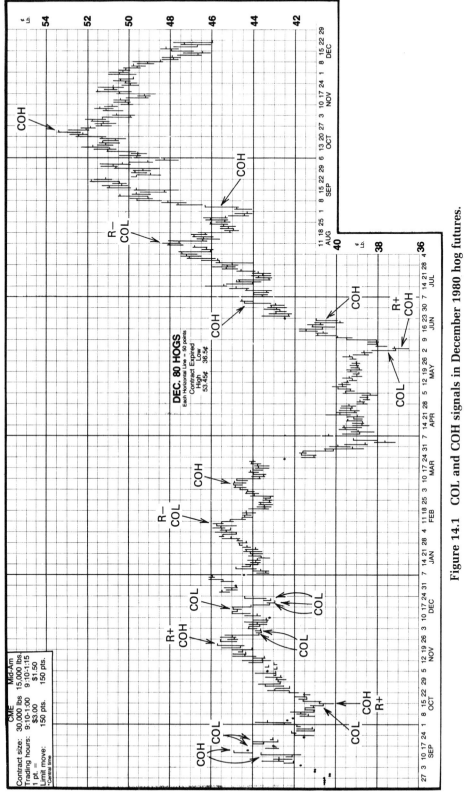

Figure 14.1 COL and COH signals in December 1980 hog futures.

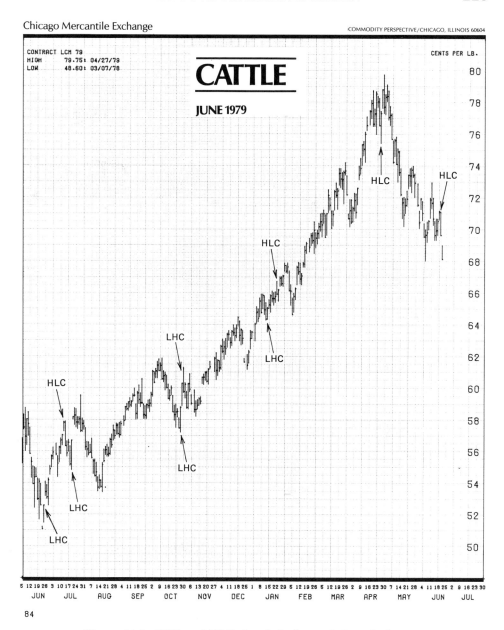

**Figure 14.2   LHC and HLC signals in June 1979 cattle futures.**

during a downtrend the market increases in bearish momentum to the point of steep downside acceleration. Assume that prices are exceptionally weak one day (or week) during the bottom window, and a limit-down move develops. The public has panicked, and a liquidation phase begins. By the end of the trading session there is more offered for sale than there are buyers. Overnight a change occurs. Prices open higher and give a COH signal as professionals step

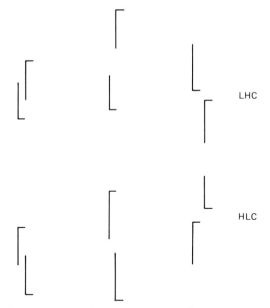

**Figure 14.3   A few more LHC and HLC signals.**

in and absorb as much selling as the public has to offer. The price that day never falls below the previous day's low (although it can). There has been *no reversal*, but a valid emotional change has most likely taken place *at the right time*. There *could* be an R+ the same day. Hence, we'd have a double signal that would bear considerably more weight. Figure 14-4 shows a few of these double signals (R+ and LHC and/or R− and HLC).

### BUYING ON LHC SIGNAL

To execute this signal it is necessary to follow many of the same methods as described for other BUY signals. The close, however, is more critical since it must not fall outside of the given 10 percent of daily range tolerance. It is often best to wait for all the facts before taking action. This means making the purchase next day on the open, or shortly thereafter.

### SELLING ON HLC SIGNAL

The opposite method is followed in this case and the same general rules apply as for other sell signals.

### THE IMPORTANCE OF CLOSING PRICES

I reiterate the importance of knowing the closing price and of evaluating signals *only on that basis*. It is often tempting to act prematurely, but you should avoid this temptation in all well-structured and disciplined programs. Unless you are certain about the closing price, put off action until the next day. If you have clearly erred in anticipating a signal, then the best time to correct the error is *as soon as possible*. The value of having many different signals is clear. One,

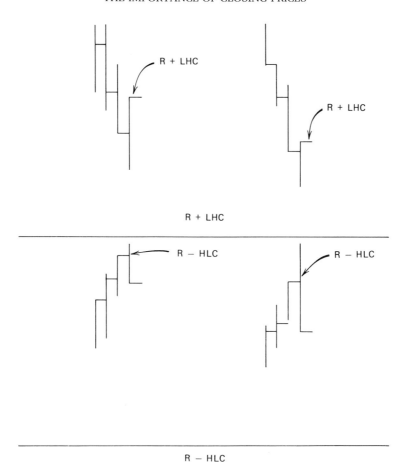

**Figure 14.4   R + LHC and R − HLC combination signals.**

all, or several will occur within the time window, but virtually all, according to my cyclic method, depend on the closing price. Because it is not possible to know the closing price until the close has come, it is always best to wait. If you are in very close touch with the market and if you can get prompt order executions on the close, then you can take your chances, so long as you remember that errors must be undone immediately (if not sooner). Experienced traders can hold on to positions, offsetting them by "legging" into a spread. This requires establishing an opposite position which may be closed out once the cycle turns.

# CHAPTER FIFTEEN

# Timing Signals IV

In the previous chapter I discussed several timing signals used during the time window to confirm a cyclic turn. More often than not, the R+, R−, HLC, and LHC signals will be sufficient for timing your market entry. On occasion, however, it is best to use another important signal that is based entirely on the closing price relationship of 3 time units (i.e., days or weeks).

As in the case of previous signals I have discussed, the three-unit signals are used only within the proper time window. In essence, then, we now have a total of four powerful timing signals to confirm changes in a cyclic trend. To review, they are R+ or R−, UBO or DBO, and 3H+ or 3L−.

## THE BASIC SIGNAL

The 3H+, 3L− signals are based exclusively on the closing prices for the past 3 days or 3 weeks. When working with daily charts, you will observe the relationship between today's closing price and the closing price of the previous three trading sessions (regardless of weekends or holidays). When using weekly data, you will use the same signal, but you will do so on the basis of weekly closing prices for the past 3 weeks as compared to the current weekly close.

## DEFINITIONS

A 3H+ signal is used to determine a cyclic upmove. Hence, it is used at a time window low. The most recent 3 days' or 3 weeks' closing prices are compared to the current close. If the current close (fourth day) is higher than the highest close of the last three days (or weeks), then a signal to buy has been given. Remember that the signal must occur within the proper time window! When the signal is diagrammed, it appears as in Figure 15-1.

The 3L− signal is used to determine a cyclic downmove. Hence, it is used at a time window high. The most recent 3 days' or 3 weeks' closing prices are compared to the current close. If the current close is lower than the lowest of the last three closes, then a signal to sell has been made. Graphically, this signal appears as in Figure 15-2. If there is no signal on the day (or week) after the 3 day period you have under observation, then you drop the oldest day from the configuration and add the current day to your 3 unit period. See Figure 15-2 for a sample of what I mean.

Remember that the 3H+ and 3L− signals do *not* depend in any way, shape, or form on the daily or weekly high but, rather, on the *closing* high of the 3 unit time span. All we are looking at is the closing price. Figures 15-3, 15-4, 15-5, and 15-6 are actual price charts that show the 3H+ and 3H− signals.

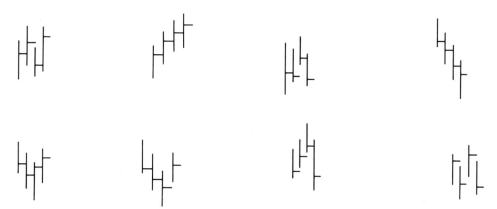

Figure 15.1    Some 3H+ signals.           Figure 15.2    Some 3L− signals.

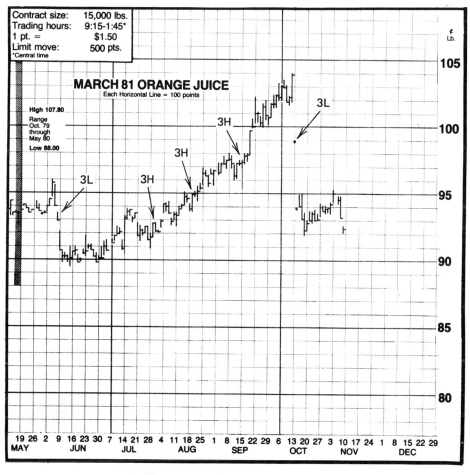

Figure 15.3    Some 3H, 3L signals.

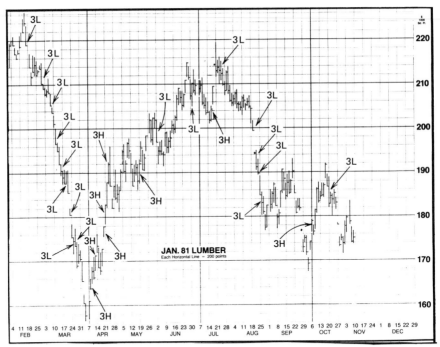

**Figure 15.4  Some 3H, 3L signals.**

**Figure 15.5  Some 3H, 3L signals.**

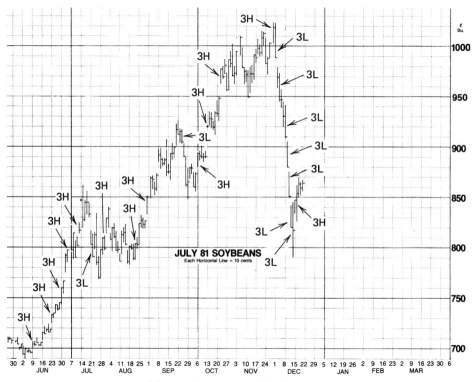

Figure 15.6    Some 3H, 3L signals.

# CHAPTER SIXTEEN

# The Possibility Of Combined Signals

Inasmuch as we now have four specific ways of timing market entry at a cyclic trend change, it is entirely possible that several signals will occur at one time. Of course, the more signals there are during any time window, the better. Turns that are especially valid tend to give many different timing signals, but remember that only one signal is necessary for market entry during the time window. At no other time are these signals used (other than several exceptions to be discussed).

Let's examine how the combination of signals might look on a price chart. Figure 16-1 shows the combination of several signals. Remember that this type of signal can take a number of different forms, but ultimately the concept remains the same. The combined R+ and LHC signal is a powerful team that often leaves gaps on the chart, particularly when it occurs on a weekly or monthly basis. As always, the specific stop loss point, discussed in Chapter 17, applies. Figure 16-2 shows a single combination of R+ and LHC signals and what generally transpires subsequent to their formation at a time window in a cyclic low.

The opposite of a combined R+LHC close signal is, of course, the R−HLC signal—in other words, a time window during which the market not only reverses down but during which prices also close on their high first and on their low next. Figure 16-3 shows the R−HLC signal. Figure 16-4 shows what can happen after this powerful combination occurs at a time window in a cyclic top.

Because there are four basic signals, it is quite possible for all to occur during one time window. In some instances, although rare, we will get a combined R+LHC−3H+ signal. I believe that this combination is even more powerful than the one previously discussed. It can take several forms, but the basic form is always the same. A combined R+LHC−3H+ signal is one during which we not only close on the high of the given time unit, after a previous close on low (COL); we also reverse up and close above the highest closing price of the last three time units (days, weeks, or months). In practice, this is not a common event. Figure 16-5 shows what a triple buy signal looks like.

Similarly, the combination of three signals at a time window top is also quite powerful. This signal hybrid is a R−HLC−3L− and looks like those shown in Figure 16-6. The frequency of such a combination is not high, but its reliability when it does occur is good. Figure 16-6 shows what can result after the triple

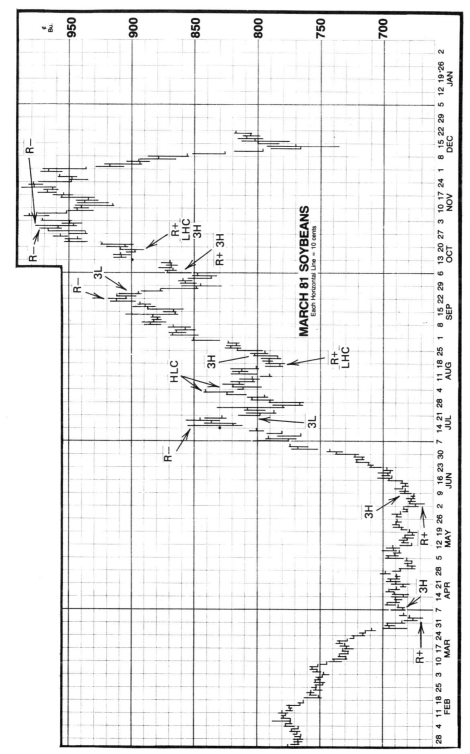

Figure 16.1   Combined signals.

237

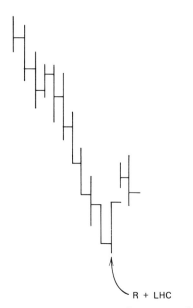

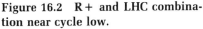

**Figure 16.2   R+ and LHC combina-
tion near cycle low.**

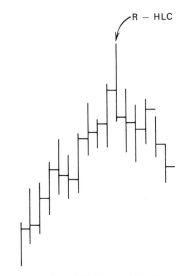

**Figure 16.3   R− HLC combination-
signals near cycle high.**

combination occurs at a time window high. In all cases remember when trading
these combined signals that the stop loss or risk method, examined in Chapter
17, must be rigorously implemented. Figure 16-7 shows an actual R − HLC3L − .

By now you are probably wondering about the possibility of a quadruple
timing signal. On the buy, or lows, this signal is a combined R + LHC−3H−UBO.
In practice, it is not as rare as one might imagine. It appears graphically as
shown in Figure 16-8. The chart in Figure 16-9 shows what can transpire after
this signal develops.

It is possible to get the quadruple signal at tops as well. It is a combined
R − HLC−3L−DBO, and it looks like the example given in Figure 16-10. It is
not nearly as uncommon as you may think, and it does carry with it a fairly
high degree of reliability. An actual price chart depicting this combination is
shown in Figure 16-11. If you use the combined signals in combination with
another trend-following method (e.g., moving average), then they should be
equally valid. They may, however, come a bit later than if you were using a
cycle window.

Combinations of signals will quite often appear at highs and lows that have
historical significance. Many major market tops and bottoms in the past 15
years have been classic examples of combined signals. I have provided you
with an illustrative sampling of several such highs and lows in Figures 16-12
through 16-14. Many of these tops and bottoms came at important seasonal and
cyclic turning points.

## USING COMBINED SIGNALS WITH SEASONALS

In an earlier section I discussed the use of seasonal trading expectations and
patterns along with timing signals. I demonstrated a method by which you can

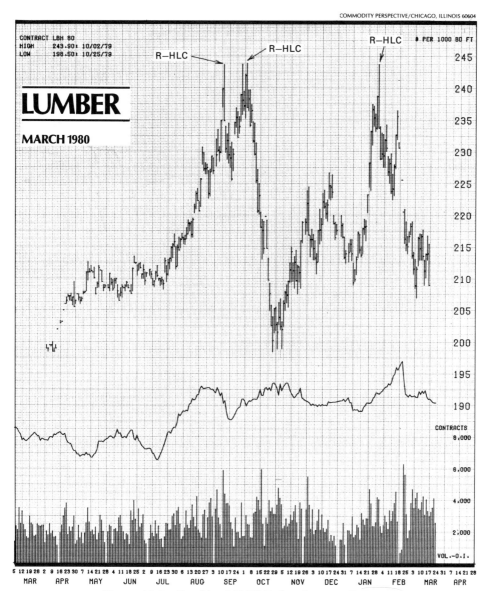

**Figure 16.4   Combined R-HLC signals at cyclic tops.**

combine seasonal reliability of trend and/or weekly probability with timing in order to maximize the potential for profit. When you use the combination of signals, your seasonal timing may be enhanced significantly. Remember one important point, however. Combined signals may frequently occur on a daily rather than a weekly basis. Here's what I mean. Assume that you are waiting for the seasonal upturn in wheat futures. You are trading the December contract. The seasonal futures composite chart for this contract is shown in Figure 16-15. Assume that you are waiting to buy during the optimum low week which, according to my composite chart, is week No. 34. This means that a

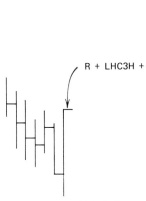

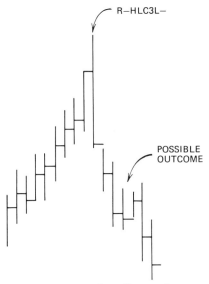

Figure 16.5  Triple buy signal combination R + LHC 3H +.

Figure 16.6  Triple sell signal combination R − HLC 3L −.

low might come in either week No. 33 or 34 (i.e., the number of weeks prior to contract expiration). It may be possible to isolate weekly timing signals from weekly charts, or it may be possible to isolate the precise day of the turn by examining and following daily charts and signals. If we can isolate our timing to the very day of the seasonal turn, we may take considerably less risk. An example of this can be seen in Figure 16-16. The 1980 December Chicago wheat delivery made its seasonal low on April 21, 1980. We knew from our studies that this was indeed the time window of a seasonal low. On precisely that day, the market flashed an R+ signal, thus indicating the high probability that a seasonal low had been seen. On even closer examination, you can see that the market also gave a UBO (short term) signal.

In late March a daily R+ signal alone was flashed. Aside from coming just a bit too early in the seasonal, this signal was a single one and, as you can see, not valid. Notice that a double signal would have been flashed in this case had the close been just a bit closer to the daily high on day No. 1. The first reason, then, for not having taken buy action on signal No. 1 was that it came too early in the seasonal. If you had been keeping weekly price charts, then the action of the week beginning March 31, 1980 would have indeed been a weekly R+ signal (see weekly chart Figure 16-17). Assuming that you had taken action to buy, your stop loss would be under the low of the week (stops are discussed in Chapter 17), and several weeks later you would have taken a loss. The very next week, however, another signal to buy occurred, and had it been followed according to the rules a profit would have resulted.

The important thing to remember is this: During the time frame of a seasonal low, there is ordinarily a preponderance of buy signals, and they are frequently

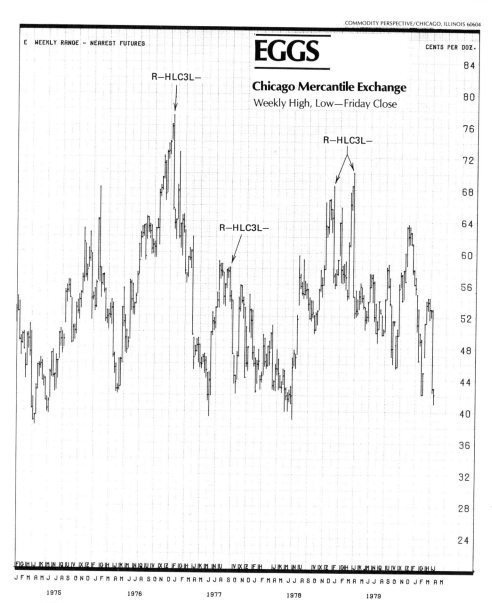

COMMODITY PERSPECTIVE/CHICAGO, ILLINOIS 60604

**Figure 16.7   R − HLC 3L − combination sell signals in weekly egg chart.**

combined signals. During the ideal time of a seasonal high, there is ordinarily a preponderance of sell signals, which may be individual or combined. Notice the many buy signals in December 1980 wheat at or about the seasonal low time that have been marked accordingly in Figure 16-16 (using our standard abbreviations).

To use the cyclic technique best, it is especially important to study signals, their various combinations, and their consequences. This alone will permit you

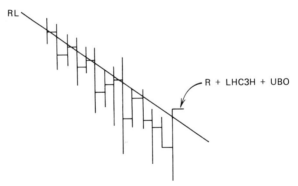

**Figure 16.8  Quadruple buy signal R + LHC 3H + UBO.**

to properly and profitably execute timing decisions, which are, after all, the very essence of commodity trading. Take some charts and spend time with them until you have trained your eye to pick out the signals, both individually and in combination. Remember that the more signals you get at one time, or within a very limited period of time, the more probable is the market move. The situation is much like one that confronts a medical doctor in his attempt to diagnose a patient. The more symptoms he recognizes, the more likely he is to reach a correct diagnosis.

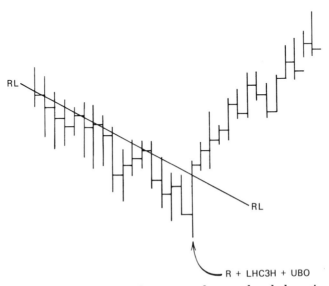

**Figure 16.9  Hypothetical upmove after quadruple buy signal.**

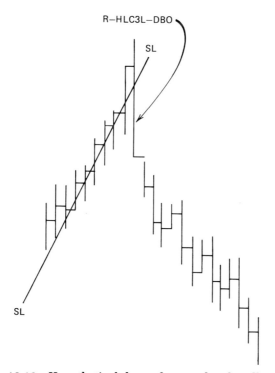

**Figure 16.10   Hypothetical drop after quadruple sell signal.**

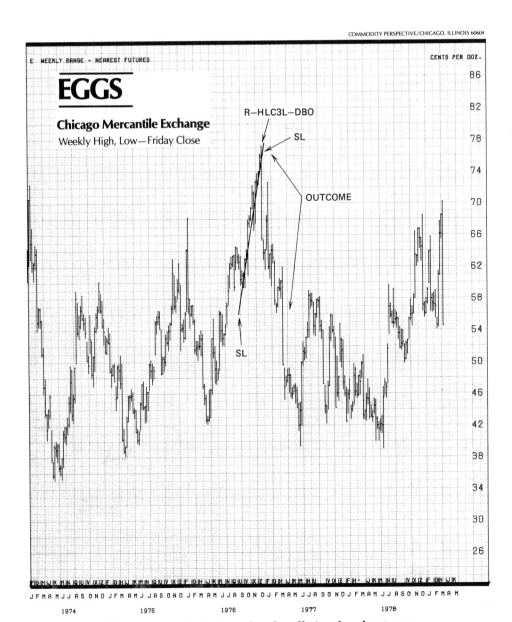

**Figure 16.11  Actual quadruple sell signal and outcome.**

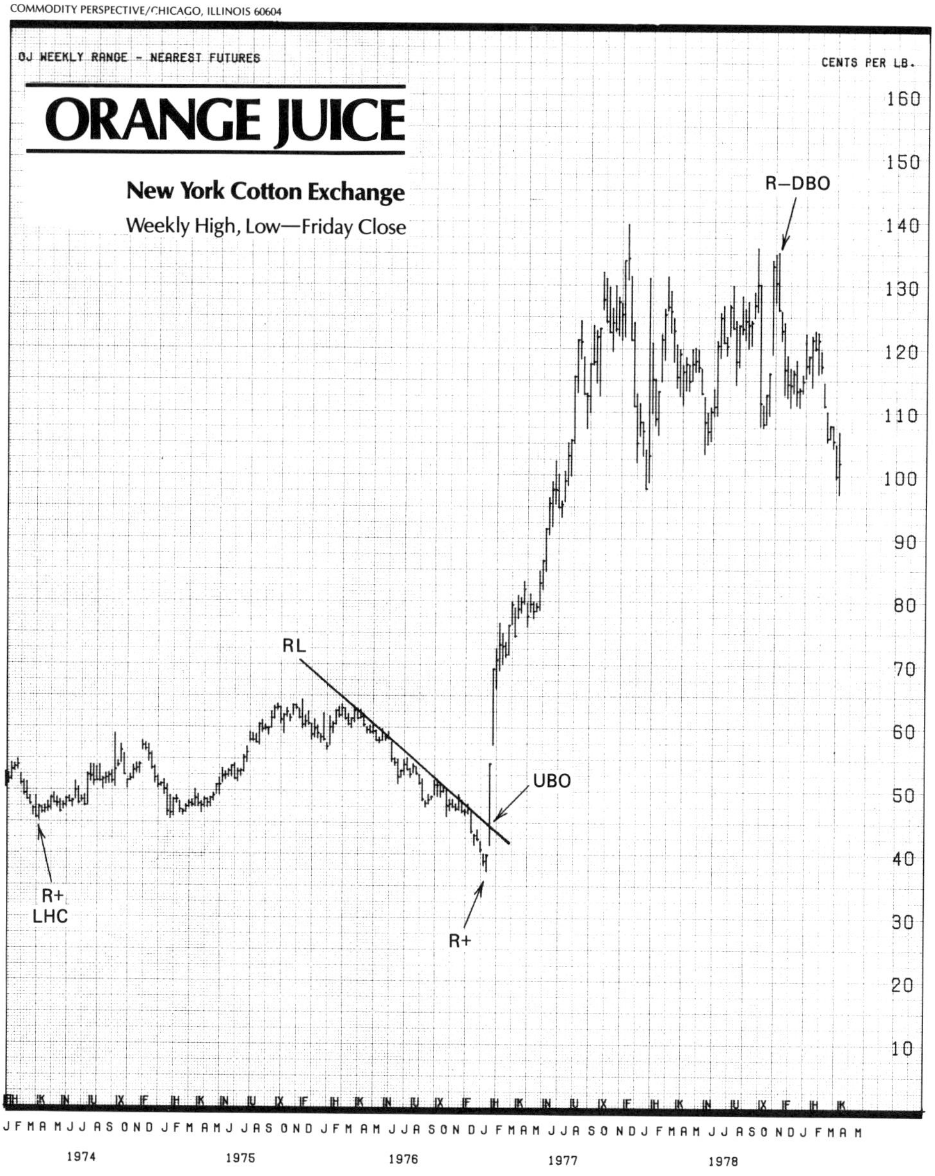

OJ WEEKLY RANGE - NEAREST FUTURES                                                    CENTS PER LB.

# ORANGE JUICE

### New York Cotton Exchange
Weekly High, Low—Friday Close

160

150

R–DBO
140

130

120

110

100

90

80

RL
70

60

UBO
50

40

R+
LHC
30

R+
20

10

J F M A M J J A S O N D J F M A M J J A S O N D J F M A M J J A S O N D J F M A M J J A S O N D J F M A M J J A S O N D J F M A M

1974          1975          1976          1977          1978

**Figure 16.12  Combined signals at major tops and bottoms in orange juice futures.**

245

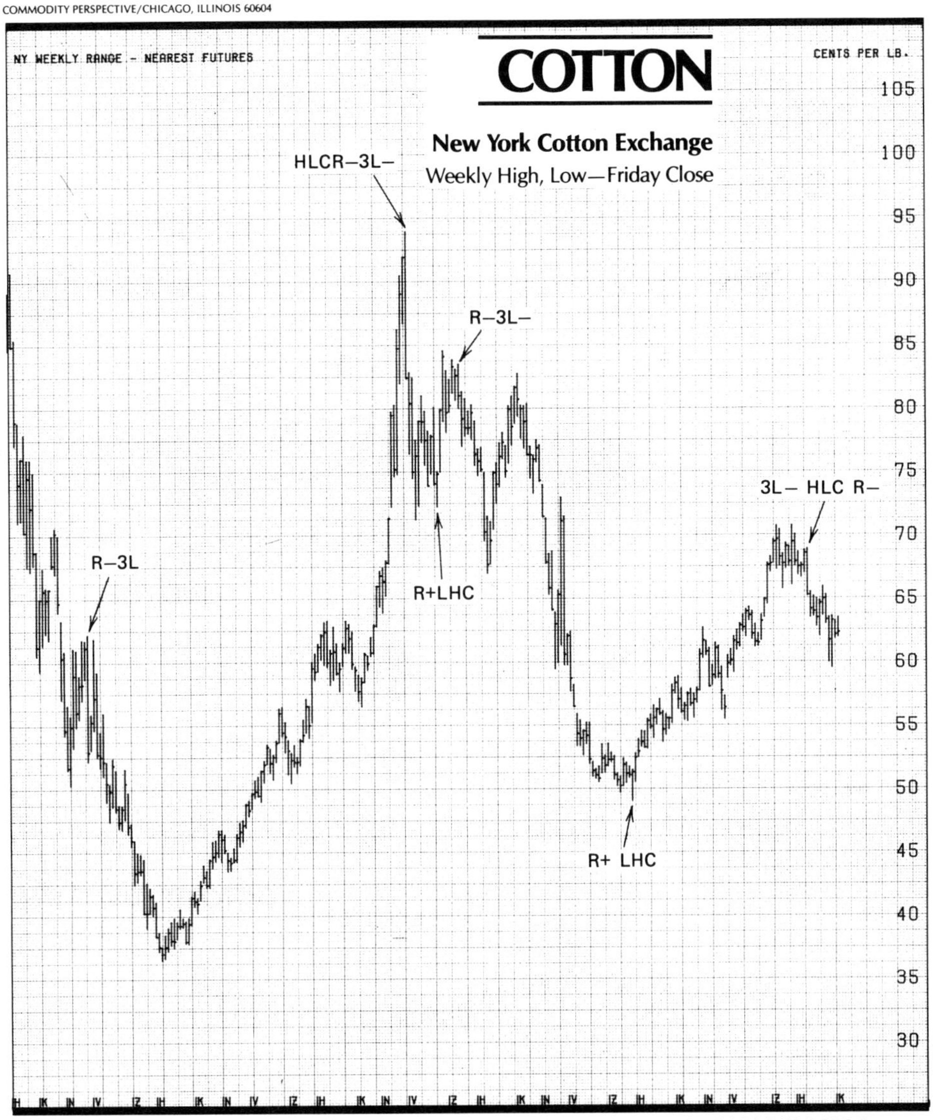

Figure 16.13  Combined signals at major tops and bottoms in cotton futures.

246

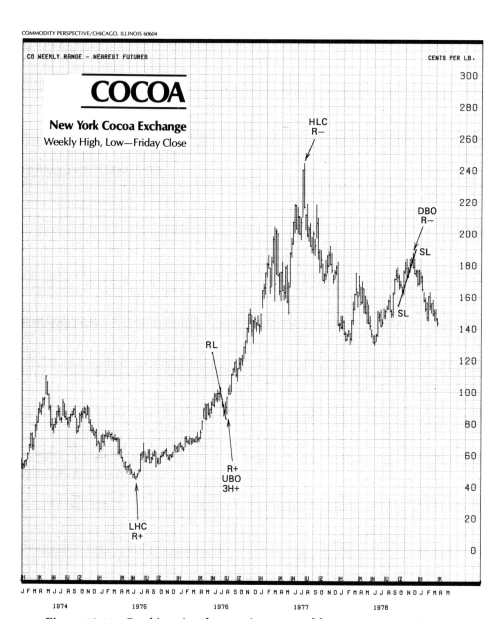

CO WEEKLY RANGE - NEAREST FUTURES                                    CENTS PER LB.

# COCOA

**New York Cocoa Exchange**

Weekly High, Low—Friday Close

HLC
R—

DBO
R—

SL

SL

SL

RL

R+
UBO
3H+

LHC
R+

300
280
260
240
220
200
180
160
140
120
100
80
60
40
20
0

J F M A M J J A S O N D J F M A M J J A S O N D J F M A M J J A S O N D J F M A M J J A S O N D J F M A M J J A S O N D J F M A M

1974        1975        1976        1977        1978

**Figure 16.14  Combine signals at major tops and bottoms in cocoa futures.**

247

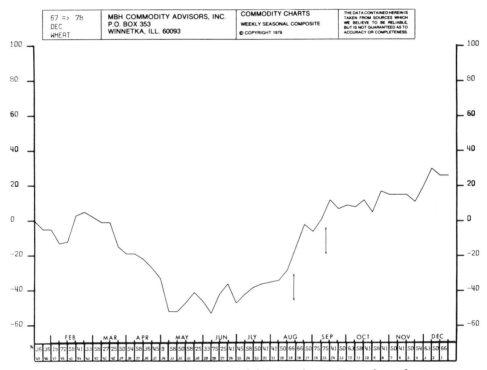

Figure 16.15    Composite seasonal futures chart—December wheat.

248

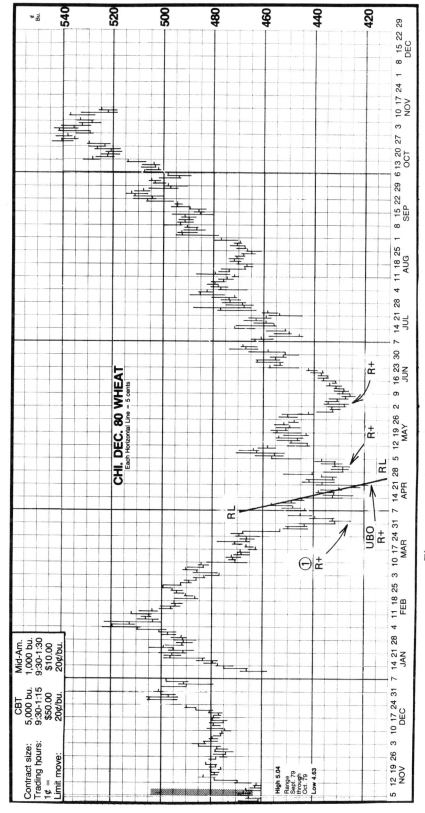

Figure 16.16    Seasonal signals in December 1980 wheat.

249

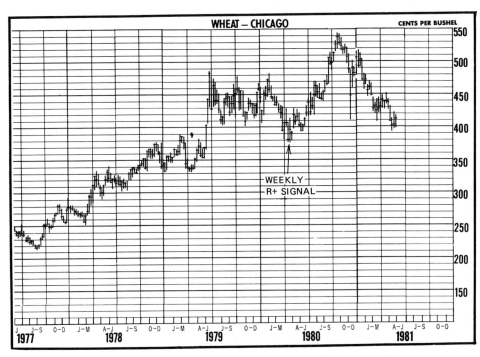

Figure 16.17   Weekly wheat chart R + signal at seasonal low.

# CHAPTER SEVENTEEN

# Stop Losses—
# Knowing When You Have
# Been Wrong

## THE VALUE OF STOP LOSSES

There are essentially three aspects of successful trading. I have covered the first two, *expectation* and *timing*, in earlier chapters. Cyclic expectation allows you to have a window on time. During the appropriate time window, it is imperative to watch for the development of proper timing signals. The timing signals are then followed accordingly in order to establish a position (long or short). Associated with expectation and timing is a third important aspect of trading—*money management*. There are many aspects of money management, but the single most specific and important one is *capital preservation*, which is normally accomplished through the use of a loss-limiting method. At the moment a timing signal occurs, the cyclic trading method also lets you know precisely how much you will risk and at what price you will need to exit your position should it move contrary to expectation.

The use of loss-limiting techniques is especially important in commodity trading because of the relatively low margin requirements. In stock trading, where margins run about 50 to 75 percent, the amount of money put up for each transaction is far greater than the 1 to 3 percent put up as margin for most commodity trades. The small amount of margin in futures trading can be gone within a matter of minutes should a market move contrary to expectation. The trader will then be called for more margin money. This means, of course, that more than your original capital can be lost when you trade the futures market. For those traders with a systematic and well-defined plan of action, such leverage can be extremely beneficial. For most traders, however, it acts as a curse. It is, therefore, necessary to limit your loss in commodity trading much earlier than you might limit a loss in trading stocks or bonds. For example, if the cost of a given futures contract is 5000 bushels at $3.00 per bushel, there is a total value of $15,000, for which perhaps $1000 might be put up as margin. Compare this to 1500 shares of a $10 stock on which the margin is about $7500. The illusion created by a small margin must be counteracted by a rigid and effective loss-limiting policy. I am quite sure that all experienced commodity traders will understand exactly what I am saying. If you do not, or if you are new to this field of speculation, then make it your first order of business to acquaint yourself with the risks of commodity trading.

Each of the timing signals discussed in previous chapters carries with it its own specific degree of risk, or stop. The stop loss is the price beyond which the position must be closed out in order to preserve capital and protect the integrity of the cyclic system. It is a predetermined point that should be dutifully followed when the time comes. Because the cyclic method, or any other trading method I have seen, is not always right about selecting a trade, it is also necessary to limit loss in order to preserve capital for the next signal or signals. I discuss the stop point for each signal along with illustrations in each case in the pages that follow. The stop points are valid for daily, weekly, or monthly signals, whichever you happen to be trading. In other words, if I refer to a stop as being "under the low of the week," this same reasoning applied to daily charts would read "under the low of the day." This is a very important point, one which tends to confuse some students. More on this later.

## LOSS LIMITING WITH REVERSAL SIGNALS

The reversal signals, as you will recall, are as follows:

*Reversal Up (R+)*   Any time unit during which prices fall below the low of the previous time unit but close higher.

*Reversal Down (R−)*   Any time unit during which prices rise above the high of the previous time unit but close lower.

The stop loss in the case of R+ would be a close below the low of the time unit during which the signal was given. Hence, if the R+ signal came at the low window of a short term cycle, one which is being followed with daily price charts, the stop would be a daily close below the low of the day the signal was given. The details of executing stop losses is discussed later. You may elect to place a "close only" stop loss (if such orders are accepted by the exchange or floor trader), or you can act on the close.

The stop loss for a reversal down (R−) signal would be a close above the high of the time unit during which the signal was given. If, for example, you are using a weekly chart and prices rise above the stop loss point during the week, this would *not* be a valid penetration of the stop. You must wait until the end of the time unit (in this case, the end of the week) before the stop can be triggered. Although prices may move above the stop during the week, they may very well pull back and close well below the stop on the last trading day of the week. This is a very important point for those who are trading on an intermediate term basis.

You can see immediately that the long term trader takes much more risk on any one position than the short term trader. The advantage is that he also tends to have considerably more profit, substantially less commission, and a much lower time input than the short term trader who must keep daily charts and act on daily signals. In any type of system there is always a tradeoff between risk and reward. The larger the reward you are seeking, the more risk you may have to take at certain critical times. Another thing to remember is that the signals, as I have pointed out many times before, must occur within the time window. You can then trigger the stop loss once the time window has passed.

Say, for example, you put on a trade within the time window for corn. You are long on a weekly reversal up signal. The time window then passes, and prices start to move up. Several weeks later the stop point is penetrated on a down move, and prices close below your stop point for the week. What to do? Simple. You get out!

Figures 17-1 and 17-2 show examples of weekly and daily reversals and the precise stop loss point for each signal. Remember that the stop loss point is for a close either *under* the low (R+) or *over* the high (R−). This means exactly what it says. For example, if the low is 59.00, then the stop will be 58.99 or lower, and not an iota more. If the market fluctuates in hundredths of a point, then the stop would be 58.999, and so on. Notice that the signals in Figures 17-1 and 17-2 are not necessarily within time windows. They are merely being used as illustrations to clarify the explanation of stop loss.

## HIGH LOW/LOW HIGH CLOSE STOPS

Recall one more time the following definitions:

*Low–High Close (LHC) signal*    Any time unit during which prices close at or within 10 percent of the high of that time unit after first having closed at or within 10 percent of the low of previous time unit.

*High–Low Close (HLC) signal*    Any time unit during which prices close at or within 10 percent of low of that the time unit after first having closed at or within 10 percent of the high of previous time unit.

In the case of an LHC signal, the stop would go under the low of the time unit during which the signal was given, closing basis. Assume the following configuration of weekly high–low closes for a 2 week period:

|       | Week 1 | Week 2 |
|-------|--------|--------|
| High  | 56.00  | 58.90  |
| Low   | 54.00  | 54.30  |
| Close | 54.03  | 58.90  |

The signal given here is clearly an LHC. The stop would be a close under the low of week No. 2, or below 54.30.

The reverse would hold true for HLC signals. The stop in this case would be a close above the high of a week during which the signal was given. Figures 17-3 and 17-4 show some LHC and HLC signals, not necessarily within time windows, and the stop points for each of the signals. Remember that the LHC and HLC signals are less frequent than any other signal. You will not find as many of them on the charts when you study the markets, but they tend to be more reliable than other signals.

## 3H AND 3L SIGNAL STOPS

The same basic principle applies to stops for this signal group. In the case of a 3H signal, defined as a close above the highest close of the last three time

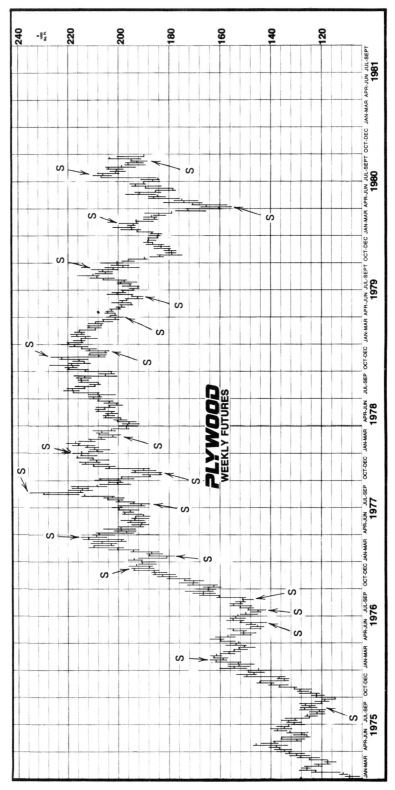

Figure 17.1  Weekly reversal stops (S).

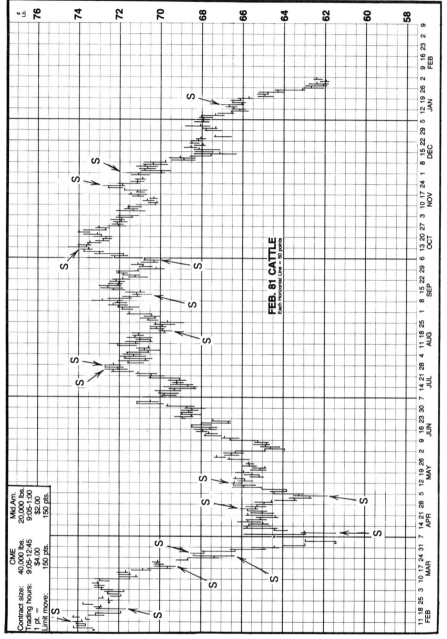

Figure 17.2  Daily reversal stops (S).

255

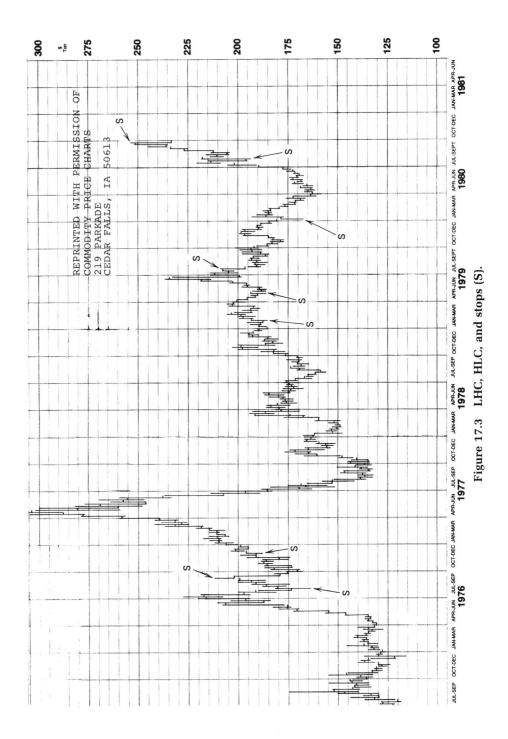

REPRINTED WITH PERMISSION OF
COMMODITY PRICE CHARTS
219 PARKADE
CEDAR FALLS, IA 50613

Figure 17.3  LHC, HLC, and stops (S).

256

**Figure 17.4   LHC, HLC, and stops (S).**

units, the stop would be a close below the low of the time unit during which this signal was given. Assume the following succession of weekly prices:

|  | Week | | | | |
|---|---|---|---|---|---|
|  | 1 | 2 | 3 | 4 | 5 |
| High | 56.20 | 55.45 | 56.75 | 55.30 | 58.45 |
| Low | 54.30 | 55.10 | 55.50 | 54.35 | 55.70 |
| Close | 55.10 | 55.30 | 56.45 | 55.10 | 57.10 |

Week No. 2 does not give us a timing signal of any kind, and neither does week No. 3. Come week No. 4, we begin to watch for a 3H signal. If prices had closed above 56.45, the highest of the last three weekly closes, we'd have a signal, the stop promptly going under 55.10, which was the low of week No. 4. But no actual signal was given. Instead, in week No. 5, the closing price of 57.10 gave us a 3H signal with a stop now under 55.70, which is the low of the week that gave us our signal.

The 3L signal stops are similar, only in reverse. Figures 17-5 and 17-6 show many examples of 3H and 3L signal stops on a weekly and daily basis, respectively. Notice that these are the most common signals, the most apt to show losses, and therefore the least reliable of the four.

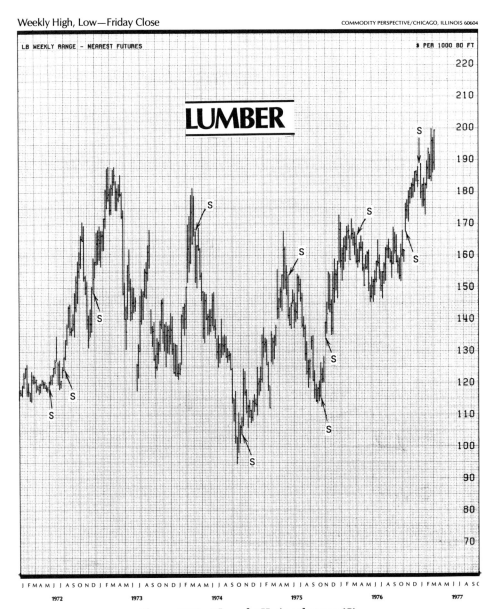

Weekly High, Low—Friday Close                    COMMODITY PERSPECTIVE/CHICAGO, ILLINOIS 60604

**Figure 17.5    3L and 3H signal stops (S).**

## UBO AND DBO SIGNAL STOPS

The stops for UBO and DBO signals are just as specific as those for 3H and 3L stops, but they are more difficult to understand. In each case the stop would refer to two full time units back from the time unit in which the signal came. Say, for example, that you had a UBO signal. To find the stop, or risk, for this signal you count back 2 time units and use the lowest closing low of all 3 time units as your closing stop. Figure 17-7 illustrates precisely what is meant. In

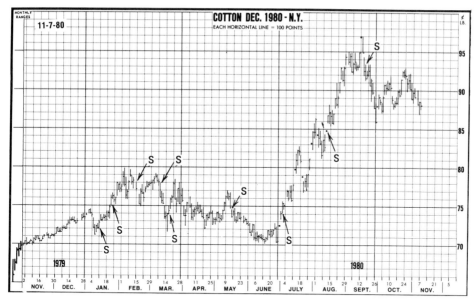

**Figure 17.6   3L and 3H signals and stops (S).**

the event of a DBO signal the reverse holds true. Figure 17-8 illustrates this point.

I have included two samples (Figures 17-9 and 17-10), to give you additional examples of UBO and DBO signal stops. Generally, you will find that the three other signals I have discussed will account for most of the entry indicators. Very often a UBO or DBO signal will come at the same time as one of the other signals. Some traders may prefer to dispense entirely with the UBO and DBO signals because they are a bit more difficult to keep on your chart and require much drawing, erasing, and redrawing of lines. You may use a system with either three or four signals. There are only a few ways in which you can pass through the time window without a signal being given, so it is not really necessary to follow the UBO and DBO signals religiously. However, you should either follow them at all times or not follow them at all. Obviously, you will have more confirmation of a turn in trend if you use all four timing indicators.

## STOPS FOR COMBINED SIGNALS

Assume that on a given week or day you get R+, LHC, and 3H signals all at once. The problem arises as to where the stop should go because there are three signals. The stop in this and all cases of combined signals goes under the *low* for that week in the buy signals and over the *high* for that week in sell signals. The concept is quite simple. Take the configuration shown in Figure 17-11, which is an R+ LHC. The stop would go under the point indicated because it is the low of the week (or time unit) during which the signals were given. Figure 17-12 shows a combined R−, HLC, and 3L signal. Notice that the stop goes above the high of the week the signals were given. Figure 17-13 shows a

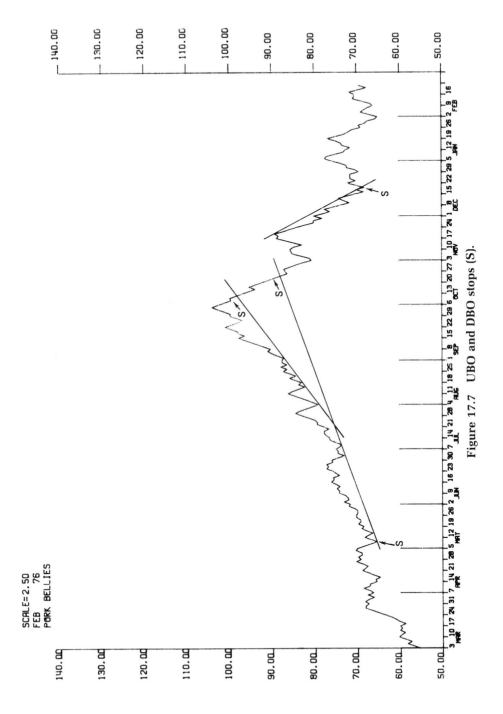

SCALE=2.50
FEB 76
PORK BELLIES

Figure 17.7 UBO and DBO stops (S).

260

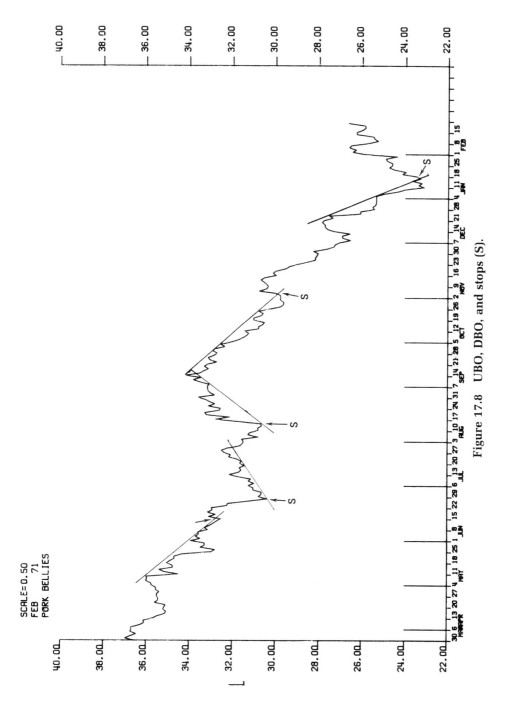

SCALE=0.50
FEB 71
PORK BELLIES

Figure 17.8  UBO, DBO, and stops (S).

261

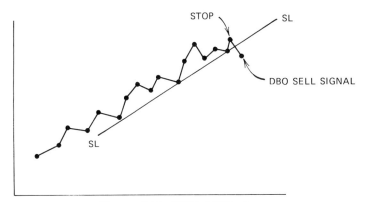

Figure 17.9   UBO, DBO, stops.

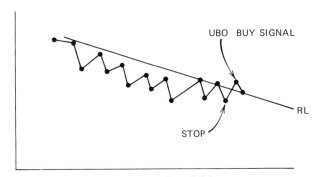

Figure 17.10   UBO, DBO stops.

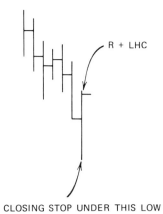

CLOSING STOP UNDER THIS LOW

Figure 17.11   Stop for R + LHC signal.

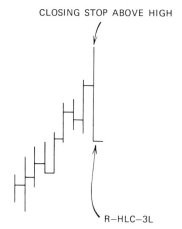

**Figure 17.12  Stop for R −
HLC 3L − signal.**

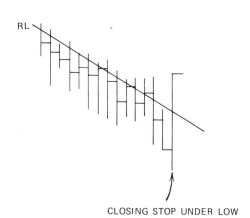

**Figure 17.13  Stop for R + LHC 3H +
UBO signal.**

combination of four signals on the buy side during a cycle window. Notice where the stop has been placed. In this case it goes under the *lowest* low of the three week period!

In the event of a combined signal, your stop will probably entail more risk. This is reasonable because combined signals tend to have more reliability and profit potential than any one signal alone. The more signals in a time window and the closer these signals come in time, the more reliable they will be and the larger the stop will probably be. As in every case, you must evaluate the amount of stop you will need to use so that you can determine whether the actual dollar risk is worth your while or is within the limits of your financial ability. Many traders would be rightly loath to take such a potentially large loss, unless the size of their account was correspondingly large.

## SUMMARIZING RISKS AND STOPS

The value of stop losses, or loss-limiting measures, has been discussed. Specific methods for using each signal have been presented to provide you with a way of cutting losses in the event that the system is incorrect in selecting a trade. As you know, no system is right 100 percent of the time. In fact, most systems are right only about 60 percent of the time. The critical element in making any system work effectively is to limit losses according to the predetermined method associated with each signal or method. The cyclic techniques I have examined, along with their specific timing entry signals, also let you know precisely how much you need to risk in each case. You know that your potential loss will be *at least* the amount indicated by stop, plus commissions. You may then evaluate whether the trade is right for you. This is something only you can determine, because only you are aware of how much overall risk exposure you can accept.

Assume that you use the cyclic concept along with other timing signals, such as point and figure or moving average indicators. In this case, you will need to develop your own loss-limiting methods. You will experience a great temptation to avoid using good principles of money management. ''If the cycle is good,'' you might rationalize, ''then a stop is not necessary.'' This type of thinking is your first step along the path to ultimate ruin. Whether you trade cycles, moving averages, lunar signals, astrological signals, the toss of a coin, or gut feel, loss limiting is a key element in success. I have said this many times before, and I will say it again because it is so important.

# CHAPTER EIGHTEEN

# Seasonal Price Cycles

The seasonal price pattern, which most commodities exhibit, can also be used profitably by traders, hedgers, and investors. If you study the price behavior of a given market over the course of time, it becomes quite clear that there are indeed repetitive price tendencies that can readily be used for predictive analysis. The farmer has known these seasonal cycles for many years. Generally, grain prices peak in late summer to early autumn, decline after harvest, make lows toward year end, and then begin a gradual rise. Virtually every market has its unique seasonal pattern.

Over time the seasonal pattern of a market may vary, but the general trend remains in effect. If you know, for example, that soybeans make their seasonal lows in October more than 80 percent of the time, you can not only have a good idea of approximately when to buy into the market, but you can also know when prices were too low for selling or for short hedging.

Let's examine a few more seasonal patterns. Figure 18-1 shows the seasonal patterns of cash copper. There are two important aspects of this chart. First, highs are often made during the October/November time frame. And second, after rising early in the year, prices usually peak by the third quarter's end.

Gold prices have a pattern as well. Lows tend to come in August, prices are higher by June, and a fairly strong seasonal upmove frequently begins in January (if you failed to capture part of the August move).

By carefully studying the frequency with which seasonal moves occur, you can determine a factor for the percentage of probability for rising or falling prices in each month. The seasonal charts discussed to this point have presented basically simple cash and/or futures patterns.

## CONSTRUCTING A SEASONAL CHART

The technique employed in constructing a seasonal chart is quite simple. The following step-by-step explanation will help you do it for a market not covered here.

*Step 1.* Determine time period you wish to study. Ideally, seasonal data should be studied from a weekly or monthly basis. The raw data you will need should be either weekly average price or monthly average price.

*Step 2.* Place data in an array as follows:

| Year | Jan. | Feb. | Mar. | Apr. | May | June | July | Aug. | Sept. | Oct. | Nov. | Dec. |
|---|---|---|---|---|---|---|---|---|---|---|---|---|
| 1953 | 50 | 60 | 70 | 50 | 40 | 35 | 25 | 20 | 25 | 30 | 40 | 50 |
| 1954 | | | | | | | | | | | | |
| 1955 | | | | | | | | | | | | |
| 1956 | | | | | | | | | | | | |
| 1957 | | | | | | | | | | | | |
| 1958 | | | | | | | | | | | | |
| 1959 | | | | | | | | | | | | |

etc.

If weekly data are used, then replace the months with week numbers. You will therefore have 52 entries for each year.

*Step 3.* In order to minimize the effects of price variance across the time span, the data must now be "normalized." The best way to do this is by working down each column, assigning to the largest entry an arbitrary value of 100, and the smallest, an arbitrary value of 0. Each of the other values is then converted to a percentage (or normalized figure). See Figure 18-2 for an example of how this is done, and then perform the same calculations for all the columns until the data have been completely analyzed.

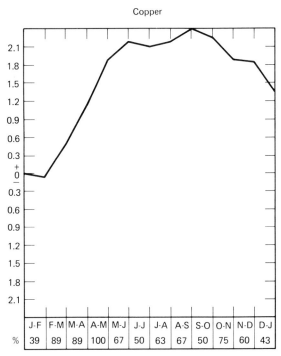

**Figure 18.1 Copper seasonal—cash.**

| Year | Raw Data for January | Converted Data |
|------|---------------------|----------------|
| 1953 | 50 | 45.4 |
| 1954 | 60 | 54.5 |
| 1955 | 30 | 27.2 |
| 1956 | 20 | 18.1 |
| 1957 | 10 | 0 |
| 1958 | 70 | 63.6 |
| 1959 | 70 | 63.6 |
| 1960 | 60 | 54.5 |
| 1961 | 80 | 72.7 |
| 1962 | 110 | 100 |
| 1963 | 45 | 31 |
| 1964 | 30 | 27.2 |
| 1965 | 20 | 18.1 |

Figure 18.2   Normalizing seasonal data

*Step 4.*   Now add all the column entries and take the arithmetical average by dividing the number of entries into the total figure. See Figure 18-3.

*Step 5.*   Plot the data on a price chart, using the monthly normalized data as the plot points. Your chart should look like the cash charts shown earlier.

*Step 6.*   To determine the percentage up or down probability you need to add another step to the data array by examining the price entry for February. If the price entry for February is larger than the price entry for January, enter a plus (+). If it is smaller, enter a minus (−). If it is unchanged, enter a zero (0). Compare each subsequent month with the previous one. When you get to December's entry, compare it to November. Then examine January and December of the previous year to see how they compare. Now count the number of plus, minus, and zero entries in each column. Then calculate the percentages of plus, minus, or zero entries to obtain the reliability reading. Say, for example, you have 10 years of data, of which there are eight plus entries and two minus

| Year | Jan. | Feb. | Mar. | Apr. | May | June | July | Aug. | Sept. | Oct. | Nov. | Dec. |
|------|------|------|------|------|-----|------|------|------|-------|------|------|------|
| 1953 | 50 | 65 | 100 | | | | | | | | | |
| 1954 | 65 | 60 | 80 | | | | | | | | | |
| 1955 | 40 | 100 | 90 | | | | | | | | | |
| 1956 | 30 | 20 | 70 | | | | | | | | | |
| 1957 | 100 | 0 | 70 | | | | | | | | | |
| 1958 | 10 | 40 | 60 | | | | | | | | | |
| 1959 | 0 | 25 | 0 | | | | | | | | | |
| 1960 | 20 | 50 | 40 | | | | | | | | | |
| Total |  |  |  | | | | | | | | | |
| Average |  |  |  | | | | | | | | | |

Figure 18.3   Summation and average of normalized data

entries in the January/February period. This means that during the period under study, prices in February were higher than prices in January 80 percent of the time.

Generally, a reading of more than 65 percent in either direction is considered reliable enough for trading purposes. Naturally, the higher a reliability reading is, the more likely will be the seasonal move. The larger your data base, the more significant your readings. A reading of 90 percent based on 10 years' data is much less meaningful than a 90 percent reading based on 25 years' data.

## THE SEASONAL RUN

Once the reliability figures have been posted (either on your own chart or one of my charts), you will begin to see reliable seasonal patterns. These are periods when a market moves in the same direction for several months and also shows high reliability readings during the move. An upmove lasting 3 months with reliability readings of +70 percent, +80 percent, and +82 percent, is a reliable seasonal run. Seasonal runs are those patterns that ordinarily provide the greatest profit potential. One can also use weekly seasonal runs.

## THE CRITICAL MONTH CONCEPT

My years of experience with seasonal patterns has led me to formulate what I call the *critical month concept* (CMC). The CMC allows the futures trader to

| Year | Jan. | | Feb. | | Mar. | Apr. | May | June | July | Aug. | Sept. | Oct. | Nov. | Dec. |
|------|------|---|------|---|------|------|-----|------|------|------|-------|------|------|------|
| 1953 | 50 | – | 20 | + | 50 | | | | | | | | 40 | |
| 1954 | + 60 | – | 50 | + | 60 | | | | | | | | 60 | |
| 1955 | + 90 | – | 40 | + | 100 | | | | | | | | 100 | |
| 1956 | – 30 | 0 | 30 | + | 40 | | | | | | | | 20 | |
| 1957 | 100 | – | 80 | – | 0 | | | | | | | | 10 | |
| 1958 | 20 | + | 50 | + | 60 | | | | | | | | 0 | |
| 1959 | 0 | 0 | 0 | + | 30 | | | | | | | | 50 | |
| 1960 | 10 | + | 100 | – | 40 | | | | | | | | 80 | |

**Figure 18.4   Reliability readings for normalized seasonal data.**

arrive at measures of *timing* and *contracyclicality*. In effect, the CMC says that in each market certain things must happen at certain times of the year. If they do, then the market can be expected to act "normally," or as it usually does. The critical months (CMs) vary for each market and serve as timing benchmarks. As an example, April is a critical month in the cattle market (as in all meats). When prices fall below April lows after the month is over, they often continue a sharp decline. When they close above their April highs, they generally begin a sharp rise to seasonal highs.

Remember, do not blindly follow CM signals. As I have said, money management is one of the keys to successful trading and must be considered. When CM signals are combined with the cyclic signals that are discussed elsewhere in this book, you will arrive at a complete analysis of the market situation.

Typically, the CMs for a given market are the usual seasonal lows or highs. In the case of soybeans, for example, the seasonal low is ordinarily in October. Another CM is January. In most markets a penetration of the January high has very bullish implications. This high can be penetrated at any time, not necessarily in February only.

## SOME GUIDELINES FOR SEASONAL TRADING

There are some time-tested rules for effectively using seasonal price cycles. Here are a few of my guidelines and suggestions:

1 Attempt to use seasonal patterns only in conjunction with other cyclic indicators.

2 If you use seasonals alone, then implement the traditional loss-limiting rules for money management.

3 Watch CM indicators and research historical charts to determine previously undiscovered CM relationships.

4 Expect shifts in the seasonal top or bottom when a long term cyclic turn is due. More details on this rule are covered later.

5 Be prepared for a contraseasonal move, or one that goes in the direction opposite from what has occurred in the past. Such deviations tend to indicate major aberrations in the entire seasonal for the given year.

6 Use seasonals for hedging purposes when they are following their scenario closely.

## SEASONAL CYCLES IN COMMODITY SPREADS

It is only logical that commodity spreads follow seasonal price tendencies as well. As you know, a spread trade is one in which the speculator holds both a long and a short position in the same (or two) closely related market(s). He hopes to profit from either a widening or a narrowing of the price difference. A spread chart, therefore, depicts net change.

The way to construct a weekly seasonal spread chart is basically similar to what is used for the construction of cash and weekly futures charts.

The January versus May soybean meal spread is a classic example of seasonal cyclicality in spreads. What the chart says, in essence, is that the time frame (marked with arrows on the chart) is one during which January meal tends to gain ground on May meal. Appendix 5 shows several seasonal spread charts and contains explanatory material on these seasonal patterns.

## WEEKLY SEASONAL ANALYSIS

The use of seasonality in the commodity markets is not a new concept. During the past few years a number of books and studies dealing with the technique have been published. In 1977 I published *Seasonal Chart Study 1953–1977—Cash Commodities*. This was one of the first serious attempts to quantify seasonals in the commodity markets. In 1979 I published *Seasonal Chart Study II—Commodity Spreads*. This report provided a week-by-week seasonal analysis of commodity spreads and isolated many highly reliable trends in a number of markets. Williams and Noseworthy (1977), in their *Sure Thing Commodity Trading*, provided speculators with a list of specific seasonal trades having high reliabilities over the past 10 years or so. This study was a pioneering effort in the isolation of specific seasonal trades in the futures market on a market-by-market basis. More recently the Grushcow and Smith book (1980) has also been published.

The combined effect of these and other efforts has been to increase the use of seasonals markedly. It is unfortunate that despite all the available few traders can use seasonal concepts to their advantage. Speculators will often seek to justify an already established position by referring to seasonals. If the seasonal does not agree with their opinion, then they will ignore the seasonal. If there is agreement, then they may double up on the position. And there are those traders who understand the concept of seasonality and are aware of key seasonal trades but who do not have the patience to trade them effectively. These latter primarily have problems with self-discipline, problems that are not discussed in this book.

My goals in this chapter are twofold: (1) to identify and define some dominant seasonal cycles, and (2) to detail possible uses of seasonal cycles in conjunction with timing signals, or individually.

## ADDITIONAL ASPECTS OF SEASONAL CYCLES

As I have previously shown, seasonal patterns occur in virtually all commodity markets. To most traders these cyclic movements are neither obvious nor meaningful, which is truly unfortunate because regularity and repetition are the cornerstones of profitable trading. All trading systems seek to isolate signals or indicators that repeat themselves frequently and with sufficient reliability to permit profitable trading. Seasonals and cycles are the ultimate factors underlying market regularirty. Those persons who have read and understood the previous chapters should be familiar with the underlying long-range cycles in each market.

The price of virtually every commodity is affected by weather, season, and growing conditions. Supply and demand are also a function of seasonal fluctuations. When crops are large, following harvest, it is natural to assume that prices may be low because of selling by growers. When demand for grain feeds is high during winter months, we can reasonably expect prices to be high. If all factors could be known, there would be errorless forecasting of prices. The markets themselves are perfect, I maintain. It is our ability to recognize and use all the price inputs that is imperfect. Hence, our forecasting ability is limited. Inasmuch as seasonal factors affect prices, it is possible, or should be, to determine if and when a given market will move up or down because of seasonality. A *seasonal pattern* is, therefore, the *tendency of a given futures market to trend in a given direction at certain times of the year*. We do not always know the reasons for seasonal price movements. Personally, I have no need to know why a market moves up or down at a given time of the year, although knowing why makes some traders feel more secure. My concern is not with the *why* of things but rather with the *that* of things. I do not know why a given market moves up 90 percent of the time during November, but I do know *that* it makes the move. My security comes from the profit I can reap by having this knowledge. Seasonal fluctuation, then, is a cyclic pattern whose period of repetitive movement is tied to the calendar year. Instead of looking for low and highs, which may come in virtually any interval of time, we look for patterns within each year. If we can know ahead of time, for example, that wheat prices are likely to make major lows for the year in April or May, we can apply various trend change indicators to ascertain precisely when the change has come about.

It was W. D. Gann who underscored the importance of seasonality in commodity futures prices. His *How to Make Profits Trading in Commodities* (1942) devotes considerable time and space to this concept. Today, with the assistance of computer technology, it is possible to determine accurately and specifically most seasonal trends in the commodity futures markets. Whereas Gann was primarily interested in using seasonal highs and lows, my interest is directed toward shorter term moves. The lack of such information has left many traders uncertain about the usual yearly pattern in each market. It is difficult to believe that even today many traders do not know what the seasonals for each market are, nor do they believe in the importance of seasonals.

## THE VARIOUS TYPES OF SEASONALS

The topic of seasonal analysis can be approached in many ways, and many price periods can be analyzed. We might, for example, seek to isolate month-by-month price tendencies in the cash market. We could also isolate monthly patterns in the futures market. Another approach would be to examine weekly patterns for potential in an overall trading plan. We could carry this analysis one more step by isolating day-to-day patterns. By so doing we might be able to answer such questions as, "What does the June cattle futures contract usually do three days before Christmas?" Or, "Is it true that meats decline several days before the Fourth of July weekend?" Such ultra short term tendencies certainly exist. And once isolated, they could prove highly profitable to many traders and hedgers.

Appendix 2 contains several computer programs that outline the step-by-step mechanics of finding a seasonal tendency in the futures market. Such analysis is also possible by manual calculation. In each case, the output is a chart or table that shows what the normal price pattern of a given market has been over a certain period. The more years of data you use, the more reliable is the outcome. If you tell me that corn prices have been up during the first week of June 100 percent of the time in the past 5 years, then I may not be too impressed. If you can say, however, that this has happened 8 out of the past 10 years, or 18 out of the past 23 years, then you've said something of potential value.

The rest of this chapter concentrates on isolating several important seasonal price tendencies in a selected number of markets. Once these tendencies have been explained, we carefully examine some price charts to see how timing and seasonals can be combined. Not all seasonals are discussed; this would take too much space. For a comprehensive analysis of weekly seasonals, I refer you to my publication *MBH Seasonal Futures Charts* (1980), which contains at least two weekly seasonal charts for most of the active commodity markets.

## UNDERSTANDING THE SEASONAL CHARTS

It is not necessary to have a background in computer programming to understand the manner in which these charts were prepared. In order for you to more fully appreciate the results and the amount of work that went into their production, I suggest you familiarize yourself with the methodology. Following, in step form, is the procedure I followed in my analysis. Although the steps were designed to be done by computer, you can use the same steps for manual calculation.

1   Take the daily history file for a given market and month, for each year on file (e.g., June live cattle 1967, 1968, 1969, 1970 . . . 1979). Read the data from tape to a disk file. If you perform this step manually, record the data in tabular form. Paper that is ruled to make 52 vertical columns for the weeks of the year is useful for this purpose.

2   Line up each contract by date. The last day of trading is treated as day 1, the second to last day as day 2, and so on so that not all contracts terminate on the same calendar day. The exchanges have specific rules for determining last day of trading, however, and most contracts will terminate on or about the same week.

3   Calculate the price change for each week using the Friday price as the last price, or the Thursday price if Friday was not a trading day. You thus achieve a record of the weekly price change for each market and year.

4   Standardize or normalize the price changes for each year to limit the effect of unusually wide or unusually small price swings. You are primarily interested in the direction of move (i.e., the trend from one week to the next). Convert the highest change to 100 and the lowest to zero. Other values will fall between zero and 100.

5   Once you have normalized the data, take the algebraic average for each column of week. This yields an index of average fluctuation per week of the year.

6   Determine the percentage of years during which the price was up or down for a given week.

7 Dump data to plotter and plot the line of the cumulative price trend, or plot manually on chart paper.

The data can be manipulated in other ways. If you plan to replicate this study on your own data base, you may wish to experiment with different techniques of lining up the data, or with different indexing arrangements.

## HOW TO READ THE SEASONAL CHARTS

Figure 18-5 is a sample chart that lists specific details to observe in each case. Refined uses are discussed later on. Here is a general overview of each chart. *Please read these instructions carefully.* You will save considerable time and frustration if you read the instructions before attempting to use or understand the charts. I have listed, in order, the key points. Refer to the numbered callouts (Figure 18-5) as you read these instructions.

1 This line lists the contract month and market which is plotted below.

2 The column headed *Years Covered* lists the years accordingly. For example, 67–79 means that 13 years of data were used in preparing this chart. If a market has not been actively traded for many years, there is a smaller data base.

3 The scale, or index, is shown along the left and right axes. This is an index of the normalized rate of change and does not have any direct bearing on actual price. It merely shows, on a relative basis, the magnitude of move from one week to the next. If, for example, the move from week 23 to 22 is high compared to previous weeks, and if the percentage reading is 85 percent, then you can expect a large weekly upmove 85 percent of the time during the week under study. A drop under the zero line merely indicates that a rather persistent bear trend usually occurs. There is no special significance associated with a market's crossing above the zero line or below it. It is simply another reference point.

4 The *weekly price plot* shows the average net change, up or down, for a given week.

5 These figures represent the weekly upside probability, on a percentage basis, for the specific week listed under the reading. For example, if the data plot (4) for a given week is up from the previous plot and the reading is 80 percent, then it is an indication that prices tend to rise this week 80 percent of the years under study. This is a strong indication of seasonality. If the percentage figure is under 65 percent and the plot is up, then the seasonal is not particularly reliable.

*If plot is down* and the percentage reading is above 65 percent, it means that although the market tends to move up more years than it moves down, the net downmove is much larger than the net upmove—thereby accounting for the down entry. If you buy, then you stand to make only a small profit.

*If plot is down* and the percentage reading is below 35 percent, it means that the market is down 65 percent or more of the years under study. In this case the downside reliability is 100 percent minus 35 percent, or 65 percent. For downside reliabilities, subtract the indicated figure from 100 to arrive at the reading. A downmove with a reading of 10 percent, for example, indicates that

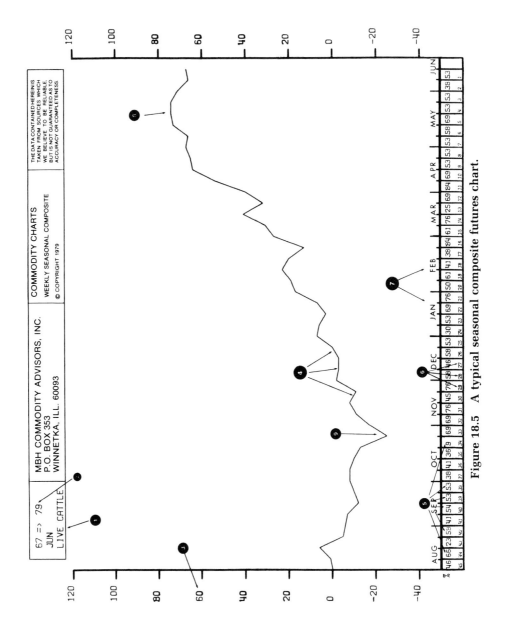

Figure 18.5   A typical seasonal composite futures chart.

the market has been down 90 percent of the years studied. Remember this simple but important rule for calculating downmove reliability.

*If plot is up* and the percentage reading is below 35 percent, it is an indication that even though most years were down for this week, those years that were up were very strong. If you sell short on this type of combination, you may take a large risk for a potentially small but reliable profit.

*If plot is unchanged (sideways)* from previous week, it is an indication that the magnitude or size of the move for this week is in equal balance between up and down. This does not necessarily mean a sideways trend for the week. Trend can be determined only by the accompanying percentage reading. If it is 65 percent, then you can expect generally higher prices. If it is under 35 percent, then you can expect a downmove. The sideways plot means only that the up and down moves are about equal in size.

6   The *week number* is the percentage probability reading. The week number shown tells you how many full weeks are left to contract expiration. The last week of trading would read "1" because it is the final week in the life of this contract. A reading of "34," for example, means that this is the thirty-fourth week prior to contract expiration. These figures are important in calculating the week and month number according to exchange expiration dates for any given year. The week numbers allow you to determine relative time for any year.

7   The *month and week* column is next. The number of weeks in any given month, using Friday as the last day of a week, will vary from year to year. Sometimes November will have five Fridays, and other years it will have four. The dates listed on these charts are for the 1979, 1980, and 1981 trading years. If you wish to adapt your chart for other trading years, then simply determine when the given contract is due to expire and work backward, using the trading week as a guide. Once you have learned to use these charts, you will find that it is not necessary to pinpoint the exact week. If a given market is conforming well to its seasonal trend, you can superimpose the actual weekly price onto the seasonal chart, and you can see whether there is a time lead or lag. A clear acetate sheet can be used for this purpose.

8   The *usual seasonal high* is indicated by the highest plot on the chart, which means that during the years under study there has been a tendency for prices to hit their contract high around this week and/or month. If a high is made during the last few weeks of a contract, prices may move even higher several months thereafter. The next contract month should be checked for this possibility. If a seasonal high is associated with high readings in the percentage column, and if a subsequent move to the downside occurs with equally reliable readings, then this is probably a highly reliable seasonal top.

9   To arrive at the *seasonal low*, simply reverse the procedure given in the preceding paragraph for seasonal highs.

## MORE DETAILS ABOUT SEASONAL CHARTS

Remember that seasonal charts are a composite or distillation of typical activity and as a result extreme highs and extreme lows during the same period in different years tend to balance each other out. The net result is a relatively even line on the seasonal chart. This is valuable information because it shows that the market is not seasonal at certain times of the year. You can then safely assume that trend is the single most reliable indicator, and you can also assume that once a trend starts, it will continue. It is best not to rely on seasonals when this occurs.

Relative highs and lows within the composite chart are not necessarily repeated in any actual year's market. Some years may look exactly like the seasonal composite charts, and others may not. A low may or may not occur at a given time, but this does not mean that the seasonal chart is incorrect. When using the seasonal charts, look for the following seven things:

1  *Very Strong Up or Down Weeks.* When I say strong, I mean reliabilities in excess of 70 percent over 10 or more years. These weeks will most probably bring you quick profits on short term trades.

2  *Long Term Up or Down Trends.* These trends can be seen in many markets. Copper and cattle are two notable examples. If a trend begins and is accompanied by high reliability readings at the start and high readings interspersed within the trend, then it is likely to be a highly valid seasonal tendency. The same is true of downmoves.

3  *Seasonal Highs and Lows.* You can estimate seasonal highs and lows by reference to the chart and in accordance with the guidelines outlined in items 8 and 9 in the foregoing list.

4  *Contraseasonal Moves.* You can spot contraseasonal moves in the actual market. If a market shows highly reliable seasonality on the composite and if this pattern fails to appear in the actual market for any given year, you can expect a further move in the contraseasonal direction. Spotting these moves is perhaps one of the most important uses of a seasonal chart.

5  *Market Turns.* You can expect market turns at certain times of the year. *Market turns* is just another term for "trend changes." If the market has been moving down and if the seasonal chart shows a downmove with a high percentage reliability followed by a large reliable upmove, then you should be on the lookout for a major trend change in the market.

6  *The Weekly Percentage Reading and How It Relates to Current Time.* As I have indicated to you previously, the weekly readings have been obtained by lining up contract data, from last trading day to first trading day. The month and week reading, which have been included along the bottom of each chart, *may not necessarily apply* to every market year. They are primarily for the 1980 expirations. In future years, or in past years, there may be a one- or two-week shift in the timing. In such cases you can calculate the period of time by working backward from the last entry (lower right hand of Figure 18-5) and counting the week number to current time. This is not a difficult task. Simply determine from the rules of the exchange when a given contract is due to expire.

After several months of use, you will find it possible to isolate the time frame rather easily. In studying actual market behavior compared to the seasonal composite, you will know if there has been a lead or lag in the current contract. This seasonal shift can occur during given years. A major seasonal low, for example, could come several weeks ahead of time as a result of various fundamentals. Be on the lookout for early tops and bottoms.

7  *High Reliability Weekly Runs.* From time to time the seasonal composites show high reliability for a span of several weeks. Such a run is typically a good period for seasonal trends. I have marked the corresponding trend with arrows on the given charts to make spotting these moves less difficult (see charts in Appendix 5). Every now and then a market may show weekly readings as follows: 69 percent, 75 percent, 68 percent, 45 percent, 78 percent, 69 percent, 50 percent, 33 percent, 78 percent, 67 percent. This is a very strong seasonal uptrend interrupted by only a few low reliability readings. The longer term trader might establish and hold a position through this seasonal up or down-trend.

## GRAINS

Corn prices usually peak during August/September and begin upmoves in May. Figure 18-6 shows the seasonal composite chart for corn for March 1967–1980. Notice that the fourth week of May shows an especially high reliability reading (78 percent). During this time frame watch for seasonal turns to the upside. By using some of the timing signals on a weekly basis, as discussed earlier, you may be able to time market entry for an upmove. Also notice that the price trend usually turns lower in August/September. You can also use timing signals to enter the short side during this time frame. Let's examine how this might have worked on the March 1981 corn delivery (see Figure 18-7).

Arrow No. 1 shows the entry point of a hypothetical long position. The timing signal is also marked accordingly. In fact, there are several timing signals (on a weekly basis) that are all marked accordingly. The position is ideally held until either a stop point has been hit or until the ideal seasonal peak has occurred. Because the composite chart indicates a usual peak in August, week No. 3, we will liquidate at that time and begin to look for sell signals or trend reversal signals. Arrow No. 2 marks the point at which we would have liquidated the long position and gone short, as well as the signal that prompted a short trade. Arrow No. 3 marks the point at which our short would have been stopped out at a loss. Hypothetically, there could have been at least two trades based on this elementary use of our seasonal composite chart. The first would have yielded an approximate profit of about $0.42. The second trade closed out at a loss of about $0.08, leaving a net profit of about $0.34 cents per contract assuming reasonable price fills.

There is yet a second way in which the seasonal chart might be used. You can examine only those weeks with favorable up or down readings and make trades accordingly. Remember that Figure 18-7 is a daily price chart. Each heavy line on the grid is a Friday, and the dates shown are Fridays. In the first example we used weekly highs, lows, and closings to find our signals. Now we'll switch to daily signals for an example of a shorter term.

Another way of looking at the seasonal chart is by simply using the high reliability weekly readings. For my purpose any reading of 65 percent or higher and any reading of 35 percent or lower is acceptable as a reliable weekly pattern. On Figure 18-6 I have marked the weekly seasonal composite for March corn A through K accordingly, with arrows pointing to the weeks that show reliable tendencies. Remember that this chart is a composite of March corn contracts

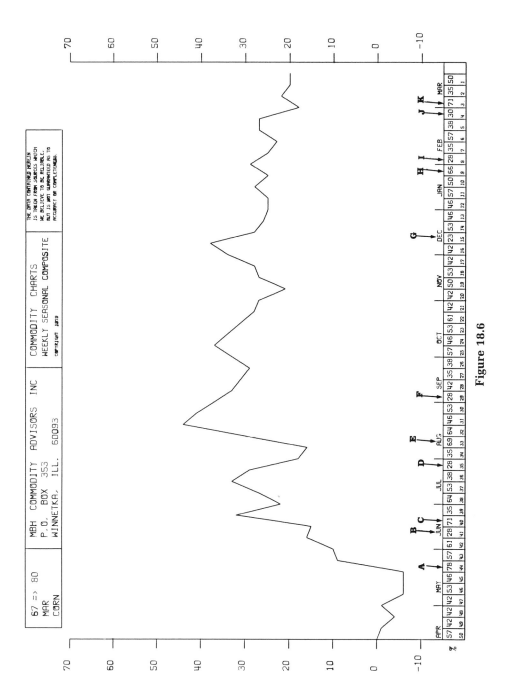

**Figure 18.6**

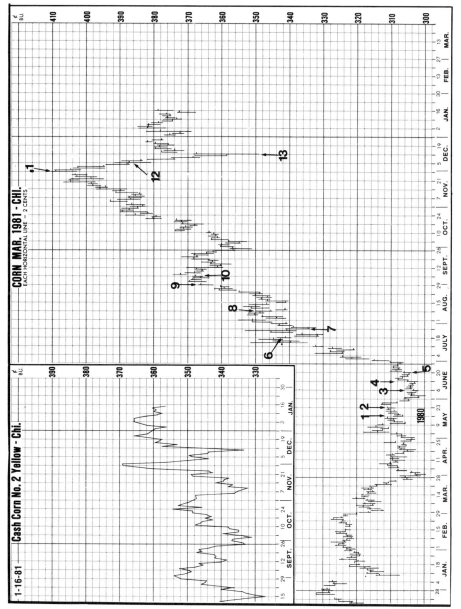

**Figure 18.7   Seasonals and March 1981—corn.**

279

from 1967 up to and including the 1980 delivery. It *does not* include any data
from the 1981 delivery of March corn. In other words, the chart should tell us
what will happen in 1981 within a reasonable degree of accuracy. If it does,
then we've got a potentially profitable seasonal on our hands.

Once the reliable weeks have been singled out, we examine the trend for
each given week. As an example, let's start with week 44, marked A on the
chart. The reading for this week is 78 percent, and the weekly plot is up. What
would we expect on the basis of these readings? The logical conclusion is that
the Friday closing price for this week has a 78 percent probability of being
higher than the Friday closing price of the week before. When the actual week
shows a holiday on Friday and/or Thursday, the last trading day of the week
is used. In other words, we will go to the current price chart (Figure 18-7,
March 1981 corn) to see if history has repeated itself. Looking at Figure 18-7,
what do we see? Arrow 1 shows the Friday close on May 14, 1980. The approximate close was 3.05¾. Arrow 2 shows the Friday close one week later, on
May 23, 1980, at a price of approximately 3.11. The net price change for this
week was, therefore, $+5\frac{1}{4}$. The probability of an upmove was high, and the
market followed its seasonal tendency.

There are two ways in which this information can be used. The trader who
wishes to act simply on the basis of a reliable seasonal can buy corn at the
close of trading on Friday of the week before the high reliability move. He can
then sell out his position on the next Friday at a profit, it is hoped. In this case
he would be successful. Another way of using this information is to watch for
one of the trend change (i.e., timing) signals on a daily basis within the period
of five trading days. As soon as the signal comes, he takes a position. The trade
is then closed out either at a loss on a stop, or at a profit on the next Friday.
When a reliable seasonal runs several weeks in duration, the position can be
added to and carried for an even longer time. In either case, the trade is strictly
short term, and the approach is specific. No attention need be paid to other
cycles, although their effects will most certainly make the weekly seasonals
more or less reliable. If an up cycle is in process when a weekly seasonal
upmove is expected, then the probability of a profit is higher. The opposite,
of coursre, holds true for a down cycle.

Now let's examine the next reliable weekly pattern (arrow marked B Figure
18-6). You'll note that the plot is *down* and the reading is 28 percent, which
means that the chances of a downmove based on historical tendencies is 72
percent (100 percent − 28 percent = 72 percent). Arrow 3 (Figure 18-7) shows
the Friday close one week before, and arrow 4 shows the Friday close of the
week in question. Instead of moving lower as expected, the weekly change was
about $0.01. A trader who established a position on Friday, June 6, 1980 and
closed it out on Friday, June 13, 1980 without any timing signal would have
shown a small loss. A trader waiting for one of our four timing signals might
have had a minor DBO signal, but there were no other timing indicators of
importance and a position should not have been taken. Hence, a loss was
avoided. This is the value of timing!

Now we'll go on to the next week, C, which shows a 71 percent probability.
The Friday close on June 13, 1980 was a daily upside reversal signal. As you'll
recall, this signal indicates a change in trend to the upside. Hence, a long

position might have been taken at that time in the expectation that the Friday close on June 20, 1980 would be higher (arrow 5). This was in fact the outcome, and we might have shown a gain of a little more than $0.01 for our efforts. This is not an impressive profit, but it is nonetheless a profit. Moreover, it is a verification of the weekly seasonal pattern. I will not outline in abbreviated form the remaining reliable weekly seasonals $D$ through $K$ and their corresponding signals, arrows 6 through 13 (Figures 18-6 and 18-7, respectively). If you have not grasped the technique I am using, then please reread the previous paragraphs. I will list seasonal, identifying letter, date, signal, date out, signal, and potential gain or loss, as follows:

1   Week 35, $-72$ percent (remember: 100 percent $-$ 28 percent $=$ 72 percent), arrow $D$. Arrow 6 DBO, short at approximately 3.41 and out on July 25, 1980, arrow 7 at $3.34\frac{1}{4}$ for a gain of $0.0675.

2   Week 33, $+69$ percent, arrow $E$, arrow 8. Weekly close below previous weekly close, but no signal.

3   Week 29, $-72$ percent, arrow $F$, arrow 9 long on August 29, 1980, 3H signal. Out on Sept. 5, 1980, arrow 10. Net gain about $0.01\frac{1}{2}$.

4   Week 15, $-77$ percent, arrow $G$. Short at $3.87\frac{1}{2}$, arrow 12 on 3L signal. Out at about 3.66, arrow 13 for approximate gain of $21\frac{1}{2}$¢.

Summing up our week-by-week seasonal trading of March corn, we can see that total profits outpaced losses when the final figures were in. Weeks during which there was no clear-cut timing signal were not used, although a higher risk trader might have used all high reliability seasonal readings, signal or not.

In the discussions of seasonals that follow I outline some highlights for each of the weekly composite charts. I have provided a current daily bar chart for each of the markets mentioned that are marked with arrows, letters, and numbers to facilitate my illustration of timing indicators, dates, and entry prices. The seasonal composite charts also show reliable seasonal weeks, which are then discussed in relation to the current contract of each market. In other words, I am first presenting the composite chart and pointing out the prominent seasonal features. Then I move to a discussion of the current chart in terms of historical seasonal weekly probabilities. What I am really doing here is translating price tendency into a real-life, trade-by-trade analysis to familiarize you with the seasonals and timing signals combination.

After a brief introduction and step-by-step analysis, I switch to a tabular presentation in which a number of abbreviations are used. To fully understand them, refer to the list that follows:

| Abbreviation | Meaning |
|---|---|
| B@ | Buy at, or long, at given price |
| SS@ | Sold short or sell short at given price |
| 3H, 3L | Timing signal to buy or sell |
| R+, R− | Reversal up, reversal down timing signal |
| LHC, HLC | High-low close, low-high close timing signals |
| UBO | Upside breakout signal to buy |
| DBO | Downside breakout signal to sell |

These timing signals are discussed in several previous chapters, and I hope you are familiar with them by now. If there is any uncertainty as to what the signals are, or what their parameters and meaning are, then refer to the various chapters in which I discuss these topics.

Above all, remember that we are dealing with a hypothetical situation. The buy/sell signals as combined with the seasonal patterns are discussed with the full knowledge that these events are being looked at with 20/20 hindsight. It's a fairly simple task to look at history and say what should have or might have been done. The results of our situation are hypothetical, and the entry/exit prices are approximate. The step-by-step analysis is provided to illustrate how decisions might be made using a combination of seasonal and cyclic data in order to optimize timing. In reality, the decision-making process might not be as straightforward as has been presented in my analysis. I believe, however, that by following the indicated signals and seasonals you can resolve any uncertainties. Remember that it takes considerable experience to employ the combined indicators effectively. Finally, I have made no deductions for such things as commissions, poor order fills, or failure to follow signals. These are all important limiting factors and must be carefully considered in using all trading systems.

## COPPER

The copper market is highly seasonal. There have been only a few years on record that failed to show a seasonal uptrend beginning sometime in the January/February period with a peak in March or April. Some of the upmoves are among the largest on record, which is why copper is an especially good market for those persons interested in trading seasonals. Figure 18-8 shows my composite weekly chart for March copper. The time span for this seasonal analysis ran from 1967 through 1980 inclusive. Weeks marked A through E are analyzed. These weeks correspond to arrows 1 through 7 on Figure 18-9, the March 1981 copper delivery. I outline the signal and seasonal information in tabular form as follows:

| Week | Arrow | Percentage of Reliability | Arrow | Commentary | Result |
|------|-------|---------------------------|-------|------------|--------|
| 47 | A | −70 | 1 | Previous Friday no signal. HLC on Monday of week. Short at 99.0, out at 97.00 | +2.00 |
| 43 | B | −70 | 2 | R⁻ and HLC double signal SS at 99.50, out at 97.50 | +2.00 |
| 42 | C | −70 | 4 | 3L arrow 3 SS at 97.50, out at 94.50 | +3.00 |
| 27 | D | +69 | 5 | LHC B at 97.70, out at 98.60, arrow 6 | +0.90 |
| 15 | E | +78 | 7 | Sharply lower close on week contrary to seasonal reading but *no* timing signal to buy | |

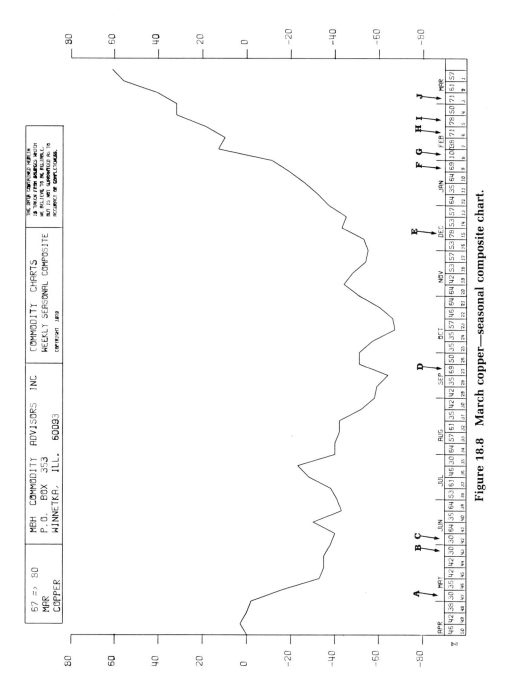

**Figure 18.8  March copper—seasonal composite chart.**

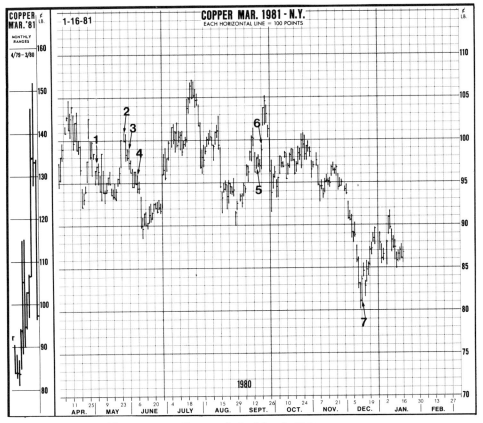

**Figure 18.9    Seasonals in March 1981—copper.**

As you can see, the five seasonal trades in March 1981 copper yielded about $0.0790 cents in potential profits before commissions. The only potential loss was seasonal E in week 15, but this seasonal failed to produce a signal. Hence, no trade would have been made.

Assume that you had entered the market in October strictly on the basis of the composite chart. As you can see, the result would have been a loss because patterns were contrary to seasonal expectations. It's very likely that the bottom in December 1981 was the seasonal low. The best way to trade seasonals is, therefore, to enter during a period of high seasonal upside reliability. On the composite chart this would have been week 15, arrow D. Because there was no signal during this week, the best alternative would have been to wait for new signals during the F, G, H, I, J period. The most likely time for such a signal would have been during the final week of January 1981.

## PORK BELLIES

The pork belly market has several reliable seasonals. Typically prices peak in August or September. A strong seasonal upmove usually begins in June following a seasonal low in May. The composite chart of February bellies covers

1967 through 1980 inclusive (Figure 18-10). The February 1981 belly chart (Figure 18-11) is marked in the fashion we have used previously. The trader who did not use signals but, rather, established positions merely on the basis of the seasonal chart would have been buying in June around the $0.43 level and taking profits in early September around the $0.70 level. The total move of over $0.30 from seasonal lows was a large move indeed and was an almost textbook case.

There were 12 reliable weekly readings. Notice that arrows *e*, *f*, and *g* in Figure 18-11 are part of a strong upside run. In the case of March 1981 bellies, the trader who bought and held at seasonal lows according to the composite chart would have done much better than the hit-and-run trader who worked only the weekly seasonal signals. The table on page 000 lists each weekly pattern and the corresponding action in March 1981 bellies.

You can easily see from this analysis that the short term trading, although profitable, was not nearly so successful as the seasonal trade put on in June and taken off in September.

| Week | Arrow | Percentage of Reliability | Arrow, Signal, and Commentary | Result |
|---|---|---|---|---|
| 35 | a | +71 | Long at arrow 2 daily R+, out by Friday 20 June 1980, arrow 3 | about even |
| 27 | b | +78 | Long at arrow 6 R+ at 62.50, out by Friday, arrow 5 for gain of | +1.00 |
| 20 | c | −72 | 3L signal on 9/26/80 SS at 65.00, out at arrow 7 at 62.50 | +2.50 |
| 19 | d | −72 | Prices rally strongly contrasonal to trend but no signal to sell short | |
| 16 | e | +76 | R+ at arrow 9 B at 70.50, out by arrow 10 for net loss | −0.60 |
| 15 | f | +71 | R+ Monday 11/03/80 B at 71.00, out at arrow *a* 68.05 | −2.95 |
| 14 | g | +71 | R+ at arrow *b* B at 66.20, out at arrow *f* 67.50, with a second R+ at arrow *c* | +1.50 |
| 13 | h | −65 | SS 11/24/80 3L at 70.60, out at 71.80 11/28/80 | −1.20 |
| 11 | i | −65 | SS arrow *h*, R− at 71.10, out at arrow *i* 68.10, or could hold since arrow *i* was also a 3L for the next week | +3.00 |
| 10 | j | −65 | SS at arrow *i*, 3L at 68.10, out at 60.30 arrow *j*. | +7.80 |
| 8 | k | +76 | 3H 12/19/80 B at 63.50, out at *k* 60.50 | −3.00 |
| 6 | l | +71 | R+ on 1/12/81 B at 52.30, out on Friday 01/16/81 at 53.20 | +0.90 |
| | | | Net gain | 8.95 |

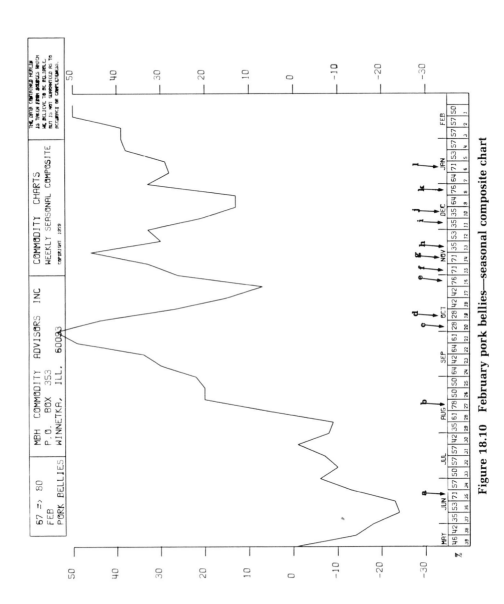

**Figure 18.10  February pork bellies—seasonal composite chart**

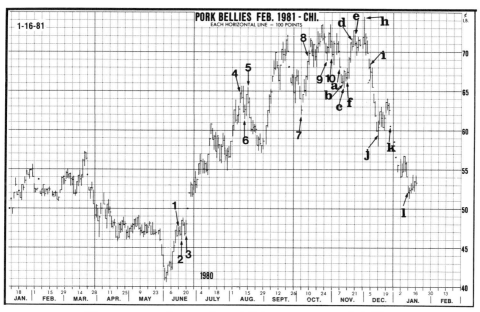

**Figure 18.11   Seasonals and February 1981 pork bellies.**

## SILVER

The strongest seasonal tendency in silver is for a low early in January with a sharply higher trend through March. Figure 18-12 shows seventeen reliable weekly readings a through q. These are detailed individually along with the current March 1981 silver chart in order to show you how the timing indicators work in conjunction with the seasonal and is done in the usual manner. Please refer to Figures 18-12 and 18-13.

| Week | Arrow | Percentage of Reliability | Arrow, Signal, and Commentary | Result |
|---|---|---|---|---|
| 47 | a | +76 | Not on our chart | |
| 40 | b | −75 | 3L 6/14/80 SS at 16.60, out arrow 2 16.70 | −0.10 |
| 38 | c | +66 | 3H arrow 3 b at 17.65, out arrow 4 at 18.25 | +0.60 |
| 34 | d | −67 | R− arrow 6 SS at 17.50, out arrow 7 at 16.80 | +0.70 |
| 30 | e | −67 | 3L arrow 8 SS at 17.15, out arrow 9 at 17.50 | −0.35 |
| 24 | f | +69 | LHC arrow a B at 21.50, out arrow b at 22.70 | +1.20 |
| 23 | g | −75 | R− arrow d SS at 19.95, out arrow c at 21.75 | +0.95 |
| 20 | h | −70 | R− arrow d SS at 19.95, out arrow e at 19.00 | +0.95 |

| Week | Arrow | Percentage of Reliability | Arrow, Signal, and Commentary | Result |
|------|-------|---------------------------|-------------------------------|--------|
| 17 | *i* | +69 | No buy signal during this week ended with arrow *f* | |
| 15 | *j* | +76 | No buy signal during this week ended with arrow *h* | |
| 14 | *k* | +76 | 3H arrow g B at 16.15, out arrow *i* at 16.75 | +0.60 |
| 13 | *l* | −70 | R− arrow *i* SS at 16.50, out arrow *j* at 17.15 | −0.65 |
| 12 | *m* | +69 | No buy signal during this week ended with arrow *m* | |
| 11 | *n* | −70 | R− arrow *k* SS at 16.70, out arrow *n* at 15.55 | +1.15 |
| | | | Net gain | 5.05 |

Because of a lack of timing indicators, not all seasonal patterns were traded. In particular, weeks 17 and 15 were large down weeks. According to the seasonal plot, they should have been large up weeks, but there was no timing signal to get on the long side. Hence, no position would have been taken by the individual using timing and seasonals together.

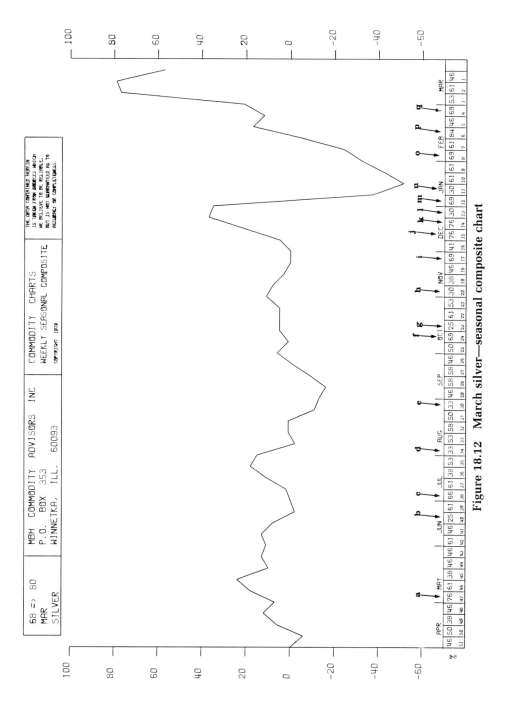

**Figure 18.12  March silver—seasonal composite chart**

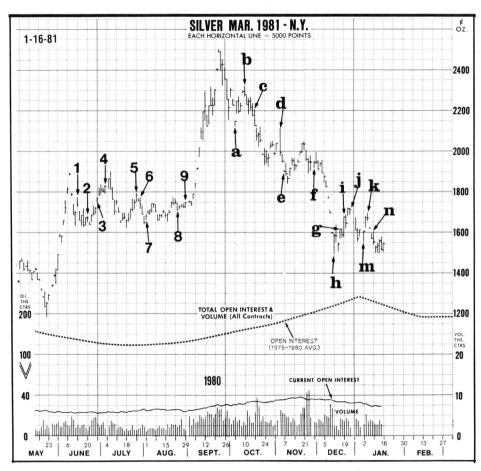

**Figure 18.13  Seasonals and March 1981—silver.**

# CHAPTER NINETEEN

# Some Observations on Money Management and Cyclic Trading

A system that does not include a sound method of money management is like the proverbial horse without a rider. No matter how intrinsically sound a given method may be, it is, as I have indicated previously, virtually useless unless it is carefully followed, faithfully implemented, and soundly managed. The old time-tested rules (e.g., as "Cut your losses and let your profits ride") are to be taken for granted. The cyclic trading methods earlier discussed, however, have their own set of money management principles that have been developed through years of experience. In some cases the dictums are relatively similar to what you have already heard and should know by now. In other instances, the suggestions I make may run contrary to what is traditionally preached. Ultimately, you will integrate what I have told you with your own tools. Remember at all times that a trading method is like a theory of scientific behavior. It will always seem sound and sensible in a book, but the manner in which theory is translated into action makes the difference between losses and profits.

## HOW MUCH CAPITAL?

A question frequently asked and one that is basic to successful trading is, "How much capital should be used?" The answer depends on several key considerations. First, it is up to the individual to decide how much risk he can take. Risk must always be defined in terms of dollars. I always recommend that a person begin by stating in dollars the total amount of money he can lose without any change in living standard. Of this amount, I then ask the individual to state how much he can lose without remorse. Generally, the response is about 20 percent the total amount of available risk capital. Say, for example, that a potential speculator has $200,000 in risk capital. My 20-percent rule then defines the amount to be used in commodity speculation as about $40,000. The acid test, to my way of thinking, is to truthfully answer the question, "Can you accept the possibility of a total loss of these funds?" Assuming the answer is affirmative, or even close to it, I then recommend this as the proper starting amount.

A second, and possibly more rational way of dealing with the issue is to decide how many markets you wish to trade. Then multiply this number by three times the current margin requirement total. Say, for example, that you want to trade the model portfolios shown in Figure 19-1. Each of the major market groupings is represented. One grain, one meat, one metal, one financial future, cotton, one wood market, and one of the food group markets has been selected. This is a very reasonable way of choosing and makes a total of seven markets. The total margin might, for example, be $12,000. This figure multiplied by three yields $36,000, which I recommend as the starting amount.

There are other methods you can use. Regardless of how you determine what is proper within the boundaries of your financial ability, observe the following simple, but necessary, guidelines:

1   Do not under margin yourself. Allow ample room for price movement against you.

2   Allow sufficient capital for several losses. The cyclic trading method I have given you is not a guarantee of success. Like any other market discipline, it requires some leeway on losses. A trader who exits the marketplace after two successive losses, either willfully or by necessity, is doomed to failure well before the start.

3   Allow sufficient capital for unexpected opportunities. There may be one or more valid signals to add to a position after the initial trade has been established. They should be followed, but sufficient margin must be available.

4   Don't go big game hunting with an air gun. Stay away from markets with a history of extremely wide price fluctuation, successive limit-up and/or down moves, and relatively high margins. If your account is large, you may be tempted to go after big game although your experience to date is insufficient. Stay away from these markets because they may rapidly absorb too much of your starting funds.

## HOW ABOUT "PYRAMIDING"?

Until I started trading commodities I was under the impression that the base of a pyramid was its widest and strongest point. As used in the commodity markets, however, the term *pyramiding* does not mean what one might expect.

| Portfolio 1 | Portfolio 2 (higher risk) |
| --- | --- |
| Corn | Soybeans |
| Live cattle | Pork belllies |
| Copper | Gold |
| T-Bonds | T-Bills |
| Cocoa | Orange juice |
| Cotton | Cotton |
| Lumber | Lumber |
| Canadian dollar | British pound |
| | Heating oil |

**Figure 19-1   Model commodity futures portfolios.**

All too often the novice trader is lured into adding additional units as soon as the initial position shows sufficient profit to meet the margin required. Hence, an initial position of 1 unit, once profitable, might permit the addition of 2 more units; the new total of 3 units might soon permit the additional purchase of six contracts; and the new total of nine units could then show enough profit for the accumulation of 12 more contracts, and so on. The use of such an inverted pyramid is something I emphatically discourage. It is more common in gambling than in informed speculation. The only time to add to a position is when there is a signal to do so! At no time should each additional trade be larger in the number of units than the starting position. If you start with five units, then each successive signal to add must result in the accumulation of not more than five additional units.

The reasoning here is simple. As long as the market continues in a given direction, signals to add will more often than not be valid. By accumulating on a linear curve, your additional units are not likely to outpace the momentum and angle of market movement. Hence, a small setback in trend will not destroy an inordinately large amount of open profit. If you follow the inverted pyramid method, however, you will always be more vulnerable to smaller and smaller setbacks in trend. An extremely small move could conceivably neutralize all (if not more than) your total profit.

## REVERSE POSITION OR TAKE PROFITS AT AN OBJECTIVE?

There are two schools of thought in the world of trend following. Some techniques require the trader to be constantly in the market, long or short. When a long position is closed out on a given signal, the same signal necessarily required the trader to get short. Getting short is possible if the trader is using the cyclic trading method I have described but not in every case. Cycle signals may occur as follows:

1  Simple buy signal.
2  Simple sell signal.
3  Signal to sell out long and go short.
4  Signal to cover short and go long.
5  Liquidation of long position on stop signal with no reversal of position.
6  Liquidation of short position on stop signal with no reversal of position.

Sometimes no new signal appears for a period following liquidation of an existing position. During this time no trading is done. If there is a reversal signal, then the position is reversed and the new trend followed. It is that simple.

Some traders prefer to follow a "hit-and-run" type of approach to cyclic trading. When they establish a position, they also determine an objective. Once they attain this time window objective (notice that it is *not* a price objective), they automatically close out the position and do nothing until a new signal appears. Of course, they could close out the position before reaching the time objective if the predetermined stop signal comes. Although this method has the advantage of being especially well suited for short term trading, it can also limit profits in a runaway type of move, up and/or down. I recommend a longer term approach for most traders.

## THE STOP LOSS

For many years the public has been advised to use stop losses. Although the intent of such advice is good, the actual use of stops no longer seems reasonable. All too often the following sequence of events occurs:

1   Trader establishes position.
2   Stop loss order is entered at what is considered a reasonable dollar loss figure or at the appropriate technical chart point.
3   At first the position moves in the expected direction (but not necessarily).
4   A sudden, but technically meaningless (and usually intraday), move hits stop, and the position is closed out.
5   The expected move then continues.

The trader who was stopped out unnecessarily feels as if there has been some foul play. Although nothing of the sort has in fact happened, there is never-theless a rational explanation. Since the late 1950s, there has been a steady growth in technical trading systems. Most systems either follow a combination of moving-average signals, specific chart points and signals, and/or traditional point-and-figure signals. At any one time several thousand stop orders may accumulate within a fairly small price range. Once that range is hit, the resulting chain reaction wipes clean the slate of resting stops, and the existing trend continues. This explanation is not necessarily the only plausible one, and I have no hard evidence for it. I have seen this happen often enough, however, to know whereof I speak. It is understandable that many individuals, all re-sponding in similar fashion to generally similar signals, can cause an erratic price move. This is how the best intentions regarding use of stop loss orders can go astray, and a once-sound rule of money management can have an effect opposite from that actually intended.

How do I propose we avoid this situation? There are several methods. My main method is to avoid the use of stops. If you do as the Romans do when you are in Rome, then you will also go under with them when the empire collapses. When I tell you to avoid the use of stops I mean simply *do not actually place the stop order with your broker.* By not having a resting stop on the books, you will not be one of the sufferers in a false reversal situation such as earlier described. This does *not* mean that you have no stop in mind. It does not mean that you will fail to limit your losses. It *does* mean, however, that you will not act at the same time as others are acting, which in and of itself is a good policy regardless.

The way in which a precise stop is determined has been covered in Chapter 17. This procedure remains unchanged. Let me emphasize that our stops are either *close only* or *next day* stops. If the cyclic method gains in popularity, then there will most likely come a time when close only stops fail to achieve their purpose. Should this occur, we will need to use another method of limiting losses that is not used by most other traders. I suggest you carefully reread the section on stops and limiting losses. Notice above all that the way in which a loss is limited should always be 180 degrees out of phase with what the general public is doing. If the public is placing stops with the broker, then you ought not do so. If the public is placing close only stops then you ought not do so. If the public is waiting until the next day's opening to liquidate a position that hits its stop point, then you ought to place your stop close only the day before, and so on.

## REMOVING PROFITS FROM YOUR ACCOUNT

Many traders do not have a predetermined plan for removing profits from the market. Often there are no profits to remove; there are only margin calls to meet. Go to the market prepared to remove profits. Not only is this a positive, winning attitude but it is also sound investment policy. Remove 50 percent of your capital each and every time you have increased your starting amount by 100 percent. Some people will argue that this practice leaves too little capital for trading. I offer this suggestion only as another conservative method for avoiding losses and enjoying profits. If you start with $40,000 and your account grows to $80,000, then remove 50 percent of the total profit, or $20,000. This leaves you with $60,000. When the account grows to $120,000, remove 50 percent of the new gain, or $60,000. You will now be left with $180,000. The money you remove will probably be needed for taxes and would have had to be removed anyway.

## MARGIN CALLS—WHAT THEY MEAN

There is an old but wise adage that cautions against meeting a margin call. There is much truth to this dictum. If you are called for additional margin, then you are probably doing something wrong. Either you have put on too many positions, carried a loss too far or too long, added to a losing position with no signal to do so, or failed to observe stop loss signals. You should liquidate all positions necessary to avoid the margin call, even if it means closing out the entire account. Do not trade again until you have discovered the source of your error(s).

## TRADING FOR LONG TERM OR SHORT TERM

The decision to trade primarily for the short term requires several prerequisites. Inasmuch as short term trading by its very nature generates many more signals and trades than does long term trading, the time input requirement is considerably greater. In addition, the trader who selects short term trading requires a greater degree of self-discipline because day-to-day events affect price behavior. The decision as to time orientation usually must be made by each trader.

My preference is for long term trades—by which I mean trades kept in excess of one month. The cyclic method, however, makes no distinction between long term or short term. The signals discussed here should function equally well in both cases.

## RISK—HOW MUCH IS TOO MUCH

One of the questions most often asked is, "How much risk is too much?" The following example illustrates an important point about risk taking. Assume that you have a signal to buy soybeans. On the basis of the signal, it is quite clear that the stop loss point for this trade requires a potential minimum loss of $2,300. The potential dollar loss is calculated according to the stop loss method presented in Chapter 17. You are now faced with a difficult decision. Although the signal to buy is valid within the cyclic timing rules, a loss of this amount might be too large for your account. A $10,000 account would lose almost 25 percent of its total account should the signal to buy prove invalid. At this rate you would have only three more chances to turn a profit. These are not good odds.

To determine how much risk is enough I recommend the 10 percent rule. Never make a trade that will require more than 10 percent of the total size of your account as a potential loss. There will be times when a loss is greater than you originally expected, but the 10 percent rule will help keep you out of trouble while keeping the odds on your side. A trade requiring more risk will also yield potentially more profit. This is not the way in which the decision must be made, however. Safe trading is like defensive driving, and preservation of capital is the single most important rule you can observe.

As you can see, it is important for all traders to maintain the correct balance between rational money management and technical discipline. Without *every* part of this system, there is no functional method. Were it not for the limitation of available funds, the use of my 10 percent rule would be unnecessary. For the trader with limited monies, strict adherence to this rule, at least early in the game, is necessary for survival.

## SPREADING TO AVOID TAKING A LOSS

An otherwise intelligent speculator will often make the grave error of spreading a position to avoid taking a loss. A spread (also called a straddle) involves being both long and short in the same market (usually) in different contract months. Another form of spread involves being long in one market and short in another related market. Frequently, a trader will fail to close out a position at the appropriate time or will be unwilling to do so when the time comes. To avoid riding the loss, or to avoid taking the loss, the trader will simply put on an opposite position in a different contract month, thereby locking in his loss with the hope that it will not become larger.

The problem with a spread is that, although it supposedly locks in the loss, the trader is now in the position of having to deal with two decisions rather than one. By locking in the loss, he has indeed bought more time. His hope is that he will eventually close out one leg (side) of the spread at or near breakeven, while riding the loss side to break even, or possibly to achieve a much smaller loss, as well. In practice, such a spread situation is rarely resolved favorably. More often than not both legs go against the trader, thereby creating an even larger loss than might have been taken earlier.

Signals to spread are quite clear in some situations. But to "leg" into and/or out of a spread, as it is called, is not usually recommended. If a loss is dealt with when the time is right, then there is no need for spreading, and hence no further grief about the loss. If a loss is not taken when prescribed, then the best time to act is immediately. In other words, correct your error as soon as you have recognized it! Once made, errors left uncorrected tend to grow into all-consuming monsters, which causes you to make even more errors. *In some instances the experienced trader will know how to use spreads as a means of avoiding or delaying a loss, but considerable skill is necessary to do so successfully.*

## SELECTION OF A BROKERAGE HOUSE

This topic is not usually mentioned under the subject of money management. In fact, I have never seen it mentioned in other market texts. Yet I consider it one of the most important aspects of this chapter. We live in unstable economic times. Within a matter of weeks there can be major changes in the financial stability and solvency of individuals and firms. Should a firm with which you have funds on deposit show signs of financial difficulty, you could in the not so distant future find that your own good money has gone down the drain with them. Although unfair, it has and will continue to happen. Assume that at some point in the future you get all your money back. If this money was your only risk funds, then you have most likely lost many market opportunities while awaiting the return of what was rightfully yours.

I have found it best to establish your account with the most financially stable and oldest firms. In many cases this means that you pay larger commissions per trade, but in the long run you are better off. If a market situation arises that threatens the financial liquidity of the brokerage community, then those houses best capitalized are the most likely survivors.

Another advantage of dealing with an older, well-established firm is that their hiring policies are generally more stringent. Hence, you are less apt to wind up with an ill-trained or unscrupulous broker. There are many horror stories about the manner in which a deceptive broker can affect the funds in a client account. In addition, the continuing supervision, both managerial and legal, tends to be more rigorous in an older line firm. Remember, I am not saying that a smaller firm cannot give you good service. The important thing is to know the firm with which you are dealing. It is vital to know its financial condition, history, reputation, and policies.

Perhaps the greatest single mistake a trader can make is to select a firm entirely on the basis of its commission charges. The cheapest, as you know, is not always the best. In fact, the cheapest may turn out to be the most costly in other ways. True, if you do not use the research services of a brokerage house, then you are entitled to a lower rate. To place funds with a financially unstable firm as a function of low commission charges is not in my experience, however, a good thing to do. Great care and a little investigation can go a long way in helping you select the right discount brokerage firm. Know your broker!

One final point about the selection of a broker deserves mention. Many traders cannot resist the temptation of outside opinion, particularly that of a broker.

Brokers are, in most cases, honest, hard-working individuals attempting to perform a service for their clients. When asked to express an opinion about a given market, they will often do so as part of the service their firm offers. Quite often, however, the customer may be swayed by such opinion, either in favor of or opposed to a trade earlier indicated by the customer's trading system. I find that most individuals do not have the necessary persistence to work through the opinions or recommendations of a broker. For such people I advise finding a broker who remains tight-lipped, acting only as an order taker. In the long run most traders are better off with such a broker because having one of that type fosters the growth of self-discipline. This is an important thing to consider when shopping for a broker. Either you decide to follow all the broker's advice, or you decide to play your own signals. Anything that falls in between is usually doomed to early failure.

## THE IMPORTANCE OF BEING PERSISTENT

Persistence is a quality not ordinarily included under the heading of money management. After all, though, one of the key elements in successful money management is the psychological attitude of the money manager. In my commodity trading seminars I am often asked, "Why are you making your trading system public . . . are you not afraid that it will become too widely known and thereby lose its effectiveness?" My answer to this natural query is always the same. In my experience there are three types of traders: (1) the one who doesn't believe anything anyone else tells him; (2) the one who believes that what I am teaching has merit but who lacks the discipline and motivation to do anything about it; (3) the one who recognizes the value of cyclic trading to the point of actually attempting it. Following several initial losses, the patience of the third dwindles to naught and he abandons the method. There are, in other words, few people in the world who even bother to implement any of my suggestions because they lack the *discipline, motivation,* or *persistence* to do so.

These three qualities lay the foundation for success in any field, commodities or whatever. And it is for this reason that I discuss them in the section on money management. Asked for ways in which I would go about developing or improving these skills, I often suggest the following:

1  Maintain a thorough and comprehensive trading record in which you list all cycles, time windows, and signals as discussed.

2  Follow each signal as if it were the highest law of the land. Do not stray from the indicators in any way, shape, or form.

3  Do not fall victim to the perils of interpretation. A signal is a signal is a signal. I have presented the timing indicators here most specifically and without any room (I hope) for misunderstanding. You must *follow* them, not *interpret* them.

4  If you have valid technical reason for making a trade and take a loss in adhering rigidly to the rules, then you have done a good job despite the loss of funds. There is only one way to respond to such a loss, and that is by trading the next signal as soon or as late as it develops. There is no other choice.

These rules hold true for any trader regardless of system, race, creed, color, sex, nationality, or market being traded. They are basic to success in commodity futures and are not subject to change, consideration, judgment, or interpretation. And they are totally necessary for effective money management.

## THE USE OF TRADING OBJECTIVES

Another popular misconception involves the use of price objectives. For years we have been told to set a price objective for each trade. Rather than price objectives, I believe we should set *time objectives* based on the cyclic time window. Why do I make this suggestion? Consider the following brief story. A trader buys gold during the seasonal low period in August. He does so on several valid technical cycle signals. He buys in the area of $500 per ounce and decides that his price objective is $720 or more. Several months later he still holds his position. In the interim gold has moved a grand total of $20 in his favor. The appropriate time for a seasonal high arrives. The high is confirmed by a cyclic top and timing signals. Here sits our trader, long in gold, expecting about $200 more on the upside, looking at clear-cut signals to sell. He is disappointed. Perhaps he has been reading the papers or listening to the gloom-and-doom philosophers and their predictions about infinitely high gold prices. True, they may be right, but they could also be wrong. And because the *market* is the only thing that is *always* right, their forecasts amount to nothing in the face of clear-cut technical evidence to sell. Several months from now the price of gold may indeed rocket skyward, but in the interim it could plummet several hundred dollars while our trader stays long, expecting sharply higher prices.

The mere act of establishing a price objective is in some respects a denial of your belief in *time* and *timing* as the key elements in cyclic analysis. The way of Zen teaches us to flow with the tide wherever it may lead. The river twists and winds its way to the end, and so does the market. We cannot tell the market where to take us and when to get there, so the act of forecasting price rather than time is a futile, infantile, and dubious achievement. By waiting for a given price, you may totally lose track of the proper time. Although it is a romantic and possibly noteworthy achievement to be correct in predicting price, it is a far greater achievement financially to be in the *right place* at the *right time*. That is why I discourage the use of price objectives.

## THE USES AND ABUSES OF MARGIN

The main attraction of commodity trading as distinct from other forms of speculation is the relatively small amount of capital required to control a large amount of goods. *Leverage*, as that is called, can be both a friend and an enemy. When you are using several hundred dollars to control several thousand dollars, both the risk and reward factor are magnified manyfold. It is the 1 to 3 percent margin that has occasioned many rags-to-riches stories as well as riches-to-rags heartbreaks. And so, the very low margin required in commodity futures is both a friend and an asset, as well as a potential liability. It all depends on your use or abuse of the privilege. Fortunately, you can use a number of techniques to circumvent the possibly destructive side of this wonderful tool.

The use of low margin gives most traders the illusion that they are not risking much. It is generally known, although not truly believed, that you can often lose more than your original investment in the commodity market. Even though you can possibly lose much more than your starting amount and this is known to be a fact, it is a fact that is generally understated by the public and by the professional community as well. Hence, you must promptly dispel the illusion that a margin of $1000 can rarely result in the loss of more than $1000. If I can help you to do so, I will be pleased. To overcome the false sense of low risk that accompanies low margin, it is necessary that you combat the concept of low margin with a disciplined approach. A technique I have always found helpful is to trade each market with twice or three times the amount required in order to cushion myself from the possible adverse consequences of a loss. Therefore, should the margin on a gold contract be $1000, I mentally assign $2000 or even $3000 to this position. In so doing, I overcome both the emotionalism and temptation that accompany low margin. I leave myself with an adequate buffer within which prices may move.

As you can see, the myth of margin is not structured for the good of the general public. In fact, low margin seems to serve the purpose of no one but the brokers and floor traders. By having margin requirements that are too low, the exchanges may be encouraging positions that are too high, thereby increasing the probability of wide price swings when traders scramble at the slightest move to liquidate positions that are too large. I urge you not to fall into the trap of low margin. You can accomplish this by the use of a double or triple margin technique described in the foregoing paragraph, by trading only about 50 percent of your total account equity, or by trading one market per major grouping (e.g., one meat, one grain, one metal).

# CHAPTER TWENTY

# Some Caveats

The commodity trading public is constantly searching for the Holy Grail. If there is even the slightest chance that a trading system will be "perfect" or "the ultimate," its promoters can probably sell it to the public at outrageously high prices, whether it is indeed perfect or not. In my years of trading I have never seen nor do I know of anyone who has developed the ultimate trading system. If it exists, it is not being sold. The cyclic technique is not a perfect system; it is merely one way of looking at reality. I do not say that it will be better for you than any other disciplined trading method. Only you can decide if, how, and why the cyclic methods are valuable within the constraints of your market approach. In fact, the success of cyclic trading itself is most likely cyclic, alternating between on the continuum of profit and loss.

Implementation of a system requires considerable effort and time. Should you wish to be well versed in fundamentals or traditional charting techniques, you must study, read, practice, experiment, and organize. You need records, books, data, charts, time, time, time, and more time. These are the prerequisites to success in any business or discipline, whether technical, religious, or educational. Hence, the cyclic method, although capable of being distilled into a text or into three days of lecture and explanation, is only a beginning. It is the inputs of organization, trial and error, and time that truly differentiate the motivated person from the intellectually lazy person. In fact, it's not nearly as much a matter of intelligence as it is drive and discipline (the three of which are not necessarily related).

I cannot, and will not, make any guarantees to you about what has been presented in this book. Because I have no control over how you use what I have given you, how the markets may change over time, or how cyclic analysis may need to improve by way of adjustment to changing conditions, I can make no definitive statements about profits, potential profits, losses, potential losses, or future performance. I can and will tell you that any form of organization and discipline is valuable in the market regardless of its orientation, outlook, philosophy, or theoretical basis. Some readers will want to examine the cyclic concepts in relation to their own market methods, which will necessarily change some of the techniques, stop points, and so on that I have given you. Such alterations are deviations from my original work. Hence, I cannot and will not be held accountable for what may result, good or bad.

Some traders may wish to use my work as a steppingstone to more sophisticated methods. Computer application of the principles discussed here is certainly possible, as Appendix 2 shows (see also Chapter 21). In fact, I have already employed my computer facilities to this end, and all the work presented here is being maintained in computerized form. The concept I have presented, however, is still only the second or third step in a series of perhaps 100 or more steps. The student of mathematics could expand on what I have said. Whether the results would be rewarding financially in terms of the time input required, I am not certain. The effort should be a most interesting and exciting one that may provide some totally new ideas and/or answers.

Great care, preservation of capital, consistency, hard work, discipline, and dedication are some of the key elements in making my method work. Should you decide to investigate how well it can work for you, either on its own or in association with another set of timing indicators or time window methods, I make the following suggestions. I hope that you will give them due consideration inasmuch as they came to me as expensive lessons, many of which had to be learned several times in succession:

1. *Get organized.*  Being well organized is truly one of the keys to success whether you use my method or any other trading system. Get your charts in order, know exactly which markets you want to follow, know if you want to trade intermediate term, short term, long term, or all three. Get your seasonal data ready.

2. *Stay up to date.*  After several losses, you will be tempted to give up on the system (this or any other system). Your data will fall behind, your charts will not be up to date. When the big move comes and the signal is right, you won't be ready. You must always keep up to date, even if you must hire someone else to keep records for you.

3. *Keep good records* of signals and trades, which is a vital feedback method that will let you know how well you are following your system, where you may have taken a wrong turn, and how you can get back on the track.

4. *Learn all signals and rules thoroughly.*  It is a good idea to have the signals and rules in card form prominently displayed or readily available. It's easy to bend the rules when you want a position to go your way. Having the rules in front of you in black and white can help you to avoid the temptation to twist rules.

The caveat I can offer you has to do with risks and losses. Too many commodity speculators, or would-be traders, pay too little attention to what can be lost. They assume that they will not lose their entire starting amount. By the time 25 percent of it has eroded, they begin to panic, worry, lose sleep, become anxious, make errors in judgment, and make emotional decisions not based at all on the trading system. If you cannot take the chance, if you cannot afford the tuition of playing the game, then don't play it because it could prove very costly. Regardless of whose trading system you follow, whether you listen to a broker, a newsletter, a market seer, or the popular press, you must accept the risk within your financial ability. Money can be lost through professional money managers as well, although possibly not as quickly. Avoid the commodity game unless you have been totally honest with yourself about risks and rewards, about losses and profits, about what will hurt you and what won't. There's a world of difference between being upset *about* a loss and being financially upset *by* a loss.

# CHAPTER TWENTY-ONE

# Using the Computer

Advances in electronic technology have brought computers into the home. Commodity and stock traders have eagerly welcomed this tool into their bag of market resources. Computers and their peripherals can help the commodity trader accomplish many things that otherwise would consume vast amounts of time. Among these are data storage, research on trading systems, hard copy graphics, monitoring of trades and equities, remote data transfer, and optimization of trading methods. Unfortunately, the field of microcomputers and minicomputers has grown more rapidly than has public knowledge regarding these wondrous tools. Many traders have purchased expensive systems that do not meet their needs, and many individuals have purchased systems whose cost does not in any way justify bottom line profit. Having been in the common computer quandary myself, I have learned through expensive experience. Many budding students of cycles are attracted to computer systems in the belief that their job of finding and tracking cycles will be facilitated. On occasion, the desired result is achieved, but more often it is not. The suggestions I make in the following pages relate to all aspects of computer use in commodity analysis, but they are particularly directed at those traders who intend to use computers in cyclic research.

## TO OWN OR TO SHARE

The first real question to answer is whether you stand to gain anything by actually owning your own computer system. It may be quite fashionable to say, "I have my own computer system," but who really benefits? There are two choices. You can buy and maintain your own system, or you can rent time on a system that is much larger than what you might be able to purchase. The outright purchase of an average system in today's microcomputer market might run you from $4000 to $8000. A minicomputer system (one step up) might cost from $10,000 to $25,000. These prices are typical in today's market. Things will change in time. As competition increases, systems will become cheaper, faster, and more sophisticated. When the hand-held calculator was introduced to the public, prices were outrageously high. Within only a few years calculators were being given away as incentives toward other purchases. Remember that outright purchase of a system does not include upkeep and maintenance costs. If the system fails, anything not under warranty must be repaired at your own expense. Manufacturers of the larger systems offer a service contract on their hardware, but the contracts are costly too.

How about renting time? There are several advantages to this alternative. First, you will have access to a very large system. If the system fails to operate, then the headache and expense of repair will not be yours. The hourly rental fees vary from one firm to another, but you pay only for what you use. The cost of programming is borne by the user in both cases. If you are proficient in computer language, then you can save considerable expense by doing the programming work on your own. If you lease time, then the company from whom the time is rented may be able to provide you with expert programming services of their own. In many cases these outfits will have a library of statistical programs, some of which you might find useful.

Another important consideration is that of confidentiality. If you own a system of your own, then your programs and results are yours and yours alone. If you come across an especially successful method, then you will not have to fear its' being stolen or copied, either by the company from whom you are renting time or by an astute programmer who knows what's been going on. The issue of confidentiality is very important, particularly in the marketplace. Trading systems that can yield handsome profits are an easy target for the unethical operator. One of the best arguments in favor of owning your own computer system is the peace of mind you will gain by knowing that your methods and research are as safe as they can be.

A final issue regarding whether to own or to rent time is the question of commodity data. To buy historical data for research purposes can prove quite costly. Once you have purchased the data, you have a storage problem. Small home computer systems can handle only relatively small chunks of data at one time. Storage of 15 years' data might require the use of many floppy disks. Before you buy a system, make certain you know how the data can be stored. As an alternative, however, a number of firms will rent you time on their computer and also maintain an up-to-date commodity data base. By renting time on their system, or by having them do your research for you, you avoid the cost of buying, storing, and maintaining your own data base.

These are just a few of the key issues in the buy versus renting time question. Each person must respond according to his or her own needs. You alone can determine how the costs balance against needs and return on capital. If there is an idea you want tested and if you feel it is good enough to keep secret, then the cost of your own system may be justified. Above all, remember that there are many hidden costs. You must always take into consideration such things as programming expenses, cost of maintaining hardware, and the expense of keeping data up to date. If your trading results and/or research will generate a profit after all costs have been deducted, then you would do well to get your own system. If you wish to test a system that may not work out, then you might be better off renting time and contracting for data and programming services.

## KEEPING GOALS IN SIGHT

Another commonly misunderstood aspect of computer technology is the amount of work actually required in testing an idea. To accurately determine whether a theory has any practical use, you need to be certain that it has been correctly programmed. Too many novices believe that commodity research using a computer is a matter of simply pressing some buttons, pulling some switches, and getting an answer. This is, of course, a gross oversimplification of the truth. The more intricate your system, the more carefully it must be tested. You need to know whether the program that has been written is actually getting at the idea you want tested. The intensive process of "debugging" or testing a program is very important in determining if it is accomplishing your intended goal. This takes time, money and effort, directly proportional to the complexity of the system being tested. In testing a theory you must always keep your goals clearly in sight, or you will spend hours and dollars needlessly.

There is yet another consideration in the area of goals. If you think that the computer can do anything you cannot do for yourself, then you are wrong. It's been my experience that the computer helps me do things faster and more accurately. Anything I want the computer to do must be spoonfed to it in programming language. If you have ideas and theories you want to check out, then you must put them into computer terminology, or you must explain them to someone who can do the translating for you. I like to think of the computer as a high-speed multifaceted brain that can do some things far more quickly and correctly than I can. Although work is now being done on computer systems that can actually go through a type of thinking or reasoning process, the computers available to most of us can only follow instructions. If you can instruct them properly and efficiently, then they will do your work for you. If you are confused about what you want to do, however, then you will most likely remain confused. In fact, your level of uncertainty may very well increase.

## CYCLIC RESEARCH USING THE COMPUTER

In Appendix 2, are some programs that can help you in the analysis of repetitive commodity price patterns. In addition, I have included some of the statistical and cyclic research material produced by the Foundation for the Study of Cycles. Remember that these programs were written for use on specific systems and need some modification if they are to be run on other systems. The programs I use are written primarily in FORTRAN and need considerable alteration if they are to be run in BASIC. The most useful applications of a computer in the area of cyclic analysis are discussed in the following paragraphs.

1. *Seasonal Patterns.* The calculation of seasonal price tendencies, either in cash or futures, whether monthly or weekly, requires considerable number pushing. Assume, for example, that you are interested in a weekly seasonal pattern over a 50 year period. If you have 52 prices per year and 50 years of data, then you have more than 2500 pieces of data. You must subtract each number from the one next to it, and then add all the price differences. Finally, you must calculate an average. The process is time-consuming, and the results might not be accurate if you were to perform the entire task by hand. An appropriate computer program for this process is relatively simple to write and even more simple to run. My system can compute 15 years of seasonal weekly data and plot a hard copy chart on the result in 5 minutes. Many home computer systems can do the same thing in about 10 minutes using a standard printer to produce the hard copy. This represents a substantial savings of time. The

same process can be done on seasonal spreads. My programs for seasonal cash and futures as well as seasonal spread calculation are contained in Appendix 2.

2. *Plotting and/or Charting.* You can easily plot and chart by using the computer and various peripheral equipment. Whether you use a plotter or a standard printer, you can obtain high quality, virtually perfect hard copy charts in a matter of minutes. If properly outfitted, your cathode ray tube (CRT) screen can display the chart, and you can make a hard copy photo of it. The various models of plotters and/or printers can make charts faster, better, and more accurately than any human being can make them manually.

3. *Finding, Projecting, and Combining Cycles.* All these operations are amenable to computer application. Some programs for doing this are provided in Appendix 2. You can instruct the computer to test a data series for the presence of a given cycle and, if it fails to find one, to move on to another cycle, and then another. This repetitive, or iterative, process can be carried on indefinitely until all possible cycles and combinations of cycles can be found. The cycles can then be mathematically recombined by the computer to plot a hypothetical chart of prices to account for all statistically valid patterns.

4. *Electronic Data Input and Output.* An important feature of computers allows you to send and/or receive data electronically, which is quicker and usually more accurate than recording manually. Instead of having to write prices in a log or record book, you electronically move the data into the computer storage facility (tape, floppy disk, or hard disk) until you need them, this saving time, expense, and storage space. Rather than keeping several thousand copies of the *Wall Street Journal* in your library, you simply have all the commodity price data stored on several disks or magnetic tapes.

5. *Keeping Track of Trades and Performance.* It is a very simple task for the computer to keep track of trades and performance if it has been properly programmed. Here, too, the amount of time and storage space are significantly reduced. When you need the information, you can easily retrieve it. In addition, a number of statistical operations can be performed to let you know such thing as your percentage of accuracy, return on capital, commissions generated, and the like.

6. *System Testing.* Among the more popular applications of a computer system is to test your system of trading. If you have a new idea about a system, whether it is cyclic or not, you can test it on the computer to see how it might have worked, assuming, of course, that you have the appropriate programs and necessary data to perform the test.

## A FEW PRECAUTIONS

If you've decided that you just can't live without a computer, then the next few points will be of interest. In time my precautions may be outdated, but for now they are sensible.

*Testing* a system can yield misleading results because your model will not have been tested in the real market. Why does this happen? First, the computer can get you in and out of the market at prices that might not have been possible in real time. Such things as gap openings, split range closing prices, sell stops, and buy stops cannot be completely reflected in a system test. The opening price, although it may be used as a computer entry point, might not have been obtainable in real time. Hence, your system test or model must be programmed to account for such error.

*System crashes and hardware failure* can and do happen. If you're trading for the short term and on-line computer use is necessary, then you will necessarily be out of the market if your hardware fails. You must either have backup equipment or an emergency plan for dealing with such problems. If you update data daily and your system is down when update time comes, then you will be thrown off your schedule. You should have a contingency plan for rectifying such difficulties.

*Loss of data* because accidental erasure or system failure is another problem. Should you lose your data through such a mishap, you must restore it. To prevent a massive headache and considerable expense, you should have backup copies of all your data and programs. In the event of theft or fire you would lose only the most recent material rather than everything. Remember that backup copies should be stored in a separate location. You should also have a schedule for making backup tapes or disks regularly.

# CHAPTER TWENTY-TWO

# Looking at the Entire Picture

Our journey through cycles has been like climbing a mountain. Having attained our goal, we can now sit back and examine the distance we have traveled. In so doing, we can obtain an overview of the entire concept. The individual parts that comprise the cyclic machinery have each been identified, examined, researched, and defined. Their specific roles in the overall cyclic network has been explained to the best of our current knowledge. A machine cannot function unless all its parts are put together, however. And they must fit properly as well. The correct procedure in working with cycles is to begin with the long term and work in the direction of the short term. What happens after the cyclic analysis has been completed is a function of the way it will be employed.

The hedger, or commercial interest, may wish to follow only long term, intermediate term, and seasonal tendencies. If he can determine the approximate time frame of a change in price trend, he can act well in advance according to what is expected. I gave the example of how such a person might have traded any of several markets, using more than the required margin in order to compensate for the degree of potential timing error. If your goal is to arrive at the most likely time for price change, then timing indications are only of secondary importance. The longer you can hold on to a position, the more likely you will be to show a profit if you have used the cycles as a guideline for entry. The commodity futures market is, however, a game of leverage and money management. Many traders cannot sit through large moves against them while they are waiting for a cycle to turn.

The issue of timing then becomes important. In fact, risk and timing are proportional considerations. The less risk you are willing to take, the more precise your timing must be. Hence, the cyclic trading system I have presented takes an important step beyond simple determination of the cycle length. By adding timing indicators to the cycle windows, the goal of limiting risk becomes more of a reality. Looking at the entire situation from an organizational point of view, we can categorize the many uses of cycles according to goals and associated inputs. Figure 22-1 lists intended use, technical inputs, and commentary. In order to optimally employ the cyclic approach, it is first necessary to determine your goals. Once you have done so, you can consult Figure 22-1 to determine how much work you will need to do.

You may decide that a combination of several objectives is best. Should this be the case, you will need to allow more time than indicated in Figure 22-1.

| Goal | Inputs | Commentary |
|---|---|---|
| Short term speculation | Daily and/or hourly charts | Requires full time attention |
| Intermediate term speculation | Weekly charts | Can be done well with only several hours input per week |
| Long term speculation | Weekly or monthly charts | Can be done well with only one hour (approximately) input per week |
| Hedging | Weekly charts | Must watch seasonal tendencies as well as intermediate cycles |
| Investing | Weekly or monthly charts | Requires minimal input per week and larger margin per trade |
| Seasonal trading | Weekly charts | Only several hours per week; same basic work as hedging |

**Figure 22.1. Outline of goals and technical inputs.**

You should also maintain several different trading accounts, one for each type of trading. Assume, for example, that you wish to trade seasonal cycles and short term cycles. Assume also that you have an interest in hedging the cattle market. My advice would be to handle all your cattle hedging transactions in one account, the seasonal trades in a totally separate account, and your short term trades in yet a third account. I recommend this because of the confusion that might result from doing several different types of trading through one account.

## WHAT YOU NEED TO GET STARTED

The more intensively and actively you want to trade, the more starting materials you need. The short term trader, therefore, needs more initial data than one who seeks to trade only long term cycles. I have listed several general requirements applicable to all traders, as follows:

1  A reliable source of price data, whether tick by tick, daily, or weekly, is necessary if you wish to follow cycles effectively. Several sources are given in Appendix 1. Such data include not only actual high, low, and closing prices but also weekly, monthly, daily, or shorter price charts. Price charts can be obtained from commercial sources, or you can make them on your own. Keeping your own charts takes more time, but it is also beneficial in other ways.

2  Have on hand a list of markets that you plan to trade. It is best to trade only several markets, so that you can keep your work to a minimum. Suggestions regarding which markets should be considered have already been made in Chapter 19.

3  Keep an outline of rules and indicators for cycle system trading until you have learned them without error or omission. These need not necessarily be the exact rules I have suggested. You may have researched a combination of

timing and cycles especially suited to your needs. Regardless of the exact timing method you employ, make certain that it is completely operational, objective, and readily available.

4    Mark your charts with the cycles, their lengths, and their time windows. At any time you should have an idea of when the next important cycle highs and lows are due. Mark your charts for every cycle in every market you intend to trade. It is best to keep these dates, or time windows, in a notebook used only for this purpose.

5    Keep a record of all trades, their outcome, stop, time objective, signal, and rationale for establishing the position. This will allow you to work back and check possible errors, deletions, or complications.

6    Make a regular routine of doing your market work. By having everything scheduled at a given time, by not deviating from this schedule too often, and by knowing in advance when and what your work will be, you will be more organized and less apt to make errors. Furthermore, your market work will not fall behind.

7    Make certain that you have the proper writing implements to keep charts up to date. If you want to follow cycles as I have suggested, then you ought to invest in several mechanical pencils of high quality—one each of black, red, and blue. In addition, purchase a professional set of compass points (or dividers), a long straightedge or ruler (about 20 inches), preferably one of transparent plastic. The best kind of chart paper and record-keeping book were discussed in Chapter 1.

8    It is best to keep you charts in a three-ring binder of appropriate size. Keep a list of the relevant cycles for the given market on each chart.

9    If you plan to trade seasonal cycles, then you must keep a list of the exact seasonal patterns for each contract month you intend to trade. Weekly seasonal futures charts are best, and it is best to keep them adjacent to the current contract month and year of the given market.

The foregoing are several of the major prerequisites for starting trading. Other necessities will appear as you become more deeply involved in cycle trading. Organization of information along the lines indicated is necessary in any form of technical trading. Many of the suggested items apply equally to other trading systems. If you have no interest in cycles as a trading method, then you might still wish to consider the many organizational suggestions made in this book. They have been learned through years of personal experience.

## HOW TO BEGIN

Let's assume that the entire field of cycles is new to you. You have read this book, and you have decided that there may actually be some potential to the cyclic method of commodity trading. You might even be considering the possibility of applying cyclic methods to other markets as well (e.g., stocks). As a novice, you may be intimidated by the magnitude of the available information. There are thousands of purported experts, hundreds of newsletters and advisory services, many brokerage houses, and countless opinions. Chart services and sources of raw data are less plentiful, but you must still make a decision about the services you really need. Here are some guidelines for the novice (some of which may apply to the seasoned trader as well):

1.   Take your time. Become familiar with your local situation regarding price data. Are prices readily available in your evening paper? Does the paper cover the markets you need? Does the paper provide weekly high, low, and close prices in the weekend edition? Should you subscribe to the *Wall Street Journal*, or should you buy it daily? If the mail is slow and you trade daily, then you must get your paper daily, unless you have another source of prices such as a quotation machine or a copperative broker.

2.   Get to know your chart services. Take a trial subscription to several services. See what they have to offer in terms of your needs. Do the historical charts (weekly or monthly) go back far enough to permit a complete analysis of cycles? Are they accurate? Can you keep them up to date on your own? Are they large and easily read? These are all important considerations. I recommend weekly charts that go back at least 8 years for intermediate term trading and daily charts for close to start of current contract. If you decide to take a chart service, then make certain it will reach you on time. How fast is the mail delivery from their location to yours?

3.   Find a broker who will cooperate. The best broker is not necessarily the one who offers the cheapest commissions. In fact, commissions, as long as they are within the industry norm, should be your last consideration unless you are a day trader. Among the things to consider in selecting a broker are the following:

1   Can he or she be reached quickly?
2   Is the broker reliable?
3   How fair are the price fills (only time will tell)?
4   Will the broker gladly give you daily and/or weekly prices when you need them?
5   Is the broker so opinionated that you stand a chance of being talked out of or into positions?
6   Will the broker act promptly and with accuracy in executing your trades?
7   Is the brokerage house well established?
8   Will your funds be secure?
9   Will interest income be given on the monies not actively used in trading?

These are only some of the things you should consider in selecting a broker.

4.   Follow only several markets, possibly even only one market. Before jumping into the cycles system whole hog, get some experience with it. Perhaps you will have difficulty putting my method into operation. You may decide that the system is not suited to your needs and temperament. Why make a large investment in time and materials until you are certain that this is the right thing for you? Spend several months studying historical price behavior of the cycles I have discussed. See if you might have used them profitably.

5.   How about a quotation machine? Many traders feel that they will need a machine for tick-by-tick data. In the majority of cases, a machine is totally unnecessary and, in fact, can be quite detrimental to the intermediate or long term trader. You will not need a quotation machine unless you decide to "scalp" or day trade the market according to an ultra short term cycle method. I especially discourage such short term trading. Hence, I do not believe that most traders, especially those having other full-time jobs, should have a price ticker.

6.   How much money should be risked? This is an individual consideration. The best rule of thumb is to avoid risking anything until you are certain you understand what you are doing, regardless of the trading method you have selected. Chapter 14 discussed in detail the subject of risk.

7.   Determine your goals. Decide whether you are interested in long term, short term, intermediate term, or seasonal trading. Once this has been done you will know exactly how much and what kind of data you should keep.

8.   Make an outline of what you will need. A checklist is invaluable in learning a new procedure or in keeping an old one flawless. By knowing exactly what needs to be done, you ensure completion of the overall task.

Other things will become clear to you in time. Only experience can help you overcome many of the small obstacles that are part of any trading system. Certain types of trading may not be practical, given other aspects of your life, family situation, and job. These factors must all be given great thought, not only in the selection of your trading method but primarily in the decision as to how actively you want to trade.

Appendix 4 contains a number of sample analyses done on back data for illustrative purposes. Going through the step-by-step examples may give you a better feel for the entire technique.

# APPENDIX ONE

# Sources of Information

Keeping your cyclic research up to date is of major importance. In addition to the daily, monthly, and/or weekly charts, which should be maintained regularly, you may wish to read about the work of others in this field.

## PUBLICATIONS AND ORGANIZATIONS

*Cycles* is a monthly publication of the Foundation for the Study of Cycles. I have referred to their work many times in this book. The cost of an annual membership is very low compared to virtually any other form of information available by subscription these days. Write to them at 124 S. Highland, Pittsburgh, Pennsylvania 15206.

*SIRE* is another group dedicated to the study of repetitive patterns. They have regular meetings and publish a synopsis of each speaker's presentation as well as, in some cases, tapes. Their address is Society for the Investigation of Recurring Events, Box 477, Linden, New Jersey 07036 U.S.A.

*Journal of Interdisciplinary Cycle Research* is another publication you may wish to receive regularly. Many of its reports relate to biological studies, but there are frequent items of interest to students of economic cycles. The publisher is Swets & Zeitlinger B.V., Heereweg 347B Lisse, The Netherlands.

## STATISTICAL SOURCES

Statistical data are also important. Most information of this nature can be obtained at no charge from various government agencies that regularly publish bulletins and economic data. Among these are the United States Department of Agriculture and the United States Department of Commerce. You might wish to write them for a listing of their statistical material. I suggest writing to the main offices in Washington, D.C.

*Standard and Poors Corporation* has compiled much of the important data relating to cycles in their monthly publication, *Statistical Abstract Service*, which is available by subscription from Standard and Poors, 345 Hudson Street, New York, New York 10014.

Daily and weekly prices in the futures markets can be obtained in any of several ways. If you wish to maintain your data on computer there are many daily update services that can send the information by telephone to keep you current at all times. If you plan to keep the data on computer, then you will need a service that is efficient, accurate, affordable, and dependable. I have found Bob Pelletier of *Commodity Systems* to be the right person for this job.

His address is Commodity Systems Inc., 150 E. Palmetto Park Road No. 515, Boca Raton, Florida 33432.

The daily prices can otherwise be obtained from the *Wall Street Journal* or the *Journal of Commerce and Commercial,* both out of New York. I do not advise using your local daily or weekend newspaper because the price quotations are often incorrect or entirely missing. Weekly high, low, and closing prices can be obtained from *Barron's,* a publication of Dow Jones & Co.

*Price charts,* should you decide not to keep your own, can be obtained from any of three excellent sources. Each service mentioned below has its own merits. To decide which will best suit your purpose, you may wish to sample all of them. (1) *Commodity Price Charts,* 219 Parkade, Cedar Falls, Iowa 50613 are publishers of weekly price charts on all active commodity markets. They regularly mail weekly charts and monthly charts during the year. The weekly and monthly charts are large and easy to read. They show high, low, and closing prices for every active market on either a weekly or monthly basis. Many of their charts have been used in this book, and you can evaluate them yourself. (2) *The Commodity Research Bureau,* 1 Liberty Plaza, New York, New York 10006, publishes price charts. They also send updated monthly high, low, close and weekly high, low, close charts on a regular basis, and their charts are accurate. Many have been used in this book so you can judge for yourself their potential value in your work. The Commodity Research Bureau has pioneered chart work since 1934 and annually publishes the *Commodity Yearbook,* a valuable source of detailed information on virtually every commodity under the sun. You ought to have this book on your desk at all times. It is a storehouse of commodity price history. CRB also maintains the CRB index to which I have referred in the text. In addition, they publish the *Statistical Abstract Service,* which updates commodity prices and data you may wish to keep on file. (3) *Commodity Perspective,* a weekly chart book, and *Financial Perspective,* a weekly chart book, are publications that cover virtually all active commodity markets and show daily high, low, and closing prices. In addition, an updated weekly high, low, and close chart for most markets is in each issue. The weekly chart is on a small scale, but it provides a handy reference for cycle watchers. The daily charts are very large and easy to update. In addition, Commodity Perspective publishes several commodity chart history books, which show price action for the previous several years. Many of their charts have been used in this publication. You may write to them at *Commodity Perspective,* 327 S. LaSalle Street, Chicago, Illinois 60604.

There are many other chart services. New ones crop up all the time. To find a good chart service, experiment with such things as speed of delivery, ease of use, accuracy, and completeness. Whichever service makes your work more efficient and thorough is the best one for you.

## NEWSLETTERS

The newsletter business is growing by leaps and bounds. I have read most of the commodity letters, of which only a few are devoted to cycles or seasonals. Most letters use a mixture of fundamentals, news, technical indicators, cycles, and anything else that is in vogue. I have found only a few to merit attention.

For serious students of cycles, and nothing else, I would advise a totally disciplined approach, one that makes it necessary for you to avoid all extraneous inputs (price data and charts excluded).

From time to time a number of newsletters touch on the subject of cycles or seasonals. You might want to examine them to see if they fit your needs. I publish two weekly cycle letters as well. For those wishing more information on how the details in this book are put into practice, I suggest writing for a copy of one or both of my cycle letters. The *MBH Weekly Commodity Trading Letter* covers all active markets, making cyclic comments, discussing timing signals, and detailing cyclic expectations. *MBH Money Market Strategies* covers cycles exclusively in currencies, interest rates, and precious metals. The letters can be obtained by writing MBH Commodity Advisors, P. O. Box 353, Winnetka, Illinois 60093. Naturally, I am biased and believe that my publications will serve you best, but only you can be the judge.

## OTHER SOURCES OF STATISTICS

Earlier I mentioned the Standard and Poors *Statistical Service* and the Commodity Research Bureau *Statistical Abstract Service* as sources of ongoing data. Their data are, for the most part, monthly. Persons wishing to obtain the most accurate data on daily futures prices should purchase the various yearbooks published by the various commodity exchanges. Both the Chicago Mercantile Exchange and the Chicago Board of Trade publish the entire year's worth of data in easily workable form. Also included are such things as cash prices, volume, open interest, shipping information and import/export data. You might also be interested in the daily price bulletin published by each exchange. You can write the exchanges for information on any of the foregoing topics at the following addresses: Chicago Mercantile Exchange, 444 W. Jackson Boulevard, Chicago, Illinois 60606; and The Chicago Board of Trade, 141 W. Jackson Boulevard, Chicago, Illinois 60604.

## THE EHRLICH CYCLE FINDER

The Ehrlich Cycle Finder was discussed in Chapter 7. You can write for details to: Ehrlich Cycle Finder Co., 2220 Noyes Street, Dept. C2, Evanston, Illinois 60201.

# APPENDIX TWO

# Computer Programs

The computer programs that follow are written for use on a Data General System working in conjunction with a Houston Instruments DP–11 Incremental Plotter. They are written in DG–Fortran IV operating under RDOS. To use these programs on another system requires modification to make them compatible with your operating software and hardware. The general procedures will be similar, however, and considerable research effort could be spared by adapting their use to your specific system configuration.

# PROGRAM: DELTA To Calculate and Plot Weekly Seasonal Futures Charts

```
C NAME = DELTA.FR
C
C          PROGRAM TO READ HISTORY FILE AND FIND:
C
C                    1. SUM OF THE DIFFERENCES BETWEEN LAST CASH PRICE
C                       OF LAST DAY OF WEEK AND LAST DAY OF NEXT WEEK.
C                    2. AVERAGE DIFFERENCE
C                    3. PERCENTAGE POSITIVE DIFFERENCES
C


C
          COMMON / IXYZ / IYDAT(21),IFILE(6)
C         DEFINE MAIN STORAGE ARRAY  'IWDATA(IW,IY,IX)'
          DIMENSION IWDATA(120,20,2),IDATA(120,2)
          DIMENSION INAM(10)
C
C         IW= WEEK NUMBER ( RELATIVE TO NOTHING )
C         IY= CONTRACT PERIOD ( RELEATIVE TO START OF HISTORY FILE )
C         IX= 1 => CASH PRICE ON LAST DAY OF TRADING WEEK
C         IX= 2 => CHANGE IN SETTLEMENT PRICE WEEK TO WEEK
C
C
C
C         DEFINE STORAGE FOR NAME OF COMMODITY
C
          DIMENSION ICNAM(10)
C
C         STORAGE FOR CONTRACT MONTHS TO ANALYZE
C
          DIMENSION IMCNT(12)

          DATA IYDAT / '6566676869707172737475767778798081828384B5' /
          DATA IFILE/ 'DP0:' /

          IY=0
          IGCN=1
          DO 55 I=1,12
55        IMCNT(I)=0
C
X         ACCEPT '<7>MOVE PRINTER CABLE TO PRINTER, THEN ENTER 0 ! ',IX
X         CALL OPEN(1,'$TTO1',3,IER)
          ACCEPT 'ENTER MONTH NUMBER? ',ICOM
          ACCEPT 'ENTER WEEK # (1=>4), THAT COMMODITY ENDS? ',IEW
          TYPE 'ENTER LAST 4 CHARACTERS OF HISTORY FILE NAME? '
          READ(11,1) (IFILE(I),I=4,5)
1         FORMAT(2A2)
```

**PROGRAM:** **DELTA To Calculate and Plot Weekly Seasonal Futures Charts** *(Continued)*

```
              ACCEPT 'ENTER STARTING YEAR? ',IYST
              ACCEPT 'ENTER ENDING YEAR? ',IYEND
              ACCEPT 'ENTER COMMODITY NUMBER? ',IC
              CALL OPEN(0,'COMNAMES',1,IER)
              IF(IER.NE.1) STOP 'CANNOT FIND COMNAMES'
      60      READ(0,3) ICN,INAM,IDECM,ICSUF
      3       FORMAT(I2,10A2,I2,A2)
              IF(ICN.NE.IC) GOTO 60
              CALL FCLOS(0)


      C
      C       CLEAR OUT ARRAY'S AND OPEN HISTORY FILE
      C
              DO 50 I=1,120
              DO 50 II=1,20
              DO 50 III=1,2
              IWDATA(I,II,III)=0
      50      CONTINUE

              IYST=IYST-64
              IYEND=IYEND-64
              DO 944 IYLP=IYST,IYEND
              IFILE(3)=IYDAT(IYLP)
              CALL OPEN(0,IFILE,1,IER)
              IF(IER.NE.1) STOP 'HISTORY FILE OPEN ERROR'
      C
      C       READ FIRST RECORD
      C
      C       ICOM=IMCNT(IGCN)
              READ(0,2) ICNAM,IDECM
      2       FORMAT(10A2,I3)

      C
      C       NOW LOOP READING EACH DAYS PRICES
      C
              IPYR=64+IYLP
              TYPE 'YEAR= ',IPYR
              IOLD=0
              ISY=0
              XDOW=0
              IY=IY+1
              IW=1
      100     READ BINARY(0) ICOMX,ICDAT,IO,IH,IL,IS
              IF(ICOMX.EQ.0) GOTO 102
              IYEAR=ICOMX/100
              IYEAR=ICOMX-IYEAR*100
              IMONTH=ICDAT/100
              IDAT=ICDAT-IMONTH*100

      C
      C       CONVERT DATE TO DAY OF WEEK
      C
              IF(IMONTH.EQ.0) GOTO 100
              CALL GDAY(IMONTH,IDAT,IYEAR,IDOW)

              IF(ISY.EQ.0) ISY=IYEAR
      C
      C       NOW CHECK FOR ZERO PRICE
      C
              IF(IS.EQ.0) TYPE 'ZERO PRICE',IYEAR,IMONTH,IDAT,IDOW
      C
```

318

## PROGRAM: DELTA To Calculate and Plot Weekly Seasonal Futures Charts *(Continued)*

```
C          CHECK FOR FIRST TIME THROUGH
C
           IF(XDOW.EQ.0) GOTO 241
C
C          TEST TO SEE IF NEW DAY NUMBER LESS THAN OLD DAY NUMBER
C
           IF(XDOW.EQ.IDOW) STOP DAY OF WEEK ERROR
           IF(XDOW.GT.IDOW) GOTO 230
C
C          THIS DAY HIGHER THAN LAST, COULD BE LAST DAY OF WEEK!
C
241        IWDATA(IW,1Y,1)=IS
           GOTO 240
C
C          START OF NEW WEEK
C
230        IW=IW+1
240        XDOW=IDOW

           GOTO 100
102        CALL FCLOS(0)
944        CONTINUE

X          DO 972 I=1,120
X          WRITE(1,802) (IWDATA(I,JJ,1),JJ=1,20)
X972       CONTINUE

           TYPE "FINISHED READING HISTORY FILES"

           DO 400 I=1,20
           J=121
           DO 410 JJ=1,120
           J=J-1
           IF(IWDATA(J,I,1).NE.0) GOTO 420
410        CONTINUE
           GOTO 400
420        K=J
           L=120
           DO 430 IL=1,K
           IWDATA(L,I,1)=IWDATA(J,I,1)
           IWDATA(L,I,2)=IWDATA(J,I,2)
           L=L-1
           J=J-1
430        CONTINUE
           II=120-K
           DO 440 J=1,II
           IWDATA(J,I,1)=0
440        CONTINUE
400        CONTINUE

C
C          NOW FIND INDEX INTO ARRAY FOR WHICH ALL WEEK ENDING SETTLEMENT
C          PRICES ARE NONZERO.
C
           DO 510 J=1,120
           DO 520 I=1,IY
           IF(IWDATA(J,I,1).EQ.0) GOTO 510
```

319

**PROGRAM: DELTA To Calculate and Plot Weekly Seasonal Futures Charts** *(Continued)*

```
520       CONTINUE
          GOTO 530
510       CONTINUE
          STOP LOGIC ERROR
530       CONTINUE
          ISTYR=I
          II=J

C
C CONVERT PRICES INTO A RANGE OF 0 TO 100
C
          DO 980 I=1,IY
          ILOW=9999
          IHIGH=0
          DO 970 J=II,120
          IF(ILOW.GT.IWDATA(J,1,1)) ILOW=IWDATA(J,I,1)
          IF(IHIGH.LT.IWDATA(J,I,1)) IHIGH=IWDATA(J,I,1)
970       CONTINUE
          XLOW=ILOW
          IF(ABS(XLOW).GT.XHIGH) XHIGH=-XLOW
          XHIGH=IHIGH
          DO 960 J=II,120
          VAL=IWDATA(J,I,1)
          PER=(VAL)*1000./XHIGH
          IWDATA(J,I,1)=PER
960       CONTINUE
980       CONTINUE

C
C         FIGURE DIFFERENCE BETWEEN LAST SETTLEMENT PRICE OF LAST WEEK
C         AND FIRST SETTLEMENT PRICE OF THE NEXT WEEK.
C
          DO 545 I=1,IY
          DO 545 J=II,119
          IF(IWDATA((J+1),1,1).EQ.0.OR.IWDATA(J,I,1).EQ.0) GOTO 546
          IWDATA((J+1),I,2)=IWDATA((J+1),I,1)-IWDATA(J,I,1)
          GOTO 545
546       IWDATA((J+1),I,2)=0
545       CONTINUE
X         DO 540 J=II,120
X         WRITE(1,802) (IWDATA(J,IJ,1),IJ=1,IY)
X         WRITE(1,802) (IWDATA(J,IJ,2),IJ=1,IY)
X802      FORMAT(1X,2016)
X540      CONTINUE

C
C         FIND SUM OF DIFFERENCE ACROSS YEAR BOUNDARIES AND
C         NUMBER OF GAINS.
C
          II=II+1

          IX=121-II
          IDATX=0
          DO 555 I=II,120
          IDATA(I,1)=0
          IDATA(I,2)=0
          ICNT=0
          DO 550 J=1,IY
          IDATA(I,2)=IDATA(I,2)+IWDATA(1,J,2)
```

```
            IF(IWDATA(I,J,2).EQ.0) GOTO 550
            IDATA(I,1)=IDATA(1,1)+1
550         CONTINUE
            DO 565 J=1,IY
            IF(IWDATA(I,J,2).LE.0) GOTO 565
            ICNT=ICNT+1
565         CONTINUE
            IYY=IDATA(I,1)
            IDATA(I,1)=ICNT*100/IYY
            IDATX=IDATX+(IDATA(I,2)/IYY)
            IDATA(I,2)=IDATX
555         CONTINUE

            IDECM=-1
            CALL DFILW('DTEMP',IER)
            CALL OPEN(0,'DTEMP',3,IER)
            IF(IER.NE.1) STOP 'CANNOT OPEN DTEMP'
            IX=IX+1
            A=0.
            IYST=IYST+64
            IYEND=IYEND+64
            WRITE(0,6) ICNAM,ICOM,IX,IDECM,IYST,IYEND,IEW
X           WRITE(1,800) ICNAM,ICOM,IX
X800        FORMAT(1X,10A2,2I6)
6           FORMAT(1X,10A2,I2,I3,4I2)
            WRITE BINARY(0) A,A
X           WRITE(1,801) A,A
            DO 2000 I=II,120
            PERC=IDATA(I,1)
            VALUE=IDATA(I,2)
            WRITE BINARY(0) PERC,VALUE
X           WRITE(1,801) PERC,VALUE
X801        FORMAT(1X,2F8.2)
2000        CONTINUE
            CALL FCLOS(0)
X           ACCEPT '<7>MOVE PRINTER CABLE TO PLOTTER, THEN ENTER 0 ! ',IX
            CALL CHAIN('DELTA1.SV',IER)
            END
```

## PROGRAM: DELTA To Calculate and Plot Weekly Seasonal Futures Charts *(Continued)*

```
C   NAME = DELTA1.FR
C
C PROGRAM TO PLOT DELTA WEEK CHANGES
C PROGRAM IS CHAINED TO FROM 'DELTA.FR'

C
C
        DIMENSION XDATA(2,60),ICNAM(10)
        COMMON /BLECH/ IMD(24),IPC,IEQ,IW(12),IMZ(53)
        DATA IMD/48HJAN FEB MAR APR MAY JUN JUL AUG SEP OCT NOV DEC /
        DATA IPC/1H%/
        DATA IEQ/2H=>/
        DATA IW/ 4,5,4,4,5,4,4,5,4,5,4,4 /
        CALL OPEN(0,'DTEMP',1,IER)
X       CALL OPEN(1,'$TTO',3,IER)
        IF (IER.NE.1) STOP 'CANNOT FIND DTEMP'
        READ(0,1) ICNAM,ICOM,ICNT,IDECM,IYS,IYE,IEW
1       FORMAT(10A2,I2,I3,4I2)
        DO 40 I=1,ICNT
        READ BINARY(0) XDATA(1,I),XDATA(2,I)
40      CONTINUE
        CALL FCLOS(0)
C
C FIND RANGE OF XDATA
C
        ZMIN=9999.0
        ZMAX=0.0
        DO 50 I=1,ICNT
        IF(XDATA(2,I).GT.ZMAX) ZMAX=XDATA(2,I)
        IF(XDATA(2,I).LT.ZMIN) ZMIN=XDATA(2,I)
50      CONTINUE
```

```
          CALL FIT(ZMIN,ZMAX,8.0,DMIN,DX)
          ORGX=1.00
          ORGY=.465
          AXY=1.465
          CALL INITAL(8,200,11,0,0,0)
          CALL FACTOR(2.)
          CALL PLOT(0.,0.,0)
          CALL PLOT(ORGX,ORGY,3)
          CALL AX(ORGX,AXY,8.0,DMIN,DX,1DECM,0)
          DLEN=(.25*ICNT)+ORGX
          CALL PLOT(ORGX,AXY,3)
          CALL PLOT(ORGX,ORGY,2)
          CALL PLOT(DLEN,ORGY,1)
          CALL PLOT(DLEN,AXY,1)
          CALL AX(DLEN,AXY,8.0,DMIN,DX,IDECM,1)

C
C NOW DRAW PERCENTAGES ON THE BOTTOM
C
          SNUM=1.
          DMARK=DLEN-.25
          II=ICNT
          DO 70 I=1,ICNT
          IF(I.EQ.1) GOTO 71
          CALL PLOT(DMARK,ORGY,3)
          CALL PLOT(DMARK,(ORGY+.50),2)
          CALL NUMBER ((DMARK-.21),(ORGY+.30),.11,XDATA(1,II),0.0,-1)
          CALL NUMBER ((DMARK-.21),(ORGY+.05),.07,SNUM,0.0,-1)
          IF(I.EQ.1) GOTO 70
          SNUM=SNUM+1.
          II=II-1
          DMARK=DMARK-.25
C
C OFFSETT NUMBER TO GET POSITIVE RANGE
71        XDATA(2,I)=XDATA(2,I)-DMIN
70        CONTINUE

          CALL SYMBOL((ORGX-.25),(ORGY+.20),.14,IPC,0.0,1)

          DMARK=ORGX
          IXM=ICOM
          IC=IEW+1
          IX=ICNT+1

210       IF(IX.LT.3) GOTO 260
          IF(IX.LT.IC) GOTO 280
          IF(IC.LT.3) GOTO 230
290       IWY=3
          IF(IC.EQ.4) IWY=2
          IF(IC.EQ.3) IWY=1
          DO 220 I=1,IWY
          IMZ(IX)=0
          IX=IX-1
220       CONTINUE
```

```
              IMZ(IX)=IXM
              IX=IX-1
              IMZ(IX)=-1
              IX=IX-1

250           IXM=IXM-1
              IF(IXM.LT.1) IXM=12
              IC=IW(IXM)
              GOTO 210

230           DO 240 I=1,IC
              IMZ(IX)=0
              IX=IX-1
240           CONTINUE
              GOTO 250

280           IC=IX
              GOTO 290

260           DO 270 I=1,IX
              IMZ(IX)=0
              IX=IX-1
270           CONTINUE

              IX=0
              DO 310 I=1,ICNT
              IF(I.NE.1) IX=1
              IF(IMZ(I)) 330,320,340
340           IPT=IMZ(I)*2-1
              CALL SYMBOL((DMARK-.21),(ORGY+.55),.11,IMD(1PT),0.0,3)
              GOTO 321
330           IF(IX.EQ.0) GOTO 321
              CALL PLOT((DMARK-.25),(ORGY+.50),3)
              CALL PLOT((DMARK-.25),(ORGY+.71),2)
321           IX=1
320           DMARK=DMARK+.25
310           CONTINUE

              CALL PLOT(DLEN,(ORGY+.50),3)
              CALL PLOT(ORGX,(ORGY+.50),2)


C
C NOW PLOT THE XDATA
C
              IFLAG=3
              DMARK=ORGX
              DO 100 I=1,ICNT
              VALUE=XDATA(2,I)/DX+AXY
              CALL PLOT(DMARK,VALUE,IFLAG)
              IF(IFLAG.EQ.3) IFLAG=2
              DMARK=DMARK+.25
100           CONTINUE
```

324

## PROGRAM: DELTA To Calculate and Plot Weekly Seasonal Futures Charts *(Continued)*

```
      YS=IYS
      YE=IYE
      CALL NUMBER((ORGX+.5),(ORGY+9.75),.14,YS,0.0,-1)
      CALL SYMBOL((ORGX+.85),(ORGY+9.75),.14,IEQ,0.0,2)
      CALL NUMBER((ORGX+1.25),(ORGY+9.75),.14,YE,0.0,-1)

      ICOM=ICOM*2-1
      CALL SYMBOL((ORGX+.5),(ORGY+9.50),.14,IMD(ICOM),0.0,3)
      CALL SYMBOL((ORGX+.5),(ORGY+9.25),.14,ICNAM,0.0,12)

      CALL PLOT(0.,0.,3)
      CALL RSTR(0)
      CALL CHAIN('DELTA2.SV',IER)
      END
```

```
C
C
C       FILE NAME 'GDAY.FR'
C
C       SUBROUTINE TO CONVERT MONTH/DAY/YEAR TO DAY OF WEEK
C
C       IM = MONTH NUMBER ( 1 => 12 )
C       ID = DATE ( 1 => 31 )
C       IY = YEAR ( 68 => 99 )
C       IW = DAY OF WEEK ( 1 => 7 )
C
C               1=MON,2=UES,ETC.


      SUBROUTINE GDAY(IM,ID,IY,IW)
      COMMON /LB/IC(12)
      DATA IC(1),IC(2),IC(3),IC(4),IC(5),IC(6),IC(7),IC(8),IC(9),IC(10),
     1IC(11),IC(12)/0,31,59,90,120,151,181,212,243,273,304,334/
      I=IY-60
      JX=I/4
      IF(JX*4.NE.I.OR.IM.GT.2) GOTO 2
      JX=JX-1
2     IMM=365*(I-3)+IC(IM)+ID+JX
      IN=IMM/7
      IW=IMM-(IN*7)+1
      RETURN
      END
```

325

## PROGRAM: SEASON To Calculate and Plot Cash Seasonal Prices

```
C          NAME = SEASON.FR
C
C          PROGRAM TO PLOT SEASONAL PRICES
C
           DIMENSION       IFILE(10),IUFD(20),A(12,50),B(2,12),IHEAD(10)
X          CALL OPEN(1,'$TTO1',3,IER)
10         TYPE 'ENTER FILENAME?'
           READ(11,1) IFILE
1          FORMAT(10A2)
           CALL STAT(IFILE,IUFD,IER)
           IF(IER.NE.1) GOTO 10
           ACCEPT 'ENTER BEGINNING YEAR OR ZERO FOR FIRST YEAR? ',NYEAR
           IF(NYEAR.EQ.0) GOTO 13
           IF(NYEAR.LT.1900) NYEAR=NYEAR+1900
13         ACCEPT 'ENTER ENDING YEAR OR ZERO FOR LAST YEAR? ',LYEAR
           IF(LYEAR.EQ.0) GOTO 15
           IF(LYEAR.LT.1900) LYEAR=LYEAR+1900
15         CALL OPEN(0,IFILE,1,IER)
           READ(0,2) IHEAD,IDECM,IYEAR
2          FORMAT(10A2,I3,I4)
           IF(LYEAR.NE.0) LYEAR=LYEAR-IYEAR-1
           IF(NYEAR.EQ.0) GOTO 19
           IF(NYEAR.LT.IYEAR) STOP 'STARTING YEAR NOT IN DATA!'
           IF(NYEAR.NE.0) NYEAR=NYEAR-IYEAR+1
           IF(NYEAR.EQ.1.OR.NYEAR.EQ.0) GOTO 19
           IM=1
           IY=1
18         READ(0,3) VALUE
           IM=IM+1
           IF(IM.LE.12) GOTO 18
           IM=1
           IY=IY+1
           IF(IY.NE.NYEAR) GOTO 18
```

**PROGRAM: SEASON To Calculate and Plot Cash Seasonal Prices**
*(Continued)*

```
C
C          NOW READ PRICES INTO ARRAY
C
19         IM=1
           IY=1
20         READ(0,3) A(IM,IY)
3          FORMAT(F12.4)
           IF(A(IM,IY).EQ.0.) GOTO 50
           IF(LYEAR.NE.0.AND.IY.GT.LYEAR) GOTO 50
           IM=IM+1
           IF(IM.LE.12) GOTO 20
           IM=1
           IY=IY+1
           IF(IY.GT.50) STOP "TOO MUCH DATA!"
           GOTO 20
50         CALL FCLOS(0)
X          DO 9000 I=1,IY
X          WRITE(1,8000) (A(J,I),J=1,12)
X8000      FORMAT(1X,12F3.2)
X9000      CONTINUE
           IY=IY-1
           YI=IY
           DO 200 I=1,12
           B(1,I)=0.
           DO 100 J=1,IY
           B(1,I)=B(1,I)+A(I,J)
100        CONTINUE
           B(1,1)=B(1,1)/YI
200        CONTINUE
C
C          FIND LARGEST NUMBER
C
           XMAX=0.
           DO 300 I=1,12
           IF(B(1,I).GT.XMAX) XMAX=B(1,I)
300        CONTINUE
C
C          NOW NORMALIZE TO 100. & FIND SMALLEST NUMBER
C
           XLOW=100.
           XMAX=100./XMAX
           DO 310 I=1,12
           B(1,I)=B(1,I)*XMAX
           IF(B(1,I).LT.XLOW) XLOW=B(1,I)
310        CONTINUE
           LOW=XLOW
           MAX=99-LOW
```

```
420         MAX=MAX+1
            IF(MAX.EQ.14) GOTO 430
            IF(MAX.EQ.35) GOTO 430
            IF(MAX.EQ.70) GOTO 430
            IF(MAX.EQ.140) GOTO 430
            IF(MAX.EQ.350) GOTO 430
            IF(MAX.EQ.700) GOTO 430
            IF(MAX.GT.700) STOP CALL GEORGE!
            GOTO 420
430         XMAX=MAX
            DX=XMAX/3.50
            IF(NYEAR.EQ.0) GOTO 500
            NYEAR=NYEAR+IYEAR-1
            GOTO 510
500         NYEAR=IYEAR
510         IF(LYEAR.EQ.0) GOTO 520
            LYEAR=LYEAR+IYEAR-1
            GOTO 530
520         LYEAR=IYEAR+1Y-1
530         CALL DFILW('TEMP',IER)
            CALL OPEN(0,'TEMP',3,IER)
            WRITE(0,4) IHEAD,IDECM,XLOW,DX,NYEAR,LYEAR
4           FORMAT(1X,10A2,I3,F12.4,F12.6,2I6)
            DO 460 I=1,12
            WRITE(0,7) B(1,I)
7           FORMAT(1X,F5.1)
460         CONTINUE
            CALL RESET
            CALL CHAIN('SEASON1.SV',IER)

            END




C           NAME = SEASONA1.FR
C
C           PROGRAM TO CHART SEASONAL PRICES
C
            COMMON /BLK/ IMN(24),1THUR,ISNL(4)
            DIMENSION         IHEAD(10),V(12)
            DATA IMN/48HJAN FEB MAR APR MAY JUN JUL AUG SEP OCT NOV DEC /
            DATA ITHUR/'-- '/
            DATA ISNL/'SEASONAL'/
            CALL OPEN(0,'TEMP',1,IER)
            READ(0,1) IHEAD,IDECM,XLOW,DX,NYEAR,LYEAR
1           FORMAT(10A2,I3,F12.4,F12.6,2I6)
            ORGX=1.0
            ORGY=.46
            CALL INITAL(8,400,11,0,0,0)
            CALL PLOT(0.,0.,0)
            IPNTR=3
            POS=ORGY+.750
            DO 100 I=1,16
```

```
            CALL PLOT(ORGX,POS,IPNTR)
            IPNTR=2
            POS=POS+.250
            CALL PLOT(ORGX,POS,IPNTR)
            CALL PLOT((ORGX+.05),POS,1)
100         CONTINUE
            ZPOS=POS
            POS=ORGX
            DO 110 I=1,12
            CALL PLOT(POS,ZPOS,IPNTR)
            IPNTR=2
            POS=POS+.333333
            CALL PLOT(POS,ZPOS,1)
            CALL PLOT(POS,(ZPOS-.05),1)
            CALL PLOT(POS,ZPOS,1)
110         CONTINUE
            APOS=POS
            POS=ZPOS
            DO 120 I=1,16
            CALL PLOT(APOS,POS,1)
            POS=POS-.250
            CALL PLOT(APOS,POS,1)
            CALL PLOT((APOS-.05),POS,1)
            CALL PLOT(APOS,POS,1)
120         CONTINUE
            CALL PLOT(APOS,ORGY,1)
            CALL PLOT(ORGX,ORGY,1)

            POS=ORGY+.750
            CALL PLOT(ORGX,POS,1)

            CALL PLOT(APOS,POS,1)
            POS=POS-.250
            CALL PLOT(APOS,POS,1)
            CALL PLOT(ORGX,POS,1)
            POS=POS-.250
            CALL PLOT(ORGX,POS,1)
            CALL PLOT(APOS,POS,1)
            DPOS=ORGY+.760
            POS=APOS
            DO 130 I=1,11
            POS=POS-.3333333
            CALL PLOT(POS,ORGY,3)
            CALL PLOT(POS,DPOS,2)
130         CONTINUE
            POSY=ORGY+.540
            DPOS=ORGX+.05
            DO 140 I=1,12
            J=(I-1)*2+1
            CALL SYMBOL(DPOS,POSY,.10,IMN(J),0.0,3)
            DPOS=DPOS+.3333333
140         CONTINUE
C           APOS=(11.*.250)+ORGY
C           CALL PLOT(ORGX,APOS,3)
C           ZPOS=ORGX+4.00
C           CALL PLOT(ZPOS,APOS,2)
C           AMAX=0.
```

**PROGRAM: SEASON To Calculate and Plot Cash Seasonal Prices**
*(Continued)*

```
C       DO 150 I=1,12
C       READ(0,2) V(I)
2       FORMAT(F5.2)
C       IF(AMAX.LT.V(I)) AMAX=V(I)
C150    CONTINUE
C       IL=0
C       IF(AMAX.LT.10.) IL=1
C       IF(AMAX.LT.1.) IL=2
C       DPOS=ORGX
C       POSY=ORGY+.290
C       DO 160 I=1,12
C       CALL NUMBER(DPOS,POSY,.09,V(I),0.0,IL)
C       DPOS=DPOS+.333333
C160    CONTINUE
C       DPOS=ORGX+.05
C       POSY=ORGY+.040
C       DO 170 I=1,12
C       READ(0,3) AMAX
C3      FORMAT(F3.0)
C       CALL NUMBER(DPOS,POSY,.11,AMAX,0.0,-1)
C       DPOS=DPOS+.333333
C       CONTINUE
        DPOS=ORGX+.16666
        IPNTR=3
        DELTA=3*.250+ORGY
        DO 180 I=1,12
        READ(0,2) AMAX
        AMAX=((AMAX-XLOW)/DX)+DELTA
        CALL PLOT(DPOS,AMAX,IPNTR)
        IPNTR=2
        DPOS=DPOS+.333333
180     CONTINUE
        CALL SYMBOL((ORGX+1.0),(ORGY+5.4),.14,ISNL,0.0,8)
        CALL SYMBOL((ORGX+1.0),(ORGY+5.2),.14,IHEAD,0.0,15)
        AMAX=NYEAR
        CALL NUMBER((ORGX+1.00),(ORGY+5.00),.14,AMAX,0.0,-1)
        CALL SYMBOL((ORGX+1.70),(ORGY+5.00),.14,ITHUR,0.0,1)
        AMAX=LYEAR
        CALL NUMBER((ORGX+1.98),(ORGY+5.00),.14,AMAX,0.0,-1)
        CALL RSTR(2)
        END
```

## PROGRAM: SEASONAL FR To Calculate and Plot Seasonal Spread Relationships Between Two Futures Contracts

```
C       NAME = SEASONAL.FR
C
C       PROGRAM TO PLOT SEASONAL SPREAD PRICES
C
        DIMENSION        IFILE(10),IUFD(20),A(12,50),B(2,12),IHEAD(10)
X       CALL OPEN(1,'$TTO1',3,IER)
10      TYPE 'ENTER FILENAME?'
        READ(11,1) IFILE
1       FORMAT(10A2)
        CALL STAT(IFILE,IUFD,IER)
        IF(IER.NE.1) GOTO 10
        ACCEPT 'ENTER BEGINNING YEAR OR ZERO FOR FIRST DATA YEAR? ',NYEAR
        IF(NYEAR.EQ.0) GOTO 19
        IF(NYEAR.LT.1900) NYEAR=NYEAR+1900
        CALL OPEN(0,IFILE,1,IER)
        READ(0,2) IHEAD,1DECM,1YEAR
2       FORMAT(10A2,I3,I4)
        IF(NYEAR.EQ.0) GOTO 19
        IF(NYEAR.LT.IYEAR) STOP 'TOO EARLY A YEAR!'
        NYEAR=NYEAR-IYEAR+1
        IF(NYEAR.EQ.1) GOTO 19
        IM=1
        IY=1
18      READ(0,3) VALUE
        IM=IM+1
        IF(IM.LE.12) GOTO 18
        IM=1
        IY=1Y+1
        IF(IY.NE.NYEAR) GOTO 18
```

**PROGRAM: SEASONAL FR To Calculate and Plot Seasonal Spread Relationships Between Two Futures Contracts** *(Continued)*

```
C
C          NOW READ PRICES INTO ARRAY
C
19         IM=1
           IY=1
20         READ(0,3) A(IM,IY)
3          FORMAT(F12.4)
           IF(A(IM,IY).EQ.0.) GOTO 50
           IM=IM+1
           IF(IM.LE.12) GOTO 20
           IM=1
           IY=IY+1
           IF(IY.GT.50) STOP 'TOO MUCH DATA!'
           GOTO 20
50         CALL FCLOS(0)
X          DO 9000 I=1,IY
X          WRITE(1,8000) (A(J,I),J=1,12)
X8000      FORMAT(1X,12F8.2)
X9000      CONTINUE
           IY=IY-1
           DO 100 I=1,IY
           DO 110 J=1,11
           K=J+1
           A(J,I)=A(K,1)-A(J,I)
110        CONTINUE
           M=I+1
           A(12,I)=A(1,M)-A(12,I)
100        CONTINUE
X          DO 9100 I=1,IY
X          WRITE(1,8000) (A(J,I),J=1,12)
X9100      CONTINUE

C
C          NOW FIND AVERAGE DIFFERENCE
C
           COUNT=IY
           DO 200 J=1,12
           B(1,J)=0.
           DO 210 K=1,IY
           B(1,J)=B(1,J)+A(J,K)
210        CONTINUE
           B(1,J)=B(1,J)/COUNT
200        CONTINUE
C
C          NOW FIND PERCENTAGE POSITIVE
C
           DO 300 J=1,12
           IC=0
           DO 310 K=1,IY
           IF(A(J,K).GT.0.) IC=IC+1
310        CONTINUE
           IP=(IC*100)/IY
           B(2,J)=IP
300        CONTINUE
```

```
C
C          FIND THE LARGEST VALUE
C
           XMAX=0.
           SUM=0.
           DO 400 I=1,12
           SUM=SUM+B(1,I)
           IF(ABS(SUM).GT.XMAX) XMAX=ABS(SUM)
400        CONTINUE
           IS=0
405        IF(XMAX.GE.14.) GOTO 410
           XMAX=XMAX*10.
           IS=IS+1
           GOTO 405
410        MAX=XMAX
420        MAX=MAX+1
           IF(MAX.EQ.14) GOTO 430
           IF(MAX.EQ.35) GOTO 430
           IF(MAX.EQ.70) GOTO 430
           IF(MAX.EQ.140) GOTO 430
           IF(MAX.EQ.350) GOTO 430
           IF(MAX.EQ.700) GOTO 430
           IF(MAX.GT.700) STOP CALL GEORGE!
           GOTO 420
430        XMAX=MAX
           DX=XMAX*2.0/3.50
440        IF(IS.EQ.0) GOTO 450
           IS=IS-1
           XMAX=XMAX/10.
           DX=DX/10.
           GOTO 440
450        CALL DFILW('TEMP',IER)
           CALL OPEN(0,'TEMP',3,IER)
           WRITE(0,4) IHEAD,IDECM,XMAX,DX
4          FORMAT(1X,10A2,I3,F12.4,F12.6)
           DO 460 I=1,12
           WRITE(0,7) B(1,I)
460        CONTINUE
           DO 470 I=1,12
           WRITE(0,6) B(2,I)
6          FORMAT(1X,F3.0)
470        CONTINUE
           COUNT=0.
           WRITE(0,7) COUNT
7          FORMAT(1X,F5.2)
           DO 480 I=1,12
           COUNT=COUNT+B(1,I)
           WRITE(0,7) COUNT
480        CONTINUE
           CALL RESET
           CALL CHAIN('SEASONAL1.SV',IER)

           END
```

```
C          NAME = SEASONAL1.FR
C
C          PROGRAM TO CHART SEASONAL SPREAD PRICES
C
           COMMON /BLK/ IMN(24)
           DIMENSION       IHEAD(10),V(12)
           DATA IMN/48HJAN FEB MAR APR MAY JUN JUL AUG SEP OCT NOV DEC /
           CALL OPEN(0,'TEMP',1,IER)
           READ(0,1) IHEAD,IDECM,XMAX,DX
1          FORMAT(10A2,I3,F12.4,F12.6)
           ORGX=1.0
           ORGY=.46
           CALL INITAL(8,400,11,0,0,0)
           CALL PLOT(0.,0.,0)
           IPNTR=3
           POS=ORGY+.750
           DO 100 I=1,16
           CALL PLOT(ORGX,POS,IPNTR)
           IPNTR=2
           POS=POS+.250
           CALL PLOT(ORGX,POS,IPNTR)
           CALL PLOT((ORGX+.05),POS,1)
100        CONTINUE
           ZPOS=POS
           POS=ORGX
           DO 110 I=1,12
           CALL PLOT(POS,ZPOS,IPNTR)
           IPNTR=2
           POS=POS+.333333
           CALL PLOT(POS,ZPOS,1)
           CALL PLOT(POS,(ZPOS-.05),1)
           CALL PLOT(POS,ZPOS,1)
110        CONTINUE
           APOS=POS
           POS=ZPOS
           DO 120 I=1,16
           CALL PLOT(APOS,POS,1)
           POS=POS-.250
           CALL PLOT(APOS,POS,1)
           CALL PLOT((APOS-.05),POS,1)
           CALL PLOT(APOS,POS,1)
120        CONTINUE
           CALL PLOT(APOS,ORGY,1)
           CALL PLOT(ORGX,ORGY,1)

           POS=ORGY+.750
           CALL PLOT(ORGX,POS,1)

           CALL PLOT(APOS,POS,1)
           POS=POS-.250
           CALL PLOT(APOS,POS,1)
           CALL PLOT(ORGX,POS,1)
           POS=POS-.250
```

# PROGRAM: SEASONAL FR To Calculate and Plot Seasonal Spread Relationships Between Two Futures Contracts *(Continued)*

```
            CALL PLOT(ORGX,POS,1)
            CALL PLOT(APOS,POS,1)
            DPOS=ORGY+.760
            POS=APOS
            DO 130 I=1,11
            POS=POS-.3333333
            CALL PLOT(POS,ORGY,3)
            CALL PLOT(POS,DPOS,2)
130         CONTINUE
            POSY=ORGY+.540
            DPOS=ORGX+.05
            DO 140 I=1,12
            J=(I-1)*2+1
            CALL SYMBOL(DPOS,POSY,.10,IMN(J),0.0,3)
            DPOS=DPOS+.3333333
140         CONTINUE
            APOS=(11.*.250)+ORGY
            CALL PLOT(ORGX,APOS,3)
            ZPOS=ORGX+4.00
            CALL PLOT(ZPOS,APOS,2)
            AMAX=0.
            DO 150 I=1,12
            READ(0,2) V(I)
2           FORMAT(F5.2)
            IF(AMAX.LT.V(I)) AMAX=V(I)
150         CONTINUE
            IL=0
            IF(AMAX.LT.10.) IL=1
            IF(AMAX.LT.1.) IL=2
            DPOS=ORGX
            POSY=ORGY+.290
            DO 160 I=1,12
            CALL NUMBER(DPOS,POSY,.09,V(I),0.0,IL)
            DPOS=DPOS+.333333
160         CONTINUE
            DPOS=ORGX+.05
            POSY=ORGY+.040
            DO 170 I=1,12
            READ(0,3) AMAX
3           FORMAT(F3.0)
            CALL NUMBER(DPOS,POSY,.11,AMAX,0.0,-1)
            DPOS=DPOS+.333333
170         CONTINUE
            DELTA=(11.*.250)+ORGY
            DPOS=ORGX
            IPNTR=3
            DO 180 I=1,13
            READ(0,2) AMAX
            AMAX=((AMAX)/DX)+DELTA
            CALL PLOT(DPOS,AMAX,IPNTR)
            IPNTR=2
            DPOS=DPOS+.333333
180         CONTINUE
            CALL SYMBOL((ORGX+1.0),(ORGY+5.2),.14,JHEAD,0.0,15)
            CALL PLOT(0.,0.,3)
            CALL RSTR(0)
            END
```

## PROGRAM: DETREND To Calculate and Plot Detrended Commodity Prices in Any Given Contract and Any Determined Moving-Average Length

```
C           NAME = DETREND.FR
C
C           PROGRAM TO PLOT ON A SPLIT CHART:
C
C           1. THE DAILY SETTLEMENT PRICE OF A COMMODITY YEAR
C           2. THE DIFFERENCE BETWEEN THE DAILY PRICE AND A MOVING AVERAGE
C
C           THE MOVING AVERAGE PERIOD IS DEFINED BY THE OPERATOR
C
C
            DIMENSION PRICE(500),DELTA(500),ICNAM(10),IUFD(20),IFILE(10)
            WRITE(10,1)
1           FORMAT(' ENTER FILENAME? ',Z)
            READ(11,2) IFILE
2           FORMAT(10A2)
30          ACCEPT "ENTER MOVING AVERAGE? ",IMA
            IF(IMA.LT.2.OR.IMA.GT.60) GOTO 30
            XMA=IMA
            ILC=0
            CALL STAT(IFILE,IUFD,IER)
            IF(IER.EQ.1) GOTO 160
            STOP "CANNOT FIND FILENAME!"
C
C           NOW FIGURE MOVING AVERAGE AND DIFFERENCE
C
160         CALL OPEN(0,IFILE,1,IER)
            READ(0,3) ICNAM,IDECM,IYEAR
3           FORMAT(10A2,I3,I4)
            IF(IDECM.EQ.0) IDECM=-1
            ICNT=0
            XLOW=32000.
            XHIGH=0.
            DHIGH=-32000.
            DLOW=32000.
100         READ(0,6) VALUE
6           FORMAT(F12.4)
            IF(VALUE.EQ.0.) GOTO 200
            ICNT=ICNT+1
            PRICE(ICNT)=VALUE
            IF(ICNT.LT.IMA) GOTO 100
            VALUE=0.
            J=ICNT-IMA+1
            DO 110 I=1,IMA
            VALUE=VALUE+PRICE(J)
```

```
            J=J+1
110         CONTINUE
            VAL=VALUE/XMA
            DELTA(ICNT)=PRICE(ICNT)-VAL
            IF(PRICE(ICNT).LT.XLOW) XLOW=PRICE(ICNT)
            IF(PRICE(ICNT).GT.XHIGH) XHIGH=PRICE(ICNT)
            IF(DELTA(ICNT).LT.DLOW) DLOW=DELTA(ICNT)
            IF(DELTA(ICNT).GT.DHIGH) DHIGH=DELTA(ICNT)
            GOTO 100
200         CALL FCLOS(0)
C
C           NOW SCALE DATE FOR PLOTING
C
            CON=1.
205         DV=XHIGH-XLOW
            IF(DV.GE.5.) GOTO 208
            CON=CON*10.
            XHIGH=XHIGH*10.
            XLOW=XLOW*10.
            GOTO 205
208         ILOW=XLOW
            IHIGH=XHIGH
210         IHIGH=IHIGH+1
            ID=IHIGH-ILOW
            J=1
            DO 220 I=1,3
            IF(ID.EQ.(J*5).OR.ID.EQ.(J*10)) GOTO 230
            IF(ID.EQ.(J*20).OR.ID.EQ.(J*40)) GOTO 230
            J=J*10
220         CONTINUE
            GOTO 210
230         XLOW=ILOW
            XHIGH=IHIGH
            DV=(XHIGH-XLOW)/5.0
            DV=DV/CON
            XLOW=XLOW/CON
            XMAX=DHIGH
            IF(XMAX.LT.ABS(DLOW)) XMAX=ABS(DLOW)
            DX=XMAX/2.0
C
C           NOW WRITE DISK FILE AND CHAIN
C
            CALL DFILW("TEMP",IER)
            CALL OPEN(1,"TEMP",3,IER)
            J=ICNT-IMA+1
            WRITE(1,4) ICNAM,IDECM,J,IMA,IYEAR,XLOW,DV,DX
4           FORMAT(1X,10A2,3I3,I4,3F9.3)
            DO 315 K=IMA,ICNT
            WRITE(1,5) PRICE(K),DELTA(K)
5           FORMAT(1X,2F9.3)
315         CONTINUE

            CALL RESET
            CALL CHAIN("DETREND1.SV",IER)
            END
```

# PROGRAM: DETREND To Calculate and Plot Detrended Commodity Prices in Any Given Contract and Any Determined Moving-Average Length *(Continued)*

```
C       NAME = DETREND1.FR
C
C       SECOND PHASE OF PROGRAM TO PLOT COMMODITY PRICES AND THE
C       DIFFERENCE BETWEEN PRICE AND MOVING AVERAGE
C
        COMMON/BLK/IDAT(2)
        DIMENSION        ICNAM(10)
        DATA IDAT/"MA= "/
        CALL OPEN(0,"TEMP",1,IER)
        READ(0,1) ICNAM,IDECM,ICNT,IMA,ICY,XLOW,DV,DX
1       FORMAT(10A2,3I3,I4,3F9.3)
        ORGY=.465
        ORGX=1.00
        ORGD=5.465
        CALL INITAL(8,400,11,0,0,0)
        CALL PLOT(0.,0.,0)
        IK=(ICNT+11)/12
        CLEN=IK
        CLEN=CLEN*.428+ORGX
        CALL PLOT(ORGX,ORGY,3)
        CALL PLOT(CLEN,ORGY,2)
        CALL PLOT(ORGX,ORGY,3)
C
C       WRITE YEARS
C
        POS=ORGX
        YEAR=ICY
        DO 70 I=1,IK
        CALL PLOT(POS,ORGY,3)
        CALL PLOT(POS,(ORGY-.15),2)
        CALL NUMBER((POS+.07),(ORGY-.15),.09,YEAR,0.0,-1)
        YEAR=YEAR+1.0
        POS=POS+0.428
70      CONTINUE
        CALL PLOT(ORGX,ORGY,3)
        CALL PLOT(ORGX,(ORGY+2.5),2)
        CALL PLOT(CLEN,(ORGY+2.5),1)
        CALL PLOT(ORGX,(ORGY+2.5),3)
        CALL PLOT(ORGX,ORGD,2)
        CALL PLOT((ORGX-.15),ORGD,3)
        CALL PLOT(CLEN,ORGD,2)
        CALL PLOT(ORGX,ORGD,3)
        CALL PLOT(ORGX,(ORGY+10.0),2)
        CALL PLOT(CLEN,(ORGY+10.0),1)
        CALL PLOT(CLEN,(ORGY-.15),1)
        YHED=ORGY+4.75
        CALL SYMBOL((ORGX+.50),YHED,.14,ICNAM,0.0,15)
        CALL SYMBOL((ORGX+2.25),YHED,.14,IDAT,0.0,4)
        VAL=IMA
        CALL NUMBER((ORGX+2.80),YHED,.14,VAL,0.0,-1)
```

**PROGRAM:** **DETREND To Calculate and Plot Detrended Commodity Prices in Any Given Contract and Any Determined Moving-Average Length** *(Continued)*

```
C
C          DRAW 5 HASH MARKS
C
           YPOS=ORGD
           DO 100 I=1,5
           YPOS=YPOS+1.00
           CALL PLOT((ORGX-.15),YPOS,3)
           CALL PLOT(ORGX,YPOS,2)
100        CONTINUE
C
C          PLOT AXIS NUMBERS
C
           CALL PLOT(ORGX,ORGD,3)
           VALUE=XLOW
           YPOS=ORGD
           DO 110 I=1,6
           CALL NUMBER((ORGX-.80),YPOS,.14,VALUE,0.0,IDECM)
           VALUE=VALUE+DV
           YPOS=YPOS+1.00
110        CONTINUE
C
C          NOW PLOT DAILY PRICES ON TOP SECTION
C
           XPOS=ORGX+.035
           IPNTR=3
           DO 120 I=1,ICNT
           READ(0,2) PRICE,VALUE
2          FORMAT(2F9.3)
           POS=((PRICE-XLOW)/DV)+ORGD
           CALL PLOT(XPOS,POS,IPNTR)
           IF(IPNTR.EQ.3) IPNTR=2
           XPOS=XPOS+.035
120        CONTINUE
           CALL FCLOS(0)
           CALL OPEN(0,'TEMP',1,IER)
           READ(0,1) ICNAM,IDECM,I,IMA,ICY,XLOW,DV,DX
C
C          NOW PLOT OTHER VALUE
C
           XPOS=ORGX
           IPNTR=3
           DO 130 I=1,ICNT
           READ(0,2) PRICE,VALUE
           POS=VALUE/DX
           POS=POS+2.50+ORGY
           CALL PLOT(XPOS,POS,IPNTR)
           IF(IPNTR.EQ.3) IPNTR=2
           XPOS=XPOS+.035
130        CONTINUE
           CALL RSTR(2)
           END
```

# APPENDIX THREE

# The Mathematics of Cycles

The mathematics of cycle analysis is a highly complex subject. There have been many attempts to work with cycles in the stock and commodity markets using various methods under the premise that price behavior is essentially repetitive. Those who are interested in a more thorough understanding of these approaches should consult the bibliography. As a starting point, the general formulas presented in this appendix should help provide an overview of the areas that can be investigated. Remember that it is not the intention of this book to provide a thorough analysis of the mathematics. However, major areas of interest are highlighted in an effort to stimulate further productive research.

## METHODS OF SEASONAL ANALYSIS

In addition to the techniques discussed in this text there are several other approaches to seasonal price analysis.

*Adjusting for inflation rate* is applicable to virtually every analytical method. Simply stated, you factor in a constant which adjusts seasonal price indexing to the inflation rate. The effect of this factor is to nullify the years in which there was an excessive price response as a function of inflation. Basically, the formula is simple and can be applied to the raw data. Consider the following application to the raw data:

$$A_i = (P \times I) - P$$

where $A_i$ is price adjusted for inflation, $P$ is raw data price, and $I$ is percentage rate of inflation expressed as a decimal. Essentially, we are "removing" the effect of inflation by subtracting from the raw data figure. The effect of the years with high inflation rates will, as a result, be lessened whereas years with a lower rate of inflation will not have as large a correcting factor. The same basic correction could be applied to futures and/or seasonal spread analysis in the futures market.

*The Holt-Winters method of components* is a more advanced method of seasonal analysis. Basically this technique applies a curve-smoothing factor to the data by separating time-series components using an exponential technique. Kaufman (1978) offers a more complete discussion of this variation. Essentially the mathematics is as follows:

$$m_t = \frac{ax_t}{s_{t-12}} + (1 - a)(m_{t-1} + c_{t-1})$$

$$s_t = \frac{bx_t}{m_t} + (1 - b)s_{t-12}$$

$$c_t = d(m_t - m_{t-1}) + (1 - d)c_{t-1}$$

Where $m_t$ is the mean to date, $c_t$ is the intermediate term trend of cyclic component, $s_t$ is the seasonal component, and $a$, $b$, and $c$, are exponential components to smooth the equation. The technique can be involved and is ideally applicable to computerized manipulation.

## CYCLIC METHODS

In addition to the basic methods discussed in this book, the advanced analytical techniques usually applied to cyclic study can help minimize the degree of error and may, in fact, result in more accurate predictive results both on a short and long term basis. Here are several areas that have gained popularity in recent years.

### CURVE FITTING

The basic approach here is to examine a historical set of data points and write an equation or set of equations which best fits the data. It is hoped that the formulas will then make a prediction of future data more possible. The basic components of each wave of curve fall into the three major categories:

Amplitude $(A)$ — the height of a curve
Frequency $(F)$ — the number of repeated wavelengths calculated as the ratio $F = 1/T$
Time (period) $(T)$ — the number of time units in each completed wavelength

It is assumed that the combination and proper manipulation of the categories will result in the successful ability to predict the next data points by using the resultant formula. Basically the following equations are applicable in working with the basic linear equation $y = a + bx$. The generalized formula for performing the analysis is expressed as

$$Y = A1 \sin(F1p + B1) + A2 \sin(F2p + B2)$$

where $p$ = the starting price point and $A$ and $B$ are variables. Those interested in taking this basic analysis to its logical conclusion are advised to study in greater detail the methodology of trigonometric curve-fitting.

### FOURIER ANALYSIS

A more thorough treatment of curve-fitting is the Fourier method. The treatment of data points is much more extensive and there are various alternate methods. Essentially the mathematics is as follows:

$$N = \sum_{i=1}^{N} y_i$$

$$y_i = 1 + \sum_{k=1}^{N/2} \left( V_k \cos \frac{2\pi ki}{(N/2)} + V_k \sin \frac{2\pi ki}{N/2} \right)$$

where

$$V_k = \frac{1}{N/2} \sum_{i=1}^{N} y_i \cos \frac{2\pi ki}{N/2}$$

and

$$V_k = \frac{1}{N/2} \sum_{i=1}^{N} y_i \sin \frac{2\pi ki}{N/2}$$

## SPECTRAL ANALYSIS

The Foundation for the Study of Cycles has worked extensively with this advanced technique. This work available to members of the Foundation, provides a thorough, step-by-step method for analyzing a data series for cyclic components. It yields cycle lengths as well as measures of statistical significance for each cycle which is found. The basic formula in spectral analysis is the trigonometric, time-based series:

$$\hat{y}_t(\omega) = \frac{1}{\pi} \left( c_0 + 2 \sum_{k=1}^{N-1} c_k \cos \omega k \right)$$

$$c_k = \sum_{t=1}^{N-k} \frac{(y_t - \bar{y})(y_{t+k} - \bar{y})}{N}$$

$$\hat{y}_t(\omega) = \frac{1}{\pi} \left( \lambda_0 c_0 + 2 \sum_{k=1}^{M} \lambda_k c_k \cos \omega k \right)$$

The full method of spectral analysis involves the use of a so-called lag window. There are several alternative methods of computing the window. One is the Tukey method:

$$\lambda_k = \frac{1}{2} \left( 1 + \cos \frac{\pi k}{M} \right)$$

## SUGGESTIONS FOR MORE ADVANCED RESEARCH

Those interested in further research on the cyclic method are encouraged to investigate material readily available from the Foundation for the Study of Cycles. The great strides made in mini- and microcomputer systems and their now reasonable cost should make such technology easily procurable for the average trader. The results, however, may not be worth the effort. Essentially, I believe that basic methods can be the most productive when all is said and done, but there are still many aspects of cyclic analysis which remain either untested or untried. There are, at the time of this writing, few sources of study which can be of value, other than those mentioned above and in earlier discussions. The area of cyclic analysis is still wide open in this sense and the rewards to those who develop effective techniques could be immense.

# APPENDIX FOUR

# Sample Chart Analyses

The charts that follow are designed to help you isolate the signals discussed in the text. The first group of charts shows daily and weekly support and resistance lines. Not all lines have been drawn in. Particular attention has been paid to those which are significant in terms of the move that followed or the time span that came before. Also shown are lines that came at or near cyclic turning points. Note that the UBO and DBO signals are not shown because there is limited space on charts. These can be easily determined by reference to the previously stated definitions.

   The second set of charts shows REVERSAL SIGNALS UP and DOWN, indicated by arrowheads (▲ ▼). This set of charts also shows HLC and LHC signals denoted by two arrows (⇈), one for each day or week of the signal. Again, the text has already explained the meaning and significance of these signals. Remember that not all reversals or HLC, LHC signals are shown. For a more thorough understanding nothing can replace practice and experience. Always remember that these are raw signals in the sense that they have not been combined with the cycle indicators.

The figures in this appendix show several different types of signals as discussed in Chapters 12 through 17.

All charts in this appendix reprinted with permission of Commodity Perspective Inc. 327 S. LaSalle, Chicago, IL. 60604

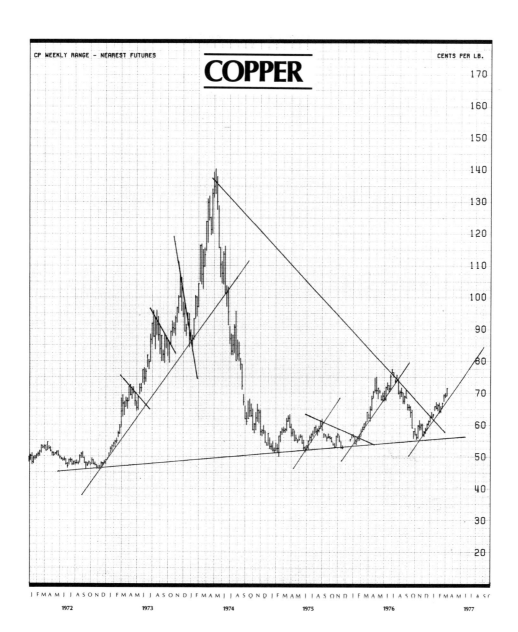

CP WEEKLY RANGE - NEAREST FUTURES

# COPPER

CENTS PER LB.

170
160
150
140
130
120
110
100
90
80
70
60
50
40
30
20

J F M A M J J A S O N D J F M A M J J A S O N D J F M A M J J A S O N D J F M A M J J A S O N D J F M A M J J A S O N D J F M A M J J A S O

1972    1973    1974    1975    1976    1977

345

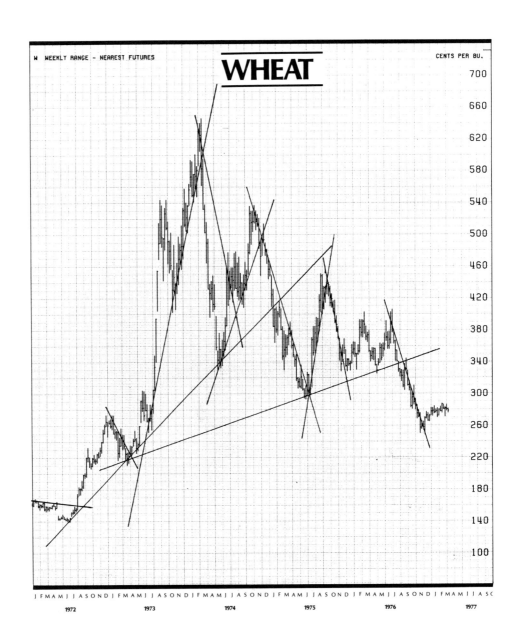

W   WEEKLY RANGE - NEAREST FUTURES

# WHEAT

CENTS PER BU.

700
660
620
580
540
500
460
420
380
340
300
260
220
180
140
100

J F M A M J J A S O N D J F M A M J J A S O N D J F M A M J J A S O N D J F M A M J J A S O N D J F M A M J J A S O N D J F M A M J J A S O

1972        1973        1974        1975        1976        1977

346

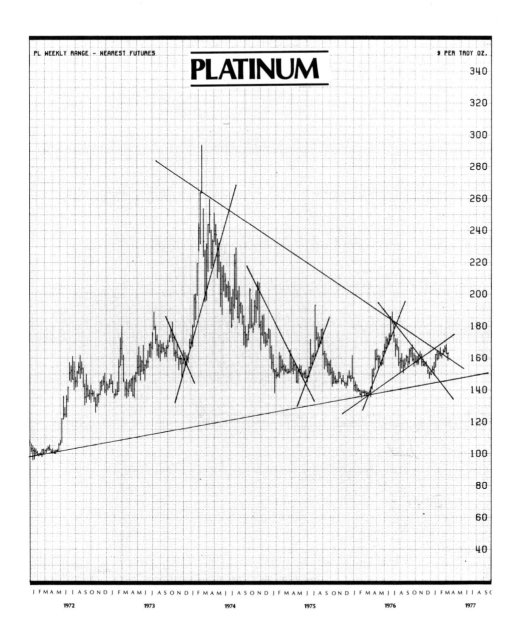

PL WEEKLY RANGE - NEAREST FUTURES

# PLATINUM

$ PER TROY OZ.

340
320
300
280
260
240
220
200
180
160
140
120
100
80
60
40

J F M A M J J A S O N D J F M A M J J A S O N D J F M A M J J A S O N D J F M A M J J A S O N D J F M A M J J A S O N D J F M A M J J A S O

1972      1973      1974      1975      1976      1977

CONTRACT TBZ 78
HIGH    93.94: 08/31/77
LOW     90.60: 12/20/78

# T. BILLS

## DECEMBER 1978

PTS OF 100 PERCENT

93.4

93.2

93.0

92.8

92.6

92.4

92.2

92.0

91.8

91.6

91.4

91.2

91.0

90.8

90.6

90.4

5 12 19 26  2  9 16 23 30  6 13 20 27  6 13 20 27  3 10 17 24  1  8 15 22 29  5 12 19 26  3 10 17 24 31  7 14 21 28  4 11 18 25  2  9 16 23 30  6 13 20 27  4 11 18 25  1  8 15 22 29
  DEC        JAN       FEB       MAR       APR       MAY       JUN       JUL       AUG       SEP       OCT       NOV       DEC       JAN

348

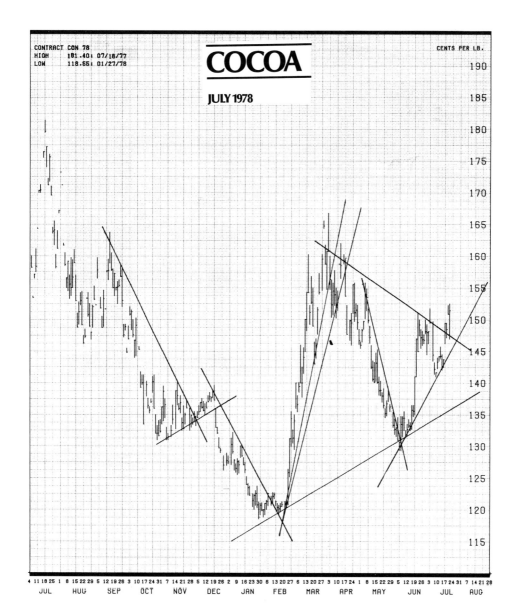

COCOA

JULY 1978

CONTRACT CON 78
HIGH      181.40: 07/18/77
LOW       118.55: 01/27/78

CENTS PER LB.

190
185
180
175
170
165
160
155
150
145
140
135
130
125
120
115

4 11 18 25  1  8 15 22 29  5 12 19 26  3 10 17 24 31  7 14 21 28  5 12 19 26  2  9 16 23 30  6 13 20 27  6 13 20 27  3 10 17 24  1  8 15 22 29  5 12 19 26  3 10 17 24 31  7 14 21 28

JUL    AUG    SEP    OCT    NOV    DEC    JAN    FEB    MAR    APR    MAY    JUN    JUL    AUG

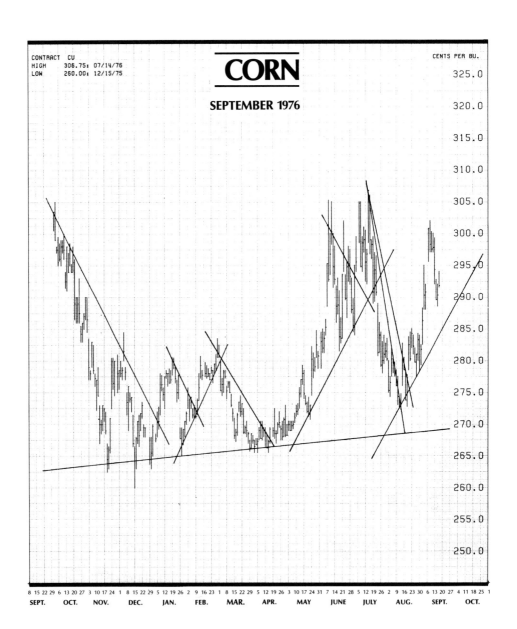

# CORN

## SEPTEMBER 1976

CONTRACT CU
HIGH    306.75; 07/14/76
LOW     260.00; 12/15/75

CENTS PER BU.

325.0
320.0
315.0
310.0
305.0
300.0
295.0
290.0
285.0
280.0
275.0
270.0
265.0
260.0
255.0
250.0

8 15 22 29 6 13 20 27 3 10 17 24 1 8 15 22 29 5 12 19 26 2 9 16 23 1 8 15 22 29 5 12 19 26 3 10 17 24 31 7 14 21 28 5 12 19 26 2 9 16 23 30 6 13 20 27 4 11 18 25 1

SEPT.   OCT.   NOV.   DEC.   JAN.   FEB.   MAR.   APR.   MAY   JUNE   JULY   AUG.   SEPT.   OCT.

CENTS PER LB.

# ORANGE JUICE

### JULY 1976

76
74
72
70
68
66
64
62
60
58
56
54
52
50
48
46

7 14 21 28  4 11 18 25  1  8 15 22 29  6 13 20 27  3 10 17 24  1  8 15 22 29  5 12 19 26  2  9 16 23  1  8 15 22 29  5 12 19 26  3 10 17 24 31  7 14 21 28  5 12 19 26  2  9 16 23 30

JULY    AUG.    SEPT.    OCT.    NOV.    DEC.    JAN.    FEB.    MAR.    APR.    MAY    JUNE    JULY    AUG.

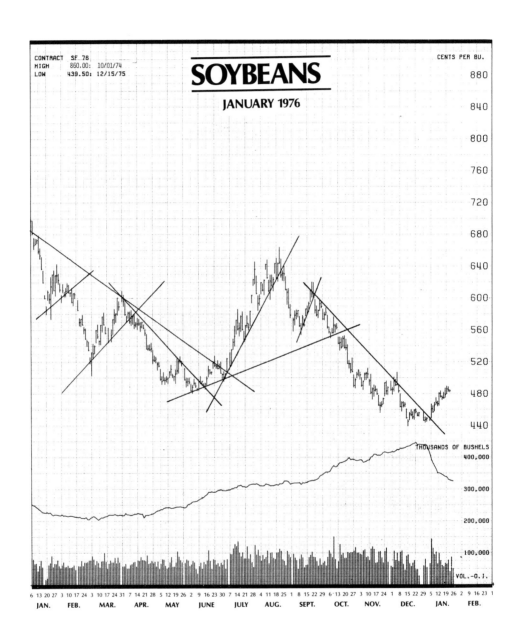

CONTRACT SF 76
HIGH 860.00: 10/01/74
LOW 439.50: 12/15/75

# SOYBEANS

## JANUARY 1976

CENTS PER BU.

880

840

800

760

720

680

640

600

560

520

480

440

THOUSANDS OF BUSHELS
400,000

300,000

200,000

100,000

VOL.-O.I.

6 13 20 27 3 10 17 24 3 10 17 24 31 7 14 21 28 5 12 19 26 2 9 16 23 30 7 14 21 28 4 11 18 25 1 8 15 22 29 6 13 20 27 3 10 17 24 1 8 15 22 29 5 12 19 26 2 9 16 23 1

JAN. FEB. MAR. APR. MAY JUNE JULY AUG. SEPT. OCT. NOV. DEC. JAN. FEB.

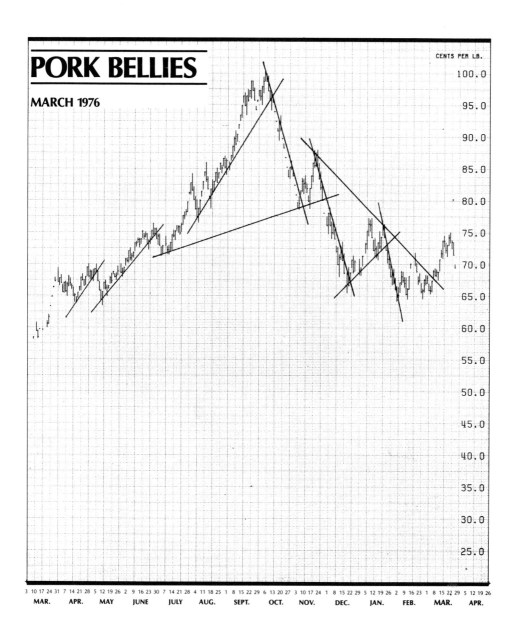

# PORK BELLIES

**MARCH 1976**

CENTS PER LB.

100.0
95.0
90.0
85.0
80.0
75.0
70.0
65.0
60.0
55.0
50.0
45.0
40.0
35.0
30.0
25.0

3 10 17 24 31 7 14 21 28 5 12 19 26 2 9 16 23 30 7 14 21 28 4 11 18 25 1 8 15 22 29 6 13 20 27 3 10 17 24 1 8 15 22 29 5 12 19 26 2 9 16 23 1 8 15 22 29 5 12 19 26

MAR.     APR.     MAY     JUNE     JULY     AUG.     SEPT.     OCT.     NOV.     DEC.     JAN.     FEB.     MAR.     APR.

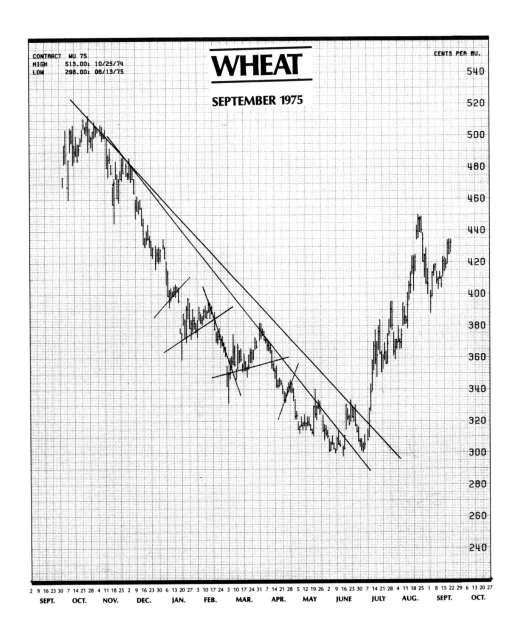

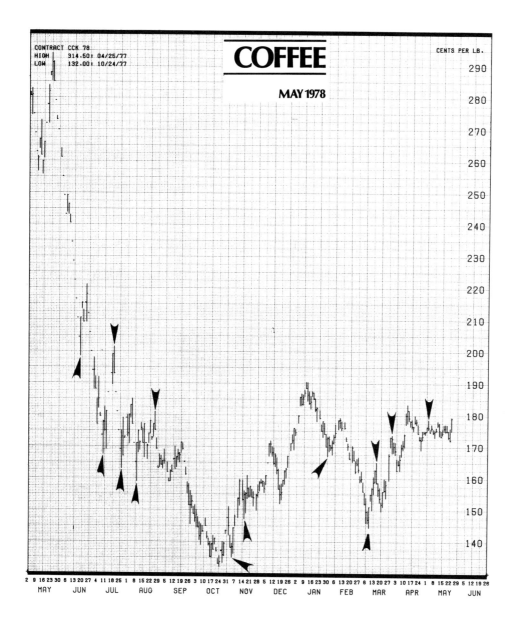

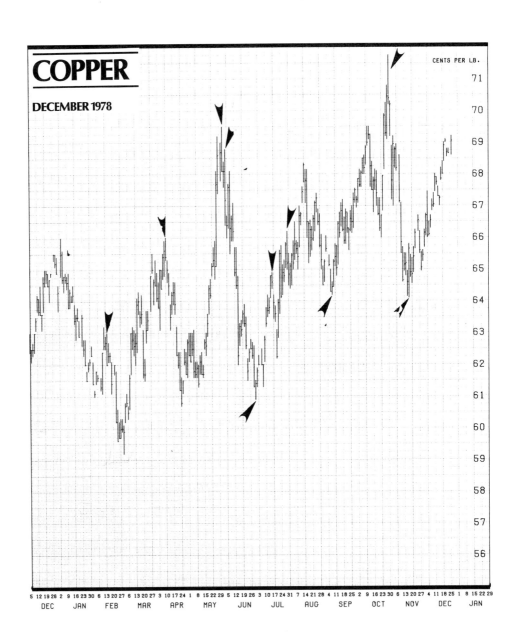

COPPER

DECEMBER 1978

CENTS PER LB.

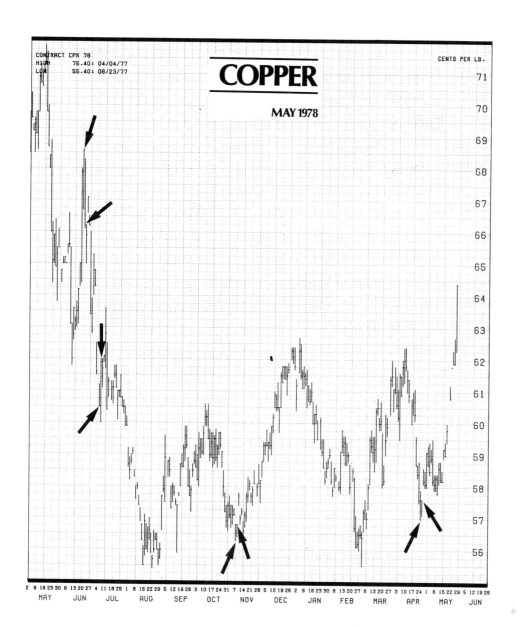

CONTRACT CPK 78
HIGH        76.40: 04/04/77
LOW         55.40: 08/23/77

CENTS PER LB.

# COPPER

**MAY 1978**

71
70
69
68
67
66
65
64
63
62
61
60
59
58
57
56

2  9 16 23 30  6 13 20 27  4 11 18 25  1  8 15 22 29  5 12 19 26  3 10 17 24 31  7 14 21 28  5 12 19 26  2  9 16 23 30  6 13 20 27  6 13 20 27  3 10 17 24  1  8 15 22 29  5 12 19 26
   MAY       JUN        JUL       AUG        SEP        OCT        NOV        DEC        JAN       FEB        MAR        APR       MAY       JUN

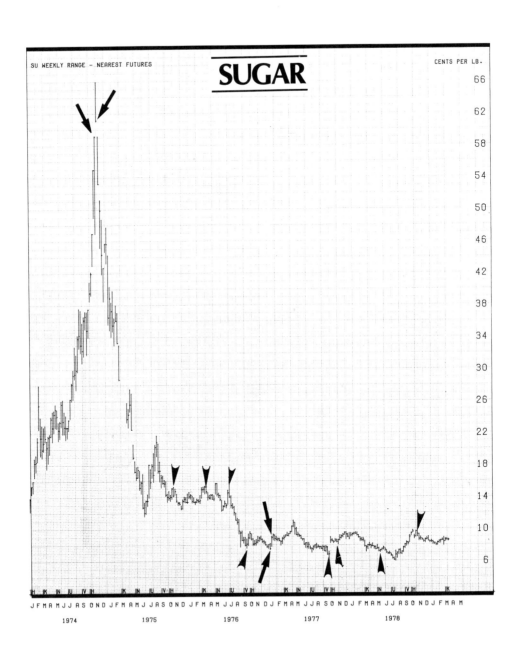

SU WEEKLY RANGE - NEAREST FUTURES

# SUGAR

CENTS PER LB.

66
62
58
54
50
46
42
38
34
30
26
22
18
14
10
6

J F M A M J J A S O N D J F M A M J J A S O N D J F M A M J J A S O N D J F M A M J J A S O N D J F M A M J J A S O N D J F M A M

1974        1975        1976        1977        1978

# APPENDIX FIVE

# Seasonal Futures Charts

The futures charts contained in this appendix were generated by computer using the methods, programs, and procedures discussed throughout the text. As time passes the charts will need to be updated inasmuch as new data will be available. This can be done either manually or by computer. They can also be ordered from MBH Commodity Advisors Inc., Post Office Box 353, Winnetka, Illinois 60093, at the going price. Some representative charts are included in this appendix. Remember that these charts are only part of a total approach to cyclic trading.

The seasonal composite spread charts were not computer generated, but follow the same basic method as indicated in Appendix 2.

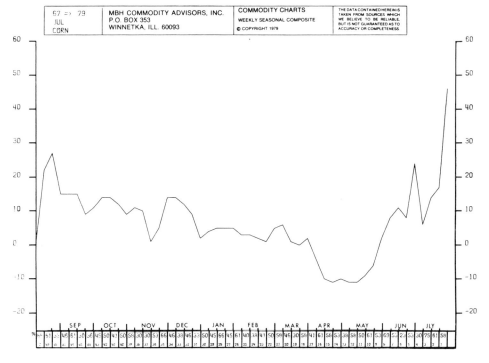

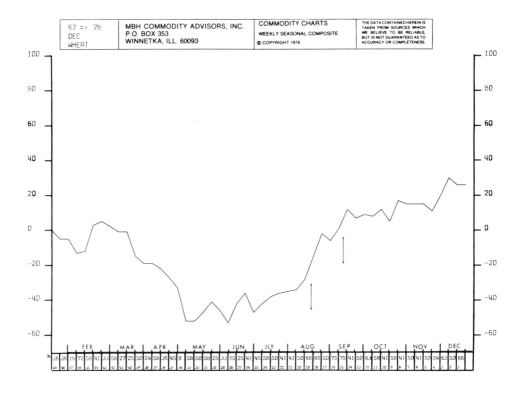

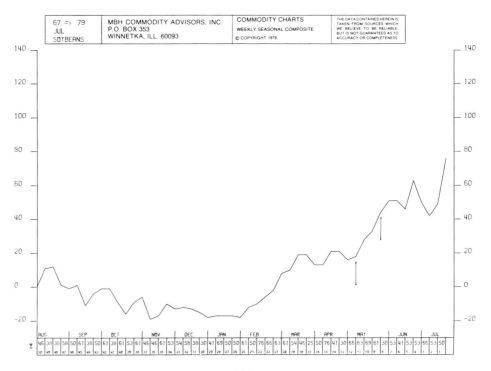

360

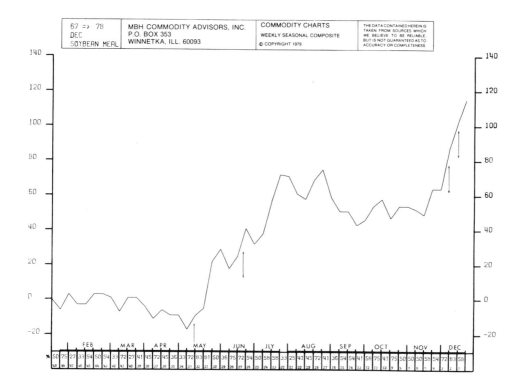

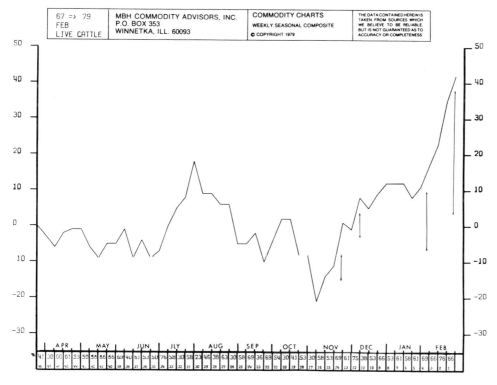

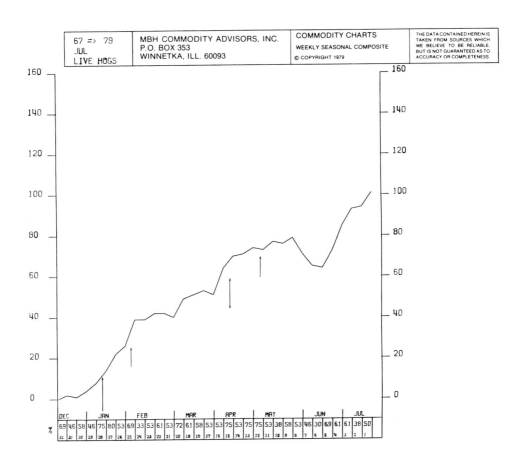

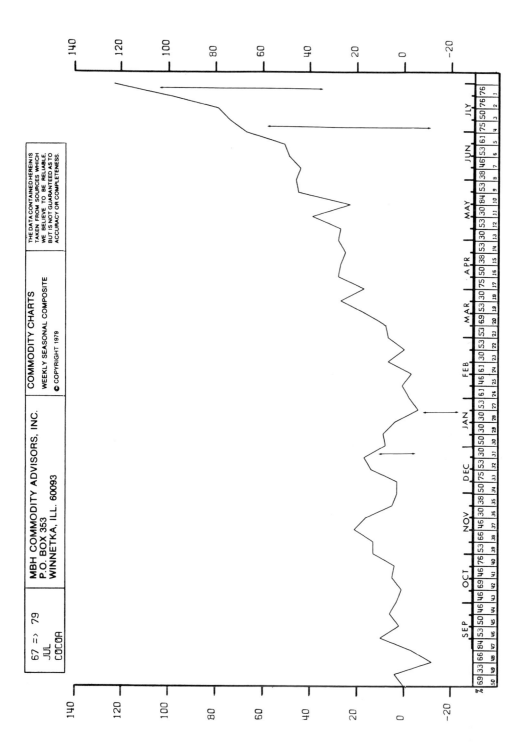

COMMODITY CHARTS
WEEKLY SEASONAL COMPOSITE
© COPYRIGHT 1979

MBH COMMODITY ADVISORS, INC.
P.O. BOX 353
WINNETKA, ILL. 60093

67 => 79
JUL
COCOA

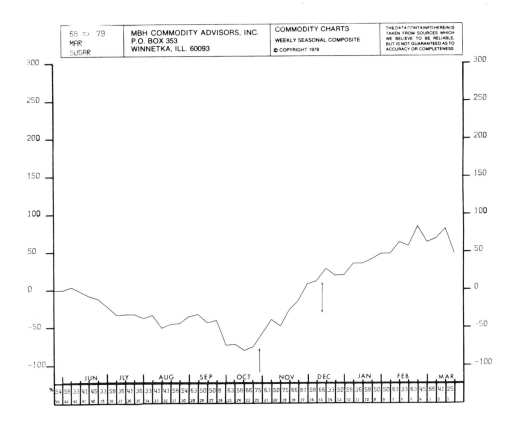

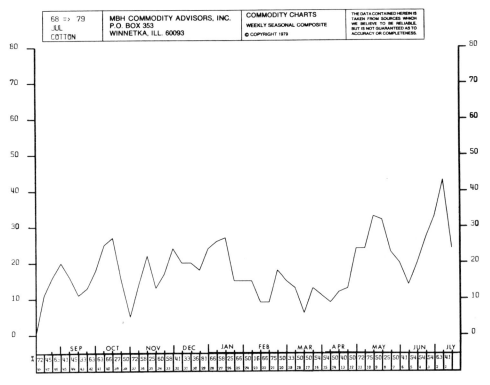

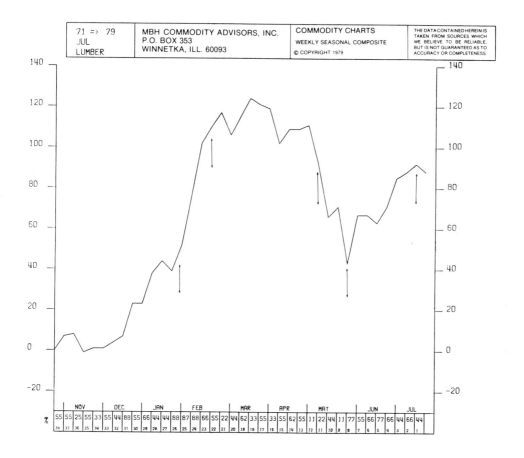

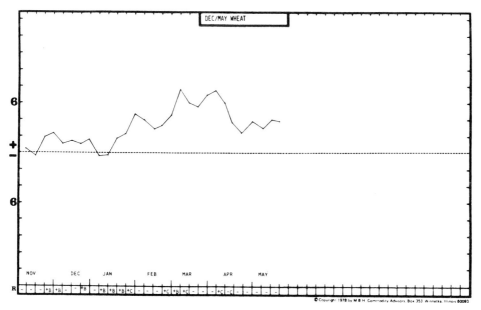

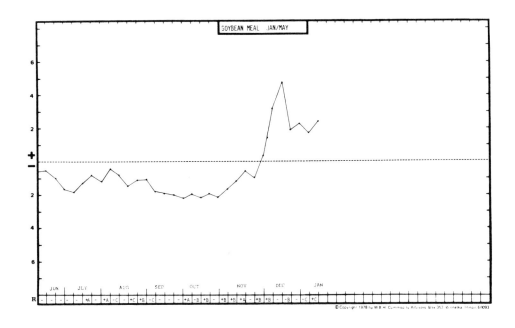

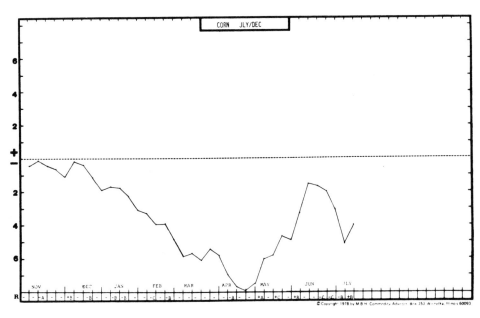

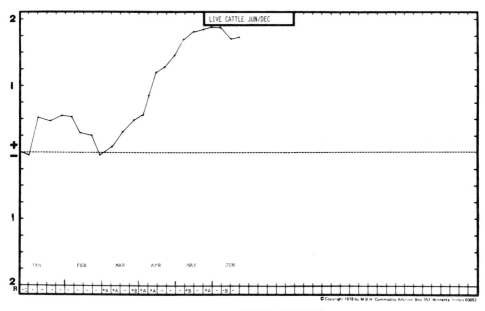

LIVE CATTLE JUN/DEC

JUN/DEC LIVE CATTLE

# Glossary of Terms

This glossary of terms is designed for use with the text of this book. The glossary items are not defined as thoroughly as they are in the text. It is important to understand that some of the definitions used in this book may differ somewhat from the manner in which you are currently using these terms. The best way to understand the concepts presented is by referring to the specific chapter(s) that discuss them in detail.

## AMPLITUDE

The height or magnitude of a given price cycle. Whereas period measures the time span from low to low, or low to high and back to low again, amplitude measures how high the cycle actually went. Clearly, a cycle that runs 52 weeks, for example, could have a much larger or smaller amplitude than another cycle of similar period. Hog prices, for example, could run 3.6 years, low to low and move from $0.13 to $0.45 as a high. The next 3.6 year cycle could then run from $0.26 low to $0.31 as a high. The amplitude of the second cycle was clearly lower than the amplitude of the first cycle, but the overall period, or cycle length, was unchanged (or approximately the same). The cycle work in this book does not consider amplitude in great detail. This subject has been left for students of advanced cycle mathematics.

## AVERAGE (MEAN)

The central tendency, mathematically defined, of a data series. In order to compute the arithmetic mean of a given cycle, you need only add all the observed cycle lengths and divide by the total number of observations. The following simple formula defines the procedure:

$$\text{average cycle length} = \frac{\text{total of all cycle lengths}}{\text{number of cycles counted}}$$

There are other measures of average tendency. Among them are the mode, the median, and the geometric mean, which are not covered in our discussions although some studies of cycle science consider them useful and relevant to their analyses.

## BAR CHART

A price chart that depicts the daily, weekly, or monthly high, low, and closing price of a given market in the form of a price bar. At times the opening price is also included. Most market technicians use bar charts in their work. This book contains many bar charts. A bar chart is used in spotting cyclic highs and lows as well as in establishing timing signals.

## CASH

A market in which actual raw commodities are traded on a day-to-day basis for immediate delivery. The cash, as opposed to futures, market does not make use of trading margins or delivery months because it is an on-the-spot immediate payment market. Cycles and seasonals are found both in cash and in futures markets. (Also called *spot market*.)

## CLOSE ONLY STOP

A stop loss order executed only on the close of trading if prices close, or are about to close, at or beyond a predetermined level. A close only stop of 45.20, for example, means that the position is to be closed out if the 45.20 level has been penetrated on the close. Frequently, it is not possible to determine if a closing price will be at the predetermined price. Exchanges or brokerage concerns will often not accept close only stop loss orders. In such cases, the position must be liquidated on the following day.

## CLOSING PRICE CHART

Also known as a close only chart. The closing price chart shows only the last, or settlement, price of a given market connected by a line. The time span can be either daily, monthly, weekly, or yearly, but only the very last price for each time unit is shown. Some market technicians use these charts instead of bar charts because they believe that the only important price for any given time span is the final price. Close only charts make it easier to spot upside and downside breakout timing signals (UBO and DBO, respectively) discussed in the text.

## CYCLE

A repetitive pattern in any natural or economic data series.

## CYCLE HIGH

The point at which prices reach a peak and begin to turn down during the proper time frame for such a turn. Many such peaks may occur during the proper time frame or time window. The correct top for cycle research purposes is the highest of these peaks. A cycle high can also be verified by timing indicators such as R−, 3L, DBO, or HLC, as discussed in the text. It is not uncommon for cyclic tops to come a bit early or late depending on other cycles that may be exerting their influence during the same time period. Highs can be selected visually or with the aid of mechanical measuring devices. Mathematical models can also be useful in selecting the high of a given cycle or cycles. The time span measured between cycle highs is less regular than the time span measured between cycle lows. (Also called *cycle peak* or *cycle top.*)

## CYCLE LENGTH

A measure of time. Whether counted in years, months, weeks, days, hours, or minutes, cycle length tells you the time or period of each cycle. There are many different ways in which the cycle length can be measured. Each market or data series contains many cycles of different lengths (i.e., time periods). You can choose the average cycle length, or you can select any given cycle and examine the length. In every case the cycle length is an approximate figure unless you can determine to the very second when a low was made. The larger the time unit, the less accurate will be your determination of cycle length. If we say that a cycle has a 6 year period, it means that a low could come at any time in the sixth year subsequent to the last low. If we say that a cycle has a length of 16 days, low to low, then this means that the low came at some point during the sixteenth day. The only way in which we can determine the most exact time frame is to measure a cycle in the number of seconds or minutes from low to low or high to high. This is a difficult thing to do, given the limitations of data. For our purposes days, weeks, months, and years are used. (Also called *time length, time span,* or *period.*)

## CYCLE LOW

The point at which prices establish a bottom and begin to turn higher during the proper time frame. There may be many attempts at a bottom during the proper time frame, or time window. The correct bottom for cycle research purposes is the lowest of all the lows during this time frame. Lows can also be verified by such timing or trend change signals as R+, UBO, 3H, and LHC, as discussed in the text. It is not uncommon for cycle lows to be influenced by other cycles that may be exerting their influence during the same time period. Lows can be selected with the aid of mechanical devices or by visual inspection. Mathematical models can also be used in selecting such lows. The time span measured between lows tends to be less variable than the time span measured between cycle highs. (Also called *cycle bottom* or *cycle trough.*)

## DAILY CHART

A daily chart that shows only the price behavior from from one day to the next. Daily price charts are used in finding and trading short term cycles, and may be bar or close only.

## EXTRAPOLATE

To predict. To extrapolate means to forecast the future on the basis of an existing or ongoing tendency that has proved to be valid. If, for example, a cycle has repeated itself 50 times, then we can extrapolate the next cycle low and high with considerable confidence. In determining the time window, we are extrapolating on the basis of current cyclic information.

## FUTURES CONTRACT

An agreement between two individuals, buyer and seller, to exchange a commodity for a given sum of money or a fixed price, at some specified time in the future. The contract is entered into with a deposit of good faith money, or margin, which actually represents a very small fraction of the actual final cost. The contract may then be held until the actual transaction is completed, or it may be sold or bought back prior to the expiration date.

## HEDGER

One who buys and or sells commodity futures contracts with the intention of protecting current supplies from depreciating in value, or for the purpose of planning needs in advance. A hedger intends either to make or take delivery on a given contract. In time, the need to make or take delivery may change as a function of price and/or demand, but it is the original intention that distinguishes a hedger from a speculator. The term *hedge* means, in essence, to protect. And this is exactly what the hedger is doing. By taking a position in the futures market, either long and/or short, the hedger's intent is to protect future needs and/or prices.

## HIGH TO HIGH

A measurement of cycle period or time across highs. A cycle can be measured either from low to high and back to low again, or from high to low and back to high again. The traditional manner of measurement is to define a cycle length or period from low to low terms because measurements of the lows vary less than measurements of highs.

## INTERMEDIATE TERM CYCLE

A cycle longer than 6 months but less than 1 year in its average length. (See *long term cycle* for more information on cycle length categories.)

## LONG TERM

The time span of a cycle. If a cycle runs longer than 1 year, it is defined for our purposes as a long term cycle. There are no firmly established rules regarding the terminology used to describe the length of a cycle other than the specific period—low to low or high to high. In other words, what may be a long term cycle to one individual may be considered relatively short term to another. The definitions used in this text may not be similar to what is found in other cycle studies.

## LOW TO LOW

A measure of cycle length from one low to the next expressed in time units. Cycles are commonly measured from low to low as opposed to measurements made between highs. Unless otherwise stated, the measurements in this text are made from one low to the next.

## MAGNITUDE

See *amplitude*. Magnitude and amplitude are used interchangeably.

## MARGIN

The amount of up front or good faith money required to establish a position, long or short, in the futures market. The actual amount required is determined by the various commodity exchanges, brokerage houses, and/or government regulatory policy. Amounts vary but generally run less than 10 percent and more than 1 percent of the total contract value.

## MONTHLY CHART

A monthly chart that shows only the price behavior from one month to the next. Monthly price charts are used in finding and trading intermediate and long term cycles, and may be bar or close only.

## PATTERN/PERIOD

Any repetitive tendency in price, whether seasonal or cyclical. The term is usually used in reference to a series of cycles or seasonal tendencies that is more complex or involved than any one cycle or seasonal. A cyclic trend that repeats several lengths over a period of time is a pattern. If, for example, a cycle of 50 months is followed by a cycle of 12 months and then another cycle of 50 months, the total series is referred to as a pattern if the next series of cycles is generally similar to the one just mentioned. (See also *cycle*.)

## PERIOD

An expression of cycle length in time units. If we say that the period of a given cycle is 22 days, we mean that the cycle spans 22 days from low to high and back to low again.

## POSITION TRADER

A trader who establishes a given market position—long, short, or spread—and holds that position for a fairly long time. There is no predetermined time length, but generally anything longer than 3 months is considered fairly lengthy in terms of futures trading and would qualify as a position trade for the purposes of this text. Other individuals may differ in their interpretation of this term. There is no firm rule regarding the actual meaning of this term, however.

## PROBABILITY

The likelihood of future repetitions of a cycle. Because cyclic science is not sufficiently advanced to permit perfect prediction of future highs and lows, each forecast or projection must be assigned a relative probability of occurrence. When a cycle has repeated itself many times with only minor variations in time, the probability of future repetitions is high. On the other hand, a cycle with only a relatively brief history is less likely to repeat itself with as high a probability.

## PROJECTION

As used in connection with cycle research, a prediction of time. In common technical usage, most technicians refer to price projections. In other words, they estimate where a given market will go in terms of price. Because cycle analysis is based on time, the projections are also based on time and not price. When a given cycle length has been determined, either from low to low or from high to high, an analyst can count forward in time and predict the approximate time period of the next low and/or high. The projection results in what we call a *time window*. The concept and technique of the time window are discussed in the text.

## RISK

A measure of potential dollar loss relative to potential profit from a given commodity transaction. Ordinarily, the trades with the highest risk trades to produce the largest dollar profit. This is not necessarily the case, however, if the trader has poor timing. It is my contention on the basis of the cyclic studies advanced in this text that risk decreases during time windows, provided the appropriate entry and exit signals are followed.

## SEASONAL PRICE TENDENCY

The tendency for prices to act in certain ways at given times of the year. Such price patterns can be examined on a monthly, weekly, or daily basis depending on the trader's goal. Seasonality is present in cash, futures, and spreads.

## SHORT TERM CYCLE

A cycle that runs less than 6 months. (See *long term cycles* for additional information regarding the time span of cycles and their categories.)

## SPECULATOR

A person who takes a position (whether in stocks, commodities, real estate or any form of capital venture) with the intention of increasing his capital over the shortest possible period of time. There has been much controversy about the difference between an investor and a speculator. For the purposes of this book, the only difference between the two is that the investor believes he is entering the market for a longer period. In reality, however, any form of market involvement involves risk and is, hence, a form of speculation.

## SPOT MARKET

Another term for a cash market, or the futures market once the contract in question comes due for delivery. A spot market is, therefore, a current or "on the spot" market as opposed to a futures market.

## TIME WINDOW

The period of time during which a cycle is most likely to change direction. In order to calculate the time window, you must compute the average cycle length, or the period between cycle lows as well as the period between cycle highs. The next cycle lows and highs are projected according to these computations. A range of ± 15 percent is then calculated as the time window for the next high and low. It is during the time window that signals of a trend change are closely watched for buying and selling opportunities.

## TIMING SIGNAL

A specific technical indicator that correlates well with changes in price trend. By examining an operationally defined set of technical market parameters (e.g., price, volume, and open interest relationships), a timing signal can be determined which, if on examination proves to be reliable in selecting market turns, is judged to be reliable or useful. For the purposes of this book, four timing signals and their various combinations have been defined for use in connection with the time window.

## TRADER

An individual who establishes positions in the markets (long, short, or spread) with the intention of fairly rapid exit. The trader is interested in capitalizing only on short term price fluctuations. The position trader, on the other hand, is interested in maintaining a position for a considerably longer period of time (see *position trader*). The terms *trader* and *speculator* are often used interchangeably.

## WEEKLY PRICE CHART

A whether bar or close only, showing the price behavior from only one week to the next. Weekly price charts are used in finding and trading intermediate term cycles.

# BIBLIOGRAPHY

Benner, S. F. *Benner's Prophecies of Future Ups and Downs in Prices.* Ohio: Dundee, 1875.

Bernstein, J. *Seasonal Chart Study, 1953–1977.* Winnetka, Ill.: MBH, 1977.

———. *Seasonal Chart Study II: Commodity Spreads.* Winnetka, Ill.: MBH, 1978.

———. *Commodities—Now through 1984.* Winnetka, Ill.: MBH, 1979.

———. *Seasonal Futures Charts.* Winnetka, Ill.: MBH, 1980.

———. *The Investor's Quotient—The Psychology of Successful Investing in Commodities and Snocks.* New York: Wiley, 1980.

Bynner, W. *The Way of Life According to Lao Tzu.* New York: Capricorn, 1944.

Commodity Perspective—Price Charts. Chicago, 1979–1981.

Commodity Price Charts. Cedar Falls, Iowa, 1978–1981.

*Commodity Yearbook(s), 1950–1981.* New York: Commodity Research Bureau.

Dewey, E. R. *Cycles—Selected Writings.* Pittsburgh: Foundation for the Study of Cycles, 197.

———. "Putting Cycles to Work in Science and Industry." New York: Foundation for the Study of Cycles, 1941. Reprinted as *Foundation Reprint No. 11,* 1945, 194.

———. "Cycles in Wholesale Prices: Cotton (a) War and Post-War Behavior (b) the 6-Year Rhythm, 1731–32 to 1947–48." *Foundation Report No. 2.* Riverside, Conn.: Foundation for the Study of Cycles, 1949.

———. "Cycle Analysis: The Moving Average." *Technical Bulletin No. 4.* Riverside, Conn.: Foundation for the Study of Cycles, 1950.

———. "Wholesale Price Cycles: The 22-Year Cycle in Wholesale Prices." *Cycles* **1**, No. 2 (September 1950), p. 18.

———. "Cycles in General Business: The 3- to 3½-Year Waves, 1790–1946." *Cycles* **1**, No. 4 (November 1950), pp. 4–14.

———. "Long Cycles in Cotton Prices." *Cycles* **1**, No. 4 (November 1950), pp. 17–19.

———. "Long Cycles in Cotton Prices—Continued." *Cycles* **2**, No. 4 (April 1951), pp. 140.

———. "Cycles in Residential Building Construction, The 18⅓-Year Cycle." *Cycles* **2**, No. 5 (May 1951), pp. 171–73.

———. "The 9.6-Year Cycle in the Acreage of Wheat." *Cycles* **2**, No. 5 (May 1951), pp. 175–77.

———. "Cycle Analysis: The Moving Average." *Technical Bulletin No. 4. Cycles* **2**, No. 10 (October 1951), pp. 295–322.

———. "War Cycles and the 6-Year Cycle in Cotton Prices, 1731–1949." *Journal of Cycle Research* **1**, No. 2 (Winter 1951–52), pp. 35–42.

———. "What Made the Benner Forecast Tick?" *Cycles* **3**, No. 3 (March 1952), pp. 90–93.

———. "Cycle Analysis for the Beginner." *Cycles* **3**, No. 3 (March 1952), pp. 97–98.

———. "The 9.6-Year Cycle in the Acreage of Wheat." *Cycles* **3**, No. 9 (November 1952), pp. 327–29.

———. "The 6-Year Cycle in Cotton Production." *Cycles* **4**, No. 1 (January 1953), p. 9.

———. "What Is Ahead for Cotton Production?" *Cycles* **4**, No. 1 (January 1953), pp. 9–13.

———. "The 9.3-Year Cycle in Wheat Prices." *Cycles* **4**, No. 5 (May 1953), pp. 139–41.

————. "Cycles in Weather." *Cycles* **4**, No. 5 (May 1953), pp. 145–46.

————. "What's Ahead for Wheat Prices?" *Cycles* **4**, No. 6 (June-July 1953), pp. 182–88.

————. "What's Ahead for Wheat Prices?" *Cycles* **4**, No. 7 (September 1953), pp. 222–27.

————. "Cycles in Wheat Prices and in Weather." *Cycles* **4**, No. 10 (December 1953), pp. 340–41.

————. "1954 Postscript—Samuel Benner's Forecast of 1875." *Cycles* **5**, No. 2 (February 1954), pp. 76–78.

————. "Cycle Analysis: The Moving Average." *Journal of Cycle Research* **3**, No. 2 (Spring 1954), pp. 27–50.

————. "The 9.3 and the 8.6-Year Cycle in Cotton Prices." *Journal of Cycle Research* **3**, No. 4 (Fall 1954), pp. 99–107.

————. "The 5.91-Year Cycle in Cotton Prices." *Cycles* **5**, No. 8 (October 1954), pp. 277–83.

————. "Effects of Moving Averages." *Cycles* **5**, No. 8 (October 1954), p. 294.

————. "The 916-Year Cycle in the Acreage of Wheat." *Cycles* **5**, No. 9 (November 1954), p. 320.

————. "The 9.3- and 8.6-Year Cycles in Copper Prices, 1784–1953." *Cycles* **5**, No. 10 (December 1954), p. 352.

————. "The $17\frac{3}{4}$-Year Cycle in Cotton Prices, 1731–1953–4." *Cycles* **6**, No. 1 (January 1955), pp. 14–17.

————. "The $5\frac{1}{2}$-Year Cycle in Corn Prices." *Cycles* **6**, No. 2 (February 1955), pp. 43–47.

————. "Non-Symmetric Cycles." *Cycles* **6**, No. 2 (February 1955), pp. 48–49.

————. "The $5\frac{1}{2}$-Year Cycle in Corn Prices—Continued." *Cycles* **6**, No. 3 (March 1955), pp. 77–81.

————. "Samuel Turner Benner—Pioneer Cycle Analyst." *Cycles* **6**, No. 3 (March 1955), p. 87.

————. "The 16- or $16\frac{3}{4}$-Year Cycle in Coffee Prices 1854–1954." *Cycles* **6**, No. 6 (June-July 1955), pp. 180–83.

————. "The 9-Year Cycle in Number of Cattle on Farms, 1867–1954." *Cycles* **6**, No. 7 (August-September 1955), pp. 201–8.

————. "The $3\frac{1}{2}$- to $3\frac{3}{4}$-Year Cycles in Corn Prices, 1720–1954." *Cycles* **6**, No. 8 (October 1955), pp. 238–48.

————. "The 3.49-Year Cycle in Corn Prices." *Cycles* **6**, No. 9 (November 1955), pp. 273–80.

————. "The 9.3- and 8.6-Year Cycles in Copper Prices." *Cycles* **7**, No. 9 (September 1956), pp. 241–49.

————. "What's Ahead for Corn Prices?" *Cycles* **8**, No. 6 (June 1957), pp. 149–58.

————. "A Projection of Five Cycles in Copper Prices." *Cycles* **8**, No. 8 (August 1957), pp. 214–15.

————. "What's Ahead for Wheat Prices?" *Cycles* **8**, No. 9 (September 1957), pp. 229–36.

————. "Long-Term Trend of Copper Prices." *Cycles* **8**, No. 9 (September 1957), p. 238.

————. "The 54-Year Cycle in Copper Prices." *Cycles* **8**, No. 9 (September 1957), pp. 238–39.

————. "What's Ahead for Interest Rates?" *Cycles* **8**, No. 10 (October 1957), pp. 253–56.

————. "What's Ahead for Commodity Prices?" *Cycles* **8**, No. 11 (November 1957), p. 295.

————. "Finding Cycles." *Cycles* **9**, No. 1 (January 1958), p. 31.

————. "The Cycle Workshop: How to Get Hints of Cycles—Continued." *Cycles* **9**, No. 4 (April 1958), p. 96.

————. "The Cycle Workshop: How to Get Hints of Cycles, the Graduated Scale." *Cycles* **9**, No. 11 (November 1958), p. 302.

————. "Some Basic Cycle Concepts." *Cycles* **10**, No. 1 (January 1959), pp. 8–10.

————. "The Three Kinds of Cycles." *Cycles* **10**, No. 5 (May 1959), p. 104.

————. "The Cycle Workshop: The Moving Average." *Cycles* **10**, No. 10 (October 1959), p. 230.

————. "Copper Prices." *Cycles* **10**, No. 12 (December 1959), p. 279.

————. "The Case for Exogenous Rhythms." *Cycles* **11**, No. 12 (December 1960), pp. 269–70.

————. "The Cycle Workshop: The Time Chart, Part 3." *Cycles* **12**, No. 12 (December 1961), pp. 325–26.

———. "The Cycle Workshop: The General Procedure of Rhythm Analysis." *Cycles* **13**, No. 1 (January 1962), pp. 17–18.

———. "The Cycle Workshop: The Periodogram, Part 1." *Cycles* **13**, No. 4 (April 1962), pp. 104–5.

———. "The Cause of the 8-Year Cycle in Business: The Theory of Professor H. L. Moore." *Cycles* **13**, No. 5 (May 1962), p. 117–21.

———. "What Is It All About? The Mystery of Cycles." *Cycles* **13**, No. 5 (May 1962), p. 128.

———. "The Cycle Workshop: The Periodogram, Part 2." *Cycles* **13**, No. 6 (June 1962), pp. 164–65.

———. "The Cycle Workshop: How Cycles Combine." *Cycles* **13**, No. 8 (August 1962), pp. 229–30.

———. "The Cycle Workshop: More About Trends." *Cycles* **13**, No. 10 (October 1962), pp. 295–96.

———. "The 54-Year Cycle in European Wheat Prices." *Cycles* **13**, No. 11 (November 1962), pp. 310–11.

———. "The Cycle Workshop: Effect of Moving Averages Upon Cycles." *Cycles* **14**, No. 2 (February 1963), pp. 45–46.

———. "The 42-Year Cycle in Cotton Prices." *Cycles* **14**, No. 5 (May 1963), pp. 125–27.

———. "The 42-Year Cycle in European Wheat Prices." *Cycles* **14**, No. 5 (May 1963), p. 128.

———. "The Cycle Workshop: The Use of the Periodic Table." *Cycles* **14**, No. 10 (October 1963), pp. 253–54.

———. "A Statement of the Problem." *Cycles* **14**, No. 11 (November 1963), p. 266.

———. "The 22.25-Month Cycle in Cotton Prices." *Cycles* **14**, No. 11 (November 1963), pp. 267–77.

———. "The Cycle Workshop: More About Periodic Tables." *Cycles* **14**, No. 11 (November 1963), pp. 281–82.

———. "Cycle Synchronies." Pittsburgh: Foundation for the Study of Cycles, November 1963.

———. "The Cycle Workshop: Definitizing the Cycle." *Cycles* **15**, No. 2 (February 1964), pp. 29–30.

———. "The Cycle Workshop: Moving Percentages." *Cycles* **15**, No. 3 (March 1964), pp. 73–75.

———. "The Cycle Workshop: The Effect of Moving Percentages Upon Cycles." *Cycles* **15**, No. 4 (April 1964), pp. 93–94.

———. "Comparative Cycle Study: Evidences of the 916-Year Cycle." *Cycles* **15**, No. 5 (May 1964), pp. 103–8.

———. "The Cycle Workshop: More About Moving Averages." *Cycles* **15**, No. 5 (May 1964), pp. 119–21.

———. "The Computer Research Program." *Cycles* **16**, No. 3 (March 1965), pp. 59–60.

———. "A Possible 9.2-Year Cycle in Cattle." *Cycles* **16**, No. 8 (August 1965), pp. 183–86.

———. "The Measurement of Cycles." *Cycles* **16**, No. 8 (August 1965), pp. 190–95.

———. "The 5.6-Year Cycle in Wheat." *Cycles* **18**, No. 5 (May 1967), p. 130.

———. "The Case for Cycles." *Cycles* **18**, No. 7 (July 1967), pp. 161–91.

Dewey, Edward R. and Mandino, Og. *Cycles*. New York: Hawthorn Books, 1971.

Edwards, R. D. and Magee, J. *Technical Analysis of Stock Trends*. Springfield, Mass.: John Magee, 1948.

Fuller, W. A. *Introduction to Statistical Time Series*. New York: Wiley, 1976.

Gilchrist, W. *Statistical Forecasting*. London: Wiley, 1976.

Granville, J. *The Granville Letter*, No. 25 and 37. Holly Hill, Florida, 1980.

Gann, W. D. *How to Make Profits in Commodities*. Pomeroy, Wash.: Lambert-Gann, 1976; orig. pub. 1942.

Gruschow, J. and Smith, C. *Profits Through Seasonal Trading*. New York: Wiley-Interscience, 1980.

Kaufman, J. *Commodity Trading Systems and Methods*. New York: Wiley-Interscience, 1978.

Kroll, S. and Shishko, I. *The Commodity Futures Market Guide*. New York: Harper & Row, 1973.

Pugh, B. *Science and Secrets of Wheat Trading*. Lambert-Gann: Pomeroy, Wash, 1978 orig. 1933.

Shirk, G. "Cycles in Industrial Bond Yields." *Cycles* **19**, No. 5 (1968).

———. "Cycles and Trends in Silver Prices." *Cycles* **25**, No. 9 (1974).

———. "Report on the Soybean Synthesis." *Cycles* **26**, No. 6 (1975).

———. "The Seasonal Cycle in Corn Prices." *Cycles* **30**, No. 2 (1979).

———. "Cycles in Interest Rates: Part 4." *Cycles* **31**, No. 9 (1980).

———. "Corn Prices: 1981 Extrapolation." *Cycles* **32**, No. 4 (1980).

———. "Cycles in Interest Rates: Part 5." *Cycles* **32**, No. 3 (1981).

Watts, A. *Tao: The Watercourse Way*. New York: Pantheon Books, 1975.

Williams, L. and Noseworthy, M. *Sure Thing Commodity Trading*. Brightwaters, N.Y.: Windsor, 1977.

# Index